A Guide to PUBLISHED LIBRARY CATALOGS

BONNIE R. NELSON

Foreword by Lee Ash

The Scarecrow Press, Inc.
Metuchen, N.J., & London
1982

Library of Congress Cataloging in Publication Data

Nelson, Bonnie R.
A guide to published library catalogs.

Includes index.
1. Library catalogs--Handbooks, manuals, etc.
I. Title.
Z710.N44 019 81-16558
ISBN 0-8108-1477-3 AACR2

Manufactured in the United States of America

TABLE OF CONTENTS

FOREWORD

The proper use of this wide-ranging reference book puts the world's written records into our hands. This seemingly all-inclusive description of major modern multivolumed catalogue sets has its limitations set forth in the preface but, even so, through the records incorporated in these magnificent works we also have reference to shorter even more highly specialized bibliographies. While many of these latter bibliographies may, as well, be catalogues of particular collections more of them are not but may locate copies of titles even these major catalogues do not include.

Thus do we truly live in a "golden age of bibliography"; or, if that phrase may not be accurate, it can certainly be said that it is a far easier and more convenient age in which to find the location of books that may not be in even the largest collections.

Now, with the advantages of interlibrary loan, international photocopying, the intelligent use of computer technologies, and the world record of the catalogued resources included in the works described herein, it would seem that any researcher can find information that might be needed and have it brought to hand quickly.

Most of us know, however, that researchers have adequate knowledge of only some of the most relevant works in their field. This is particularly true of younger scholars who will not yet have spent the necessary years developing their subject bibliographies. Lest I be misunderstood, I do not mean to proceed from this and imply that librarians are any better at the scholar's job. Unfortunately, fewer and fewer librarians are knowledgeable "book persons," for a variety of reasons not pertinent to this statement.

Through the hundreds of wonderful catalogues listed by Bonnie Nelson though, millions of books are brought into view. Careful study of her introduction, as well as the arrangement and the critical descriptions and analyses of the vagaries of each catalogue separately, along with the book's subject index, will be rewarding to the librarian.

In beginning a search for an obscure title the first step might be to find out what library has which appropriate catalogue that ought to be examined, a task generally passed on to a research or state library, but which often should be the researcher's own responsibility, especially if extensive lists are to be compiled. This excellent guide may be able to save any scholar hours of time and miles of travel, and provide widely extended horizons for any subject.

I do not want to close this Foreword without a note of my own appreciation of the various publishers of these catalogues and their courageous investments in them, and of the cooperation they have had from libraries that permitted publication of their records. Without their mutual assistance (in some cases catalogues were refiled at the publisher's expense, or a portion of the cards were retyped) these great sets could not have been published, Ms. Nelson's guide would have been a lesser one, and the world of readers would be that much poorer.

Instead, now we have a golden chain that links the world of books and, in this book, a key to the gates that open on them. This book does more: it gives the push through those gates so that we may revel in the garden of the mind that they enclose.

Lee Ash
Library Consultant

Bethany, Connecticut
July 1981

PREFACE

This book grew out of the interest in published library catalogs that developed from my realization that the major bibliography and index to the literature of my field of specialization in librarianship, anthropology, was a published library catalog--the catalog of the Peabody Museum of Archaeology and Ethnology at Harvard University. Curiosity and the event of working at New York University's Elmer Holmes Bobst Library, which has an extraordinary collection of published library catalogs, led me to explore other catalogs that I thought might be helpful for research in anthropology. The result was an article that appeared in RQ in Winter, 1979, "Anthropological Research and Printed Library Catalogs." My interest in library catalogs as research tools for anthropologists rapidly grew to an interest in published library catalogs in general--in what they are and what they can do. The present book is the result of this absorption.

I have included in it only major, modern catalogs. By major I mean these catalogs that describe significant collections, generally multi-volume catalogs. By modern I mean those catalogs published in the last 20 years, rather than the numerous catalogs published in the 19th and early 20th century, when the printed book catalog was almost the norm for libraries. I have included very few of the thousands of printed catalogs of collections of rare books and manuscripts that exist in the United States and abroad, but I have on occasion violated my own rules of exclusion to describe a catalog that by its content or organization seems sufficiently unusual to merit attention, or a catalog that seems to complete or complement a larger or later work.

The catalogs were discovered and selected with the help of the catalogs of those publishers specializing in the production of these costly works, and also with the help of preliminary versions of A Checklist and Union Catalog of Holdings of Major Published Library Catalogs in METRO Libraries by George Thompson (New York: New York Metropolitan Reference and Research Library Agency, 1980. METRO Miscellaneous Publication, no. 27). A few additional titles were found by my perusal of the card catalogs and reference shelves of the major research libraries in New York City, and by checking Robert L. Collison's Published Library Catalogues: An Introduction to Their Contents and Use (London: Mansell Information Pub., 1973).

I have examined all but a handful of the published catalogs listed here, and that handful has been described on the basis of photocopies of the introductions of the catalogs and sample pages plus, in some cases, reviews. These photocopies and, occasionally, physical volumes of the catalogs were secured for me through inter-library loan with the enormous help of Paula Jescavage, who heads that department at N. Y. U. 's Bobst Library. The libraries of New York City, however, are among the best in the world, and probably nowhere else would I have been able to find such a collection of published library catalogs as exists in this city. I thank the bibliographers of New York University, The New York Public Library, and Columbia University, in particular, for purchasing these catalogs.

A very special debt of gratitude is owed to George Thompson who, besides providing me with drafts of his Checklist and of his pamphlet Using Printed Book Catalogs (Boston: G. K. Hall), also shared freely his truly encyclopedic knowledge of published library catalogs and of bibliography in general. His discussions with me helped focus my examination of the catalogs and refine my insight into them.

I also wish to thank Arnold Markowitz, who helped me organize this project. And I extend my appreciation to my other colleagues at New York University and now at John Jay College of Criminal Justice of the City University of New York for their tolerance of my obsession with my subject and for their many helpful words of advice. I also thank John Jay College and the City University of New York for extending me a brief, paid research leave, and I enthusiastically encourage other universities to make such leaves available to librarians.

Finally, I do not quite know how to thank my husband, Robert Nelson, who has cheerfully looked after the running of our household for the year and a half this work has been in progress, not to mention the years of research and education preceding it, and who has, in addition, read every page of this work at least three times. I could not have done without his encouragement and counsel.

INTRODUCTION

> The ideal catalog would give under every subject its complete bibliography, not only mentioning all the monographs on the subject, but all works which in any way illustrate it, including all parts of books, magazine articles, and the best encyclopedias that treat of it; in short, the catalog would lay out just that course of reading which a man who thoroughly studied the subject, with a view not only to learn it, but to master the history of its treatment by others, would be obliged to pass through.
>
> --Charles A. Cutter[1]

> The catalog is designed to show what books are contained in a particular collection, and nothing more. Persons in want of further information, are expected to seek for it in bibliographical dictionaries, literary histories, or similar works.
>
> --Charles C. Jewett[2]

Cutter and Jewett, those two giants of librarianship in nineteenth-century America, expressed two opposing viewpoints about the function of the card catalog in the library. This dichotomy of opinion among librarians has never been resolved, as the diversity of catalogs described in the following pages attests. What is important, however, is less whether the scale of opinion has tipped one way or the other than that the variety of attempts to resolve this debate has resulted in the creation of a variety of catalogs, and that their publication and availability to researchers provides a range of opportunities for the discovery of information that would not exist had libraries fully standardized their operations.

The works described in this Guide to Published Library Catalogs have generally been published within the last twenty years, and are reproductions of catalogs actually in use in libraries, yet there is still a range from simple author catalogs like the Catalog of the Melville J. Herskovits Library of African Studies to the complex subject catalog of the Ibero-American Institute in Berlin, which is in four parts with five indexes.

History of the Published Library Catalog

The earliest library catalogs were lists, in manuscript, of the books in the library, arranged sometimes by the authors' names, sometimes by important words in the title, sometimes by broad subject, and often simply by the arrangement of books on the shelves (by size, order of acquisition, subject, and so on). With the advent of the printing press these lists were printed and distributed as book catalogs, enabling scholars at other locations to discover the holdings of the library. The major disadvantage of these book catalogs was that they were frozen in time, obsolete as soon as they were printed. Nevertheless they persisted for several hundred years as the dominant form of the catalog, often being updated with inserted paper slips. Book catalogs, in printed and manuscript form, began disappearing with the introduction of the easily modified card catalog in the latter half of the nineteenth century. The cost involved in publishing lists of the holdings of libraries, while at the same time maintaining a separate card catalog, was prohibitive, and the published book catalog very nearly disappeared from the scene.

What accounts, then, for the rebirth of the printed book catalog in the second half of the twentieth century? Part of the explanation lies in the major advantage that the printed book catalog has always had over the card catalog: it is portable and available to any library that obtains a copy, while a card catalog is accessible only in one fixed geographic location. The other major reason for the resurgence of the printed book catalog was the introduction of new reproduction technology, which enabled card catalogs to be photographed as they exist and then reproduced in book form, whereas in the past the production of a book catalog required that each entry be set in type and printed. The tremendous success of The National Union Catalog in the 1950's pointed up the interest that libraries had in discovering where particular titles were held. Later the firm of G. K. Hall developed techniques to reproduce card catalogs more cheaply, and found that libraries would pay to acquire the catalogs of other major research libraries. G. K. Hall's success is apparent from the fact that nearly three-quarters of the catalogs described in the following pages were published by this one firm.

Types of Catalogs

The predominant form of catalog listed here is the dictionary catalog, which has been the prevailing form of catalog in American libraries since the end of the nineteenth century. In such a catalog books and other works are listed under the author of the book, the title of the book, and the subject or subjects of the book, and all three types of entry are interfiled into one alphabetical or dictionary-type arrangement.

Another form of catalog, less popular but actually very similar, is the divided catalog, in which cards for the authors and the titles of books are arranged alphabetically in one list, while cards for the subjects of books are listed in a separate alphabetical arrangement. There can be variations on this theme, with authors separated from titles to form a third catalog, for instance, or with works about individuals being filed with authors' names in a "Names" catalog.

The chief problem with dictionary and divided catalogs, however, is that most of them use very specific subject headings and works on similar subjects, such as "Abused wives" and "Wife abuse," will not be found near each other but may be separated by the entire alphabet.

A radically different form of catalog, often used in combination with a separate author catalog, is the classified catalog. In this form the works are arranged in the catalog in a logical subject order, placing similar books together, rather than relying on the vagaries of the alphabet. In libraries (like most North American libraries) that shelve books according to a subject classification system, such as the Dewey Decimal classification or that of the Library of Congress, the shelflist--or catalog of cards arranged in the same order as the books are arranged on the shelves--is a classified catalog. Some libraries have published their shelflists. The two most notable examples are the publication of the Library of Congress's shelflist in microform and the ongoing publication of the shelflist of Harvard University's Widener Library. A lesser-known example is the published shelflist of the Union Theological Seminary Library, arranged according to its own locally-developed classification system. This catalog has also been published, rearranged into an alphabetical list by main entry, becoming a simple author catalog.

Such shelflists are useful for grouping related items together--the effect is very much like browsing on the shelves of an open-stack library. They have, however, one major flaw. Since a book can be placed on a shelf in only one place, the shelflist can list a book in only one place. A book that is about more than one subject, or that falls somewhere between two subjects, must summarily be assigned to one place in the classification, and the reader who thinks to look only in the other subject areas will not find it.

There are classified catalogs, however, that use classification systems designed to organize the catalog, rather than to organize the books on the shelves. In these catalogs, several classification numbers may be assigned to a work, or different classification numbers may be assigned to different parts of a work, such as chapters in a book, or articles in journals. The Classed Catalog of the American Museum of Natural History is an example of one such catalog. Here, the classification system is based on a classification of scientific subjects; a single item may be classed in several different places; and many analytical entries for chapters in books and articles in journals are included. The Research Catalog of the American Geographical Society is arranged by large and small regions of the world; one of the guides to the catalog is a series of maps depicting the classification numbers for each region.

A hybrid form of catalog closer to the dictionary catalog, but with elements of the classified catalog, is the alphabetico-classed catalog. It is little used now, but all of the published catalogs of The New York Public Library show remnants of the alphabetico-classed system once employed there. In this type of catalog broad subjects are arranged in alphabetical order and then subdivided by more specific subjects. The heading "Naval History," for example, contains works on the naval history of different countries and different wars, subdivided by country or period. Works about different types of dogs will be listed together with subdivisions rather than dispersed through the alphabet depending on whether the works are about Afghans or wolfhounds, army dogs or police dogs. However, even The New York Public Library has abandoned the alphabetico-classed concept in favor of the specific subject headings represented by Library of Congress Subject Headings, which has become, by far, the most used list of subject headings in the United States, and probably in the world.

Another method employed to group related subjects together, even when Library of Congress Subject Headings are used, is to invert the heading so that the noun part of the heading comes before the adjective. The Conservation Library of the Denver Public Library uses this technique so that works on polar bears and black bears, for example, will not be separated by most of the alphabet, but will appear next to each other as "Bears, Black" and "Bears, Polar."

An alternative method of grouping related material together in a catalog, especially in small specialized libraries, is simply to ignore very specific subject headings in favor of more general ones. This has been done by the John G. White Department of the Cleveland Public Library in its Catalog of Folklore, Folklife, and Folk Songs. This library uses Library of Congress subject headings and, in fact, uses LC printed cards, but often ignores, in favor of more general headings, the specific subjects the Library of Congress assigns. For example, the library lists all material about the folklore of North American Indians together under the subject heading "Indians of North America--Folklore and legends," where the Library of Congress would list each work under the name of the individual tribe it concerned. The result is that the Catalog of Folklore, Folklife, and Folk Songs is rather inconvenient for the reader who is looking for material on Cree folklore only, but provides the reader who is seeking material on the folklore of all North American Indians with a bibliography he or she could not find in any other catalog.

Materials Found in Library Catalogs

The diversity in the types of catalogs that exist is matched by the diversity of the types of materials listed in the catalogs. Most libraries include only books and serials in their catalogs; sometimes even serials are listed separately. But some libraries include all of the many kinds of items that are found in libraries: books, journals, series, pamphlets, microforms, government documents, manuscripts, slides, photographs, tapes, records, and other multimedia materials. An excellent example is the catalog of the Dance Collection of The New York Public Library, in which the majority of the items listed are non-print materials. The Catalog of the Old Slave

Mart Museum and Library in Charleston, South Carolina includes realia, actual artifacts of slave life.

Many libraries collect these types of materials, but because of budgetary constraints or philosophical objections, do not list them in their catalogs, relying on printed guides, reference librarians, or the researcher's own knowledge to direct individuals to the material. United States government documents, for example, may be collected by a library through its participation in the document depository system, but are often kept in a special collection with only the Monthly Catalog of U.S. Government Publications for access, and may never appear in the library's catalog. A good number of published catalogs, however, treat documents of the United States and other governments as they do any other publication, providing full author, title, and subject cataloging.

Microform collections are another underutilized resource in most libraries because they often consist of hundreds of individual works that libraries cannot afford to catalog separately. Early American printed books and early English printed books have been reproduced in several different microform collections that are owned, but generally not individually cataloged, by numerous libraries. The catalogs of the libraries that own the original titles, such as the Folger Library in Washington, D.C., provide the best means of access to these microform collections.

Other collections of microforms also pose problems. To illustrate, the University of Florida at Gainesville Latin American Collection owns 2,896 reels of microfilm of the General Records of the United States Department of State, pertaining to Latin America, including Consular Despatches, Diplomatic Despatches, Decimal File, and Notes from Foreign Legations. This tremendous wealth of material is represented in their catalog by just two cards, indicating only that the library owns the set. But some libraries do catalog titles in microform collections individually. The catalog of the Latin American Collection of the University of Texas provides entries for each of the types of microfilmed diplomatic records available for each Latin American country, and in addition lists them under subject headings for the foreign relations of the United States and the countries involved.

Some libraries also catalog parts of works--chapters in books, articles in journals, and the like--as separate entities, to be given author, title, or subject entries. This "analytical cataloging" is a very expensive and time-consuming procedure, and the practice in most libraries is to catalog the work only as a whole--as a monograph or serial title--and to hope that periodical or other indexes or bibliographies will list the separate units within the work. But a number of the catalogs listed in this Guide include analytics. A striking example is the Southeast Asia Subject Catalog of the Library of Congress, in which a majority of the entries are analytics.

Many libraries, like The New York Public Library, practiced

analytical cataloging extensively in the past, but now catalog only monographs or serials. These catalogs are still useful as retrospective bibliographies of periodical literature, particularly for the period before the flourishing of periodical indexes. Other libraries, like the Avery Architectural Library of Columbia University, continue to catalog individual periodical articles, and their catalogs of these articles, upon publication, have become the standard periodical indexes in their fields.

Using Published Library Catalogs

The variety in the form and content of the published catalogs is what makes them so interesting and so useful as a group. One of their most obvious uses is to simply locate a copy of a known title before either traveling to a library or requesting the title on interlibrary loan. Catalogs that include author and title entries are most satisfactory for this purpose. Or a researcher doing in-depth work on a particular subject may check the published catalog of a library specializing in the subject to determine if a long trip to that library would be worthwhile. A catalog with subject entries would be useful for this purpose. Published catalogs can also be used for compiling bibliographies, or checking bibliographical references, or as an aid in cataloging.

One of the most rewarding uses of published library catalogs is to identify material in one's own library that cannot be found through its card catalog. I have already indicated how government documents and items in microform may be identified in this way. Similarly, catalogs that include analytics for periodical articles or parts of books may lead scholars to works in serials or in monographs that are owned by their own libraries. And catalogs that provide very detailed cataloging of each title, with many points of access, can help rectify an incomplete or erroneous bibliographical reference.

An even more common difficulty is that most college and research libraries in the United States and in many foreign countries now use Library of Congress subject headings exclusively. Simply by consulting a published catalog that uses a different system of subject headings, a researcher might be able to identify material that may be owned by but cannot be located in his or her own library. The catalog of the Peabody Museum of Harvard University, for example, uses an alphabetico-classed system of subject headings taken from the language of anthropology. These headings, while somewhat outdated, are still closer to the terms that anthropologists use than the subject headings employed by the Library of Congress. Finding an ethnography of a people in a particular part of the world, which can be quite a chore using LC subject headings, is comparatively simple using the Peabody Museum catalog.

Other library catalogs may use many more subject headings when cataloging a particular book than the Library of Congress or those following its cataloging model do. The book Artists of the Nineties is given eleven subject headings in the catalog of the Prints Division of The New York Public Library, one for each chapter of the book, while the Library of Congress assigns only one, "Artists, English."[3] Even when libraries do use Library of Congress subject headings, they may use many more than LC would assign. The Arctic Institute of North America may assign twenty or more subject headings to one book, while the Library of Congress would commonly assign at most two or three. Therefore, a researcher may be able to locate a book under the subject headings she or he considers appropriate for the subject in one of the published library catalogs, and then search the catalog of the local library by author or title to find that library's copy of the book.

This Guide to Published Library Catalogs was written to help readers expand the limits of their own libraries by describing these published library catalogs. For each catalog the following information is provided, where appropriate: subjects covered, languages included, dates of material included, types of materials (e.g., books, periodicals, government publications, rare books, theses, multimedia material, etc.), presence of analytical entries for articles in journals or parts of books, the arrangement of the catalog, the types of subject headings used, the cataloging and classification systems used, and any special features that might be of interest. Catalogs have not been compared in detail in the coverage of particular subjects, since even the most cursory comparison made it obvious that no library was complete on any subject and even the largest collection lacked numerous titles that smaller ones owned. This, of course, means that all the catalogs are valuable.

The Guide is arranged into 33 different subject categories, not according to any previously developed classification system, but simply based on my attempt to group similar catalogs together. There is, in addition, a subject index listing the specific subjects covered by the catalogs, to the extent that they could be identified as specialties of the libraries. The index of libraries lists the names of the libraries and institutions that are represented by the catalogs in every combination and permutation of their names that I could think of, to enable readers to find the catalogs with whatever information they have. The forms of entry in the text, however, generally follow Library of Congress practice, and I have provided the Library of Congress catalog card number where I could obtain it.

The Future of the Published Library Catalog

As useful as published library catalogs may be, it is likely that they will again become a relic of the past. For a time it appeared that book catalogs would become even more important with the introduction of computer technology that could produce a printed catalog from information stored in machine-readable form (there are several examples of these catalogs in this volume), but libraries have discovered that computer-output microform (COM) is cheaper and more convenient. It is true that any of these computer-produced catalogs can be sold to or exchanged with other libraries, but the rationale for this exchange is missing because the source of the machine-readable bibliographic information is, in most cases, a cataloging system with a database that is shared with hundreds of other libraries. The major bibliographic utilities, like OCLC and RLIN, not only enable libraries to share cataloging burdens by maintaining and making available the cataloging records of the Library of Congress and all participating libraries, but also, in the process, make available to libraries information on which libraries own particular titles. Furthermore, these bibliographic utilities are working towards making it possible for researchers not only to identify the locations of known titles but also to discover titles on particular subjects listed in the database by searching for particular subject headings or for keywords that might appear in titles.

These new computer databases do not by any means render existing published catalogs obsolete, however. Most research libraries cannot afford to convert their existing card catalogs into machine-readable form and the information contained in them will probably never (or at least not for the foreseeable future) be available in the bibliographic utilities. Even if they can convert the information for books and serials, it is doubtful that the detailed analytical entries or the unusual subject headings can be converted. The sharing of computer cataloging has required that libraries adopt uniform standards of cataloging and uniform subject headings, a change that has likely improved the level of cataloging in general, but has also eliminated the use of those locally developed subject headings and cataloging methods that make these published catalogs so valuable for finding information on specific subjects. The variety of catalogs that resulted from the great philosophical debates of the nineteenth century will be unlikely to survive the new technology and the pressure on library budgets of the late twentieth century.

1. GENERAL CATALOGS

Some of the greatest research libraries in the world have published their catalogs, including the Library of Congress (13, 19, 20), the Bibliothèque Nationale (18), the British Library (formerly the British Museum Library) (3-5), The New York Public Library (15-16), and Harvard's Widener Library (9). This is not a new phenomenon--the British Museum Library has been issuing editions of its published book catalog since the nineteenth century--but with the advent of computer technology most of these libraries have frozen their catalogs, switched to some form of computer-produced catalog, and published their frozen catalogs partly for purposes of preservation, as well as for dissemination of knowledge.

Of these major catalogs, those of the Library of Congress list the most titles and have the most complete and consistent cataloging information. Most are not strictly speaking the catalogs of the Library of Congress, but are union catalogs of the holdings of libraries around the United States, with the bulk of the entries provided by the Library of Congress. The most difficult to use is perhaps the catalog of the Bibliothèque Nationale, since each volume covers a different time period. Only The New York Public Library has produced full dictionary catalogs, both in the frozen, pre-1972 catalog, and in the new, computer-produced catalog. Harvard University's Widener Library catalog is also computer-produced, but it takes the form of a shelflist, published in parts by subject, with each part containing its own author and title index. There is no cumulative listing for the entire library, and only the humanities and social sciences are included in the Widener Library.

Also described in this chapter are several catalogs of general newspaper and periodical collections, as well as catalogs of bibliographies and of reference books.

1. Boston. Public Library. Catalog of the Large Print Collection. 336 p. Boston: The Library, 1976 (LC 76-26121).

This catalog lists over 1,500 fiction and non-fiction titles of works available at the Boston Public Library in large print. The arrangement is alphabetical by title under broad categories. For example, under "Fiction" are the categories: General, Historical Novels, Mystery, Westerns, etc.; under "Non-Fiction" may be found: Arts, Health and Science, History, etc. There is an author index in the back. The catalog itself is in large print.

2. Boston. Public Library. Dictionary Catalog of the General Library, Boston Public Library. 61 vols. Cambridge, Mass.: General Microfilm Company, in cooperation with the Trustees of the Public Library of the City of Boston, 1975- (LC 75-4676). Supplemented by periodic computer-produced book catalogs.

This is the catalog of the circulating collection of the General Library of the Boston Public Library as of January 1, 1975. It represents approximately 300,000 titles and 700,000 volumes. The policy of the library is to maintain a well-rounded, general-interest circulating collection for the people of Boston and the state of Massachusetts.

This is a dictionary catalog of authors, titles, subjects, and added entries. Cataloging practices and classification systems have changed over the years. Both Dewey and Library of Congress classification systems are represented on the cards, as are standard subject headings from Boston Public Library's own list (used in the early years of the library), Sears list of subject headings, and Library of Congress headings.

3. British Library. The British Library General Catalogue of Printed Books to 1975. London: Clive Bingley and K. G. Saur. 1979- (projected to be completed by the end of 1984 and to have approximately 360 volumes) (LC 79-40543).

This catalog incorporates in one alphabet all of the earlier General Catalogues of the British Museum Library, including the photolithographic edition that was begun in 1956 plus its supplements. Also included are additions and corrections made in the working catalog of the British Library up to the time of publication of each volume. The completed work will list some seven million titles.

The British Library was founded in 1973 as the national library of the United Kingdom. It is actually the renamed Library of the British Museum, which originated in 1753, and it contains eight and a half million volumes on all subjects. This General Catalogue is the official record for all books published in the United Kingdom up to 1970 and for most books published from 1971 to 1975. Subsequent acquisitions are not included in the catalog because in 1975 the British Library began cataloging in machine-readable form according to the MARC standard.

The British Library, according to Sheehy, "is particularly important because of the extent and richness of its collections in all fields and in all languages, and also because its possession of the copyright privilege helps make it the most comprehensive collection of British publications in existence. Its catalog, therefore, is an indispensible bibliographic source for the scholar and librarian."[4] In addition, the British Library has "a larger collection of European imprints up to 1900 than most major libraries in the countries themselves. German and French publications are particularly well represented" [Introduction].

This is a name catalog, both personal and corporate, with a few title entries. Works by and about individuals are included under the name of the individual. Works by and about corporate entities--for example, countries and cities--are also included under the name. The result is that parts of the catalog have become major subject bibliographies, running to several volumes, complete with subdivisions and indexes. This is the case for individuals such as Aesop, Shakespeare, and Dickens, and for places like England and London, as well as for some other topics like the Bible, and for some categories of works such as Liturgies and Hymnals. In the photolithographic edition, entries under "Bible" ran for three volumes; under "England," for five volumes; under "London," for three volumes; and each of these contained its own index.

Periodicals are listed under the main entry; under the title, if it is distinct from the main entry; and under the heading "Periodical Publications," a major category in the catalog.

Also included in the catalog are many cross-references (acting as added entries) for joint authors, editors, etc. In most cases entries are not as complete as in American catalogs, details such as some imprint information, number of pages, and notes, being omitted.

4. British Library. Newspaper Library. Catalogue of the Newspaper Library, Colindale. 8 vols. London: British Museum Publications, Ltd. for the British Library Board, 1975 (LC 77-352221).

The Newspaper Library at Colindale contains approximately a half-million volumes and parcels of daily and weekly newspapers and periodicals. Included are: London newspapers, 1801- ; English provincial, Scottish, and Irish newspapers, 1700- ; and a large collection of Commonwealth and foreign newspapers. The library does not contain London newspapers published before 1801, newspapers in Oriental languages, or more than a few periodicals published less frequently than weekly.

Volumes one to four of this catalog are arranged geographically--volume one, London; volume two, England and Wales, Scotland, Ireland; volumes three and four, overseas countries--and volumes five to eight alphabetically by title. Entries provide dates of publication, notes on title changes and mergers, and cross-references. Although the publication date of this catalog is 1975, it includes titles added only through 1970-71. Most of the newspapers listed are English-language periodicals, although just about all languages, except Oriental languages, are included.

5. British Museum. Department of Printed Books. Subject Index of the Modern Works Added to the Library, 1881-1900. Edited by G. K. Fortescue. 3 vols. London: The Trustees, 1902-1903. Supplements: 1901-1905. 1906; 1911-1915. 1918; 1916-1920. 1922; 1921-1925. 1927; 1926-1930. 1933; 1931-1935. 2 vols., 1937; 1936-1940.

2 vols., 1944; 1941-1945. 1953; 1946-1950. 4 vols., 1961; 1951-1955. 6 vols., 1974; 1956-1960. 6 vols., 1965-66.

This is a companion series to the British Library General Catalogue of Printed Books (see 3), acting as a subject index to much of that catalog. It is not an easy catalog to use. First, any thorough subject search requires looking in twelve different places because of the proliferation of uncumulated supplements. Second, there is no list of the subject headings used, although there are many cross-references, and the headings tend to be very broad, with many subdivisions. The arrangements under the subheadings are neither chronological nor alphabetical.

Subject headings used in the General Catalogue of Printed Books, such as personal names, names of places, and kinds of works, like "Bible," "Liturgies," etc., are not repeated in the Subject Index. Also not included are works that appear unclassifiable, such as collections of literature.

Later supplements provide increasingly detailed notes on the types and organization of the subject headings used.

Since the Index covers works added to the library only since 1880, many of the earlier titles in the British Museum Library are not included.

6. California. University. Library. Author-Title Catalog. 115 vols. Boston: G. K. Hall, 1963 (LC 73-153193).

This is the author-title catalog of the University of California at Berkeley as of 1963. Included in this catalog are the holdings of the General Library with its twenty specialized subject branches, the Bancroft Library on Western Americana, the Library of the School of Law, plus others. Not included here are the collections of the East Asiatic Library in Chinese, Japanese, Korean, Manchu, and Mongolian; nor the scores and sound recordings of the Music Library. The catalog represents some 2,850,000 bound volumes covering all subjects and most languages. United States government documents were cataloged until the mid-1950's, and there is a strong collection of California state documents. Serials are included in the catalog, often with information concerning which issues are held. There are references to the correct form of entry. The Library of Congress system is the classification used by the library.

7. Chicago. Center for Research Libraries. The Center for Research Libraries Catalogue: Monographs. 5 vols. Chicago: Center for Research Libraries, 1969-70 (LC 76-13486). Supplement. 2 vols., 1974.

________. The Center for Research Libraries Catalogue: Newspapers. 176 p. Chicago: Center for Research Libraries, 1969 (LC 72-13485).

_______. The Center for Research Libraries Catalogue: Serials. 2 vols. Chicago: Center for Research Libraries, 1972. Supplement, 1978.

The Center for Research Libraries was founded in 1949 by a group of ten midwestern universities with the help of grants from the Carnegie Corporation and the Rockefeller Foundation. By 1978 it had over 165 members and associate members and a collection of over three million volumes. Its policy is "to acquire directly by purchase, exchange or gift, those materials not readily available in the members' own collections and whose use can be shared without handicap" [Introduction, Center for Research Libraries. Handbook. Chicago, 1978].

The published catalogs of the center are main-entry catalogs only. There are cross-references to the correct form of names, and Anglo-American cataloging rules are followed. The Serials Catalogue has some cross-references for changes in title and includes entries for newspapers, which are also listed in the Newspaper Catalogue.

The Center for Research Libraries maintains comprehensive collections of the following, although they are not included in the catalogs: foreign doctoral dissertations; books in English printed before 1641, and books, pamphlets, or broadsides printed before 1801; foreign government documents; post-1951 state documents; non-depository U.S. government documents; post-1954 United Nations documents; college catalogs and administrative reports from 1950; annual reports of railroads and corporations; children's books, comic books, and textbooks; and publications of scholarly significance from Ceylon, India, Indonesia, Nepal, Pakistan, and Yugoslavia.

8\. Columbia University. Libraries. Library Service Library. Dictionary Catalog of the Library of the School of Library Service. 7 vols. Boston: G. K. Hall, 1962 (LC 63-2444). First Supplement. 4 vols., 1976.

This is probably the nation's foremost collection of books and journals pertaining to library service. The library dates back to 1876, when the collection was begun by Melvil Dewey. In 1962, when the original catalog was published, the collection totaled 75,000 volumes of monographs, pamphlets, serials, government documents, and research reports, as well as some tape recordings. The titles are mostly in English, with other European languages also extensively collected.

Within the field of library service, the emphasis is on library resources and bibliographies; readers' services and technical services; the organization and administration of libraries; the history of libraries and their function in society; the history of books and book making; juvenile literature, including an important historical collection of children's books; and information science.

Library of Congress subject headings are used in this dictionary catalog, and approximately half of the cards are Library of

Congress printed cards. Before 1967 the Dewey Decimal classification was used; in 1967 the Library of Congress classification was adopted.

9. Harvard University. Library. Widener Library Shelflists. vol. 1- . Cambridge, Mass.: The Library; distributed by Harvard University Press, 1965- .

Harvard University's Widener Library houses one of the greatest collections of works in the humanities and the social sciences in the world. In 1964 the Widener Library developed a system for converting its manuscript sheaf shelflists to machine-readable form. It has elected to publish each section of the shelflist upon its conversion to make it available to the scholarly community.[5] These published Widener Library Shelflists, now numbering 60 volumes, are the result.

The shelflist records are very brief--consisting of author (sometimes with abbreviated first names), title (also often shortened and sometimes partly abbreviated), place and date of publication, number of volumes, and call number. Language is usually indicated, and monographs are distinguished from serials where possible. Each volume of the published shelflist contains a reproduction of that part of the classification schedule being published. In later volumes this is preceded by a brief outline of the schedule as well. This is followed by the actual listing of the shelflist by classification number, with subheadings regularly interspersed and repeated at the top of every page. There is also a chronological listing of titles by date of publication, and an alphabetical listing by author and title (the earlier volumes include title entries for anonymous works only). Each volume also contains statistical summaries listing the number of titles and volumes included, the number of titles in each language, etc.

The shelflists have all the limitations of a classified arrangement--each work is listed only once, works are not always where the reader expects to find them, and subjects which the reader thinks should be contiguous may not be. There is also no general or specific index to the classification system as a whole or to the individual parts. On the positive side, however, these shelflists represent major bibliographies, arranged by subject, of 40 different fields in language, literature, history, and some of the social sciences. While there are no subject indexes in the volumes, the author and title indexes enable the reader to look up a known work in a field, find the call number, and use that to locate other, similar works, much the way tracings are used in a card catalog.

The outlines of the classification system used in the shelflists are quite clear and should not present any difficulty in use. The classification is Harvard's own system, developed sometime after 1877. It has both influenced and been influenced by the Library of Congress classification, and many of the arrangements within subjects are similar, although the notation is different. In July, 1976 the Widener Library adopted the Library of Congress classification system, and works cataloged since that date will not be included in the published shelflists.

The shelflists include many dissertations and many rare books that are not now housed in the Widener Library. Only books and serials are included; there are no analytical entries.

At this writing, the following shelflists have been published:

v. 1 Crusades. 1965 (superseded by v. 32)
v. 2 Africa. 1965 (superseded by v. 34)
v. 3 Twentieth Century Russian Literature. 1965 (superseded by v. 28-31)
v. 4 Russian History since 1917. 1966 (superseded by v. 28-31)
v. 5-6 Latin America and Latin American Periodicals. 1966 (see 175)
v. 7 Bibliography and Bibliography Periodicals. 1966 (see 10)
v. 8 Reference Collections Shelved in the Reading Room and Acquisitions Department. 1966 (superseded by v. 33)
v. 9-13 American History. 1967 (see 102)
v. 14 China, Japan, and Korea. 1968 (see 204)
v. 15 Periodical Classes. 1968 (see 11)
v. 16-17 Education and Education Periodicals. 1968 (see 334)
v. 18 Literature: General and Comparative. 1968 (see 145)
v. 19 Southern Asia: Afghanistan, Bhutan, Burma, Cambodia, Ceylon, India, Laos, Malaya, Nepal, Pakistan, Sikkim, Singapore, Thailand, Vietnam. 1968 (see 205)
v. 20 Canadian History and Literature. 1968 (see 133)
v. 21 Latin American Literature. 1969 (see 176)
v. 22 Government. 1969 (see 344)
v. 23-24 Economics and Economics Periodicals. 1970 (see 357)
v. 25 Celtic Literatures. 1970 (see 138)
v. 26-27 American Literature. 1970 (see 161)
v. 28-31 Slavic History and Literatures. 1971 (see 146)
v. 32 General European and World History. 1970 (see 78)
v. 33 Reference Collections Shelved in the Reading Room and Acquisitions Department. 1970 (see 12)
v. 34 African History and Literatures. 1971 (see 234)
v. 35-38 English Literature. 1971 (see 162)
v. 39 Judaica. 1971 (see 253)
v. 40 Finnish and Baltic History and Literatures. 1972 (see 139)
v. 41 Spanish History and Literature. 1972 (see 177)
v. 42-43 Philosophy and Psychology. 1973 (see 261)
v. 44 Hungarian History and Literature. 1974 (see 142)
v. 45-46 Sociology. 1973 (see 316)
v. 47-48 French Literature. 1973 (see 140)
v. 49-50 German Literature. 1974 (see 141)
v. 51-52 Italian History and Literature. 1974 (see 143)
v. 53-54 British History. 1975 (see 77)
v. 55 Ancient History. 1975 (see 56)
v. 56 Archaeology. 1979 (see 57)
v. 57 Classical Studies. 1979 (see 58)

v. 58 Ancient Greek Literature. 1979 (see 55)
v. 59 Latin Literature. 1979 (see 148)
v. 60 Geography and Anthropology. 1979 (see 40)

10. Harvard University. Library. Bibliography and Bibliography Periodicals. 1066 p. Cambridge, Mass.: distributed by Harvard University Press, 1966 (LC 66-31367). (Widener Library Shelflist v. 7)

This volume of the Widener Library shelflist includes the B class (Bibliography) and the BP class (Bibliography Periodicals) arranged in call number order with an author-title index and a listing by imprint date. Subjects covered are the science of bibliography, book arts, publishing, freedom of the press, copyright, and the history of libraries. General bibliographies, library catalogs, and publishers catalogs are included. Bibliographies and library catalogs on specific subjects are classed with the subject and so do not appear in this volume.

The B class contains 18, 500 titles and the BP class 1, 200 titles. The great majority of the works are in English, followed in number by German, French, and other languages.

For a further discussion of the Widener Library shelflists see 9.

11. Harvard University. Library. Periodical Classes. 758 p. Cambridge, Mass.: distributed by Harvard University Press, 1968 (LC 68-14152). (Widener Library Shelflist v. 15)

This catalog lists approximately 25, 700 periodical titles, or about half of the periodicals and serials in Harvard's Widener Library. Represented here are the separate periodicals classes of the Harvard Library classification scheme. Periodicals have not been treated very consistently in this classification, and the other half of the Widener Library periodicals have been classed with the books on the same subjects.

Included in this list are general periodicals in English, French, German, Greek, Italian, Dutch, Portuguese, the minor Romance languages, Scandinavian, Slavic, and Spanish. Also in this volume are periodicals on the following subjects: ancient history, bibliography, the church, economics, education, Egyptology, history, learned societies, philology, Latin America, and science. However, Latin American periodicals are also included in volumes five and six of the Widener Library shelflists, Latin America and Latin American Periodicals (see 175); bibliography periodicals may also be found in volume seven of the Widener Library shelflists, Bibliography and Bibliography Periodicals (see 10); and education periodicals may be found in volumes sixteen and seventeen, Education and Education Periodicals (see 334).

As in all the Widener Library shelflists, the arrangement is by classification number, with an added listing by title. For more information on the Widener Library shelflists see 9.

12. Harvard University. Library. Reference Collections Shelved in the Reading Room and Acquisitions Department. 130 p. Cambridge, Mass.: distributed by Harvard University Press, 1970 (LC 77-128715). (Widener Library Shelflist v. 33)

This catalog is in two parts. The first part is a classified arrangement and the second an alphabetical arrangement by author and title. Included here is that part of the Widener Library shelflist that contains the RR and the Ref classes. RR includes the 4,000 reference books shelved in the main reading room of the Widener Library. Ref contains 600 bibliographical and other reference sources used in book selection and shelved in the Resources and Acquisitions Department. These are largely sales catalogs, national bibliographies, and trade catalogs. The subjects covered are in the humanities and social sciences, like the Widener Library in general.

This volume supersedes volume eight of the Widener Library shelflists.

For a fuller discussion of the Widener Library shelflists see 9.

13. The National Union Catalog, Pre-1956 Imprints: A Cumulative Author List Representing Library of Congress Printed Cards and Titles Reported by Other American Libraries. 685 vols. London: Mansell, 1968-1980 (LC 67-30001). Supplement. v. 686- , 1980- .

The National Union Catalog: A Cumulative Author List Representing Library of Congress Printed Cards and Titles Reported by Other American Libraries. Washington: Library of Congress. Monthly, with quarterly, annual and quinquennial cumulations:

________. 1965-1967. 125 vols. Totowa, N.J.: Rowman and Littlefield, 1970-1972 (LC 76-141020).

________. 1968-1972. 104 vols. Ann Arbor, Mich.: J. W. Edwards, 1973.

________. 1973-1977. 135 vols. Totowa, N.J.: Rowman and Littlefield, 1978.

The Library of Congress published catalogs are the most important and certainly the most well-known of the published library catalogs. Their significance lies not only in the fact that the Library of Congress is the world's largest library, but also in the fact that since the published catalogs are union catalogs, they represent not only the holdings of the Library of Congress, but the reported holdings of hundreds of other North American libraries as well. They have long been used by librarians to locate copies of known titles, and they can be used very profitably in conjunction with other published library catalogs, with the latter being used to identify titles on particular subjects, and The National Union Catalog to find other, nearer, or more convenient copies of the title.

The National Union Catalog has a long and rather complicated history. By 1901 the Librarian of Congress had recognized the desirability of distributing to great research libraries around the country a copy of every card printed for the LC catalogs, and also the need for the Library of Congress to receive a copy of every card printed by several of the great research libraries so that important reference works could be located. To meet the first requirement, an expensive project was developed of maintaining, in various libraries around the country, a depository catalog of cards printed by the Library of Congress and representing its holdings. To reduce the expense of this maintenance, and to make the duplicate catalogs available to more libraries, the Association of Research Libraries sponsored the 1946 publication of A Catalog of Books Represented by Library of Congress Printed Cards Issued to July 31, 1942 (Ann Arbor, Mich.: Edwards Brothers, Inc.), an author listing of the printed cards that the Library of Congress had produced for its own titles. The reception of the publication was so enthusiastic that the Library of Congress decided to continue the publication project.

Meanwhile, the Library of Congress had been maintaining a union catalog of books acquired by the major research libraries. Regional union catalogs in Cleveland and Philadelphia were incorporated into this union catalog in the mid-1940's. After this was designated in 1948 as the National Union Catalog, the entire catalogs of the libraries of Yale and the University of California at Berkeley were copied and added to it, along with the North Carolina Union Catalog. However, the National Union Catalog was available only in Washington, so the American Library Association's Board of Resources of American Libraries recommended that the book catalog of author cards being published by the Library of Congress, and now called Library of Congress Catalog--Books: Authors, be expanded to include the holdings of other libraries as reported in the National Union Catalog. This was done beginning in January of 1956. The expanded publication was named The National Union Catalog: A Cumulative Author List; it included titles and holdings of books with imprint dates subsequent to 1955. The National Union Catalog has been appearing serially ever since and has been cumulated into several quinquennial and larger published catalogs.

The success of this publication led to the decision to publish The National Union Catalog, Pre-1956 Imprints, which replaces A Catalog of Books Represented by Library of Congress Printed Cards and its supplements; The Library of Congress Author Catalog, 1948-1952; The National Union Catalog, 1952-1955 Imprints; and The National Union Catalog, A Cumulative Author List, 1953-1957. The National Union Catalog, Pre-1956 Imprints includes only works published before 1956, available in the Library of Congress or one of the more than 700 participating libraries, and reported by the libraries up to 12 months before the publication of the volume in which they are included. The following libraries have endeavored to report every cataloged item in their collections printed before 1956: the University of Chicago Library, Harvard University Library, Yale University Library, the John Crerar Library, and The New York Public Library. Other libraries have reported their holdings selectively.

The NUC, Pre-1956 Imprints contains entries for books, pamphlets, maps, atlases, microforms, and music. Serials are also included, but the holdings are not as comprehensive as the Union List of Serials or New Serial Titles. Manuscript collections are not included (these are listed in The National Union Catalog of Manuscript Collections; see 25), but cataloged individual manuscripts are included if they have been reported by the libraries that own them. Not included in the catalog are phonorecords, motion pictures and filmstrips, and books for the blind (i. e., those books published in Braille, in raised type, etc.). Holdings of United States Federal and state documents, United Nations documents, and League of Nations documents have not been reported consistently.

The National Union Catalog, Pre-1956 Imprints includes works printed or written in Latin alphabets and in Greek or Gaelic. Works in Cyrillic, Arabic, Hebrew, Chinese, Japanese, Korean, the Indic alphabets, and other languages not using the Latin alphabet are represented only by LC printed cards, since the transliteration used by other libraries has not been uniform. However, works in Cyrillic published before 1956 have subsequently been listed in the Cyrillic Union Catalog in Three Parts (see 150) and in The Slavic Cyrillic Union Catalog (see 149).

This is a main-entry catalog with cross-references and some selected added entries. All entries have been edited for consistency and uniformity with Library of Congress practices. For Pre-1956 Imprints this has almost invariably meant agreement with the American Library Association's Cataloging Rules for Author and Title Entries (1949 edition). Also included with each entry are the symbols for the libraries that own the title. These symbols are explained on the inside covers of each volume of The NUC, Pre-1956 Imprints, and in the beginning of the first volume of each of the subsequent cumulations.

Volumes of The National Union Catalog, Pre-1956 Imprints began appearing in 1968. The project was completed in 1980, but the publisher has begun issuing supplements to it for works printed before 1956 but reported after the appropriate volumes had gone to press; this includes acquisitions of cooperating libraries reported as late as August, 1977, and LC cards reported as recently as August, 1979. The supplements include new titles, new editions of titles already listed, new added entries and cross-references and, at the end of each volume, a register of additional locations for titles listed in the basic set. For post-1955 works, the separately published Register of Additional Locations should also be searched for information on holding libraries.

Since 1958, titles in Cyrillic and Hebraic alphabets reported to The National Union Catalog and not represented by LC printed cards have been included in transliteration. Also included in The NUC are post-1955 imprints from the National Library of Medicine, which also published its own catalogs from 1948 to 1965 as supplements to the Library of Congress Catalogs, and which, in January, 1966, started publishing its Current Catalog, a computer-produced book catalog (see 428).

Subject access to the titles in The National Union Catalog cataloged by the Library of Congress after 1950 is available through the Library of Congress Catalog--Books: Subjects (see 19). Title access to all titles cataloged and classified by the Library of Congress from 1897 to 1978 is now available using the Cumulative Title Index to the Classified Collections of the Library of Congress: 1978 (Arlington, Va.: Carrollton Press, 1980). This work, in 132 volumes, is arranged by title and provides the name of the author or other main entry, the date of publication, the complete LC classification number, and the LC card number.

14. New York (City). Public Library. Branch Libraries: Catalogs of the Branch Libraries. New York, 1972- .

This is a computer-produced book catalog of the holdings of the Branch Libraries system of the New York Public Library. It includes adult materials cataloged for the system since 1972 and all materials cataloged for the Mid-Manhattan Library, the central library of the Branch Libraries system. It contains, therefore, a mixture of popular and scholarly titles through the undergraduate level. Included are books, phonorecords, cassette tapes, and serials.

The catalog is divided into three parts: Names, which includes works by and about individuals and corporate bodies; Titles; and Subjects. Main entries, which may be in the Names or Titles catalog, are given full bibliographic information; added entries receive abbreviated information.

15. New York (City). Public Library. Research Libraries. Dictionary Catalog of the Research Libraries of The New York Public Library, 1911-1971. (800 vols. projected). New York: The New York Public Library, printed and distributed by G. K. Hall, 1979- .

The New York Public Library is a merger of three libraries: the Astor Library, which was established in 1849 under the will of John Jacob Astor; the Lenox Library, established by a gift from James Lenox; and the Tilden Trust, established in 1887 under the will of Samuel J. Tilden. In 1895, under authorization granted by the New York State Legislature, they were consolidated into The New York Public Library, Astor, Lenox and Tilden Foundations. The New York Public Library maintains two library systems: the Branch Libraries in Manhattan, the Bronx, and Staten Island, which are supported by New York City; and the Research Libraries, mainly supported by endowments and private gifts. Today, the Research Libraries (formerly called Reference Department) house over five million books, ten million manuscripts, 125,000 fine prints, 250,000 maps, 360,000 recordings, 150,000 pieces of sheet music, and countless newspapers and periodicals. Works are in more than 3,000 languages and dialects. The New York Public Library ranks without question as one of the world's great libraries.

The Research Libraries closed its public catalogs on December 31, 1971, when it adopted Anglo-American Cataloging Rules and Library of Congress subject headings. At the time of closing, the main Public Catalog had over ten million cards, and the total number of cards in all the catalogs, including those maintained by the different divisions of the Research Libraries, was 30 million.

It is expected that the publication of all 800 volumes, representing the main Public Catalog, will be completed by 1985.

Of the published catalogs of the great research libraries, this is the only one that is a full dictionary catalog. The Library of Congress, the British Museum Library, and the Bibliothèque Nationale have published only main-entry catalogs. NYPL's catalog has author, title, subject, and sometimes form entries (e.g., "Fiction, American" or "Bibliography--Catalogues--Libraries"). There are also series entries for monographs in series whether they are kept together or scattered on the shelves. New York Public's cataloging differs in some respects from Library of Congress practice. Where Library of Congress and American Library Association rules called for entry of institutions under place, NYPL entered under name. Otherwise, practices tend to be similar. The New York Public Research Libraries use their own classification systems: the Billings classification is used for older books, and a "fixed order" class for the newer ones; i.e., the books are shelved by size. Newer subject headings in the catalog tend to be Library of Congress headings; older ones are based on the alphabetico-classed system developed at Harvard during the nineteenth century. These headings tend to be very broad, general subjects subdivided by smaller subjects. Also, rather than entering works on an aspect of a country under the place, subdivided by the subject, NYPL reversed this order, yielding headings like "Economic history--U.S."

There are two different kinds of entries in the catalog: entries for books and book sets; and "index" entries, or page analytics for periodical and journal articles, listed mostly under subject but sometimes under the name of the author as well. Indexing of periodical articles began in 1897 and dropped off as periodical indexes appeared. In 1939, 3,769 periodicals were indexed regularly, and 30,689 entries were prepared. By 1968, according to the Introduction, 5,000 periodical titles were indexed regularly, but only 2,340 entries were prepared, and these were primarily for biographies, autobiographies, or bibliographies.

The Introduction to the catalog includes a guide to the filing system and a description of the subject headings used. There is also a separately published work, Subject Headings Authorized for General Use in the Dictionary Catalogs (Boston: G. K. Hall, 1959, 2 vols.), which lists the subject headings and has a long introduction explaining their theory and practice.

The Dictionary Catalog lists works in all languages, transliterating those in non-Roman alphabets. Despite the 1911 of the title, most of the titles date from the nineteenth as well as the twentieth century, and some are much earlier.

Many of the various divisions and collections of the Research Libraries have published their catalogs separately. However, the

Dictionary Catalog of the Research Libraries duplicates much that is contained in the separately published catalogs. The following list indicates how much of the smaller catalogs have been reproduced in the larger one.

Division/Collection Catalog	Dictionary Catalog of the Research Libraries
Dictionary Catalog of the History of the Americas (see 111)	The Research Libraries Catalog contains all entries of the smaller catalog except some periodical articles on American Indians.
Catalog of the Arents Collection of Books in Parts and Associated Literature	The Research Libraries Catalog does not include any entries for this collection.
Dictionary Catalog of the Art and Architecture Division (see 291)	The Research Libraries Catalog contains all entries in the smaller catalog except most entries for periodical articles.
Dictionary Catalog of the Slavonic Division (see 147)	The Research Libraries Catalog contains all entries of the smaller catalog except for materials in the Cyrillic alphabet.
Dictionary Catalog of the Henry W. and Albert A. Berg Collection of English and American Literature (see 164)	The Research Libraries Catalog does not include any entries for this collection.
Dictionary Catalog of the Dance Collection (see 302)	The Research Libraries Catalog contains entries for books and periodicals only, and not for multimedia material.
Catalog of Government Publications (see 346)	The Research Libraries Catalog contains all entries.
Dictionary Catalog of the Jewish Collection (see 256)	The Research Libraries Catalog contains all entries except for materials in the Hebrew alphabet.
Dictionary Catalog of the Local History and Genealogy Division (see 107)	The Research Libraries Catalog contains entries for books and periodicals only.
Dictionary Catalog of the Manuscript Division (see 109)	The Research Libraries Catalog does not include any entries for this division.
Dictionary Catalog of the Map Division (see 47)	The Research Libraries Catalog does not include any entries for this division.

Dictionary Catalog of the Music Collection (see 303)	The Research Libraries Catalog contains entries for books and periodicals only, and none for scores, librettos, and the like.
Dictionary Catalog of the Oriental Division (see 197)	The Research Libraries Catalog contains all entries except for materials in Oriental alphabets.
Dictionary Catalog of the Prints Division (see 292)	The Research Libraries Catalog does not include any entries for this division.
Dictionary Catalog of the Rare Book Division (see 110)	The Research Libraries Catalog contains most entries for books and periodicals.
Dictionary Catalog of the Schomburg Collection (see 242)	The Research Libraries Catalog does not include any entries for this collection.
Dictionary Catalog and Shelf List of the Spencer Collection (see 28)	The Research Libraries Catalog contains entries for all books of the Spencer Collection, but not for other types of materials.
Catalog of the Theatre and Drama Collections (see 304)	The Research Libraries Catalog contains all entries for books and periodicals, including printed plays, but not for the material listed in Part III, Non-Book Collections.
Catalog of the Arents Tobacco Collection	The Research Libraries Catalog contains no entries for this collection.

16. New York (City). Public Library. Research Libraries. Dictionary Catalog of the Research Libraries: A Cumulative List of Authors, Titles, and Subjects Representing Materials Added to the Collections Beginning January 1, 1972. New York: New York Public Library, 1972- (LC 73-174930).

The New York Public Library closed its catalog on December 31, 1971. The old catalog is being photoreproduced as a giant, 800-volume book catalog by the New York Public Library and G. K. Hall (see 15). This is the new catalog, produced by computer in book form, and in a variety of very easy-to-read typefaces. It is a dictionary catalog of main entries, added entries, distinctive titles, and subject entries, and conforms to Anglo-American Cataloging Rules and Library of Congress practices. Library of Congress subject headings are used. Main entries have full bibliographic descriptions, except tracings; other entries are somewhat abbreviated. Filing is word by word and is based on the simplest possible rules to permit computer filing.

This catalog includes entries for works in almost all the different divisions and collections of The New York Public Library Research Libraries. G. K. Hall has published the catalogs of many of these divisions and collections. Most of them have been supplemented to 1972, when this new computer-produced catalog began. In general, these divisional catalogs, with their specialized cataloging practices and many analytics, are no longer being maintained. The single exception is the Schomburg Center for Research in Black Culture; works added to this collection may still receive added notes and special subject headings, and books may be analyzed.

Included in the catalog are books, microforms, music scores, some sheet maps, motion pictures, and phonorecords. Works in almost all languages can be found, including, in separate alphabets, Hebrew since 1975, and Cyrillic since 1977. Before these dates, these languages were included in the catalog but in romanized form.

The catalog is issued as a paperbound set with cumulating supplements. From time to time the basic volumes are reissued to include all supplements.

17. New York (City). Public Library. Research Libraries. Guide to Festschriften. 2 vols. Boston: G. K. Hall, 1977 (LC 77-153165).

This catalog lists Festschriften, collected essays in honor of scholars by colleagues, friends, and students, or works of collected essays on the occasion of anniversaries of learned societies, institutions, and corporations.

The catalog is in two parts. Volume one, titled The Retrospective Festschriften Collection of The New York Public Library: Materials Cataloged through 1971, is a main-entry catalog. There are often extensive notes giving names of contributors and titles of essays. The New York Public Library is especially strong in Festschriften in the fields of art, Black studies, business, dance, economics, finance, history, Judaica, linguistics, literature, literary history and criticism, music, Orientalia, philosophy, science and technology, Slavic studies, and theatre.

Volume two, titled A Dictionary Catalog of Festschriften in The New York Public Library (1972-1976) and the Library of Congress (1968-1976), is a computer-produced dictionary catalog of main entries, subject entries, and some other secondary entries. It includes all Festschriften that were available at the time in the MARC data base.

18. Paris. Bibliothèque Nationale. Catalogue général des livres imprimés: auteurs. v. 1- . Paris: Impr. Nationale, 1900- .

_______. Catalogue général des livres imprimés: auteurs--

collectivités-auteurs--anonymes, 1960-1969. v. 1- . Paris: Impr. Nationale, 1972- .

This is an alphabetical catalog of personal authors, with cross-references. There are no title or corporate title entries and so no entries for anonymous works, periodicals, society transactions, or government publications. Sheehy calls this "an important modern catalog, the value of which cannot be overestimated"[6] and praises the excellence of the cataloging, which is much more complete than that of the British Library catalog (see 3). The catalog is most comprehensive for French publications but is also very strong in other Romance-language and classical materials.

The catalog has been published volume by volume in alphabetical order over the last 80 years, with each volume representing the works in the library in that part of the alphabet up to the publication of the volume; volume 227, Wood-Wuze, was published in 1977. This policy resulted in the catalog's major flaw: works of authors whose names begin with the letter "A" are represented only through 1900; works of those with names in the middle of the alphabet may have imprint dates 50 years later, leading to a chronologically imbalanced catalog. The catalog has not yet been completed but, beginning with volume 189, no new imprints after 1959 have been included in the basic catalog.

The supplements to the catalog of the Bibliothèque Nationale include anonymous works, joint authors, and corporate authors.

19. United States. Library of Congress. Library of Congress Catalog--Books: Subjects; A Cumulative List Represented by Library of Congress Printed Cards. Washington, 1950- (LC 50-60682). Quarterly with annual and quinquennial cumulations:

________. 1950-1954. 20 vols. Ann Arbor, Mich.: J. W. Edwards, 1955.

________. 1955-1959. 22 vols. Paterson, N.J.: Pageant Books, 1960.

________. 1960-1964. 25 vols. Ann Arbor, Mich.: J. W. Edwards [n. d.].

________. 1965-1969. 42 vols. Ann Arbor, Mich.: J. W. Edwards, 1970.

________. 1970-1974. 100 vols. Totowa, N.J.: Rowman and Littlefield, 1976.

This is a subject catalog of works represented by Library of Congress printed cards. For the most part these are titles held by the Library of Congress, but also included are titles owned by other American libraries participating in LC's cooperative cataloging program. These relatively few libraries are not to be confused with the more than 700 libraries that simply report their holdings to The National Union Catalog. Library of Congress Catalog--Books: Subjects, therefore, is neither the subject catalog of the Library of Congress nor the subject complement to The National Union Catalog, but simply LC printed cards arranged in subject order.

Included in it are entries for books, pamphlets, periodicals and other serials, maps, and atlases. Works in all languages written in the Arabic, Cyrillic, Gaelic, Greek, Hebraic, Indic, or Roman alphabets, or in Chinese, Japanese, or Korean characters are included.

The subject headings used are, of course, taken from or based on Subject Headings Used in the Dictionary Catalogs of the Library of Congress. See and see-also references are included. One especially interesting feature of the catalog is the inclusion of belles-lettres under subject headings indicating the literature and literary form of the work; e.g., "French Fiction," "Peruvian Poetry," and "Fiction in English."

20. United States. Library of Congress. Shelflist of the Library of Congress. Available in approx. 248 reels of microfilm from United States Historical Documents Institute, Arlington, Va., or in microfilm or approx. 3229 microfiches from University Microfilms International, Ann Arbor, Mich., 1978-79.

The Shelflist of the Library of Congress lists, in LC classification order, every title cataloged and classified by the Library of Congress up to the time of filming in 1978 and 1979. These total 6.8 million titles, making this "the world's largest card catalog."[7] The catalog has all of the advantages and disadvantages of any shelflist; works are arranged in a subject order, but each work is listed only once.

Most of the shelflist cards provide full author and title, date and place of publication, publisher, tracings, and notes, as well as the classification number. This is an exact copy, however, of the working shelflist of the Library of Congress, and many of the cards are covered with pencilled notes, or provide only the briefest of information.

There are two guides available to the Shelflist. One, User's Guide to the Library of Congress Shelflist Reference System, by Nancy Olson (Arlington, Va.: United States Historical Documents Institute, 1980), describes the catalog in microfilm as published by the Historical Documents Institute and provides the reel numbers for each part of the classification. The other, The Library of Congress Shelflist: A User's Guide to the Microfiche Edition, edited by Linda K. Hamilton (Ann Arbor, Mich.: University Microfilms International, 1979, 2 vols.) provides a list of which call numbers may be found on which microfiches and also provides a brief index to the Library of Congress classification system. Both guides also give the history of the shelflist at the Library of Congress.

Both guides also suggest that the Shelflist can best be used in combination with several indexes that have been published separately. The Combined Indexes to the Library of Congress Classification Schedules by Nancy Olson (Arlington, Va.: United States Historical Documents Institute, 1974) is a 15-volume index by subject keyword, personal name, and geographic name to the Library of Congress classification, and thus serves as a detailed subject index to the shelflist. Most subjects and names have more than one classification number associated with them. The Cumulative Title Index to the Classified Collections of the Library of Congress: 1978 (Arlington, Va.: Carrollton Press, 1980, 132 vol.) lists, by title, all works cataloged and classified by the Library of Congress from 1897 to 1978. It provides the main entry, the date of publication, the LC card number, and the complete classification number, and thus acts as a title index to the shelflist. By locating a known work through the Cumulative Title Index or through the National Union Catalog (which can serve as an author index to the Shelflist for works cataloged by the Library of Congress), one may easily find others on the same subject in the shelflist, since they should be in the same classification.

2. MANUSCRIPTS, RARE BOOKS, AND BOOK ARTS

Most of the manuscript and rare book catalogs have been included in the chapters on the subjects they cover and are represented here only by cross-references to their entries in those chapters. In this section are listed catalogs of rare books and manuscripts that cover all subjects, as well as catalogs on the history of printing and on the art of the book.

One of the most impressive recent catalogs of rare books is the Catalog of the Rare Book Room of the University of Illinois at Urbana-Champaign (23), a main-entry catalog representing over 100,000 books.

The largest catalog on the history of printing and the book arts is the Dictionary Catalogue of the History of Printing from the John M. Wing Foundation in the Newberry Library (29). The most unusual, however, is the Imprint Catalog in the Rare Book Division of The New York Public Library (27), which is arranged by the name of the city where each rare book in The New York Public Library was printed.

For manuscripts, the most useful catalog is the National Union Catalog of Manuscript Collections (25), issued annually, which provides information on which libraries hold different manuscript collections.

American Antiquarian Society, Worcester, Mass. Catalogue of the Manuscript Collections of the American Antiquarian Society. 4 vols. Boston: G. K. Hall, 1979. (see 97)

American Antiquarian Society, Worcester, Mass. Library. A Dictionary Catalog of American Books Pertaining to the 17th through 19th Centuries. 20 vols. Westport, Conn.: Greenwood Pub. Corp., 1971. (see 98)

American Philosophical Society, Philadelphia. Library. Catalog of Manuscripts in the American Philosophical Society Library. 10 vols. Westport, Conn.: Greenwood Pub. Corp., 1970. (see 391)

Amistad Research Center. Author and Added Entry Catalog of the American Missionary Association Archives. 3 vols. Westport, Conn.: Greenwood, 1970. (see 224)

Archives of American Art. The Card Catalog of the Manuscript Collections of the Archives of American Art. 10 vols. Wilmington, Del.: Scholarly Resources, 1981. (see 273)

Arthur and Elizabeth Schlesinger Library on the History of Women in America. The Manuscript Inventories and the Catalogs of the Manuscripts, Books and Pictures. 3 vols. Boston: G. K. Hall, 1973. (see 249)

Boston. Public Library. Canadian Manuscripts in the Boston Public Library. 76 pages. Boston: G. K. Hall, 1971. (see 130)

Boston. Public Library. A Catalog of the Defoe Collection in the Boston Public Library. 200 p. Boston: G. K. Hall, 1966. (see 154)

Boston. Public Library. Manuscripts of the American Revolution in the Boston Public Library. 157 p. Boston: G. K. Hall, 1968. (see 99)

California. University. Bancroft Library. A Guide to the Manuscript Collections. 2 vols. Berkeley: Univ. of California Pr., 1963- . (see 120)

California. University. University at Los Angeles. William Andrews Clark Memorial Library. Dictionary Catalog of the William Andrews Clark Memorial Library. 15 vols. Boston: G. K. Hall, 1974. (see 156)

California. University, Santa Barbara. Library. The William Wyles Collection. 5 vols. Westport, Conn.: Greenwood, 1970. (see 100)

Cashel, Ireland (Diocese). Library. Catalogue of the Cashel Diocesan Library. 635 p. Boston: G. K. Hall, 1973. (see 258)

21. Columbia University. Libraries. The History of Printing

from Its Beginnings to 1930: The Subject Catalogue of the American Type Founders Company Library in the Columbia University Libraries. 4 vols. Millwood, N.Y.: Kraus International Publications, 1980 (LC 80-13377).

The American Type Founders Company began its library and museum of printing arts in 1908 at the instigation of its advertising manager, Henry L. Bullen, who then served as librarian and curator. The collection was deposited with Columbia University in 1936, purchased by Columbia in 1941, and later dispersed among the other collections in Columbia's library.

The catalog was compiled by Bullen and his wife, Grace Bullen. It is in the main a subject catalog, with some author and catchword-title entries. The compilers probably used no authority list for the subject headings, and several headings must be checked to find information on a subject. However, at the beginning of the first volume there is a list of approximately 2,000 subject headings used in the catalog, with some see and see-also references.

Works listed in the catalog range over a variety of subjects associated with printing, such as the artistic, technical, and economic aspects of printing; political aspects of freedom of the press and the effects of government regulation; typographical unions; trade publications; journalism; and the history of books, printing, and libraries. These are discussed in books, pamphlets, periodicals, manuscripts, ephemera, broadsides and leaflets, photographs, portraits, incunabula, and rare books. Dates of the material range from the fifteenth century to 1933. There are many analytics for periodical articles (predating the Graphic Arts Index) and for essays in books.

Cornell University. Libraries. The Cornell Wordsworth Collection. 458 p. Ithaca, N.Y.: Cornell University Pr., 1957. (see 157)

Cornell University. Libraries. Petrarch: Catalogue of the Petrarch Collection. 737 p. Millwood, N.Y.: Kraus-Thomson Organization, 1974. (see 136)

Cornell University. Libraries. Witchcraft: Catalogue of the Witchcraft Collection. 644 p. Millwood, N.Y.: Kraus-Thomson Organization, 1977. (see 259)

22. Edinburgh. University. Library. Index to Manuscripts; Edinburgh University Library. 2 vols. Boston: G. K. Hall, 1964 (LC 77-377769).

The Library of the University of Edinburgh was founded in 1580. At the time of publication of this catalog its manuscript collections totalled over 8,000 bound volumes and 28,000 separate letters and pieces.

This catalog indexes the post-medieval collection. It is a dictionary catalog of personal names, place names, and subjects. The collection is especially strong in literary and historical materials. Included are Edinburgh University lectures and class notes. Most of the materials listed here date from the eighteenth and nineteenth centuries.

Folger Shakespeare Library, Washington, D.C. Catalog of Manuscripts of the Folger Shakespeare Library. 3 vols. Boston: G. K. Hall, 1971. (see 158)

Folger Shakespeare Library, Washington, D.C. Catalog of Printed Books of the Folger Shakespeare Library. 28 vols. Boston: G. K. Hall, 1970. (see 159)

German Baroque Literature: A Descriptive Catalogue of the Collection of Harold Jantz; and a Guide to the Collection on Microfilm. 2 vols. New Haven: Research Publications, 1974. (see 137)

Greenwich, Eng. National Maritime Museum. Guide to the Manuscripts in the National Maritime Museum. London: Mansell, 1977- . (see 73)

Harvard University. Graduate School of Business Administration. Baker Library. Kress Library of Business and Economics. Catalogue. 5 vols. Boston: Baker Library, 1940-1967. (see 356)

Hebrew Union College--Jewish Institute of Religion. American Jewish Archives. Manuscript Catalog of the American Jewish Archives. 4 vols. Boston: G. K. Hall, 1971. (see 254)

Hispanic Society of America. Printed Books, 1468-1700, in the Hispanic Society of America. 614 p. New York: The Society, 1965. (see 180)

23. Illinois. University at Urbana-Champaign. Library. Rare Book Room. Catalog. 11 vols. Boston: G. K. Hall, 1972 (LC 73-180423). First Supplement. 2 vols., 1978.

The rare books in the University of Illinois Library were not established as a separate collection until 1937. By 1971 the Rare Book Room housed a collection of nearly 100,000 volumes. The most significant part of the collection is the Milton Collection, with 100 seventeenth-century editions of works by John Milton and approximately 3,000 volumes of works about him. Also worthy of note are the collections on British historical, economic, and literary works of the eighteenth century; works on the history of science, particularly geology; the Baskette Collection on freedom of expression; the Meine Collection of American Humor, Local Color, and Folklore; and the H. G. Wells Collection, containing 61,000 letters representing the correspondence of Wells described in about 24,000 cards; and a collection of approximately 1,800 books, pamphlets, periodicals, newspapers, and ephemera relating to Sir Winston Churchill.

The catalog is an alphabetical catalog of main entries, with added entries for some titles, illustrators, translators, editors, and compilers. Certain of the special collections named above are listed separately as appendices.

India Office Library. Index of Post-1937 European Manuscript Accessions. 156 p. Boston: G. K. Hall, 1964. (see 207)

Institute of Chartered Accountants in England and Wales, London. Library. Historical Accounting Literature. 386 p. London: Mansell, 1975. (see 358)

International Federation of Film Archives. Union Catalogue of Books and Periodicals Published Before 1914. Bruxelles: Cinémathèque Royale de Belgique, 1967. (see 288)

Keats-Shelley Memorial, Rome. Catalog of Books and Manuscripts at the Keats-Shelley Memorial House in Rome. 667 p. Boston: G. K. Hall, 1969. (see 163)

London. University. Goldsmiths' Company Library of Economic Literature. Catalogue of the Goldsmiths' Library of Economic Literature. 2 vols. London: Cambridge Univ. Pr., 1970-1975. (see 360)

24. London. University. Library. The Palaeography Collection. 2 vols. Boston: G. K. Hall, 1968 (LC 74-152793).

The Palaeography Collection in the University of London Library was consolidated in 1955. Included in this catalog are works on the study of manuscripts, papyri, and archives; catalogs and published facsimilies of manuscripts; and works on all aspects of the medieval book. There are analytics for articles in periodicals, in Festschriften, and in books. Titles listed are in Greek, Latin, and Western European languages, but not in Slavonic or Oriental languages.

The catalog is in two parts. Volume one is an author catalog of personal and corporate authors. Rules for entry are based on those of the British Museum Catalogue. Added entries are in the form of cross-references to the main entry.

Volume two is a subject catalog. Subject headings are based loosely on those of the Library of Congress, with substantial modifications. There is a list of the subject headings used, with _see_ references and subdivisions, at the beginning of the subject catalog.

Mariners' Museum, Newport News, Va. _Catalog of Maps, Ships' Papers and Logbooks._ 505 p. Boston: G. K. Hall, 1964. (see 41)

Massachusetts Historical Society, Boston. Library. _Catalog of Manuscripts of the Massachusetts Historical Society._ 7 vols. Boston: G. K. Hall, 1969. (see 104)

Michigan. University. William L. Clements Library. _Author/Title Catalog of Americana, 1493-1860, in the William L. Clements Library._ 7 vols. Boston: G. K. Hall, 1970. (see 105)

National Museum of Natural History. Department of Anthropology. National Anthropological Archives. _Catalog to Manuscripts at the National Anthropological Archives._ 4 vols. Boston: G. K. Hall, 1975. (see 63)

25. _The National Union Catalog of Manuscript Collections, 1959/61- ._ Washington: Library of Congress, 1962- (LC 62-17486).

This is a serially-issued catalog of collections of manuscripts in the Library of Congress and participating libraries. "A collection is defined as a large group of papers (manuscript or typescript, originals or copies, of letters, memoranda, diaries, accounts, logbooks, drafts, and the like, including associated printed or near-print materials) usually having a common source and formed by or around an individual, a family, or a corporate entity, or devoted to a single theme" [Introduction]. Included are transcripts or recordings of oral history interviews, beginning with the 1970 annual.

The entries are prepared by Library of Congress catalogers from information supplied by the participating libraries, and edited to conform to _Anglo-American Cataloging Rules._ Each entry contains a main heading consisting usually of the name of the individual or family around whom the collection revolves, a title for the collection, a physical description of the size or extent of the collection, the location of the collection (the owning or holding library), and a brief annotation indicating the scope and content of the collection.

The entries are listed together with entries for other collections from the same institution. The order is by card number, however, and the institutions are not arranged in alphabetical order, although there is an index to the card numbers for each institution.

A major part of each catalog is the subject index to the collections. Usually these indexes cover more than just one volume of the catalog, but include the collections listed in the volumes for the previous year or two as well. The index includes names of individuals as subjects or collectors, names of places discussed in the collections, and topical subjects describing the contents of the collections. These subject headings are not standard Library of Congress subject headings, but many cross-references are provided for aid.

New York (City). Botanical Garden. Library. Catalog of the Manuscript and Archival Collections and Index to the Correspondence of John Torrey. 473 p. Boston: G. K. Hall, 1973. (see 412)

New York (City). Public Library. Berg Collection. Dictionary Catalog of the Henry W. and Albert A. Berg Collection of English and American Literature. 5 vols. Boston: G. K. Hall, 1969. (see 164)

New York (City). Public Library. Manuscript Division. Dictionary Catalog. 2 vols. Boston: G. K. Hall, 1967. (see 109)

26. New York (City). Public Library. Rare Book Division. Catalog of Special and Private Presses in the Rare Book Division. 2 vols. Boston: G. K. Hall, 1978 (ISBN 0-8161-0097-7).

More than 1,200 special presses, book clubs, and book designers are represented in this collection by about 15,000 books and pamphlets, dating from the eighteenth century to the present. Most of the works are from the United States, Canada, and the British Isles, but presses from Europe, South America, Australia, and New Zealand are also represented. Presses range from the eighteenth-century press of John Baskerville and Horace Walpole's Strawberry Hill Press to the modern presses of Lewis and Dorothy Allen, Walter Hamady's Perishable Press, Richard-Gabriel Rummonds' Plain Wrapper Press, Claire Van Vliet's Janus Press, and new presses like Mason Hill, Tideline, and Whittington. Book designers listed include John Henry Nash, William Goudy, and Bruce Rogers. Some of the book clubs are: Book Club of California, Grolier Club, Limited Editions Club, and the Roxburghe Club.

The catalog is arranged alphabetically by name of press and, under the press, alphabetically by the author of the book. There is a list of the presses, book clubs, etc. represented in the collection.

New York (City). Public Library. Rare Book Division. Dictionary Catalog of the Rare Book Division. 21 vols. Boston: G. K. Hall, 1971. (see 110)

27. New York (City). Public Library. Rare Book Division. The Imprint Catalog in the Rare Book Division. 21 vols. Boston: G. K. Hall, 1979 (LC 79-101770).

This catalog is unusual because entries are not for authors, titles, or subjects, but for imprints. The catalog is arranged alphabetically by the Anglicized name of the city, town, or ship where the work was printed. Within the city the arrangement is chronological, and then alphabetical by author. There are cross-references from mythical towns, and from alternate forms of a town's name. There are over 320,000 cards for books and newspapers printed in over 12,000 cities and towns, dating from the fifteenth century to the twentieth.

Included in the catalog are entries for all the books in the Rare Book Division plus all the cataloged books in the Spencer Collection of Illustrated Books and Fine Bindings (see 28), as well as important books in other parts of The New York Public Library. Earliest imprints are emphasized, and the catalog is most complete for printing done in the United States and Latin America. All books published before the following dates in the general collections of The New York Public Library are included here: 1600 for European books; 1700 for English printing; 1800 for Americana regardless of where printed; and 1820 for American imprints. Some of the entries refer only to copies of title pages in the collection; the library does not own the rest of the book. Other entries have been cut from auction catalogs and are for works not owned by The New York Public Library at all.

Guide cards in the catalog give the name of the city and information about it, such as the name and date of the first printer, the first newspaper, and the first almanac. Unfortunately, the guide cards are not always easy to find, and there are no running headings at the top of the page for the names of cities, making the locating of a particular city difficult. However, the catalog can be invaluable for establishing the authorship of a book when only the place and date are known, or for an overview of what was being printed in a particular place at a particular time.

28. New York (City). Public Library. Spencer Collection. Dictionary Catalog and Shelf List of the Spencer Collection of Illustrated Books and Manuscripts and Fine Bind-

ings. 2 vols. Boston: G. K. Hall, 1971 (LC 73-175479).

The Spencer Collection is devoted to the art of book illustration, illuminated manuscripts, and book making. It was created by the 1912 bequest of William Augustus Spencer, who left his personal collection of 232 illustrated French books, produced from 1880 to 1910, to The New York Public Library. At the time of publication of the catalog, the collection had over 6,000 titles in manuscripts and printed books, especially European books and Oriental illustrated books. These latter, however, do not appear in the dictionary catalog but only in the shelf list.

The dictionary catalog contains author, title, and subject cards. In addition, and of particular interest, it has form headings, such as "Bindings, 16th Cent., French," followed by the name of the individual or family who produced the work; or "Etchings," or "Festival Books," all of which succeed in bringing together those types of works. Titles dated from the seventh century to the twentieth century.

The shelf list is in two parts, in two separate appendices. Appendix I, Shelf List of Printed Books, is arranged alphabetically by country, and within country by date, enabling the reader to find listed together examples of illustrated books from particular places and times. Appendix II, Shelf List of Manuscripts and Oriental Printed Books, is in three parts: 1) manuscripts in the Latin alphabet; 2) manuscripts in non-Latin alphabets; 3) Oriental printed books.

New York (City). Union Theological Seminary. Library. Catalogue of the McAlpin Collection of British History and Theology. 5 vols. New York, 1927-30. (see 268)

Newberry Library, Chicago. Bibliographical Inventory to the Early Music in the Newberry Library. 587 p. Boston: G. K. Hall, 1976. (see 305)

Newberry Library, Chicago. A Catalogue of the Everett D. Graff Collection of Western Americana. 854 p. Chicago: Univ. of Chicago Pr., 1968. (see 123)

29. Newberry Library, Chicago. John M. Wing Foundation. Dictionary Catalogue of the History of Printing from the John M. Wing Foundation in the Newberry Library. 6 vols. Boston: G. K. Hall, 1961 (LC 64-314). First Supplement. 3 vols., 1970.

The John M. Wing Foundation of the Newberry Library maintains a collection of over 23,000 volumes on the history of printing. It was started by a Chicago printer and publisher named John Mansir

Wing, who left his library, together with an endowment, to the Newberry Library. "There are three main lines of acquisition: a collection of books illustrating the development of the printed book, important historically or for excellence in design or workmanship; an extensive library of the bibliographies, monographs, histories, and other background works essential to the serious study of the history of printing; and a collection of type specimens, printers' manuals, works on papermaking, bookbinding, illustration, and the other arts and crafts ancillary to printing" [Introduction]. Included are rare books, incunabula, calligraphy, archives, and documents. Works are in all Western European languages, and some have imprint dates as early as the fifteenth century. Not all the works in the collection are included in the published catalog, however.

This is a dictionary catalog. Personal entries are of several kinds: 1) autographs, bookplates, and other evidence of provenance; 2) works by an author; 3) books designed, illustrated, published, etc., by a person; 4) works about a person. Cards are annotated and may contain information that is difficult to find elsewhere, such as previously unidentified designers of books, notes on the typefaces designed by individuals, and information about a particular book.

The fifth volume is a separate catalog of additional entries for all incunabula and for books chosen as examples of printing or publishing. Volume six is a chronological file of these holdings.

Because of the annotations, the chronological file and file of place names, and the library's attempt to research information on individuals responsible for the production of a book, the catalog is a valuable research tool even if the user has no access to the collection.

Oklahoma. University. Library. The Catalogue of the History of Science Collections of the University of Oklahoma Libraries. 2 vols. London: Mansell, 1976. (see 382)

Philadelphia. Free Library. Hampton L. Carson Collection. Catalog of the Hampton L. Carson Collection Illustrative of the Growth of the Common Law. 2 vols. Boston: G. K. Hall, 1962. (see 347)

Philadelphia. Library Company. Afro-Americana, 1553-1906. 714 p. Boston: G. K. Hall, 1973. (see 245)

Royal Commonwealth Society. Library. Manuscript Catalogue. 193 p. London: Mansell, 1975. (see 82)

Saint David's University College, Lampeter, Wales. Library. A Catalogue of the Tract Collection of the Saint David's University College. 315 p. London: Mansell, 1975. (see 84)

Scholes, Robert E. The Cornell Joyce Collection. 225 p. Ithaca, N.Y.: Cornell Univ. Pr., 1961. (see 166)

Scotland. National Library, Edinburgh. Shelf-Catalogue of the Blaikie Collection of Jacobite Pamphlets, Broadsides and Proclamations. 42 p. Boston: G. K. Hall, 1964. (see 87)

30. Scotland. National Library, Edinburgh. A Short-Title Catalogue of Foreign Books Printed up to 1600; Books Printed or Published Outside the British Isles Now in the National Library of Scotland and the Library of the Faculty of Advocates, Edinburgh. 545 p. Edinburgh: H. M. Stationery Office, 1970 (LC 77-579020).

The title of this catalog is a good description of its contents. It is arranged by author or other main entry. Official publications are listed under the name of the country responsible; publications of corporate bodies are under the name of the city or country where located; and university theses are listed under the name of the university. There are liberal cross-references to preferred forms of names.

The library was founded in 1682 as the Library of the Faculty of Advocates, and was intended to be principally a legal library. It was transferred to the state in 1925, becoming the National Library of Scotland. It is now one of the four largest libraries in Great Britain, with holdings of over three million books and pamphlets.

Sophia Smith Collection. Catalogs of the Sophia Smith Collection, Women's History Archive. 7 vols. Boston: G. K. Hall, 1975. (see 251)

Union Catalogue of Scientific Libraries in the University of Cambridge: Books Published Before 1801. 9 microfiches. London: Mansell, 1977. (see 385)

United States. Library of Congress. Rare Book Division. Catalog of Broadsides in the Rare Book Division. 4 vols. Boston: G. K. Hall, 1972. (see 117)

United States. Library of Congress. Rare Book Division. Children's Books in the Rare Book Division. 2 vols. Totowa, N.J.: Rowman and Littlefield, 1975. (see 338)

Yale University. Library. Yale Collection of German Literature.

<u>German Baroque Literature.</u> 2 vols. New Haven: Yale Univ. Pr., 1958-1969. (see 152)

Yale University. Library. Yale Collection of Western Americana. <u>Catalog of the Yale Collection of Western Americana.</u> 4 vols. Boston: G. K. Hall, 1962. (see 129)

3. GEOGRAPHY, MAPS, VOYAGES AND EXPLORATION

Much of our knowledge of the geography of the earth has been acquired through the efforts of the early explorers, and from maritime expeditions, concerned as they were with mapping and describing the coasts, the oceans, and the land masses. The catalogs of the libraries that deal with geography, cartography and maps, and voyages and exploration, therefore, have been considered as a group here.

One of the largest geography libraries in the world is that of the American Geographical Society, which has published its catalog with supplements to keep it up to date (31). Its arrangement is primarily a geographic one, befitting its subject, and this is probably the first catalog one should refer to for geographic information on different regions of the world.

For those scholars particularly interested in the polar regions, the three largest polar libraries in the world have all published their catalogs. Of these, the Scott Polar Research Institute's catalog (50) is the largest and most comprehensive, but not the easiest to use because its classified arrangement is difficult to learn. However, it catalogs large numbers of periodical articles, as does the Arctic Institute of North America's catalog (34), which is arranged in dictionary format and has the advantage of assigning many subject headings to each item cataloged. The Stefansson Collection <u>Dictionary Catalog</u> (51) is the least current of the three.

There are many catalogs of maps and atlases. The largest are the catalogs of the British Museum's Map Room (35), The New York Public Library's Map Division (47), and the National Map Collection of Canada (46) which specializes in maps of that country. Maps appearing in books and periodicals are indexed in the American Geographical Society's <u>Index to Maps in Books and Periodicals</u> (33) and, to some extent, in the catalog of The New York Public Library's Map Division, which includes, along with maps published individually, maps appearing in non-cartographic publications.

31. American Geographical Society of New York. <u>Research Catalogue.</u> 15 vols. Boston: G. K. Hall, 1962 (LC 63-4293). <u>First Supplement: Regional Catalogue.</u> 2 vols., 1972. <u>First Supplement: Topical Catalogue.</u> 2 vols., 1974. <u>Second Supplement.</u> 2 vols., 1978.

This catalog represents the largest special collection in the Western Hemisphere in the field of geography. [8] All aspects of geography are covered, including travel and exploration, mathematical geography, physical geography and geology, human geography (including population, economic geography, and political geography), the history and methodology of geography, and cartography.

The catalog is a classified one, arranged according to the society's own geographic classification scheme, which breaks the world up into geographic regions: North America, South America, Europe, Africa, Asia, Australasia, Polar Regions, Oceans, and Tropics. These are further divided into subregions, and then into topical divisions and subdivisions. There is an initial two-volume section of general items divided topically. Guides to the systematic classification and maps of the regions are provided and must be consulted before the catalog can be used with any success. Works may be assigned more than one topical classification number (I have noticed as many as three for one work) and so appear in more than one place in the catalog, but most items have only one entry. There is no author index, making it very difficult to locate a known work.

Included are books, pamphlets, and government documents. Maps are not included, but a separate Index to Maps in Books and Periodicals has been published (see 33). There are analytical entries for selected periodical articles and chapters in edited volumes. The majority of the works are in English. The second supplement covers works published through 1976.

The collection is now housed in the University of Wisconsin-Milwaukee Library.

32. American Geographical Society of New York. Dept. of Exploration and Field Research. Catalogs of the Glaciology Collection. 3 vols. Boston: G. K. Hall, 1971 (LC 75-29394).

As the title implies, the subject of interest here is glaciology, and the related fields of climatology, hydrology, and geology. There are three separate catalogs.

Volume one is an Author/Title Catalog, really an author main-entry catalog, containing 20,000 entries.

Volume two is a classified Subject Catalog with 18,000 entries. The classification system is based on the Universal Decimal Classification for use in Polar Libraries. There is an alphabetical index to subjects and a numerical list of subjects. Items are sometimes given two classification numbers so they may be found under two different subjects in the catalog.

Volume three is a Geographic Catalog with 15,000 entries. Its main divisions are the continents, with some exceptions necessary because of the glaciological point of view (e.g., "Arctic" is a main division). These main regions are further broken down in subdivisions and second subdivisions. There is a breakdown of the geographic classification at the front of the volume, and there are numerous guide cards listing, for each second subdivision, the main division, and the subdivision involved.

Cards in this catalog are included from four sources: 1) Glaciology Department staff; 2) Library of Congress printed cards; 3) U. S. Army Cold Regions Research and Engineering Laboratory; and 4) the Scott Polar Research Institute (which has published its own catalog, see 50).

Included in the catalogs are entries for books, periodicals, reprints, maps, photographs, unpublished reports, and a great many technical reports. Most of the entries are analytics for journals or series. There are many annotations.

The dates for the entries are mostly from this century, and languages covered include English, Russian, and other European languages. Most of the titles in foreign languages have been translated.

33. American Geographical Society of New York. Map Department. Index to Maps in Books and Periodicals. 10 vols. Boston: G. K. Hall, 1968 (LC 68-5087). First Supplement. 603 p., 1971. Second Supplement. 568 p., 1976.

This extremely useful catalog indexes individual maps appearing in books and periodicals. Entries are arranged according to subject and geographical-political division in one alphabet. Within these subjects the arrangement is chronological. As an example of the hard-to-find information that can be located through this index, the subject heading "Ethnography," which is subdivided geographically, provides access to maps showing the distributions of native populations.

Each entry in the catalog gives the name of the map, the page on which it is to be found in the book or periodical, and full bibliographic information if the source is a book. Volume one lists the principal periodicals indexed, an international group of specialized geographical and cartographic journals. The First Supplement has a List of Areas Indexed giving name changes and cross-references for geographic areas.

Works indexed are in all the European languages and cover the nineteenth and twentieth centuries.

34. Arctic Institute of North America. Library. Catalogue of the Library of the Arctic Institute of North America, Montreal. 4 vols. Boston: G. K. Hall, 1968 (LC 73-180997). First Supplement. 902 p., 1971. Second Supplement. 2 vols., 1974. Third Supplement. 3 vols., 1980.

The Arctic Institute of North America, now part of the University of Calgary in Alberta, Canada, has "one of the three largest polar libraries in the world" [Preface]. It is chiefly concerned with the polar regions--in particular the Arctic or subarctic--with cold weather research, with oceanography, and with snow and ice studies. The library collects in the physical, biological, and social sciences, in technology, and in general interest materials. Beginning with the Second Supplement special efforts have been made to improve holdings in the social sciences, especially concentrating on northern peoples and community development.

This is a dictionary catalog of authors, subjects, added entries, and some titles. Subject headings used are similar to those of the Library of Congress, but generally many more are provided for a work than the Library of Congress would assign; the Preface states that twenty or more subject headings may be given to any one work. Many see and see-also references are provided. There are analytics for articles in the nonpolar serials--the 1968 catalog alone analyzes 4, 500 articles--while articles in polar journals are listed in the Institute's publication, Arctic Bibliography. Also analyzed are books, speeches, reports, and newspapers. Microfilms, tapes and recordings, master's and doctoral theses, papers presented at meetings, and unpublished studies are included. Maps are not listed. Works are primarily in English and Russian, and the Library of Congress's transliteration system for the Russian alphabet is followed. Titles span the period from 1599 to the 1970's; post-1978 material is available in a computer database called Arctic Science and Technology Information System (ASTIS).

35. British Museum. Dept. of Printed Books. Map Room. Catalogue of Printed Maps, Charts, and Plans. Photolithographic edition complete to 1964. 15 vols. London: British Museum, 1967 (LC 68-91645).

________. ________. Corrections and Additions. 55 p. London: British Museum, 1968.

British Library. Map Library. Catalogue of Printed Maps, Charts, and Plans: Ten Year Supplement, 1965-1974. 1380 columns. London: British Museum Publications, 1978 (LC 79-307082).

This is a dictionary catalog of "maps, atlases, globes and related materials, including literature on them" [Introduction]. Maps are entered under the name of the place, area, or geographic feature depicted; one map may be entered under two or more such names. There are cross-references from variant forms of geographic names. Under the geographic unit, subheadings divide the maps and atlases by type; e. g., agricultural maps, ethnographic maps, military atlases, and physical maps. There are also added entries under the names of surveyors, cartographers, engravers, compilers and editors, and publishers. The maps date from the seventeenth to the twentieth centuries.

36. California. University. Bancroft Library. Index to Printed Maps. 521 p. Boston: G. K. Hall, 1964 (LC 65-4745). First Supplement: Catalog of Manuscript and Printed Maps in the Bancroft Library. 581 p., 1975.

The Index to Printed Maps is a catalog of maps of California, the Western United States, and Mexico and Central America, in the Bancroft Library of the University of California at Berkeley. The maps date from the sixteenth to the twentieth centuries, although most are of the nineteenth century. This is an author and subject catalog, interfiled. The author is usually the cartographer, and the subject is generally a geographic entity, although there are selected topical headings, such as "Real Estate Maps" and "Railroads." The information given for each map includes the cartographer (if known), the title or subject of the map, the company or agency publishing it, the date, the size, and often the scale, projection, and color. Maps are classified using a modification of the Library of Congress classification system. There are some annotations.

The supplement, Catalog of Manuscript and Printed Maps in the Bancroft Library, is very different from the original volume. A new collecting policy was instituted in 1972. While the emphasis remains on Western North America, maps of all areas are collected if they were published before 1800, and of Western North America if they were published up to 1900. In 1970 a new method of classifying and cataloging maps was adopted. Maps are now entered under headings composed of area, subject (if any), date, and scale; added entries are provided for cartographer and publisher. The classification system used now is the University of California Map Classification System. In addition, individual maps from atlases and other books are indexed.

Great Britain. Ministry of Defence. Naval Library. Author and Subject Catalogues of the Naval Library, Ministry of Defence, London. 5 vols. Boston: G. K. Hall, 1967. (see 72)

37. Greenwich, England. National Maritime Museum. Library. Catalogue of the Library. vol. 1- . London: Her Majesty's Stationery Office, 1968- (LC 75-470799).

The National Maritime Museum Library was first assembled between 1928 and 1934. By 1968 it contained over 50,000 volumes on every aspect of maritime affairs. The catalog of the library is being issued in several parts according to subject. So far, five catalogs have been issued:

1. Voyages and Travel. 1968 (see 39).
2. Biography. 2 vols., 1969 (see 74).
3. Atlases and Cartography. 2 vols., 1971 (see 38).
4. Piracy and Privateering. 1972 (see 76).
5. Naval History; Part One: The Middle Ages to 1815. 1976 (see 75).

38. Greenwich, Eng. National Maritime Museum. Library. Atlases and Cartography. 2 vols. London: HMSO, 1971 (LC 74-862838) (Its Catalogue of the Library, 3).

The first part of this catalog is a list of atlases arranged by national origin of its maker, and within each country by name of individual cartographer. For each atlas all of the important maps contained in it are listed. At the end of the first part are listed works about cartography. Most of the items listed in Part One are old and rare, dating from the fifteenth century, although most of the imprint dates range from the sixteenth to the eighteenth century. There are 765 entries.

Part Two is a geographic index to individual maps in the atlases. Included in the index entry are the name of the cartographer and the entry number of the individual atlases and maps the index refers to.

39. Greenwich, Eng. National Maritime Museum. Library. Voyages and Travel. 403 p. London: HMSO, 1968 (LC 72-470679) (Its Catalogue of the Library, 1).

This is a short-title catalog with 1,204 entries, many with annotations. Included here are accounts of naval voyages from the sixteenth century onwards. The arrangement is by area of the world and, within area, by date. The beginning of each geographic section has a chronology of the major voyages to that region of the world with dates of the voyage, name of individual in charge, name of ship or ships, and area covered. There is an index of ships and a general index that lists mostly names of individuals involved in voyages. This is an excellent source of information for what voyages were made to different parts of the world and for who was involved in each voyage.

40. Harvard University. Library. Geography and Anthropology. 270 p. Cambridge, Mass.: distributed by Harvard University Press, 1979 (LC 79-617). (Widener Library Shelflist v. 60)

Two classes are listed in this volume of the shelflist of the Widener Library. The first, AN, has 1,600 entries for books of a general nature relating to anthropology and ethnology. Most of Harvard's books in these subjects are in the Tozzer Library of the Peabody Museum of Archaeology and Ethnology, which has published its own catalog (see 61). The second class, Geog, has about 7,400 entries for general works on geography, including theory, methods, and history of geography as a science; descriptive geographies of the whole world; general voyages and travels covering the whole world; and descriptive geography of and travels throughout Europe in general, the Arctic and Antarctic regions, and regions, like the tropics, which are not included in one of the history classes. Most of the works are in English, although there are many titles in German, French, Russian, and other languages. About half of the works were published before 1900, and all were cataloged before 1976, when Widener Library switched to the Library of Congress classification system.

For a further discussion of the Widener Library shelflists see 9.

41. Mariners Museum, Newport News, Va. Catalog of Maps, Ships Papers and Logbooks. 505 p. Boston: G. K. Hall, 1964 (LC 65-8799).

This is actually three separate catalogs. The first is a Map Catalog. This is a dictionary catalog with entries under the subject of the map, the name of the mapmaker, and the title of the map, if the title is distinctive. Following this is a chronological arrangement of older maps dating from 1500 to 1830. Over 1,600 maps are described in 5,400 cards.

The second catalog is a Catalog of Ships' Papers, listing over 2,000 dating from the seventeenth century. The papers include plans, specifications, licenses, captain's letters, journals, and broadsides. There are 4,300 cards with entries for the name of the ship, the captain, and general subjects such as "Clipper Ships."

The third catalog is of Log Books, Journals, Account Books, Letter Books. 278 items dating back to 1741 are listed in 900 cards. There are entries for the name of the ship, the captain, or the writer of the journal.

42. Mariners Museum. Newport News, Va. Catalog of Marine Photographs. 5 vols. Boston: G. K. Hall, 1964 (LC 65-6592).

This is a classified catalog of over 100,000 photographs of marine subjects. There are photographs of original scenes as well as photographs of paintings, drawings, plans, etc. The classification is based on the subjects of the photographs, such as types of ships, naval engagements, wars, portraits, ornaments of ships, etc. There is a Guide to Subjects and Classifications, which describes how each of the major classes is arranged, and a brief index to the classification system. There is also an Appendix that contains brief files of the names of artists, photographs of interiors of vessels, and photographs of shipwrecks.

There is generally only one entry per photograph. The cards often give detailed information, especially for ships, whose former names, owners, and reasons for demise might be listed. There are cross-references to the correct form of a name.

43. Mariners Museum, Newport News, Va. Catalog of Marine Prints and Paintings. 3 vols. Boston: G. K. Hall, 1964 (LC 65-84734).

This catalog contains entries for approximately 10,000 prints and paintings owned by the Mariners Museum. These include scenes of sailing ships, harbors and dockyards, flags, disasters, naval battles, steamships, whaling and fishing, etc.

Extensive information is provided on each card including: the name (of the ship, the individual, or the place depicted); the dates of existence of ships; the date of the scene depicted; the type of medium of the print or painting; the category of the scene (whether ship, portrait, harbor, etc.); the title of the scene; the name of the individual or individuals responsible (painter, publisher, etc.); and the size.

The catalog is in two parts. Volume one is a main-entry catalog. The main entry is usually the name of a ship or a place. Volumes two and three contain secondary entries. One main entry may have many secondary entries. These include entries for names of individuals; of ships depicted in battle scenes, disasters, etc.; of artists and publishers; of shipbuilders; and subject entries, such as "Naval Battles." A very thorough cataloging job has been done here.

44. Mariners Museum, Newport News, Va. Library. The Mariners Museum, Newport News, Virginia: Dictionary Catalog of the Library. 9 vols. Boston: G. K. Hall, 1964 (LC 76-356576).

The Library of the Mariners Museum has one of the finest collections on maritime subjects. Its holdings' special strengths are in shipbuilding, navigation, voyages and exploration, naval history, and merchant shipping.

This is a dictionary catalog of authors, titles, and subjects that uses Library of Congress subject headings. Library of Congress printed cards are often used, and no subject headings are added or changed. Titles are mostly in English, although other European languages are included, and date back to the fifteenth century, but most titles were published in the nineteenth or twentieth century. There are analytics for articles in the U.S. Naval Institute Proceedings, Virginia Cavalcade, United Service, Naval Chronicle, and other selected periodicals. Articles are fully cataloged. At the time of its publication, the catalog represented a library of 44,000 volumes.

The ninth volume is a supplement containing three separate files: 1) a chronological file of books, 1497-1825; 2) uncataloged books; and 3) Fleet Lists, Ship Owners and Shipyards, a catalog of names of shipping companies and owners, compiled from the journals Belgian Shiplover, Marine News, Sea Breezes, and Steamboat Bill of Facts, which have been indexed through 1963 or 1964.

45. Michigan. University. William L. Clements Library. Research Catalog of Maps of America to 1860 in the William L. Clements Library. 4 vols. Boston: G. K. Hall, 1972 (LC 73-157170).

This is a catalog of maps of America, designed to facilitate research in historical cartography, the history of map printing, discovery and exploration of the New World, settlement and trade,

American colonial history, the American Revolution, transportation routes, and the opening of the West. It includes both separate printed and manuscript maps and many analytical entries for maps in atlases and in printed books. Especially noteworthy are the early French and Dutch atlases and separate map sheets, and the eighteenth-century British manuscript maps.

The catalog is in three parts. Volumes one and two are arranged alphabetically by name of cartographer and title of map, with names and titles interfiled. The second section, volumes three and four, is a Geographic Area Catalog, composed of city, county, state, and regional designations. Also included in the Geographic Catalog are four subjects: Canals, Forts, Indians, and Railroads. The last section, at the end of volume four, is a list of atlases, arranged in two parts: by name of publisher, and chronologically. The card format and the cataloging system were designed for and by the Clements library.

The catalog of the book collection of the Clements library has been published separately (see 105).

46. National Map Collection. Catalogue of the National Map Collection, Public Archives of Canada, Ottawa, Ontario. 16 vols. Boston: G. K. Hall, 1976 (LC 76-379551).

The National Map Collection contains the world's largest and most comprehensive record of Canadian mapping from the discovery of North America to the present. In 1976 the collection numbered approximately 750,000 items, but only about 10 to 15 percent of the collection is listed in the catalog. This is a catalog of maps and atlases, mostly of Canada, and of North America in general. Listed are early maps of North America, geographic maps, city and town plans, political maps, maps of Indian reservations, and maps of transportation, especially railroads. There are entries for individual maps in atlases and books. The maps date mostly from the eighteenth, nineteenth, and twentieth centuries.

The catalog is in three parts. The first and major part (volumes 1-12) is a geographically classed catalog called the Area Catalogue. There is a guide to the classification schedule and an introduction to using the catalog in the beginning of volume one. The classification system used was developed within the National Map Collection. Entries give date, title, imprint, cartographer, description of insets and illustrations, a physical description, and supplementary notes. Many of the entries are quite detailed.

The second part of the catalog (volumes 12-16) is an author catalog, arranged alphabetically. Only a brief title and a call number are provided; it should be considered an author index to the Area Catalogue. The third part of the catalog (end of volume 16) is an alphabetically arranged subject catalog. The subject headings were developed by the National Map Collection. Again, this catalog should be considered as only an index to the Area Catalogue.

47. New York (City). Public Library. Map Division. Dictionary

Catalog of the Map Division. 10 vols. Boston: G. K. Hall, 1971 (LC 78-173371). Supplemented by Bibliographic Guide to Maps and Atlases: 1979- . Boston: G. K. Hall, 1980- .

This is a catalog of maps, atlases, and other cartographic publications, from early rarities to modern maps. There are analytics for many atlases and for maps and articles in non-cartographic books and periodicals.

The Map Division has been a depository for the U. S. Army Topographic Command. It has extensive holdings of maps issued by foreign governments; navigation charts, antedating 1900, of the U. S. Hydrographic Office, the U. S. Coast Survey, and the U. S. Coast and Geodetic Survey; seventeenth- and eighteenth-century world atlases, facsimile atlases, and historical, regional, and thematic atlases; and comprehensive coverage of nineteenth-century county atlases and New York City atlases from the middle of the nineteenth century. The library is particularly strong in the history of cartography and the techniques of map making.

This is a dictionary catalog. Most of the subject entries are geographic place names, but there are topical entries such as "Canoeing" (for maps of canoe routes), "Canals," "City Plans," and "Minerals." There are also entries for map makers. Entries for individual maps generally give complete imprint data as well as scale, size, and other notes.

48. Scotland. National Library, Edinburgh. Shelf-Catalogue of the Lloyd Collection of Alpine Books. 94 p. Boston: G. K. Hall, 1964.

Included in this catalog are books on mountaineering and the Alps in general, bequeathed to the National Library of Scotland by Robert Wylie Lloyd. The works are mostly in English, although some titles are in French, German, Italian, or Latin. Most of the works were printed during the nineteenth and twentieth centuries, although a few are much older.

This is a checklist, and entries provide only author, brief title, and place and date of publication. As a shelflist, it is arranged in order as the books are arranged on the shelves. Since this order is dictated primarily by size, the catalog is rendered almost useless.

49. Scotland. National Library, Edinburgh. Shelf-Catalogue of the Wordie Collection of Polar Exploration. 191 p. Boston: G. K. Hall, 1964 (LC 65-6076).

This is a catalog of books presented by Sir James Mann Wordie to the National Library of Scotland in 1959. Subjects of the books include polar and sub-polar exploration, geology, biology, whale fishing, and the Eskimo way of life. Most of the works are in English, with some in German and Scandinavian languages. The works date from the second half of the nineteenth century to the first four decades of the twentieth.

This is a checklist and only author, title, and place and date of publication are given for each book. The 1,700 titles are arranged in the same order in the catalog as the volumes are on the shelves. Since the shelf order is dictated primarily by size, the catalog is of little practical use.

50. Scott Polar Research Institute, Cambridge, England. Library. The Library Catalogue of the Scott Polar Research Institute, Cambridge, England. 19 vols. Boston: G. K. Hall, 1976 (LC 76-377369).

The Scott Polar Research Institute is a sub-department within the Department of Geography of the University of Cambridge. The library is the largest single collection of its kind in the world, covering the whole field of knowledge, particularly the sciences and the social sciences, applying to the polar regions. In the Northern Hemisphere this includes the Arctic Ocean and islands, particularly Greenland, Svalbard, and Iceland; and Arctic and sub-Arctic regions of the circumpolar continents of North America, including Alaska and Canada; and of Eurasia, including the USSR and Scandinavia. In the Southern Hemisphere the region covered is the Antarctic continent and off-shore islands, the Southern Ocean, and sub-Antarctic islands. Related topics include snow and ice in all parts of the world and polar animals like seals, whales, reindeer, and penguins.

The library contains 13,000 books, 900 current periodical and serial titles, and more than 21,000 pamphlets and article reprints. The library catalogs monographs, articles from selected journals and serials, contributions to conference proceedings, preprints and pamphlets, and published and unpublished theses. Titles of serials are not included in the catalog although individual journal articles are. Also not included here are the library's catalogs of maps and charts, newspaper clippings, photographs, transparencies, movie films, tapes, manuscripts, pictures, and polar relics.

The catalog is divided into an author catalog (volumes 1-7), a subject catalog (volumes 8-14), and a regional catalog (volumes 15-19). The subject arrangement is a classified one, using modified Universal Decimal Classification (UDC). The regional classification also uses modified UDC. Works are often given more than one classification number, separated by colons, to allow them to appear in more than one place--usually in both the subject catalog and the regional catalog. The majority of the entries appear to be analytics, and almost all have short descriptive annotations. Although there is an outline of the UDC classification provided, as well as an index of subjects, it can be difficult to find individual specific subjects in the catalog.

The catalog includes cards from the Antarctic Bibliography and the Cold Regions Bibliography, originating from the Office of Polar Programs, Washington, D. C., and from the Cold Regions Research and Engineering Laboratory, Hanover, N. H.

Works are in English, Russian, and other European languages and are mostly recent--i. e., twentieth century--in origin.

51. Stefansson Collection. Dictionary Catalog of the Stefansson Collection on the Polar Regions in the Dartmouth College Library. 8 vols. Boston: G. K. Hall, 1967 (LC 67-5979).

The major emphasis of this collection is the history of polar exploration, both of the Arctic and Antarctic. Also included are works on the history, biography, description, and travel of Alaska. The materials included here are "the product of the long-sustained and dedicated gathering by the Arctic explorer, Vilhjalmur Stefansson" [Preface] and were transferred to Dartmouth College in 1951. Stefansson worked with the collection until his death in 1962, and the catalog represents the collection as of that date.

This is a difficult catalog to use because of the nature of the cataloging. Although this is a dictionary catalog, subject entries often consist merely of see references to main-entry cards. Nevertheless, there are worthwhile analytics for journal articles and lists of tables of contents for lengthy runs of some journals. Also valuable are tape-recorded lectures and interviews, as well as diaries and correspondence.

52. United States. Library of Congress. Geography and Map Division. The Bibliography of Cartography. 5 vols. Boston: G. K. Hall, 1973 (LC 73-12977). First Supplement. 2 vols., 1979.

This has been called "the most comprehensive cartobibliography ever published" [Introduction]. It was begun by Philip Lee Phillips, who became the first Chief of the Library of Congress's Division of Maps and Charts in 1897. By 1922 the bibliography included 30,464 titles. It was not maintained extensively after Phillips retired, but interest picked up again in the 1950's and by the time the bibliography was published, it had about 90,000 entries.

This is a catalog of books, pamphlets, and analytical entries for chapters in books and articles in journals. Some 200 geographical, cartographical, and related journals have been analyzed regularly since the early 1950's. Titles date from the early nineteenth century to 1971, and are in English and other Western European languages.

The bibliography is strongest on cartography in America, the history of cartography, modern cartographic techniques, thematic cartography, private and commercial map publishing, and biographies of cartographers. It does not include highly technical books or articles on cartographic techniques, general works on topical or regional geography, general works on travel or exploration, guidebooks, gazetteers, nor geographical dictionaries. The Geography and Map Division's atlas holdings may be found in A List of Geographical Atlases in the Library of Congress (see 53).

The catalog is arranged alphabetically by author and subject. It does not conform to professional cataloging standards, or standard subject headings, but there are many see and see-also references.

The division was formerly called the Map Division.

53. United States. Library of Congress. Map Division. A List of Geographical Atlases in the Library of Congress, with Bibliographical Notes. Washington, D. C.: Government Printing Office, 1909- (LC 09-35009).

As its title suggests, these volumes list and describe the geographical atlases held by the Library of Congress. Eight volumes have been issued so far, from 1909 to 1974. Most of them provide very full bibliographic descriptions of the atlases and often list the tables of contents for atlases published before a particular date. Indexing tends to be very thorough, although indexes do not always appear in the volume or volumes they index. The volumes are described individually below:

Volumes one and two (Titles 1-3265) were compiled under the direction of Philip Lee Phillips and published in 1909. The first volume is the actual list of atlases, arranged in the following order: 1) world atlases of special subjects; 2) world atlases arranged chronologically; 3) atlases of particular areas arranged geographically. The atlases date from the fifteenth century to 1908 and were published worldwide in many languages, including Slavic. Each atlas is described in great detail and each map in each atlas is listed. The second volume is an index volume containing first a detailed author list, complete with birth and death dates for each cartographer; and second a detailed geographic and personal name index.

Volume three (Titles 3266-4087), compiled under the direction of Philip Lee Phillips and published in 1914, supplements volumes one and two, but cumulates the author list.

Volume four (Titles 4088-5324), compiled under the direction of Philip Lee Phillips, was published in 1920 and supplements the first three volumes. The author list is cumulative for volumes one to four.

Volume five (Titles 5325-7623), compiled by Clara Egli LeGear and published in 1958, describes 2,326 world atlases acquired between 1920 and 1955, including many published before 1920. It lists all maps in atlases published before 1820. The author list and subject indexes refer only to this volume.

Volume six (Titles 7624-10254), compiled by Clara Egli LeGear and published in 1963, describes 2,647 atlases of Europe, Asia, Africa, Oceania, the polar regions, and oceans received between 1920 and 1960. The tables of contents of those atlases published before 1820 are provided. Many Chinese, Japanese, and Korean atlases are listed. The volume has its own author list and subject- and added-entry index.

Volume seven (Titles 10255-18435), compiled by Clara Egli LeGear and published in 1973, describes 8,181 atlases of the Western Hemisphere received between 1920 and 1969. It provides the full tables of contents for most atlases published before 1870. The author list refers only to this volume.

Volume eight, published in 1974, is the index volume for volume seven.

4. ANCIENT HISTORY AND CLASSICAL STUDIES

This group of catalogs represents collections on the archaeology, history, and literatures of the ancient world, most often the world of ancient Greece and Rome and civilizations bordering them. Most of the collections on the ancient Near and Middle East, however, are included in chapter 14, "The Middle East," and collections on the art of the ancient world may be found in chapter 21, "Art and Architecture."

The major collection in this chapter is that of the Deutsches Archäologisches Institut, Rome (the German Institute of Archaeology in Rome) (54), with over 90,000 volumes. Several volumes of Harvard University's Widener Library shelflist are also included. Together they represent about 42,000 titles--the major part of Harvard University's collection on ancient history and classical studies.

American School of Classical Studies at Athens. Gennadius Library. Catalogue. 7 vols. Boston: G. K. Hall, 1968. (see 66)

54. Deutsches Archäologisches Institut. Römische Abteilung. Bibliothek. Kataloge der Bibliothek des Deutschen Archaeologischen Instituts, Rom: Autoren- und Periodica Kataloge (Catalogs from the Library of the German Institute of Archaeology, Rome: Author and Periodical Catalogs). 7 vols. Boston: G. K. Hall, 1969 (LC 73-202658).

________. Kataloge der Bibliothek des Deutschen Archaeologischen Instituts, Rom: Systematischer Katalog (Catalogs from the Library of the German Institute of Archaeology, Rome: Classified Catalog). 3 vols. Boston: G. K. Hall, 1969 (LC 73-205023).

________. Kataloge der Bibliothek des Deutschen Archaeologischen Instituts, Rom: Zeitschriften--Autorenkatalog (Catalogs from the Library of the German Institute of Archaeology, Rome: Author Catalog of Periodicals). 3 vols. Boston: G. K. Hall, 1969 (LC 73-202659).

The German Institute of Archaeology in Rome was founded in 1829 as the Instituto di Corrispondenza Archeologica in Rome. By the time its library's catalog was published it had over 90,000 volumes, including 1,305 periodicals, of which 590 were currently received. The subjects covered include classical archaeology; classical philology, epigraphy, and numismatics; all ancient Mediterranean cultures; the prehistory of middle and northern Europe; and early Christian and Byzantine archaeology.

Of the published catalogs, the Autoren- und Periodica Kataloge have the most complete listing of the library's holdings. The author catalog contains only main entries--i.e., author entries and some title entries for works without authors--and the cataloging information is rather brief, usually consisting of the author, title, place and date of publication, and publisher. Cataloging practices have varied over the years, and many of the entries are handwritten. Titles date from the eighteenth to the twentieth century. Volume seven is the periodicals catalog.

The Systematischer Katalog is not a shelflist or an arrangement by a classification system, but consists simply of logically arranged headings with alphabetically arranged subheadings underneath. Each of the three volumes has its own table of contents, in German, which must be closely examined before using the catalog in order to find the proper headings. There are about 1,200 different categories in all. The first volume includes over 300 pages of book reviews arranged alphabetically by author of the book reviewed. This catalog covers works published from the late 1950's to 1969.

The Zeitschriften--Autorenkatalog covers the same period. It consists of over 30,000 entries, arranged by author, for articles in periodicals and Festschriften, and for book reviews. Coverage is limited to the fields of classical archaeology and related sciences and to Greek and Latin epigraphy. The major problem here is that the names of the periodicals in which the articles appear are usually abbreviated and there is no explanation of what the abbreviations stand for.

Most of the works listed in all the catalogs are in German and Italian, although other European-language works are also included.

Dumbarton Oaks. Dictionary Catalogue of the Byzantine Collection of the Dumbarton Oaks Research Library. 12 vols. Boston: G. K. Hall, 1975. (see 281)

55. Harvard University. Library. Ancient Greek Literature. 638 p. Cambridge, Mass.: distributed by Harvard University Press, 1979 (LC 79-9989). (Widener Library Shelflist v. 58)

This volume of the Widener Library shelflist covers ancient Greek literature, including anthologies of literature and works by and about individual authors. All Greek authors of the ancient period are classified here regardless of subject. Works are primarily in

Greek, English, Latin, and German. Greek words are transliterated. The majority of the books were published before 1900, and all were cataloged before July, 1976, when the Widener Library switched to the Library of Congress classification system.

The catalog is divided into three parts: a shelflist arrangement, according to Harvard's own classification scheme; a chronological arrangement by date of publication; and an author-title listing. There are 19,800 titles listed in the catalog.

For further information about the Widener Library shelflists see 9.

56. Harvard University. Library. Ancient History. 363 p. Cambridge, Mass.: distributed by Harvard University Press, 1975 (LC 75-21543). (Widener Library Shelflist v. 55)

Two major classes are included in this volume of Harvard University's Widener Library shelflist. The AH class includes works on the history of the countries of the ancient world, primarily those areas around the Mediterranean that were part of the Greco-Roman sphere of influence, such as Arabia; Armenia; Asia Minor, including Assyria and Babylonia; Greece and Macedonia; and Rome and the Roman Empire in North Africa and Europe. Works on the history, civilization and social life, government and law, religion, economic conditions, geography and travels, and various peoples of these areas are listed. The Eg class provides for the history and literature of ancient Egypt. Periodicals relating to these two classes are also included.

Other volumes of the Widener Library shelflists are closely related to the subjects covered here, including volume 56, Archaeology (see 57); volume 58, Ancient Greek Literature (see 55); volume 59, Latin Literature (see 144); and volume 57, Classical Studies (see 58). For a more general discussion of the Widener Library shelflists see 9.

More than 11,000 titles are listed in this volume. Works are in English, German, Latin, and French, with the greatest number in English and the fewest in French. Approximately half of the titles were published before 1900. The volume is divided into three parts: a shelflist arrangement, a chronological arrangement, and an author-title listing.

57. Harvard University. Library. Archaeology. 442 p. Cambridge, Mass.: distributed by Harvard University Press, 1979 (LC 79-555). (Widener Library Shelflist v. 56)

This is the Arc class of the Harvard classification scheme, which covers prehistoric archaeology and prehistoric civilization, including reports of excavations and books on the reconstruction of ancient buildings and objects. However, books recounting historical events and describing civilizations of the ancient world are classed in history, mostly in the AH class, which is in volume 55, Ancient

History, of the Widener Library shelflists (see 56). Also not included in this volume are works that are in the Fine Arts Library of the Fogg Art Museum (see 285), and works in the Tozzer Library of the Peabody Museum of Archaeology and Ethnology (see 61), which contains most of Harvard's collection of prehistoric archaeology.

Works are primarily in English, French, German, and Italian, and over half of the 14,300 entries are pre-1900. All titles were cataloged before 1976, when the Library of Congress classification was adopted. The volume is divided into three parts: a classified listing, a chronological listing, and an alphabetical author-title listing. For a fuller discussion of the Widener Library shelflists see 9.

58. Harvard University. Library. Classical Studies. 215 p. Cambridge, Mass.: distributed by Harvard University Press, 1979 (LC 79-948). (Widener Library Shelflist v. 57)

Included in this volume of the Widener Library shelflist is much of what is usually considered to be classical Greek and Roman studies, namely the history and theory of classical scholarship, the history of classical literature (but not works about individual authors), classical arts and sciences, classical rhetoric, classical prosody, classical inscriptions, and classical mythology and religion. However, anthologies of Greek and Latin literature and works by and about Greek and Roman writers are classed in Ancient Greek Literature, volume 58 of the Widener Library shelflist (see 55), or in Latin Literature, volume 59 of the shelflists (see 144). Works on ancient Greek and Roman history and civilization are found in volume 55, Ancient History (see 56), and works on classical archaeology are in volume 56, Archaeology (see 57).

Titles are primarily in German, English, Latin, French, and Italian, with German books the most common and Italian the least. About half of the 6,700 entries were published before 1900, and all were cataloged before July, 1976, when the Widener Library switched to the Library of Congress classification system. For further information on the Widener Library shelflists see 9.

Harvard University. Library. Latin Literature. 610 p. Cambridge, Mass.: Harvard Univ. Pr., 1979. (see 144)

London. University. Warburg Institute. Catalog of the Warburg Institute Library. 12 vols. Boston: G. K. Hall, 1967. (see 264)

5. ANTHROPOLOGY, AMERICAN INDIANS, AND FOLKLORE

Only a small percentage of the catalogs that list significant holdings of works on anthropology, American Indians, and folklore are included in this chapter. Anthropology as a discipline is so broad and overlaps so many other subjects that a comprehensive listing of the catalogs with resources in anthropology would include titles from most of the collections in history, area studies, and some of the sciences.[9] Consult the index for detailed listings of catalogs that treat anthropology, ethnology, physical anthropology, archaeology, and linguistics.

The most comprehensive catalog of works on anthropology is the catalog of Harvard University's Tozzer Library of the Peabody Museum of Archaeology and Ethnology (61), which is listed in this chapter.

The Dictionary Catalog of the Ayer Collection of Americana and American Indians in the Newberry Library (64) is the largest catalog devoted exclusively to American Indians, but many of the libraries listed in chapter 8, "American History," and in chapter 9, "The American West," also have valuable collections of materials on American Indians. The New York Public Library's Dictionary Catalog of the History of the Americas (111) is perhaps the most significant of these.

The Catalog of Folklore, Folklife, and Folk Songs (60) is included in this section because so much of the material in it is ethnographic in nature. However, many other catalogs include a great deal of material on folklore and folklife, and again the index should be checked to locate them.

59. Biblioteca Nacional de Antropología e Historia, Mexico. Catálogos de la Biblioteca Nacional de Antropología e Historia (Catalogs of the National Library of Anthropology and History). 10 vols. Boston: G. K. Hall, 1972 (LC 74-225152).

This is a dictionary catalog specializing in the anthropology and history of Mexico and the rest of Latin America. It is particularly strong in Mexican anthropology and archaeology, with many entries under the names of individual archaeological sites. The library was originally part of the Museum of Antiquities and Natural History, founded in 1823 by Lucas Alamán, the historian and politician, and renamed the National Museum in 1825. It became oriented towards the anthropological sciences after 1880, under new directors of the museum. Holdings of the library currently total around 300,000 volumes.[10]

The catalog lists pamphlets, doctoral dissertations, and Mexican government documents, as well as books. There are many analytical entries for periodicals, especially Spanish-language journals and serials. Subject headings used are modifications of Library of Congress headings, translated into Spanish. Entries are primarily in Spanish, with English, German, French, and other languages included.

60. Cleveland. Public Library. John G. White Dept. Catalog of Folklore, Folklife, and Folk Songs; John G. White Department of Folklore, Orientalia, and Chess, Cleveland Public Library. Second edition. 3 vols. Boston: G. K. Hall, 1978 (LC 80-108734).

This catalog contains only the folklore material of the John G. White Department, representing approximately 36,000 volumes of monographic and serial publications. (For the chess collection see 373). "The purpose of the folklore collection is to facilitate study of the cultures and lives of the peoples of the world in the context of historic and popular traditions" [Introduction]. Subjects covered include ethnology; folktales, ballads, songs, stories, etc.; folk experience--i.e., manners and customs, rites, ceremonies, vocational practices, etc.; and folk beliefs and superstitions--i.e., magic, witchcraft, legends of saints and gods, and the like. There are especially strong holdings on the Arabian Nights, Chapbooks, Robin Hood, ballads and songs, and proverbs.

According to the Introduction, entries generally conform to Library of Congress cataloging practices. Most entries are under subjects, using 1,100 subject headings developed by the library. There are some title and uniform title entries. The subject headings tend to be broad, and even when the library uses LC printed cards, the subject headings assigned to the books are often not the ones that the Library of Congress assigns. For example, under the subject heading "Indians of North America--Folklore and legends" are pages of entries for works that the Library of Congress lists only under the names of the individual tribes concerned. The result is that similar works which would be scattered throughout the alphabet in the catalogs of most libraries are brought together in this catalog.

Works are in most Western languages, including Russian, and generally were published in the nineteenth and twentieth centuries, with many rare books included. There are some analytics for journals, serials, and books.

61. Harvard University. Peabody Museum of Archaeology and Ethnology. Library. Catalogue: Authors. 26 vols. Boston: G. K. Hall, 1963 (LC 64-2646).

_______. Catalogue: Subjects. 27 vols. Boston: G. K. Hall, 1963 (LC 64-2645).

_______. First Supplement (authors and subjects). 12 vols., 1970. Second Supplement (authors and subjects). 6 vols., 1971. Third Supplement (authors and subjects). 7 vols., 1975. Fourth Supplement (authors and subjects). 7 vols., 1979.

_______. Index to Subject Headings. Revised edition. 237 p. Boston: G. K. Hall, 1971.

This important library (now called the Tozzer Library), emphasizes American--particularly Mexican and Central American--archaeology and ethnology, but holdings cover the entire world in the subfields of prehistoric archaeology, ethnology, and physical anthropology. This is "believed to be the strongest collection in the U. S. for prehistoric archaeology generally, anthropology, and ethnology."[11]

The author catalog includes personal authors, editors, translators, names of museums, societies, and journals, and the contents of monographic series. There are also works about authors and critical replies to their works, but not book reviews.

The subject catalog uses what is essentially a classified arrangement that is primarily geographic with subject divisions and subdivisions. Works on somatology (physical anthropology) and technology are listed both under these broad headings (or a subdivision of them) and under the geographic region to which they apply. The index to the subject headings should be consulted before using the subject catalog. The subject headings date from the nineteenth century and are in the process of being revised. There should be major changes in subject cataloging in the fifth supplement, although at this time plans for a fifth supplement appear to be uncertain.

One of the most important features of these catalogs is the extensive analytics provided. Festschriften and conference proceedings are analyzed, and periodicals have been indexed since the early twentieth century, although, since the criteria for what is indexed depend more on the content of the article than on the journal in which it appears, coverage of different journals is erratic. The second supplement contains a list of journals that have been analyzed between 1970 and 1971, but there is no indication of the extent to which each has been indexed. The third and fourth supplements contain additions to this list.

In spite of the drawbacks of archaic subject headings and erratic coverage of journals, most specialists in anthropology use these catalogs as the index of first choice for identifying material by anthropologists and about anthropological subjects.

62. Huntington Free Library and Reading Room, New York. Dictionary Catalog of the American Indian Collection, Huntington Free Library and Reading Room, New York. 4 vols. Boston: G. K. Hall, 1977 (LC 78-302051).

This is the catalog of the library of the Museum of the American Indian, Heye Foundation. The American Indian collection was organized in 1930 by George G. Heye, Director of the Museum of the American Indian, and by Archer M. Huntington, who also endowed it.

The collection includes over 35,000 volumes on the anthropology, art, archaeology, history, and current affairs of all Indians in the Western Hemisphere. The library is especially strong in holdings of anthropological papers of universities and museums in the United States, Canada, and Latin America; in journals of most of the U.S. historical and archaeological societies; in manuscripts, codices, and field notes of anthropologists associated with the Museum of the American Indian; in U.S. and Canadian government reports; and in Indian-language dictionaries and Bibles, Indian autobiographies and biographies, and Indian newspapers. The catalog does not include manuscript and vertical file materials. There are entries for selected journal articles and parts of series.

The depth of the indexing and the quality of the cataloging vary widely with the changes in staff and administration that have occurred over time. The subject headings used are the library's own; often they are modifications of, or inversions of Library of Congress subject headings. When Library of Congress printed cards are used, the library will usually have changed the LC-assigned subject headings.

63. National Museum of Natural History. Department of Anthropology. National Anthropological Archives. Catalog to Manuscripts at the National Anthropological Archives, Dept. of Anthropology, National Museum of Natural History, Smithsonian Institution. 4 vols. Boston: G. K. Hall, 1975 (ISBN 0-8161-1194-4).

This catalog lists about 40,000 individual items in over 6,000 collections of manuscripts in the National Anthropological Archives. The archives are heavily weighted towards materials on the American Indian. Many of these were collected by Bureau of American Ethnology employees and collaborators between 1879 and 1965. They include vocabularies, grammar notes, linguistic texts, journals and field notes, administrative records and correspondence, files of the Bureau of American Ethnology, and maps. Also included is material from other anthropological museums and from anthropologists in general. Material dates from 1848 to 1975.

The catalog is in three major parts. First is a file for manuscripts concerning Indians of America north of Mexico, arranged alphabetically by name of tribe, linguistic group, or sometimes name of individual, with a few general subject headings. Second is a file labelled "Miscellaneous," with material on peoples not included in the first file, arranged geographically. The third file is a shelflist of the manuscript collections arranged by accession number. There is also a very small file of drawings, arranged alphabetically by name of artist, located at the end of the catalog.

New York (City). Public Library. Reference Dept. Dictionary Catalog of the History of the Americas. 28 vols. Boston: G. K. Hall, 1961. (see 111)

64. Newberry Library, Chicago. Edward E. Ayer Collection. Dictionary Catalog of the Edward E. Ayer Collection of Americana and American Indians in the Newberry Library. 16 vols. Boston: G. K. Hall, 1961 (LC 76-4986). First Supplement. 3 vols., 1970. Second Supplement. 4 vols., 1980.

This collection was begun by Edward E. Ayer in 1880 and donated to the Newberry Library in 1911. Ayer was originally motivated to find out everything he could about the Indians of North America and their contacts with white men. Strengths of the collection now include pre-Columbian discoveries; early exploration; Spanish, Portuguese, French, English, Dutch, Italian, and Swedish colonization; missionaries; Indian wars and captives; history of Latin America; and archaeology and ethnology of all the Indian tribes of the Americas. Also included are works on the histories of the Philippines and the Hawaiian Islands.

This is a dictionary catalog of authors and subjects. Library of Congress subject headings are used, and there are many see and see-also references. There are some analytics for reprints or extracts of journal articles and for proceedings and papers of meetings, and there is some subject indexing for parts of books.

Included are government documents, music scores, pamphlets, and many rare books. Works have imprint dates ranging from the sixteenth to the twentieth century and are primarily in English, Spanish, and French, but many other languages are included.

The Greenlee Collection (see 184 and 185) and the Graff Collection (see 123) are housed within the Ayer Collection, but they are not included in this catalog. The Philippine Collection, which is included in this catalog, has also been published in a classified catalog (see 210).

65. United States. Department of the Interior. Library. Biographical and Historical Index of American Indians and Persons Involved in Indian Affairs. 8 vols. Boston: G. K. Hall, 1966 (LC 77-5470).

As its title indicates, this is a valuable index to "Indian tribes, individuals, events, and other items of an historical nature" [Preface]. It indexes books, journal articles, and United States government documents, including laws. Most of the entries are for names of individuals--Indian chiefs, historically prominent Indians, personnel of the Bureau of Indian Affairs, etc.--but there are many special features. For example, under the subject heading "Agencies" is a list of the different Indian agencies and who the agents or superintendents were at different times; the heading "Agents" provides an alphabetical list of Indian agents with dates and locations of appointments; and "Battles" yields a bibliography of books and articles on various Indian battles.

Each entry in the catalog contains a reference to a publication likely to have been printed in the second half of the nineteenth century or the first quarter of the twentieth. "The entries do not always follow standard bibliographic forms, and frequently the alphabetizing is informal within a single letter" [Preface].

6. WORLD AND EUROPEAN HISTORY

The British, in their colonization of large parts of the non-European world, collected books and other printed works about the areas they were administering. Some of the largest library collections of world history are the result of the British expansion into empire. These include the Catalogue of the Colonial Office Library (69), the two catalogs of the Foreign Office Library (70-71), and the three catalogs of what is now the Royal Commonwealth Society (81-83). All of these catalogs have arrangements that will appear unusual to researchers used to American library catalogs, but most include entries for periodical articles and other materials that should make the effort of using them worthwhile.

Other major catalogs in this section are the volumes of Harvard University's Widener Library shelflist on British History (77) and on General European and World History (78). Both of these are arranged in call number order with author, title, and chronological listings, and both represent important collections in their fields.

Many of the catalogs of history collections are also catalogs of the literature of the same area. If the emphasis of the catalog is on literature, its description will not be found in this chapter; in its place is a cross-reference to the complete description of the catalog. Catalogs that list works on the history and literature of a particular part of the non-European world will be found in the chapter on that geographic area.

66. American School of Classical Studies at Athens. Gennadius Library. Catalogue. 7 vols. Boston: G. K. Hall, 1968 (LC 70-3154). First Supplement. 872 p., 1973.

This library is the creation of the Greek diplomat, scholar, and bibliophile, Joannes Gennadius (1844-1932) in memory of his father, George Gennadius. The original collection given to the American School was 27,000 volumes, but it had doubled in size by 1968 when the catalog was photographed. Gennadius intended the library to represent "the history and achievement of Greece in its entirety, from earliest antiquity to the present" [Introduction], including classical and Byzantine civilizations, Turkish domination of Greece, the struggle for independence, and the kingdom of Greece.

The library's areas of special strength are in early editions of the classical, patristic, and Byzantine authors; Greek grammars; modern Greek literature, especially to 1900 (the First Supplement is much stronger on twentieth-century Greek authors); the beginnings of classical archaeology (1750-1825); Byzantine art and archaeology; travel books on the Greek East and the Levant in general, to 1900; Greek Bibles; Eastern Orthodox Churches; early printed materials on Turkish history; Greece under the Turcocratia; the Greek War of Independence; the early kingdom of Greece; Byron and Byroniana; and the Eastern question. There is an attempt to avoid duplicating the holdings of the American School's Davis Library, which contains the collection of classical authors.

This is a dictionary catalog, with entries for authors and subjects, as well as titles for anonymous works. The Greek and Roman letters are filed together in one alphabet; the filing rules and the forms of Greek names are explained in the Introduction. Although major place names and classical writers are entered in the familiar English forms, many of the names of people and places appear only in Greek, and a knowledge of Greek is certainly a help in using the catalog. Other subject headings are in English, but there are few cross-references and no list of subject headings. The catalog includes a few manuscripts and many rare books; the library contains over half of the 60-odd Greek books printed in the fifteenth century. Languages included in the catalog are first Greek, then English, and then other Western European languages.

67. Cincinnati. University. Library. Catalog of the Modern Greek Collection, University of Cincinnati. 5 vols. Boston: G. K. Hall, 1978 (LC 78-104566).

This collection began at the University of Cincinnati when Carl W. Blegen, Professor of Classical Archaeology, began collecting for the University works of Greek scholars on ancient Greek authors, history, and archaeology. Since 1953, during the life of the Farmington Plan, the University of Cincinnati had responsibility for buying scholarly books published in Greece on all subjects except law, medicine, and agriculture, but has on its own also acquired works on law and agriculture. The collection covers mostly modern Greece, including modern Greek literature from the eleventh century to the present; modern Greek language; Greek history since 1453; the history of the Greek church; folklore, comprising all aspects of popular Greek culture; and Byzantine history and civilization.

Works are mostly in Greek, although English and other European-language works on the subject are also acquired. Titles were published for the most part in the twentieth century, but some early imprints of works in Greek printed outside of Greece are included. There are 20,000 volumes in the collection, which is especially strong in extensive holdings of serial and periodical publications, including complete runs of old, short-lived periodicals, some of which cannot be found even in Athenian libraries.

The library uses the Library of Congress classification system and ALA and Anglo-American cataloging rules, with many cross-references to proper forms of names. This is a dictionary catalog, using Library of Congress subject headings.

Dumbarton Oaks. Dictionary Catalogue of the Byzantine Collection of the Dumbarton Oaks Research Library. 12 vols. Boston: G. K. Hall, 1975. (see 281)

68. Genoa. Biblioteca Civica Berio. Catalogo della Raccolta Colombiana, Berio Civic Library, Genoa (Catalog of the Columbus Collection). Second edition. 151 p. Boston: G. K. Hall, 1963 (LC 64-5514).

This collection is devoted to Christopher Columbus and his voyages. The Columbus room was established in the Berio Civic Library in Genoa in 1892 through funds from the Municipal Council of Genoa and donations from citizens. The first catalog of the library was published in 1906 (Cervetto, Luigi Augusto. Catalogo delle Opere Componente la Raccolta Colombiana Esistente nella Civica Biblioteca Berio di Genova. Genova, stab. Folli Pagano, 1906). For this new, revised catalog of 3,156 cards, all entries were retyped on 3 x 5 cards. Titles date from the sixteenth to the early twentieth century and consist largely of rare books and pamphlets. There are also entries for articles in 78 periodicals held by the Berio Library. Works are mostly in Italian, and the arrangement is by main entry.

69. Great Britain. Colonial Office. Library. Catalogue of the Colonial Office Library, London. 15 vols. Boston: G. K. Hall, 1964 (LC 65-51806). First Supplement, 1963-1967. 894 p., 1967. Second Supplement. 2 vols., 1972.

Third Supplement issued as:
Great Britain. Foreign and Commonwealth Office. Library. Accessions to the Library, May 1971-June 1977. 4 vols. Boston: G. K. Hall, 1979.

The catalog of the Colonial Office Library was a union catalog servicing three departments: the Colonial Office, the Commonwealth Relations Office, and the Department of Technical Cooperation. In 1968 the Library was merged with the Foreign Office Library to form the Foreign and Commonwealth Office Library; the second and third supplements represent material added to the combined collections. Material collected by the Foreign Office Library before 1968 can be found in the separately published Foreign Office Library catalogs (see 70 and 71).

The aim of the Colonial Office Library was to maintain an extensive collection of material on the dependent territories of the British Empire and later, when the Empire dissolved, to obtain material on the independent countries of the British Commonwealth.

All subjects are covered, including the history, geography, economics, politics, sociology, natural history, and technology of these areas.

The 1964 catalog is in five parts. There is a pre-1950 catalog of sheaf entries, divided into a subject catalog and an author index, and a post-1950 card catalog, divided into an author-title catalog, a subject catalog (using Library of Congress subject headings), and a classified catalog (arranged by the Library of Congress classification system). The author catalogs include some titles and persons as subjects of biographies. Both pre- and post-1950 catalogs contain entries for books, pamphlets, reports, official publications of Great Britain and the colonies (or former colonies), periodical titles, and periodical articles. The pre-1950 catalog is especially rich in entries for pamphlets and journal articles.

The supplements do not continue the subject catalog, and have analytics for only a few selected journals. In the classed catalog journal articles are listed only with the classification number for the journal.

70. Great Britain. Foreign Office. Library. Catalogue of Printed Books in the Library of the Foreign Office. 1587 p. London: HMSO, 1926 (LC 26-22011).

This is the catalog of the Library of the British Foreign Office as it stood in 1926. It has not been superseded by the later Catalogue of the Foreign Office Library, 1926-1968, published by G. K. Hall in 1973 (see 71). Subjects of interest to the Foreign Office were world history and world affairs, foreign affairs, and political science. This is a dictionary catalog with many see and see-also references for authors and subjects. Only brief cataloging information is provided. Dates range from the seventeenth century to 1926, and titles are in English as well as other European languages.

71. Great Britain. Foreign Office. Library. Catalogue of the Foreign Office Library, 1926-1968. 8 vols. Boston: G. K. Hall, 1972 (LC 73-160726).

This catalog picks up where the earlier Catalogue of Printed Books in the Library of the Foreign Office, published in 1926 (see 70) left off. The emphasis of the catalog is on British external affairs, especially the politics, government, history, economic development, and international relations of foreign countries.

The catalog is in four parts. Volumes one and two are an author catalog, including added entries for editors, joint authors, etc. Volumes three and four are a subject catalog; the subject headings used are based on Sears subject headings, but are extensively modified. Finally, volumes seven and eight are a classified catalog arranged by the Dewey Decimal classification and subdivided by a two-letter country symbol. Unfortunately, there is no list of the country symbols. Items may be listed under more than one classification number.

Many British and foreign government publications are included in the catalog, as are numerous pamphlets; titles are in English and other Western European languages. There are no analytics for books or journals.

In 1968 the Foreign and Commonwealth Offices merged, and subsequent additions to the combined library collections are included in the second and third supplements of the Catalogue of the Colonial Office Library (see 69).

72. Great Britain. Ministry of Defence. Naval Library. Author and Subject Catalogues of the Naval Library, Ministry of Defence, London. 5 vols. Boston: G. K. Hall, 1967 (LC 74-168386).

All aspects of maritime affairs are covered here--voyages, navigation, hydrographic surveys made before 1795, geography, history, biography, sailing, the art of war, etc. Works from the nineteenth and twentieth centuries are included and are mostly in English. There are many rare books, long runs of periodicals, some manuscripts, and some analytical entries for journal articles.

This is a divided catalog. The first two volumes are the Author Catalogue and volumes three to five are the Subject Catalogue. The library uses its own classification system and the subject catalog is arranged according to this classification. There is a table of contents at the beginning of volume three which serves as a guide to the approximately 130 major divisions. There are, in addition, 676 subdivisions. Large sections, like "History--Naval," which occupies nearly 200 pages, are subdivided by such headings as "Espionage," "Shipwrecks," etc., but there is no clue as to how these subdivisions are arranged, and the reader needs sharp eyes to spot the tiny guide cards which separate one subdivision from another. The Biography section, which is also quite extensive, is arranged by date of publication of the biographies, making it very difficult to find a particular biography. However, biographies are also listed in the author volumes under the name of the subject of the biography.

73. Greenwich, Eng. National Maritime Museum. Guide to the Manuscripts in the National Maritime Museum. Edited by R. J. B. Knight. vol. 1- . London: Mansell, 1977- (LC 78-303849).

Thus far only the first volume of this guide to the manuscript collections of the National Maritime Museum has been published. It is titled The Personal Collections and lists the personal papers of 300 people connected with the Royal Navy and the merchant shipping industry. The arrangement is alphabetical by name of individual, with a short biographical sketch of the individual and brief descriptions of the contents of the papers included. There is a chronological index and a general index of topics, events, and individuals mentioned in the private papers.

74. Greenwich, Eng. National Maritime Museum. Library. Biography. 2 vols. London: HMSO, 1969 (LC 79-512438) (Its Catalogue of the Library, 2).

This is a short-title catalog with 1,463 entries for biographical materials, many with annotations. The biographies are of individuals involved in maritime affairs. Part One contains sections on collective biographies, Navy Lists, and individual biographies. The general index to Part One lists authors and individuals discussed in collective biographies and in some sections of the biographies of other individuals. Also listed in the index are places and events.

Part Two is a reference index of individual biographies to be found in 21 different biographical sources ranging from Isaac Asimov's Asimov's Biographical Encyclopedia of Science and Technology, through the Dictionary of National Biography to The Trafalgar Roll. Thus it serves as a composite index to naval biographies.

75. Greenwich, Eng. National Maritime Museum. Library. Naval History; Part One: The Middle Ages to 1815. 209 p. London: HMSO, 1976 (LC 77-372896) (Its Catalogue of the Library, 5).

The title of this catalog is quite descriptive of its subject matter. This is primarily a catalog of rare books, with many analytical entries for articles in periodicals, for a total of 2,318 entries. The arrangement is chronological by century, and within century by topic. There is very detailed descriptive cataloging for the books, and many short annotations as well. At the end there is an alphabetical index of names (including authors) and subjects. Imprint dates range from the sixteenth century to the 1970's, and titles are mostly in English, but also in other Western European languages.

76. Greenwich, Eng. National Maritime Museum. Library. Piracy and Privateering. 174 p. London: HMSO, 1972 (LC 73-167555) (Its Catalogue of the Library, 4).

The basis of this catalog is the celebrated Pirate Library formed by the late Dr. Philip Gosse and acquired by the National Maritime Museum in 1939. The subject matter of the catalog, as its title indicates, is pirates, piracy, and privateering. It includes rare books, British government documents, monographs, and many analytics of journal articles on pirates and privateering, dating from the seventeenth to the twentieth centuries, for a total of 585 entries. Most of the titles are in English; some are in French and in other Western European languages.

The arrangement is by author, with some keyword title entries for works without authors. There is fairly detailed descriptive cataloging for each book, and many works have annotations. There is a subject index of persons and events described in the works in the catalog.

77. Harvard University. Library. British History. 2 vols. Cambridge, Mass.: distributed by Harvard University Press, 1975 (LC 75-21542). (Widener Library Shelflist v. 53-54)

Included in this section of the shelflist of Harvard University's Widener Library are more than 45,000 titles on the history, civilization, government and administration, foreign relations, religious history, geography and description, general social life and conditions, and various peoples of the British Isles. Lee Ash called this "an outstanding collection; noteworthy subdivisions include Civil War materials and those on Canning, Nelson, and Walpole."[12] Most special aspects of social conditions are classed with sociology in volumes 45-46 of the Widener Library shelflists (see 316), and all aspects of economic history and economic conditions are classed with economics in volumes 23-24 of the shelflists (see 357) except for works on the general economic history and conditions of Ireland, which may be found in these volumes.

Close to 90 percent of the titles are in English, and about half were published before 1900. The catalog is in three parts: a classified, or shelflist arrangement; a chronological listing; and an alphabetical listing by author and title. For further information on the Widener Library shelflists see 9.

Harvard University. Library. Finnish and Baltic History and Literatures. 250 p. Cambridge, Mass.: Harvard Univ. Pr., 1972. (see 139)

78. Harvard University. Library. General European and World History. 959 p. Cambridge, Mass.: distributed by Harvard University Press, 1970 (LC 73-128714). (Widener Library Shelflist v. 32)

Like the other volumes of the Widener Library shelflists, this is arranged in three parts. First there is a classified arrangement by class number, second a chronological arrangement, and last a listing by author and title. In this case, the classified arrangement includes four classes of the Harvard Library classification scheme. The Crus class covers the Crusades and the Latin Orient and updates and replaces volume one of the Widener Library shelflists, which covered only the Crusades. The HP class includes scholarly journals devoted to European or world history and covering the whole field of history of the medieval and modern periods. Also included here are general periodicals on the contemporary political, economic, and social questions of Europe in general or the world as a whole. The H and HB classes provide for world history and the history of Europe in general. The classification for World War I, in particular, is extremely detailed. Not included here are works on the ancient period, on the history of individual countries, or on most European wars before World War I, which are classed with particular countries.

About 37,000 titles are included; more than half of them are in English, but there are also many titles in German, French, and Russian. Most of the titles are from the twentieth century, but significant numbers of books date back to the sixteenth and seventeenth centuries, with 1502 the earliest.

Harvard University. Library. Hungarian History and Literature. 186 p. Cambridge, Mass.: Harvard Univ. Pr., 1974. (see 142)

Harvard University. Library. Italian History and Literature. 2 vols. Cambridge, Mass.: Harvard Univ. Pr., 1974. (see 143)

Harvard University. Library. Slavic History and Literatures. 4 vols. Cambridge, Mass.: Harvard Univ. Pr., 1971. (see 146)

79. Johann Gottfried Herder-Institut, Marburg. Bibliothek. Bibliothek des Johann Gottfried Herder-Instituts, Marburg/Lahn, Germany: Alphabetischer Katalog. 5 vols. Boston: G. K. Hall, 1964 (LC 65-85879). First Supplement. 2 vols., 1971.

The Johann Gottfried Herder-Institute Library was founded in 1950 and is the largest library specializing in East Central Europe. The original catalog lists 70,000 volumes and the supplement adds another 30,000.

East Central Europe is defined to be the countries of Estonia, Latvia, Lithuania, Poland, and Czechoslovakia. The library collects works on the inhabitants of the area and their history from prehistoric times to the present, including: cultural life, law and government, economics, religion and the church, art and literature, and ethnography. Excluded are the natural sciences, technology, and medicine.

In general, this is a main-entry catalog, although some works are entered under added entries as well. There are no subject entries at all. The arrangement is according to the German rules for alphabetical catalogs. Works with no author are listed not under the first word of the title, but under the first noun in the nominative case in the title. Monographs in series may be found both under the name of the author and the name of the series. There are entries for books, serials, periodicals, and newspapers, including 1,100 current periodicals. Titles are mostly in German and the Slavic languages.

80. Munich. Osteuropa-Institut. Bibliothek. Alphabetischer Katalog: Autorenkatalog in 8 Bänden. (Alphabetical

Catalog of the Library of the Institute for East European Affairs: Author Catalog in 8 Volumes). 8 vols. München: Omnia-Mikrofilmtechnik Ziffer, 1975 (LC 76-487370).

The Institute for East European Affairs was founded in Munich in 1952 to conduct research on Eastern Europe. The emphasis is on the Soviet Union and on Poland, particularly their history, geography, economy, sociology, and law. Natural sciences and medicine are excluded. The library has recently emphasized works on Czechoslovakia as well.

As of December, 1974 the library contained 93,000 titles, including 706 current periodicals and newspapers. The cataloging is done according to Prussian cataloging rules, and the catalog contains entries for or references from authors, significant titles, second or third authors, editors, etc. Information about which issues of serials and periodicals are held is provided. Besides books, maps, atlases, microforms, and records are included.

New York (City). Public Library. Slavonic Division. Dictionary Catalog of the Slavonic Division. 44 vols. Boston: G. K. Hall, 1974. (see 147)

New York (City). Union Theological Seminary. Library. Catalogue of the McAlpin Collection of British History and Theology. 5 vols. New York, 1927-1930. (see 268)

Pontifical Institute of Mediaeval Studies. Library. Dictionary Catalogue of the Library of the Pontifical Institute of Mediaeval Studies. 5 vols. Boston: G. K. Hall, 1972. (see 269)

81. Royal Commonwealth Society. Library. Biography Catalogue of the Library of the Royal Commonwealth Society. By Donald H. Simpson, librarian. 511 p. London: Royal Commonwealth Society, 1961 (LC 61-66062).

This catalog aims to include, in one volume, all of the biographical material available in books and periodicals in the Library of the Royal Commonwealth Society in London. Books published to 1960 and periodicals published to 1959 are included. Here may be found references to biographies of individuals born in, or actively connected with, countries of the Commonwealth, and persons in the United Kingdom who have been of significance in Imperial affairs.

The catalog is arranged in several parts. First, there is an alphabetical section arranged by name of individual biographee. Then there is a section for collective biographies arranged geographically by name of country. Here are listed both natives of the country in question and names of individuals associated with the country.

Also listed here are names of individuals associated with the country for whom references may be found in the alphabetical section. Finally, there is an author index.

Generally, each individual biographee is identified by birth and death dates and a brief identifying phrase, such as "Settler in Can." or "Fr. expl.," followed by references to books or articles in books or in periodicals where that individual's biography may be found.

The catalog is supplemented by the Subject Catalogue of the Royal Commonwealth Society, London (see 83).

82. Royal Commonwealth Society. Library. Manuscript Catalogue. Edited by Donald H. Simpson. 193 p. London: Mansell, 1975.

This catalog supersedes references to manuscripts listed in the published catalogs of the Royal Commonwealth Society, which are: Subject Catalogue of the Library of the Royal Empire Society, 1930-1937, and Subject Catalogue of the Royal Commonwealth Society, 1971 (see 83); and Biography Catalogue of the Library of the Royal Commonwealth Society, 1961 (see 81). Manuscripts is used here to include handwritten documents; typescripts; original drawings, paintings, and maps; photographs; photocopies; collections of photographic prints; and printed books with manuscript annotations.

The arrangement is geographic. Under each geographic heading there are see-also references to related archival materials. The arrangement within each geographic division is by the name of the individual author of the material or by the subject of the material. Each entry has either very detailed descriptions of the items included or a paragraph or two describing the general contents of the collection. There are references to printed copies of the items or published works describing the items.

In general, the subject matter of the manuscripts is the English in various parts of the British Empire in the eighteenth and nineteenth centuries.

83. Royal Commonwealth Society. Library. Subject Catalogue of the Library of the Royal Empire Society, formerly Royal Colonial Institute. By Evans Lewin. 4 vols. London: The Society, 1930-37 (LC 30-12746).

________. Subject Catalogue of the Royal Commonwealth Society, London. 7 vols. Boston: G. K. Hall, 1971 (LC 70-180198). First Supplement. 2 vols., 1977.

The Royal Commonwealth Society began in 1868 as the Colonial Society, changed its name to the Royal Colonial Institute, became the Royal Empire Society, and finally, again with changing British fortunes, adopted its present name. The library has collected material about the Mideast, India, other parts of Asia, Africa, the Americas (particularly Canada), Australia, New Zealand, and the

Pacific. The emphasis is on the countries that made up the British Empire, many of which are now part of the Commonwealth. Subjects covered include the geography, history, politics, economics, ethnology, literature, and arts of these areas.

The 1971 Subject Catalogue of the Royal Commonwealth Society supplements the earlier Subject Catalogue of the Library of the Royal Empire Society, and also supplements a separate Biography Catalogue of the Library of the Royal Commonwealth Society, published in 1961 (see 81). Both subject catalogs are arranged geographically, with subject subdivisions, and within subject by date of publication. Each volume has its own table of contents. The 1930-37 catalog includes an author index in each volume. Next to the name of each author are his dates of birth and death (where known) and a descriptive phrase, such as "Explorer in S. W. Afr."

Both catalogs include entries for books, pamphlets, official publications of Great Britain and of Commonwealth countries, and papers read before societies. Both also have extensive analytical entries for journal articles and for essays in books. Manuscripts are included in the catalogs, but the separately published Manuscript Catalogue (see 82) is a more complete listing of the library's manuscript holdings.

The 1971 catalog includes, in the seventh volume, a catalog of biographies to supplement the 1961 Biography Catalogue, and also separate catalogs of publications on voyages and travels, and on World Wars I and II.

84. Saint David's University College, Lampeter, Wales. Library. A Catalogue of the Tract Collection of the Saint David's University College, Lampeter. Edited by Brian Ll. James. 315 p. London: Mansell, 1975 (LC 76-353069).

This is the catalog of a collection of tracts, or pamphlets, held at Saint David's University College. It was originally the collection of the Bowdler family. The tracts were printed from 1520 to 1843, but most are from the period 1641-1720, "the great age of pamphlet-writing in English" [Foreword]. Most of the tracts deal with religious controversies or political crises, but they also include any subject of public interest. The collection consists of 11,395 pieces described in 8,692 entries. The entries are arranged chronologically, and a study of the catalog alone yields a good impression of which issues were absorbing public attention at varying times. There is also an index of authors and titles.

85. St. Louis. Public Library. Heraldry Index of the St. Louis Public Library. 4 vols. Boston: G. K. Hall, 1980 (ISBN 0-8161-0311-9).

The Heraldry Index of the St. Louis Public Library was begun in 1927. By the time the catalog was published it contained 102,000 entries for illustrations of coats of arms or other insignia found in approximately 860 different works in the library. Large compilations, arranged in alphabetical order, such as Burke's General Armory, Rietstap's Armorial Général, and Fairbairn's Crests are not indexed in this catalog.

The emphasis of the catalog is on coats of arms from the British Isles. In fact, until 1961, only English-language sources were indexed, but since 1961 works in French, German, Dutch, Russian, and Danish have been indexed, and coats of arms from all over the world have been included.

In the works indexed, many of the illustrations of coats of arms are accompanied by genealogies of the particular family who used the arms. (The St. Louis Public Library has also published its genealogy catalog; see 114). The Introduction points out that although all coats of arms that appear in this index have been ascribed to an individual or a family, it cannot necessarily be said that the ascription is correct.

Most sources have been assigned code letters, and the codes, with the authors and titles they represent, are provided at the beginning of the first volume.

86. Scotland. National Library, Edinburgh. Catalogue of the Lauriston Castle Chapbooks. 273 p. Boston: G. K. Hall, 1964.

This is the catalog of a collection, in the National Library of Scotland, of over 500 volumes of chapbooks from the bequest of Mr. and Mrs. W. R. Reid of Lauriston Castle. Over half of the volumes are composites, containing up to 20 pieces, and a total of about 1, 600 titles are listed. Almost all of the works were printed in the British Isles, and most of them are on Scottish subjects. Most of the works are in English, and they bear imprint dates from the seventeenth to the twentieth centuries. This is a dictionary catalog of authors and subjects, with some cross-references.

87. Scotland. National Library, Edinburgh. Shelf-Catalogue of the Blaikie Collection of Jacobite Pamphlets, Broadsides and Proclamations. 42 p. Boston: G. K. Hall, 1964 (LC 74-154055).

The Blaikie Collection was formed by Walter Biggar Blaikie (1847-1928) and on his death was presented to the National Library of Scotland. Blaikie was a printer and a recognized authority on the Jacobite period. His collection covers both attempts of the House of Stuart to reinstate itself on the throne of Great Britain--that of James III in 1715, and of his son, Charles Edward, in 1745. It contains historical works on the rebellions; contemporary poems, satires, and sermons, many in French; session papers and acts of Parliament; pamphlets; and similar material. There are 754 entries arranged in order as the books stand on the shelves; i. e., by size. As a result, it is nearly impossible to make any use out of the catalog.

Williams Library, London. Early Nonconformity, 1566-1800: A Catalog of Books in Dr. Williams's Library. 12 vols. Boston: G. K. Hall, 1968. (see 271)

7. TWENTIETH-CENTURY WORLD HISTORY AND WORLD WARS

The attempt to understand the causes and results of the devastating wars of the 20th century has resulted in the formation of several great collections about these wars and about the nature of war and peace in general. The most comprehensive of these collections is the library of the Hoover Institution on War, Revolution, and Peace, which has published its library catalogs in several parts. The Catalog of the Western Language Collections, included in this chapter (93), is a mammoth, 63-volume dictionary catalog of works on the two world wars and on war and revolution around the world. The other two major collections on this subject are in Germany: the Bibliothek für Zeitgeschichte in Stuttgart (95) and the library of the Institut für Zeitgeschichte in Munich (89). Both have separate author and classified subject catalogs, both contain many entries for periodical articles (the library in Munich is especially rich in periodical analytics), and both contain mostly works in German. The library in Stuttgart is the older and larger of the two collections.

Also of great interest are The New York Public Library's collections on World War I (90) and on World War II (91), and a very unusual collection, the G. Robert Vincent Voice Library at Michigan State University (96), which contains sound recordings of some of the important individuals and events of this century.

88. Foreign Relations Library. Catalog of the Foreign Relations Library. 9 vols. Boston: G. K. Hall, 1969 (LC 75-6133). First Supplement. 3 vols., 1980.

The Foreign Relations Library was established in 1930 as the Council on Foreign Relations Library. The nucleus of the collection was the library of David Hunter Miller, a student of foreign affairs, an official of the Department of State, and a staff member of the U. S. Delegation to the first Paris Peace Conference (1919). The aim of the library is to cover "all phases of international relations since 1918" [Preface], but some pre-World War I material is also included.

In 1969 the collection totalled approximately 55,000 volumes. Bound periodicals and a collection of League of Nations documents and of unbound United Nations documents do not appear in the catalog, but documents of other international organizations are cataloged and do appear, including: the Council of Europe, the European Communities, the International Court, the Organization for Economic Cooperation and Development, and the Nordic Council. Also included are government documents, especially of the United States (including treaties and hearings involving international relations), books, pamphlets, and mimeographed reports.

The catalog is in dictionary form, including authors, subjects, and some titles. Library of Congress subject headings are used but often adapted or expanded, and when LC-printed cards are used, subject headings are often added to those the Library of Congress has assigned. There are generous see and see-also references. Under the subject heading "Bibliography" with its several subdivisions are listed not just separately published bibliographies but also books which include significant bibliographies on a subject. All Western languages are included.

The library is located in New York City.

89. Institut für Zeitgeschichte, Munich, Bibliothek. Alphabetischer Katalog (Library of the Institute for Contemporary History, Alphabetical Catalog). 5 vols. Boston: G. K. Hall, 1967 (LC 76-460217). Erster Nachtragsband (First Supplement). 847 p., 1973.

________. Biographischer Katalog (Biographical Catalog). 764 p. Boston: G. K. Hall, 1967 (LC 72-217206). Erster Nachtragsband (First Supplement): Biographischer Katalog, Landerkatalog. 588 p., 1973.

________. Länderkatalog (Regional Catalog). 2 vols. Boston: G. K. Hall, 1967 (LC 72-191851). (see Biographischer Katalog for supplement).

________. Sachkatalog (Subject Catalog). 6 vols. Boston: G. K. Hall, 1967 (LC 76-460216). Erster Nachtragsband (First Supplement). 2 vcls., 1973.

The Institute for Contemporary History was founded in 1950 for the purpose of examining the pre-history and history of National Socialism in Germany, the period of Hitler's emergence and power. The library collects mainly on German history of the periods of the Weimar Republic, of National Socialism, and of post-1945 Germany, within the context of European and world history of the twentieth century. To provide a framework for the study of the history of this period, it also collects on general and German history of the nineteenth century, political science, economics and economic history, law and government, national defense policy and military science, Judaic studies, sociology, the cultural history of the recent past, and a broad range of belles-lettres. By 1966 the library contained nearly 52,000 volumes of books and serials, most of them in German.

The catalog is in four parts. All contain numerous analytical entries for articles in journals and yearbooks. The Alphabetischer Katalog contains individual entries for monographs, separates, periodicals, and serials, arranged alphabetically by author and title. There are many see references provided.

The Biographischer Katalog lists writings about people in alphabetical order by name of the subject of the biography.

The Regional Catalog (Länderkatalog) contains works about geographical areas. It is arranged alphabetically by the German name of the country or of the geographic region (such as Westeuropa--West Europe). There is an outline of the countries and regions covered in German and in English. Germany is not listed, but the individual states of Germany, both pre- and post-1945, are listed individually. Within each region or country the works are subdivided by broad subjects.

The Sachkatalog (Subject Catalog) is a classified catalog. The first volume provides both a synopsis of the classification system and a detailed breakdown of the classification, indicating which parts are found in each volume. Both are provided in German and in English. Within each class the most recent literature is listed first.

Kiel. Universität. Institut für Weltwirtschaft. Bibliothek. Catalogs. 207 vols. Boston: G. K. Hall, 1966-1968. (see 359)

Marx Memorial Library. Catalogue of the Marx Memorial Library, London. 3 vols. Boston: G. K. Hall, 1979. (see 368)

90. New York (City). Public Library. Reference Department. Subject Catalog of the World War I Collection. 4 vols. Boston: G. K. Hall, 1961 (LC 62-1672).

This catalog contains 58,000 subject cards about World War I taken from the general public catalog of the Reference Department of the New York Public Library. The subject headings used are the library's own and are listed in the front of volume one, with cross-references. Under the main heading "European War, 1914-1918," there are over 1,000 subdivisions running from "Addresses, sermons, etc." through "Women's work." The catalog is strong in periodicals, bibliographies, formal and informal histories, printed archives, military history, and economic aspects of the war. Included are 11,000 pamphlet titles and numerous entries for periodical articles in scholarly journals. Much of the material listed here was collected during and immediately after World War I. Works are in all Western European languages, particularly English, French, and German.

91. New York (City). Public Library. Research Libraries. Subject Catalog of the World War II Collection. 3 vols. Boston: G. K. Hall, 1977 (LC 77-153166).

This catalog consists of 43,000 entries under the subject heading "World War, 1939-1945" with its 200 major subdivisions, as well as several thousand cards under related headings. A list of the subject headings used, which are New York Public Library's own headings, is provided. Many of these subject headings are identical to Library of Congress headings; where they differ there is often a cross-reference from the LC headings to the NYPL heading that is used. Although this is primarily a subject catalog, there are a few main entries.

The catalog represents a collection of 22,000 volumes about World War II. The collection is especially strong on military, naval, and aerial history and operations; prisoners and prisons; concentration camps, atrocities, war crimes and trials; and diplomatic history and post-war planning. It is also good on economic aspects of the war, such as industries, finance, lend-lease, rationing, raw materials, and transportation; communication and propaganda; effect of the war on literature, art, music, and philosophy; and the economic, political, and social aspects of post-war problems, including demobilization, reparations, territorial questions, and peace treaties. The collection includes more than 3,000 personal narratives. Works treating the war in fiction, poetry, and drama are listed under literary form headings, such as "Novels" or "Plays."

The catalog includes material cataloged through 1971 in Roman alphabets, especially in English and German. Books and book-like material, including microforms and pamphlets, are listed. There are some analytics for proceedings, parts of books, and journal articles.

92. Royal Institute of International Affairs. Library. Index to Periodical Articles, 1950-1964, in the Library of the Royal Institute of International Affairs. 2 vols. Boston: G. K. Hall, 1964 (LC 65-9436). Index to Periodical Articles, 1965-1972. 879 p., 1974. Index to Periodical Articles, 1973-1978. 718 p., 1979.

The Library of the Royal Institute of International Affairs, located in London, is "the leading specialist collection in Great Britain dealing with international affairs from 1918 onwards" [Introduction]. International affairs includes international politics, economics, and jurisprudence.

The library receives 600 periodicals and indexes about one-third of them, since none of the available indexes were sufficient for the library's needs. The arrangement of the index is according to the library's own (Chatham House) classification system. This has an initial subject breakdown, but most of the index is a geographic arrangement, subdivided by the same topical classes as are found at the beginning of the index. The classification system, with subject and geographic indexes to it, is included in the first volume. Also listed in the first volume are the most important of the journals indexed.

The 1950-1964 index has over 30,000 entries; the 1965-1972

supplement adds another 18,000; and the 1973-1978 supplement 15,000 more.

93. Stanford University. Hoover Institution on War, Revolution, and Peace. The Library Catalogs of the Hoover Institution on War, Revolution, and Peace, Stanford University: Catalog of the Western Language Collections. 63 vols. Boston: G. K. Hall, 1969 (LC 77-17709). First Supplement. 5 vols., 1972. Second Supplement. 6 vols., 1977.

The Hoover Institution on War, Revolution, and Peace "is a center for documentation and research on political, social, and economic change in the twentieth century" [Preface]; its library is a research library specializing in foreign and international affairs. The institution was founded after World War I by Herbert Hoover, who donated money, as well as materials collected while he was Director of the American Relief Administration, to Stanford University to start a collection on the Great War. Much of the material in the Hoover Institution was collected during and after World Wars I and II specifically for the collection.

Besides great collections on the two world wars and twentieth-century European history in general, the Hoover Institution has major holdings as follows: it has substantial material on the Russian Revolution and communist revolutions around the world; "the materials on Nazism and fascism in the Hoover Institution comprise the best resources in the United States on these subjects" [Preface]; the collections on the colonies of the European countries in Africa are the basis of a major African collection; and an extensive collection on Latin America has been developed since Castro's revolution in Cuba. The library also has major strengths in its holdings on Asia, in both Western and foreign languages.

The catalogs of the Hoover Institution are issued in separate parts. Periodicals and serials in Western languages are in a separate catalog (see 94), as are materials in non-Western languages. The latter include the catalogs of the Chinese collection (see 213), of the Japanese collection (see 214), of the Arabic collection (see 198), and of the Turkish and Persian collections (see 199).

The Catalog of the Western Language Collections actually includes materials in all languages except those named above. Most of the material is in English, German, French, Spanish, and the Slavic languages, but there is also material in Swahili and other less frequently published languages, and a separate section of material in Indonesian. Titles in the Cyrillic alphabet are transliterated.

"The areas of major coverage [in the Western language collections] are Eastern and Western Europe, the Middle East, Africa South of the Sahara, Latin America, the Far East (i.e., Western language material on the Far East), and, to a more limited extent, United States and Great Britain. For these last two countries the focus of materials is primarily on their participation in the two world wars and in peace settlements, their radical movements to the left and right, their military preparedness, and their influence in international affairs. The major comprehensive collections are concerned with Germany, France, Russia, and Africa" [Foreword].

The Western languages catalog itself is in several parts. The main catalog includes books, pamphlets, addresses, and some government publications. It is a dictionary catalog of authors, titles, and subjects, following Library of Congress rules and subject headings, with some modifications and expansions. Many cross-references are included.

There are also several separate catalogs included here. The Catalog of Government Documents and Society Publications, which is in five volumes, includes, besides publications of governments, publications of private and semi-official organizations. The arrangement is by country. There is a Vault Catalog of rare or unique printed and manuscript material arranged by: 1) corporate authors, and 2) country or broad subject. Finally, there is a Catalog of Special Collections, containing personal papers and archival materials, arranged by name of individual or organization, with a subject index.

The 1969 Catalog of the Western Language Collections contains more than one million cards. The First Supplement contains 87,000 entries representing 25,000 books added between July, 1969 and June, 1971. The Second Supplement represents another 26,000 books, pamphlets, and official documents. The supplements do not update the separate catalogs of government documents or special collections.

94. Stanford University. Hoover Institution on War, Revolution, and Peace. The Library Catalogs of the Hoover Institution on War, Revolution, and Peace: Catalogs of the Western Language Serials and Newspaper Collections. 3 vols. Boston: G. K. Hall, 1969 (LC 79-17893).

This is a separate catalog of the Library of the Hoover Institution on War, Revolution, and Peace (see 93) that lists only serials. All languages in the Roman and Cyrillic alphabets are included; works in the Cyrillic alphabet are transliterated.

The Serials Catalog lists 26,000 titles in 36 languages and includes serial publications of all kinds, except newspapers. The arrangement is alphabetical by language, and within language alphabetical by title.

The Newspaper Catalog lists 6,500 titles from 125 countries, including 1,000 Russian-language newspapers. They are arranged by country, except for the Slavic newspapers, which are arranged by language. Within country or language the titles are arranged alphabetically.

Lack of running headings or a table of contents makes it difficult to find a particular language or country in the catalogs.

95. Stuttgart. Bibliothek für Zeitgeschichte. Bibliothek für Zeitgeschichte--Weltkriegsbücherei, Stuttgart: Alpha-

betischer Katalog (Library for Contemporary History--World War Library, Stuttgart: Alphabetical Catalog). 11 vols. Boston: G. K. Hall, 1968 (LC 74-223544).

________. Systematischer Katalog (Classified Catalog). 20 vols. Boston: G. K. Hall, 1968 (ISBN 0-8161-0175-2).

The Library for Contemporary History was founded in 1915 by the Swabian industrialist, Richard Franck. His goal was to collect all printed historical materials on the Great War: leaflets, placards, newspapers, periodicals, and books. The library today aims to collect comprehensively in international literature on twentieth-century history, especially wars, revolutions, political science, military science, and the disputes of international politics. The library is located in Stuttgart, and is supported by the State and Federal governments of Germany. At the time of publication of the catalog, the collection totalled 160, 000 volumes plus a photo collection and a pamphlet and placard archives. Most of the titles are in German, as well as in other European languages.

The alphabetical catalog consists mainly of author entries, with some title entries included.

The classified catalog contains 350, 000 cards in three parts: Subject Area, or general subjects; History Area, or historical subjects; and Country Area, or regional subjects. The last, more than half of the catalog, consists of geographic headings subdivided by topical subjects and periods. The historical section is broken down into large chronological divisions and further subdivided by topics and regions. The introduction to the classification system is very confusing and not much of an aid in using the catalog. There is a detailed breakdown of the classification system as well as a subject index to it; both are in German only. There are no running headings at the top of the page to indicate what classification number you are looking at, and the class numbers do not appear on the cards. There are guide cards for the subdivisions, but they do not indicate what major division they are in. There is no table of contents for each volume to detail what classification numbers start on which pages. The only indication of which numbers are in which volumes is on the inside cover of the volume. The result is that just finding your way to the right page of the catalog can be a major problem.

The Introduction does indicate that one book may be assigned two or three different classification numbers and, if necessary, chapters may be cataloged individually. There are also analytical entries for important articles in periodicals.

96. Vincent (G. Robert) Voice Library. Dictionary Catalog of the G. Robert Vincent Voice Library at Michigan State University, East Lansing, Michigan. Edited by Leonard E. Cluley and Pamela N. Engelbrecht. 677 p. Boston: G. K. Hall, 1975 (LC 75-319951).

This collection was originally the private library of G. Robert

Vincent, a specialist in sound, who worked in Edison's laboratory, established his own sound and recording studio in the 1920's, operated the multilingual interpreting system at the Nuremburg War Crimes Trials, and was Chief Sound and Recording Officer for the United Nations. The catalog lists recordings, mostly on tape, of the voices of famous people, and the sound of famous events. The collection is rich in recordings representing the history of radio, the First and Second World Wars, American isolationism, the Nuremburg trials, the United Nations, and American politics up to and including Watergate. It includes the voices of Theodore Roosevelt, Jane Addams, William Jennings Bryan, Florence Nightingale, Sarah Bernhardt, Admiral Peary, Kaiser Wilhelm, P. T. Barnum, Ellen Terry, Woodrow Wilson, and American astronauts, among many others.

This is a dictionary catalog with entries for the author (speaker), added entries, titles, and subjects. Entries tend to be very descriptive of content, although they do not say how long the tapes run. The subject cataloging is not as extensive as might be wished for, considering the amazing range of material.

8. AMERICAN HISTORY

American history is a favorite subject of American libraries, and many libraries have published their catalogs of special collections on this subject. The major catalogs are Harvard University's Widener Library shelflist on American History (102) and The New York Public Library's Dictionary Catalog of the History of the Americas (111). The Library of Congress, of course, has the largest collection in the world on this topic, and the various catalogs it publishes should be consulted for specific titles or subjects.

Discussed in this chapter are rare book catalogs of Americana, the most important being the catalogs of the American Antiquarian Society (98), the William Wyles Collection (100), the William Clements Library (105), The New York Public Library's Rare Book Division (110), and the Library of Congress's collection of broadsides (117). Complementing these are the manuscripts catalogs of the American Antiquarian Society (97), the Massachusetts Historical Society (104), with its emphasis on New England, and The New York Public Library's Manuscript Division (109), which has manuscripts on all subjects but is especially strong on Americana.

Also described in this chapter are numerous collections on local history and genealogy. Discussions of library catalogs that list works pertaining particularly to the history of the Western United States appear in the following chapter.

97. American Antiquarian Society, Worcester, Mass. Catalogue of the Manuscript Collections of the American Antiquarian Society. 4 vols. Boston: G. K. Hall, 1979 (LC 80-107440).

The manuscript collections of the American Antiquarian Society were cataloged under a grant from the National Endowment for the Humanities, awarded in 1972. The result is this dictionary catalog listing important source material for the study of American history from the seventeenth century to 1877. It contains excellent resources in the following areas: the history of the early American book trades, book selling and book collecting; early New England diaries; eighteenth- and nineteenth-century New England elites--especially religious, political, and military leaders; and voluntary associations and families in central Massachusetts from 1750 to 1870.

Collections of manuscripts are given a main-entry card with a short description of the collection, plus added entries for significant individuals and subjects. Some collections have been cataloged item by item; these individual items also appear in a separate chronological file in volume four. There are added entries for some occupations, certain types of records (e.g., account books, diaries, and sermons), and geographical locations. There are also subject entries. Subject headings are based on Library of Congress subject headings; the society's authority list of subject headings is provided in the beginning of volume one of the catalog. There are liberal see and see-also subject references in both the authority list and in the catalog itself.

98. American Antiquarian Society, Worcester, Mass. Library. A Dictionary Catalog of American Books Pertaining to the 17th through 19th Centuries. 20 vols. Westport, Conn.: Greenwood Publishing Corp., 1971 (LC 76-103820).

The title of this catalog is a fair description of its contents. Included are American imprints prior to 1821 and later works pertaining to seventeenth- through nineteenth-century America. There are first editions of American literary authors, many works of American genealogy, and extensive and detailed listings of publications of the first to the sixteenth Congress, and of American presidents and government departments to 1820. There are also numerous state and local documents, but most of the society's collection of state documents is not included. Textbooks, pamphlets, and addresses are included, but almanacs, broadsides, and local directories are not. The library contains sixty per cent of the total of books and pamphlets known to have been printed in the United States before 1821, and is the source of the Readex Microprint Corp. project, Early American Imprints, 1639-1800.[13]

The American Antiquarian Society catalog is a dictionary catalog that uses Library of Congress subject headings with some adjustments. There are many subject entries for each work, especially for works of genealogy. This is one of the catalogs interesting just to skim through, revealing as it does the concerns of early Americans as reflected in the books they produced and read.

99. Boston. Public Library. Manuscripts of the American Revolution in the Boston Public Library: A Descriptive Catalog. 157 p. Boston: G. K. Hall, 1968 (ISBN 0-8161-0825-0).

Included here are manuscripts, mostly letters, written from 1763 to 1784, concerning the American Revolution. Most are of American origin, but some come from British, European, and West Indian sources. The catalog is arranged chronologically, with an author and subject index. There are 1,238 different items or groups of items.

100. California. University, Santa Barbara. Library. The William Wyles Collection. 5 vols. Westport, Conn.: Greenwood Publishing Corp., 1970 (LC 70-19247).

The William Wyles Collection is a special collection of works in three main areas. First, and primarily, it includes works about Abraham Lincoln. Second, it holds works about the Civil War, covering the period between the Missouri Compromise of 1820 and the withdrawal of troops from the South in 1876--including military studies of the war, war memoirs, governmental reports and regimental histories, and works on Blacks in the United States, African culture, American slavery, and emancipation. Third, the collection covers the westward expansion of the United States to the Pacific and across the Pacific to the Orient, including state histories, journals of state historical societies, and accounts of early treks across overland trails.

Most of the entries represent books or pamphlets, although there are some analytics for articles detached from magazines, and for chapters or essays in books. This is a divided catalog: the Author-Title Catalog is in three volumes, and the Subject Catalog is in two volumes. Entries follow Library of Congress practices, but the Abraham Lincoln subject headings were developed by the staff. There are many see references. Items in the collection are in English and were published mostly in the nineteenth century. The collection is non-circulating.

101. Florida. University, Gainesville. Libraries. P. K. Yonge Library. Catalog of the P. K. Yonge Library of Florida History. 4 vols. Boston: G. K. Hall, 1977 (ISBN 0-8161-0019-5).

The P. K. Yonge Library of Florida History is a collection of Floridiana spanning five centuries of the state's history. It is the largest collection of Floridiana known to exist, containing over 20,000 books, 185 periodical subscriptions, and 654 newspapers on microfilm. The collection also contains manuscripts, microfilm collections, and maps, as well as pamphlets and Federal and state documents. Particular subject strengths include geography, colonial history, politics, Indians, archaeology, and anthropology, as well as the colonial history of neighboring Southeastern states.

This is a dictionary catalog of authors, titles, subjects, and added entries. Library of Congress subject headings are used with modifications--the principal one being that "Florida" is generally not used as a subject heading; instead, what would normally be subdivisions under the name of the state are used as subject headings. There are many analytics for articles in periodicals, both national and local, and some analytics for parts of books.

102. Harvard University. Library. American History. 5 vols. Cambridge, Mass.: distributed by Harvard University

Press, 1967 (LC 67-30955). (Widener Library Shelflist v. 9-13).

This catalog lists the American history collection of Harvard University in call number order arranged according to Harvard's own classification scheme. There is also a listing by author or title and a chronological listing by date of publication.

In an introductory essay to this catalog, John A. Riggs, the late Charles Warren Bibliographer in American History in the Harvard University Library, states that "only the Library of Congress excels Harvard in its general overall strength" of the American history collections. Harvard began building its American history collection in the nineteenth century and has amassed an especially valuable collection of pamphlets and tracts, particularly on slavery and the Civil War. It also has a valuable special collection on Mormonism and another on Theodore Roosevelt. In general, these volumes list the US classification of the Harvard Library classification system, covering the history of the United States and works dealing with North America or with the Western Hemisphere as a whole, including government and administration, foreign relations, religious history, U. S. civilization in general, description and travel, social customs, and peoples. It does not include economic history and conditions, American literature, or material on Hawaii.

Almost 84, 000 titles are listed here, including 22, 000 pamphlets in tract volumes. Many U. S. government documents are included.

For a further discussion of the Widener Library shelflists see 9.

103. Haverford College. Library. <u>Quaker Necrology.</u> 2 vols. Boston: G. K. Hall, 1961 (LC 61-4958).

This is simply a file, maintained by Haverford College, in Haverford, Pennsylvania, of references to 59, 000 death notices appearing in any of four Quaker periodicals: <u>The Friend</u> (1828-1955), <u>Friends Intelligencer</u> (1844-1955), <u>Friends Review</u> (1848-1894), and <u>Friends Journal</u> (1955-1960). The arrangement is alphabetical by name of the deceased, and entries include the name of the periodical and the volume, year, and page reference. States covered by these notices are Pennsylvania, New Jersey, and Delaware, and to some extent Maryland, New York, Ohio, and Indiana.

Illinois. University at Urbana-Champaign. Illinois Historical Survey. <u>The Mereness Calendar: Federal Documents on the Upper Mississippi Valley, 1780-1890.</u> 13 vols. Boston: G. K. Hall, 1971. (see 122)

104. Massachusetts Historical Society, Boston. Library. <u>Catalog of Manuscripts of the Massachusetts Historical Society.</u> 7 vols. Boston: G. K. Hall, 1969 (LC 73-16664). <u>First Supplement.</u> 2 vols., 1980.

The Massachusetts Historical Society aims to collect such materials as would "mark the genius, delineate the manners, and trace the progress of society in the United States" [Introduction]. It is one of the major manuscript depositories in the country; its manuscript collections illuminate the history of the United States, especially of New England, and include the Adams family papers. The society began collecting manuscripts in 1791 and continues building its collections today. The manuscripts date back to the eighteenth and nineteenth centuries.

This is a dictionary catalog with entries under personal and corporate names and, to a lesser extent, under subjects and geographic areas. Some of the major subject headings are "Indians," "United States. History. Revolution," and names of major cities, especially Boston. Most entries describe individual letters or other documents, and often describe the subject matter of the documents. Many of the individual collections of manuscripts have been cataloged in depth, others have been cataloged selectively, and others by main entry only.

105. Michigan. University. William L. Clements Library. Author/Title Catalog of Americana, 1493-1860, in the William L. Clements Library, University of Michigan, Ann Arbor, Michigan. 7 vols. Boston: G. K. Hall, 1970 (LC 73-156668).

This catalog contains 100,000 cards representing 30,000 books published from 1493 to 1860 on the subject of America. Included are works on New World discovery and exploration, early settlements, Indian troubles, wars for empire, the American Revolution, the Old Northwest, the War of 1812, political parties, economic theory and trade, science, literature and music, reform movements, Texas and the Mexican War, and westward migration.

The first five volumes of this catalog are an author-title catalog, with occasional personal subject entries. Volumes six and seven form a chronological catalog with the main-entry cards arranged by date of publication. Works are primarily in English but include other Western European languages. Broadsides, pamphlets, speeches, sale catalogs, and publications of colonies, states, and the United States government are all included.

The catalog of the map collection of the Clements Library has been published separately (see 45).

106. New England Historic Genealogical Society. The Greenlaw Index of the New England Historic Genealogical Society. 2 vols. Boston: G. K. Hall, 1979 (ISBN 0-8161-0312-7).

The New England Historic Genealogical Society, in Boston, Massachusetts, is the oldest genealogical society in America. Its aim is "collecting, preserving, and occasionally publishing genealogical and historical matter relating to New England families" [Introduction], but it collects representative material from throughout the United States as well.

The Greenlaw Index was compiled by William Prescott Greenlaw, librarian of the Society for 35 years, from works in the Society's library. It is an analytical index by family name, in about 35,000 cards, of genealogical information in works printed from 1900 to about 1940. Family histories, town and county histories, and to some extent studies in periodicals are indexed. Entries supply the first name of the principal ancestor, main towns in which the family resided, time periods covered in the source, fractions of a page or number of pages of data given, and dates of publication.

The Greenlaw Index continues two other genealogical guides, the Index to American Genealogies (also known as Munsell's Genealogical Index), which covers from the 1820's to 1900, and the Newberry Index (see 113), which is strongest from 1896 to 1918. However, it provides more complete information than either of these.

107. New York (City). Public Library. Local History and Genealogy Division. Dictionary Catalog of the Local History and Genealogy Division. 18 vols. Boston: G. K. Hall, 1974 (LC 75-307060).

Included in this collection, as its name implies, are local histories and works on genealogy and heraldry. There are published county, city, town, and village histories for all areas of the United States, the United Kingdom, and the Republic of Ireland. Genealogy holdings include published American genealogies, manuscript genealogies, genealogical collections, and such source material as bibliographies, church records, city directories through 1869, census records, land records, cemetery records, and probate records. The United Kingdom and Ireland are covered to a lesser extent than the United States, but more than Europe. Materials on heraldry and vexillology (the study of flags) are collected comprehensively for all areas.

There are over 100,000 volumes in the collection. Microforms and pamphlets are included in the catalog, but much ephemeral material is not listed. There are many analytical entries for journal articles and essays in books.

This is a dictionary catalog. The subject headings used are the library's own, and consist mostly of place names. The local histories included in this catalog are also listed in United States Local History Catalog (see 108) in a geographically-based shelflist arrangement.

108. New York (City). Public Library. Local History and Genealogy Division. United States Local History Catalog: A Modified Shelf List Arranged Alphabetically by State, and Alphabetically by Locality within Each State. 2 vols. Boston: G. K. Hall, 1974 (LC 75-313771). Supplemented by Bibliographic Guide to North American History: 1977- . Boston: G. K. Hall, 1978- .

The title of this catalog is a succinct description of its contents and arrangement. It is a sort of appendix to the Dictionary Catalog of the Local History and Genealogy Division (see 107). It contains only local (city, town, and village) histories of areas in the United States, and only those local histories that are cataloged and separately bound monographs and serials. Cataloged pamphlets of local history in the Division--which number 10,000--are not included, but are listed in the Dictionary Catalog.

The advantage of this catalog is its arrangement, which is alphabetical by state and, within each state, alphabetical by name of locality. Material cataloged through the end of 1971, when the library switched to Anglo-American Cataloging Rules, is included.

109. New York (City). Public Library. Manuscript Division. Dictionary Catalog. 2 vols. Boston: G. K. Hall, 1967 (LC 68-4776).

This is a catalog of the manuscript collection of the New York Public Library, ranging from Babylonian clay tablets to twentieth-century writings. The manuscripts are in the fields of history, literature, exploration, and science. In particular, the holdings are strong in discovery and settlement of the Americas; colonial Latin America; colonization, Revolution, and early Federal period in North America; New York State and City history; exploration of the Grand Canyon; Burgess family papers on early nineteenth-century Persia; Aleutian folklore and the Kamchadal language; Greek, Latin Medieval, and Renaissance manuscripts; correspondence of early nineteenth-century scientists and engineers; archives of organizations; and literary manuscripts. There are appendices of special collections which deal with Herman Melville, the anti-slavery movement, the movement for Irish independence, and music.

This is a dictionary catalog of names, subjects, geographic areas, and kinds of manuscripts--account books, autograph albums, diaries, maps, etc. The subject headings used are New York Public Library's own; there are many see and see-also references. Many entries are simply indications of the existence of a large collection; some are very detailed, with annotations of the type of material in a collection or information identifying individuals. The Manuscript Division collections include more than nine million pieces; the catalog contains only 24,000 cards and should be considered to be only a guide to the collection.

110. New York (City). Public Library. Rare Book Division. Dictionary Catalog of the Rare Book Division. 21 vols. Boston: G. K. Hall, 1971 (LC 74-173370). First Supplement. 754 p., 1973.

This catalog represents 90,000 rare books and pamphlets from the fifteenth century to today's private and special presses. The major strength of the collection is in historical Americana, from the discoveries of Columbus and Vespucci to the westward expansion of the United States. It includes a notable collection of sixteenth-century accounts of the exploration and settlement of the New World and of voyages and travels to all parts of the world. Also of note is a collection of Latin American printing from 1543 to 1800; editions of the Bible from the fifteenth to the nineteenth centuries in many languages; the William Barclay Parsons Collection of early scientific periodicals; the Spencer Collection of illustrated books and fine bindings (also described in its own catalog, see 28); and collections of cookery and of literature. Volume 21 is an appendix which lists the library's 20, 000 broadsides in chronological order, from 1215 to 1971.

This is a dictionary catalog of authors, titles, and subjects. New York Public Library's own subject headings are used. These are based on an alphabetico-classed system, whose headings tend to be very broad and to employ geographic and topical subdivisions. In recent years, however, there has been a trend toward use of Library of Congress headings. The supplement contains material cataloged through December, 1971, when the library switched to Anglo-American Cataloging Rules.

111. New York (City). Public Library. Reference Department. Dictionary Catalog of the History of the Americas. 28 vols. Boston: G. K. Hall, 1961 (LC 61-4957). First Supplement. 9 vols., 1974.

This catalog represents the American history collection of the New York Public Library. Both North and South American history is covered and the collection is especially strong in national and state histories of the United States and of other countries of the Americas, slavery in the U. S., U. S. foreign relations, immigrant groups, and American Indians. This last subject occupies two full volumes of the original catalog. The collection has comprehensive holdings of state historical society publications. The catalog includes entries for ephemera, government documents from North, South, and Central America, documents of state governments of the United States, pamphlets, and some photographs. Materials are in many languages, although English predominates. There are no entries for genealogy or United States local history, which are listed in the Dictionary Catalog of the Local History and Genealogy Division (see 107).

This is a dictionary catalog that uses New York Public Library's own subject headings. These headings are based on an alphabetico-classed system developed in the nineteenth century, but since 1925 there has been a tendency towards adoption of Library of Congress subject headings. There are many good cross-references, and there is an excellent introduction explaining the scope of the collection and the filing system. The library has been providing analytics for collections and monographic series since 1866, and since 1897 it has been subject-indexing many articles in scholarly periodicals.

The supplement covers material added through 1972, when the library switched to Anglo-American Cataloging Rules and began a computer-produced book catalog (see 16).

112. New York (City). Public Library. Research Libraries. Dictionary Catalog of Materials on New York City. 3 vols. Boston: G. K. Hall, 1977 (LC 78-300452).

This catalog has been formed by the extraction of approximately 42,000 cards dealing with New York City from the main public catalog of the Research Libraries of the New York Public Library. In large part it consists of that segment of the catalog that begins with "New York" and "New York (City)," excluding entries for "New York (Colony)" and "New York (State)," but including entries for institutions whose names begin with "New York." The first volume gives a list of the subject subdivisions under the general heading "New York" and a list of other subjects that have been included because they are geographically subdivided with entries for New York, e.g., "Airports--U. S.--N. Y.--New York." The subject headings are the library's own, based upon an alphabetico-classed system.

The policy of the library has been to acquire materials in virtually every subject area relating to New York City, from local history to political, social, and economic aspects of the city's life, and from the colonial period to the present. Pamphlets, New York City government documents, and dissertations are included, as are analytical entries for articles in periodicals.

113. Newberry Library, Chicago. Genealogical Index of the Newberry Library. 4 vols. Boston: G. K. Hall, 1960 (LC 60-51633).

"In March, 1896, the catalogue department of the Newberry Library began work upon the preparation of a genealogical index that should contain in time all the surnames, principally in the United States, that had appeared in historical and genealogical periodicals, compilations, and books in the library's collections. These entries ranged from a mere mention of a name in a list of representatives 'or some other honorable connection,' to a family history of several hundred pages" [Foreword]. In 1915 this index, which became known as the Wall Index, had 683,431 entries; by the time of its reproduction it had nearly one million entries. Coverage is strongest for the Midwest and the East.

The catalog is arranged by surname (e.g., "Bosworth family," "Taylor family," etc.) with reference to the source of information. Family listings are divided geographically. References to allied families are given, and there are cross-references to variant spellings. Some of the entries are to widely available works, such as publications of state historical societies, while others are to material available only at the Newberry Library. In all cases the bibliographic information given in the entries is very sketchy; often it consists of merely the name of a county, the author's last name and first initials, and a date. Sometimes a page reference is given; sometimes the note "see index" (i.e., the index to the work). It may be desirable to use this catalog in tandem with The New York Public Library's Dictionary Catalog of the Local History and Genealogical Division (see 107). In this latter catalog full bibliographic information can be found for most works cited in the Genealogical Index by searching under either the author or the county reference given by the Index.

114. St. Louis. Public Library. Genealogical Material and Local Histories in the St. Louis Public Library. Revised edition by Georgia Gambrill, Reference Department. 356 p. St. Louis, 1965 (LC 68-4741). First Supplement. 1971.

This is a catalog of local histories, family histories, regimental histories, biographical registers, records and rosters of immigration, and the like, maintained by the St. Louis Public Library. Most of the material deals with Missouri, Illinois, and most states east of the Mississippi. The arrangement is by type of material, and the table of contents must be checked in order to use the catalog. There are no author or other indexes. There are some entries for articles in periodicals and for parts of books. The supplement includes material added to the library through July, 1971.

The Heraldry Index of the St. Louis Public Library has been published separately (see 85).

115. United States. Library of Congress. Genealogies in the Library of Congress: A Bibliography. Edited by Marion J. Kaminkow. 4 vols. Baltimore, Md.: Magna Carta Book Co., 1972 (LC 74-187078). Supplement 1972-1976. 285 p., 1977.

This catalog of the Library of Congress's genealogical material brings up to date American and English Genealogies in the Library of Congress, published in 1910 and 1919. Besides American and English works, it also includes Canadian, Irish, Welsh, Scottish, Australian, Latin American, Polish, German, Dutch, Scandinavian, French, Spanish, Italian, Portuguese, and Asian sources. It includes all entries from the Family Name Index, a 60-drawer card catalog located in the Local History and Genealogy Room of the Library of Congress. There are references to printed books, and to works in diverse formats, such as typescripts and manuscripts. The catalog serves three functions: 1) it lists genealogical materials; 2) it acts as an index to genealogies in sources not usually considered genealogical; and 3) it acts as a guide to nonprinted manuscripts not in the Library of Congress's Manuscript Division.

The arrangement is by family name. Names that are pronounced alike although spelled differently are grouped together. There are many references to works listed under different family names that contain information about the family originally sought.

Local histories found in the Local History and Genealogy Room are listed in United States Local Histories in the Library of Congress: A Bibliography (see 116).

116. United States. Library of Congress. United States Local

Histories in the Library of Congress: A Bibliography. Edited by Marion J. Kaminkow. 4 vols. Baltimore: Magna Carta Book Co., 1975 (LC 74-25444). Volume 5: Supplement and Index. 1975 (c. 1976).

This catalog lists works on local history in the Library of Congress. It includes all books classified in the local history portion of the library's shelflist (F1-975) through mid-1972. The supplement includes works cataloged from 1972 to the beginning of January, 1976. The books in this class deal with the history and description of states, cities, towns, counties, and other localities of the United States. Most genealogies are not included but are listed in Genealogies in the Library of Congress: A Bibliography (see 115).

The arrangement is in order by classification number; that is, by region, subdivided by state, subdivided by city, county, or other local division. The beginning of each state's listings is preceded by the reproduction of the Library of Congress classification schedule for that state. At the end of each state's listings there is a "Supplementary Index of Places," which indexes, by name of town, books that treat several localities and are therefore not cataloged under each specific locality. Volume 5, the Supplement and Index, has an index of names, primarily of individuals who are authors, editors, or subjects of the works listed in the catalog.

117. United States. Library of Congress. Rare Book Division. Catalog of Broadsides in the Rare Book Division. 4 vols. Boston: G. K. Hall, 1972 (LC 72-6563).

This is a catalog of over 28,000 broadsides and leaflets held in the Rare Book Division of the Library of Congress. These items were printed from 1527 to 1971, but there are few items for these later years. The majority of the pieces were produced in the United States, although several thousand of foreign origin are included; of these, Great Britain and Mexico are especially well represented.

The subject matter of these broadsides varies a great deal. Generally, they discuss current, topical concerns; they may be advertisements, menus, political statements, election notices, and the like. Among the broadsides that may be found in this collection are: an item denouncing an individual as a "lyar, a puppy"; an announcement of lost oxen; and an appeal for information on "a young lady who saved the life of an English Baronet." Included are nearly 200 items printed in Virginia before 1800 and 246 items relating to the Continental Congress.[14]

The catalog is arranged in three parts. There is a shelflist, which is a geographical arrangement; an author/title catalog, which includes material in other collections in the Library of Congress; and a chronological file, arranged by date of printing. The chronological catalog is a fascinating study in itself, mirroring as it does the concerns of American society of the time. Many of the catalog cards seem to contain the entire text of the broadsides they describe.

118. United States. Military Academy, West Point. Library. Subject Catalog of the Military Art and Science Collection in the Library of the United States Military Academy with Selected Author and Added Entries, Including a Preliminary Guide to the Manuscript Collection. 4 vols. Westport, Conn.: Greenwood, 1969.

The subject of this collection is military art and science, including "all aspects of the evolution of warfare on land, at sea, and in the air" [Introduction]. It is richest in material on the land aspects of warfare. Most of the collection centers on United States military history, but it is also strong in works about European wars. Works are mostly in English, but other Western European languages are included. The collection dates back to the American Revolution, but most titles were published in the nineteenth or twentieth century.

The catalog is a "modified dictionary approach." Most of the entries are subject entries, but there are some main entries. In general, subject headings follow Library of Congress practice, but they may be inverted or otherwise modified. When Library of Congress printed cards are used, subject headings are occasionally added to the ones listed on the cards. Journals are not listed, but there are some analytical entries for articles in journals.

The preliminary guide to the manuscript collections, mentioned in the title, is at the end of the last volume of the catalog. Both analyzed and unanalyzed collections are included. The arrangement is generally by name of individual; it is particularly strong in items on cadets of West Point.

9. THE AMERICAN WEST

Taken as a group, these catalogs constitute an extraordinary bibliography of the history of the Western United States. The Bancroft Library catalog (119) is the largest and most comprehensive collection of the history of the American West as a whole, but the other catalogs represent more thorough collections on particular states or regions of the West. All the catalogs have valuable resources on the exploration, settlement, people, and events of the Western half of the United States.

119. California. University. Bancroft Library. Catalog of Printed Books. 22 vols. Boston: G. K. Hall, 1964 (LC 67-52922). First Supplement. 6 vols., 1969. Second Supplement. 6 vols., 1974. Third Supplement. 5 vols., 1979.

The Bancroft Collection was begun in the mid-nineteenth century by a Californian bookseller named Hubert Howe Bancroft. The subject matter of his collection was originally limited to the history of California, but it grew to include all of the western half of North America, including Mexico and Central America. Bancroft made no attempt to judge quality, believing that "the most worthless trash may prove some fact wherein the best book is deficient, and this makes the trash valuable" [Introduction].

Strengths of the collection are in the social sciences, especially history, religion, politics, economics, and social conditions of the region. There are over 230 pages of entries on American Indians. The collection is also particularly strong in material on Mormons, the Catholic Church in Mexico, early California printing, voyages and travels, government publications of New Spain, and the pioneer West.

This is a dictionary catalog that uses Library of Congress subject headings with some slight changes. Works are mostly in English, followed in number by Spanish and other Western languages. There are analytics for some major Western periodicals without indices and for some special issues of newspapers, as well as for collections of pamphlets. Maps are listed in a separate catalog (see 36), as are the manuscript collections (see 120).

The First Supplement adds a large collection on Mexico, the Yates collection of communist materials and related items on labor and politics, and analyzes pamphlets on San Francisco. The Second Supplement adds more collections on Mexico, including pamphlets on the Revolution of 1910-1925, and also includes the Koundakjian Collection of American Wit and Humor.

The Bancroft Library collection is also included in the 1963 Author-Title Catalog of the library of the University of California at Berkeley (see 6).

120. California. University. Bancroft Library. A Guide to the Manuscript Collections. Edited by Dale L. Morgan and George P. Hammond. vol. 1- . Berkeley: Published for the Bancroft Library by the University of California Press, 1963- (LC 63-16986).

Volume one. Pacific and Western Manuscripts (except California)
Volume two. Manuscripts Relating Chiefly to Mexico and Central America (1972).

This is what has been published so far of the catalog of the manuscript collections of the Bancroft Library of Western Americana. Volume one deals with the history of the West, mostly in the nineteenth century. Much of the material in it derives from dictations of individuals and from documents collected by Hubert Howe Bancroft, the bookseller and collector, in the course of writing his histories of the West. Additional archival material was added to the collection by the University of California. Volume one is arranged by state or geographical area, and covers Oregon, Washington, Canada (especially British Columbia and the Yukon), Arizona, New Mexico, Utah and the Mormons, Nevada, Idaho, Montana, Alaska, Colorado, Wyoming, Hawaii and Pacific Ocean areas, and Texas. There is a detailed index of names of individuals, organizations, places, and some subjects.

Volume two, Manuscripts Relating Chiefly to Mexico and Central America, is arranged in alphabetical order by author or, if there is no author, by title or subject. There is also a detailed index of persons, places, and subjects.

Both volumes contain brief descriptions of the manuscript or group of manuscripts listed. The Catalog of Printed Books of the Bancroft Library has been published separately (see 119).

California. University. Bancroft Library. Index to Printed Maps. 521 p. Boston: G. K. Hall, 1964. (see 36)

121. Denver. Public Library. Western History Department. Catalog. 7 vols. Boston: G. K. Hall, 1970 (LC 70-24055). First Supplement. 859 p., 1975.

The Western History Department of the Denver Public Library collects books, pamphlets, government documents, serials, maps, manuscripts, newspapers, Western periodicals, and photographs and prints on the history of the West. However, the collections of maps, manuscripts, newspapers, Western periodicals, and photographs and prints are not included in this catalog. The department's emphasis is on the history of the Rocky Mountain region, especially its fur traders, cattle industry, mining operations and promotions, railroads, Indians, outlaws, and exploration.

This is a dictionary catalog of authors, titles, added entries, and subjects. The catalog uses Library of Congress subject headings and the Dewey Decimal classification. There are many see and see-also references for names and subjects. Particularly useful here is the subject analysis for chapters of books.

Most of the books were published in the nineteenth and twentieth centuries, and they are generally in English.

122. Illinois. University at Urbana-Champaign. Illinois Historical Survey. The Mereness Calendar: Federal Documents on the Upper Mississippi Valley, 1780-1890. 13 vols. Boston: G. K. Hall, 1971 (ISBN 0-8161-0915-X).

The Mereness Calendar is an annotated guide to manuscripts, surveys, published and unpublished reports, and correspondence to and from government agencies, as well as relevant Senate and House reports, relating to the history of the Upper Mississippi Valley. Agencies covered include the Department of State, the Senate, the Post Office Department, the Department of the Interior, and the War Department, including the records of the Quartermaster General, Adjutant General, and Chief of Engineers. The Department of the Interior has the largest collection of cards in the Calendar, with over 100,000 entries (out of the total of approximately 300,000) divided among its Indian Office, General Land Office, and Office of the Secretary of the Interior.

Records are arranged by agency and then chronologically within agency. The Calendar is particularly important for research on the American Indian, pioneering, railroads, government affairs, and other aspects of the westward expansion of the United States.

The Illinois Historical Survey, in which the Mereness Calendar is located, is a manuscript collection and research division of the University of Illinois Library. The Survey was established in 1909 with the aim of collecting and preserving a wide range of historical materials and promoting the study of the "Old Northwest" in American history.

123. Newberry Library, Chicago. A Catalogue of the Everett D. Graff Collection of Western Americana. Compiled by Colton Storm. 854 p. Chicago: published for the Newberry Library by the University of Chicago Press, 1968 (LC 66-20577).

The subject matter of the Graff Collection is America west of the Mississippi. It is particularly strong in works on gold rushes, travel, surveys, the cattle industry, army camps, outlaws, and law enforcement. Included are books, manuscripts, maps, newspapers, and pamphlets, most of which were printed in the nineteenth century.

This is a main-entry catalog, with an index of titles, broad subjects, and names of individuals. The descriptive cataloging is very detailed, with notes on the physical size, appearance, and collation of a work. Often there are discussions of the background or importance of the work and an evaluation of its contents. There are 4,800 numbered entries.

124. Powell, Donald Moore. The Arizona Index: A Subject Index to Periodical Articles About the State. Compiled by Donald M. Powell and Virginia E. Rice. 2 vols. Boston: G. K. Hall, 1978 (ISBN 0-8161-0090-X).

The Arizona Collection at the University of Arizona Library, begun circa 1903, holds one of the most extensive collections of printed materials about Arizona. The Arizona Index was started in 1951 "in an attempt to help the user locate information in a select list of periodicals not indexed in standard works such as Readers' Guide" [Introduction]. The list of these periodicals, containing approximately 120 titles, is provided in the index. In addition, other journals are indexed occasionally for articles on Arizona. The journals range from scholarly titles such as Western Historical Quarterly and American Anthropologist, to business publications like Arizona Business, to recreational magazines like Arizona Highways and Outdoor Arizona, to local daily newspapers. The index attempts to cover Arizona in all aspects--recreation, history, Indians, business, social life, water and natural resources, and politics. A few pamphlets, government documents, and books are also included in the index.

This is a subject index that uses Sears List of Subject Headings with additions and special subdivisions. Individuals are indexed as subjects. There are many see and see-also references. Articles are in English and appeared from the 1890's to the mid-1970's.

125. Texas. University at Austin. Barker Texas History Center. Catalog of the Texas Collection in the Barker Texas History Center, The University of Texas at Austin. 14 vols. Boston: G. K. Hall, 1979 (ISBN 0-8161-0273-2).

This collection was begun in the 1890's and now contains approximately 110,000 volumes on the greater Texas region. "Efforts have been made in collection development to acquire everything possible relating to Texas and Texans and written by or about Texans within the following five subject groups: social and behavioral sciences, languages and literature, humanities, fine arts, and science and technology" [Introduction]. Included are books, periodicals, speeches, Texas government documents, dissertations, pamphlets, serials (with holdings indicated), and microfilms in English, Spanish, and all the non-English languages of Texas, including German, French, and Swedish. Imprint dates range from the sixteenth century to the present, but the emphasis is on the nineteenth and twentieth centuries. Of particular interest are rare materials imprinted in or dealing with the Southern and Western United States that provide extensive coverage of the Civil War, slavery, Reconstruction, and Southern political and social conditions in the late nineteenth century.

The catalog is in two parts: an author/title catalog in volumes 1-9, and a subject catalog in volumes 10-14. The subject catalog uses Library of Congress subject headings with modifications. Recently cataloged materials are classified in the Library of Congress classification.

126. Washington (State). University. Library. The Dictionary Catalog of the Pacific Northwest Collection of the University of Washington Libraries, Seattle. 6 vols. Boston: G. K. Hall, 1972 (LC 74-157790).

This collection was begun circa 1905, when the library began seeking anything relating to the state or territory of Washington, including, in addition to books and serials, official documents, newspapers, files, maps, and pictures. The scope was later widened to include the area covering what is now the states of Washington, Oregon, Idaho, and Montana, and the Province of British Columbia, as well as, still more recently, Alaska and the Yukon. Works dealing with California and the Southwest are not collected. The library has almost a complete collection on maritime voyages to the Northwest Coast, and is also particularly strong in the subjects of the fur trade, missionaries, immigration, Indians, settlement, the cattle trade, mining, agriculture, shipping, the lumber industry, the building of trails and roads, and the establishment of schools, churches, and benevolent fraternal organizations.

This is a dictionary catalog of authors, titles of books and serials, subjects, and added entries. See and see-also references were used until 1962. Library of Congress subject headings are used with adaptations. Included in the catalog are microforms, dissertations, some manuscripts, official publications of the state and territory of Washington and of its local governments, and many rare books. There are some entries for periodical article reprints. Titles are mostly in English and are from the nineteenth and twentieth centuries.

127. Wisconsin. State Historical Society. Library. Author-Title Catalog; Including the City Directory Catalog, Atlas Catalog (Publishers), Atlas Catalog (Geographic), Newspaper Catalog and Newspaper Catalog (Labor). 22 vols. on 600 sheets of microfiche. Westport, Conn.: Greenwood, 1974.

The State Historical Society of Wisconsin maintains a collection for the study of American history in general and Wisconsin and Middle

Western history in particular. This is an author-title catalog only, with added entries; the Subject Catalog of the Library has been published separately (see 128). Included here are entries for books, pamphlets, United States and Wisconsin government publications, sermons, addresses, and microforms. There are analytical entries for works in series, including series in microform.

There are several separate catalogs included with the Author-Title Catalog. The Atlas Catalog (Publishers) is an author-title catalog of atlases of the United States and the world. The emphasis is on atlases of the Midwest. Many of the titles were published in the seventeenth and eighteenth centuries.

The Atlas Catalog (Geographic) is a subject catalog of atlases. The subject headings are mainly for geographic entities, but there are also topical headings, such as "Automobiles--Road Guides."

The City Directory Catalog lists mainly nineteenth-century city directories. The arrangement is by state, and then by city within state. Many of the entries were copied from the National Union Catalog and include the NUC symbols for holding libraries.

The Newspaper Catalog lists many nineteenth-century newspapers from all over the country. Many of the titles are on microfilm, but some are represented by only one or two issues (the library's holdings are listed). The arrangement is by state, and by town or city within the state.

The Newspaper Catalog (Labor) contains entries for radical newspapers and newspapers of labor unions. Most of the papers were printed in the twentieth century and are held in microform.

128. Wisconsin. State Historical Society. Library. Subject Catalog of the Library of the State Historical Society of Wisconsin, Madison, Wisconsin; Including the Pamphlet Subject Catalog Beginning in Volume 22. 23 vols. Westport, Conn.: Greenwood, 1971 (LC 78-161601).

The charter of the State Historical Society of Wisconsin calls for the society to promote "a wider appreciation of the American heritage with particular emphasis on the collection, advancement, and dissemination of knowledge of the history of Wisconsin and the Middle West" [Introduction]. The library was begun in 1854 and by 1971 had over one million items of books, periodicals, pamphlets, broadsides, and government publications. However, the maps, broadsides, manuscripts (except those collections in microform), photographs, and most government documents are not listed in this catalog. The library takes as its province the history of the United States, its territories and possessions, and Canada, but excludes the subjects of education, literature, the arts, and science and technology. Its particular strengths are in works on American Indians, the Revolutionary War, the Civil War, the trans-Mississippian West, the old Northwest, denominational and church history, state and local history, radical social movements, ethnic groups, Blacks, and genealogy.

This is a subject catalog only; the Author-Title Catalog has been published separately (see 127). Library of Congress subject headings are used, but the subject cataloging is admitted to be inconsistent. There are extensive see and see-also references. Included in the catalog are Wisconsin obituaries since 1846 and biographical sketches published in Wisconsin county histories before 1955. There are also selected analytics for other articles in Wisconsin periodicals and learned journals.

Pamphlets are listed in two places. Those acquired through 1967 are cataloged with the books in the subject catalog. Those acquired after that date are in a separate Pamphlet Subject Catalog. In this separate catalog are described advertisements, leaflets, political pamphlets, and the like. Each pamphlet may have four or five or even more subject headings assigned. Although the date this catalog began is 1968, most of the pamphlets in it date from before that year.

129. Yale University. Library. Yale Collection of Western Americana. Catalog of the Yale Collection of Western Americana. 4 vols. Boston: G. K. Hall, 1962 (LC 63-1576).

The subject matter of this collection is the American West, defined as the area covering all states of the United States west of the Mississippi River, as well as the western provinces of Canada. The collection's strongest subjects are Texas and the Mexican War, the Plains, the Rockies, and the Pacific Northwest. Most of the entries are for rare books, including some pamphlets and some bound magazine articles.

This is primarily a main-entry catalog. There are many added entries, particularly for individuals named in books. Subject headings are used very sparingly. Also included in the catalog is a shelflist. Its arrangement is primarily geographical, divided by region, then by state within region, and then, within each state, chronologically.

10. CANADIAN HISTORY

The largest of the libraries on the history of Canada is the Library of the Public Archives of Canada (131). The published catalog of this collection, however, is only an author-title catalog and provides no subject approach. The Catalogue of the Glenbow Historical Library (132) and the catalog of the Library of the Provincial Archives of British Columbia (134) are both dictionary catalogs, but both specialize only in the history of Western Canada. The only published catalog, therefore, with a subject approach to Canadian history in general is the published shelflist on Canadian History and Literature of Harvard University's Widener Library (133), but even this is not one of Harvard's strongest collections.

130. Boston. Public Library. Canadian Manuscripts in the Boston Public Library; a Descriptive Catalog. 76 p. Boston: G. K. Hall, 1971 (LC 72-173375).

Included in this catalog are entries for 633 Canadian manuscripts or groups of manuscripts, arranged chronologically, with short descriptions. Most of the manuscripts are letters. There is an index, consisting mostly of names of individuals, but also of places and subjects. Dates of the manuscripts range from 1631 to 1930. The emphasis is on political and economic relations between New England and the Maritime Provinces in the eighteenth century, and on the Abolitionists and the antislavery movement.

131. Canada. Public Archives of Canada. Library. Catalogue of the Public Archives Library, Public Archives of Canada, Ottawa, Ontario. 12 vols. Boston: G. K. Hall, 1979 (ISBN 0-8161-0316-X).

The Public Archives Library collects printed primary and secondary source material relevant to the history of Canada, including: "books on cartography, discoveries and exploration of North America and New France extending to the gulf of Mexico, journals and diaries of explorers and missionaries, narratives of early travelers, life in Upper and Lower Canada and in the Maritimes, the discovery and settlement of the West, Indian, American and European Wars, and the Rebellions of 1837-1838, 1869-1885. Also covered are elections, trade and commerce, education, railways, canals, and religious fields of the Canadian experience" [Introduction]. The library maintains an extensive collection of early government documents of colonial and provincial governments, and a special collection of pamphlets published in Canada, the United States, France, and England.

Included here are the Author-Title Catalogue of the library and, in the last three volumes, a chronological catalog of pamphlets from 1493 to 1950. The Author-Title Catalogue conforms to Anglo-American cataloging rules on forms of entry. Publications in languages other than French are cataloged in English; French-language publications are cataloged in French. The catalog also includes printed material held in the various divisions of the Public Archives Branches.

132. Glenbow-Alberta Institute. Library. Catalogue of the Glenbow Historical Library. 4 vols. Boston: G. K. Hall, 1973 (LC 74-154304).

The Glenbow Historical Library, in Calgary, Alberta, specializes in the history and development of Western and Northern Canada, more recently focusing on the Prairie region of Canada. Also collected by the library are sports and natural history books without a regional preference; material on Canadian art, ethnology, and cultural history; and material about native peoples, ethnic groups, political movements, and local histories.

This is a dictionary catalog of books and some ephemera. Microforms, government documents, periodicals, and archival materials are not included in the catalog. Library of Congress subject headings are used, and the classification system is the Dewey Decimal Classification. Most of the titles are in English.

133. Harvard University. Library. Canadian History and Literature. 411 p. Cambridge, Mass.: distributed by Harvard University Press, 1968 (LC 68-22417). (Widener Library Shelflist v. 20)

This volume in the Widener Library shelflist series covers the history and literature of Canada. History is defined as civilization, government and administration, religious affairs, geography and travel, and peoples. Economic and financial affairs, some special aspects of social conditions, and many government documents are not included. Literature is defined as literary histories, anthologies, and works by and about individual authors, as well as works relating to Canadian literature in both English and French.

The catalog is in three parts: the first is arranged by classification number according to the Harvard classification system; the second is by author and title; and the third is chronological. There are about 10,200 monograph and serial titles listed here--about 7,300 in English and 2,600 in French.

For a further discussion of the Widener Library shelflists see 9.

National Map Collection. Catalogue of the National Map Collection, Public Archives of Canada. 16 vols. Boston: G. K. Hall, 1976. (see 46)

134. Provincial Archives of British Columbia. Library. Dictionary Catalogue of the Library of the Provincial Archives of British Columbia, Victoria. 8 vols. Boston: G. K. Hall, 1971 (LC 71-173372).

The Provincial Archives of British Columbia is the oldest archival institution in Western Canada. Its library includes books, pamphlets, periodicals, and government publications of British Columbia and of Canada. The catalog has analytics for long runs of defunct periodical titles as well as for current titles.

The library includes works relating to British Columbia, Canada west of the Great Lakes, the Northwest and Yukon Territories, Arctic exploration, and the neighboring states of Washington, Oregon, Idaho, Montana, and Alaska. The library also serves as a research collection for the Human History Section of the Provincial Museum, and therefore includes printed material on anthropology, archaeology, and ethnography.

This is a dictionary catalog of 170, 000 cards. Library of Congress subject headings are used. Pamphlets receive the same cataloging treatment as books.

135. Université Laval, Quebec. Centre d'études nordiques. Bibliographie de la péninsule du Québec-Labrador. Compiled by Alan Cooke and Fabien Caron. 2 vols. Boston: G. K. Hall, 1968 (ISBN 0-8161-0758-0).

Commissioned by the Centre d'Etudes Nordiques, this bibliography of its holdings "aims at comprehensive coverage of the literature related to the Quebec-Labrador peninsula and its near-shore islands" [Introduction]. It covers geography, natural history, exploration, mining, geology, history, and Indians of the area.

Entries include United States and Canadian government documents, archival material, and analytics for journals, as well as books. Works are in French and English and were printed from the eighteenth century to the early 1960's.

The catalog is in two parts. The first volume contains main entries arranged alphabetically by author. The second volume is an index of short-title cards filed by author under alphabetically arranged subject headings. Individuals as subjects are listed in the second volume.

The subject headings appear to be the compilers' own and are in French, but the English translation of the heading is provided. Where the English and French terms are cognates, no cross-reference from the English term to the French is provided. However, where the terms are significantly different, such a cross-reference is given. Subject headings tend to be broad, with no subdivisions, and entries under each subject may go on for pages. As there are no running headings on the tops of the pages, and the subject headings are not listed on the cards, it is sometimes difficult to find the sought-for place in the subject catalog.

Washington (State). University. Library. The Dictionary Catalog of the Pacific Northwest Collection. 6 vols. Boston: G. K. Hall, 1972. (see 126)

11. CONTINENTAL LANGUAGES AND LITERATURE

Most of the published catalogs on the literature of the continent of Europe come from Harvard University, whose publication of the shelflist of the Widener Library has given scholars a major resource in this area. However, the fact that these catalogs are shelflists limits the number of ways that information can be located, as has been explained in the general discussion of the Widener Library shelflists (9). Thus, even though Harvard's Slavic collection ranks second only to that of the Library of Congress, the researcher will probably have more success using The New York Public Library's Dictionary Catalog of the Slavonic Collection (147) when searching for works on a subject. The latter describes 194,000 volumes of materials in 724,000 entries, while Harvard's shelflist of Slavic History and Literature (146), although listing 115,000 titles, has only one subject entry (the shelflist entry) for each title (author, title, and chronological lists are also included). In addition, The New York Public Library catalog includes analytical entries for parts of books and for periodical articles, providing further access to the actual content of the collection, rather than to the names of works only.

American School of Classical Studies at Athens. Gennadius Library. Catalogue. 7 vols. Boston: G. K. Hall, 1968. (see 66)

Cincinnati. University. Library. Catalog of the Modern Greek Collection. 5 vols. Boston: G. K. Hall, 1978. (see 67)

136. Cornell University. Libraries. Petrarch: Catalogue of the Petrarch Collection in Cornell University Library. 737 p. Millwood, N.Y.: Kraus-Thomson Organization, 1974 (LC 74-3398).

This is a revision of the 1916 catalog of Cornell's Petrarch collection. The first part of the catalog consists of works by Petrarch, arranged alphabetically by title of work. The second part consists of works about Petrarch, arranged by author or other main entry. There is an index of authors, editors, translators, commentators, illustrators, and titles. The catalog does not contain the detailed "analytical disquisitions" of the 1916 catalog, but it does provide references to them, as well as detailed bibliographic notes. There are analytics for articles in periodicals. The collection now totals approximately 5,000 volumes, published from the fifteenth to the twentieth century. Most of the works are in Italian, Latin, or other European languages, and are quite rare.

The Introduction by Morris Bishop contains an interesting account of the life of Willard Fiske, who assembled the original collection, and a shorter history of the life and work of Mary Fowler, who edited the original Petrarch catalog in 1916.

137. German Baroque Literature: A Descriptive Catalogue of the Collection of Harold Jantz; and a Guide to the Collection on Microfilm. 2 vols. New Haven: Research Publications, 1974 (LC 74-23640).

This is a catalog of literary works of the German Baroque period, covering roughly the years 1616-1745. It is arranged in three main divisions. The main body of 3,169 clearly Baroque works is preceded by a selection of 317 works that are a kind of prelude to the Baroque, and followed by a selection of 144 post-Baroque works. Within these divisions the arrangement is alphabetical by author, with separate sequences for pseudonymous works and title main entries. Authors' names are usually given in the form they most preferred; titles, where exceedingly long, have been abbreviated; places of publication have been standardized; and dates have been verified. The collation information is quite extensive. Included are indexes of names, portraits, illustrators, and titles.

This collection complements the Yale Collection of German Baroque Literature, which was collected by Curt von Faber du Faur, and whose catalog of it has also been published (see 152). Both collections have been microfilmed by Research Publications.

Harvard University. Library. Ancient Greek Literature. 638 p. Cambridge, Mass.: Harvard Univ. Pr., 1979. (see 55)

138. Harvard University. Library. Celtic Literatures. 192 p. Cambridge, Mass.: distributed by Harvard University Press, 1970 (LC 69-11162). (Widener Library Shelflist v. 25)

Included in this volume of the printed shelflist of Harvard University's Widener Library are the literatures of the Irish, Gaelic, Welsh, Cornish, Manx, Breton, and Gaulish languages. Specifically, one may find individual works, anthologies, and literary history and criticism. Also included are non-literary texts written in or translated into these languages. Approximately 8,000 titles are included, about 5,500 of them in Celtic languages, 700 in English, and the rest in other languages.

Following the shelflist arrangement is a listing by author

and title, and then one arranged chronologically by date of publication.

For further information on the Widener Library shelflists see 9.

139. Harvard University. Library. Finnish and Baltic History and Literatures. 250 p. Cambridge, Mass.: distributed by Harvard University Press, 1972 (LC 72-75829). (Widener Library Shelflist v. 40)

Included in this section of Harvard University's Widener Library shelflist are works on the history and literature of Finland and of the Baltic states of Estonia, Latvia, and Lithuania. The history classification includes political history, foreign relations, government, religion, civilization, geography and travel, general economic and social conditions, and peoples of the region. Literature classes include works in all the languages of the area except Hungarian, and include literary history, anthologies, and works by and about individual authors. Also included is a section of government documents. Over half of the titles are in Finnish or Latvian, followed in number by Russian, Lithuanian, etc. Only 507 of the 8, 600 titles are in English. The classified arrangement is followed by a chronological listing and then an author-title listing.

For further information on the Widener Library shelflists see 9.

140. Harvard University. Library. French Literature. 2 vols. Cambridge, Mass.: distributed by Harvard University Press, 1973 (LC 72-93949). (Widener Library Shelflist v. 47-48)

Listed in this volume of Harvard University's Widener Library shelflist are nearly 52, 000 titles representing historical and critical works on French literature, and anthologies and individual literary works written in French. Included are works on the history of the French drama and theatre, and works by and about European authors writing in French. There is a good Provençal collection.[15] However, books relating to the literature of French-speaking areas outside of Europe are classed elsewhere. More than three-quarters of the titles listed here are in French. English, German, and other languages are also represented. Almost one-third of the works listed were published before 1900.

The catalog is in three parts: first, a classified, or shelflist arrangement; second, a chronological listing; and third, an author-title listing. For a further discussion of the Widener Library shelflists see 9.

141. Harvard University. Library. German Literature. 2 vols. Cambridge, Mass.: distributed by Harvard University Press, 1974 (LC 73-82347). (Widener Library Shelflist v. 49-50)

This section of the shelflist of Harvard's Widener Library covers the history of the German language, German literature, literary anthologies, and works by and about individual European authors writing in German and its dialects. "The Hofmannsthal and Rilke collections are most noteworthy."[16] Of the 46,000 titles listed here, only 4,500 are in English; almost all of the rest are in German. Like the other volumes of the Widener shelflists, this one is divided into a classified listing, a chronological listing, and an author-title listing. For a more detailed discussion of the Widener Library shelflist series see 9.

142. Harvard University. Library. Hungarian History and Literature. Cambridge, Mass.: distributed by Harvard University Press, 1974 (LC 72-83390). (Widener Library Shelflist v. 44)

Listed here are over 6,500 works found in Harvard University's Widener Library on the history and literature of Hungary. History titles include works on the civilization, government and administration, religious affairs, geography and description, general economic and social conditions (special aspects of economic and social conditions are classed elsewhere), and various peoples of Hungary. The category of Hungarian literature includes literary periodicals and societies, literary histories, anthologies of literature, and works by and about individual authors. The majority of the works are in Hungarian.

This volume is arranged in three parts: first, a classified, or shelflist arrangement; second, a listing arranged chronologically by date of publication; and third, an alphabetical listing by author and title. For further information on the Widener Library shelflists see 9.

143. Harvard University. Library. Italian History and Literature. 2 vols. Cambridge, Mass.: distributed by Harvard University Press, 1974 (LC 74-78747). (Widener Library Shelflist v. 51-52)

Listed in this section of the shelflist of Harvard University's Widener Library are over 72,000 titles on Italian history and literature. The history classification includes works on the government and administration, religious affairs, civilization, social life and customs, and geography and description of peninsular Italy, Sicily, and Sardinia, as well as Malta, Monaco, and San Marino. All aspects of the economic and financial affairs of these areas are classified elsewhere in the Widener Library shelflist. The literature classification includes literary histories, anthologies, and works by and about authors writing in Italian. "Collections on Dante, Petrarch, and Tasso are noteworthy, as is 19th-century drama."[17] General periodicals and documents are also listed here in their own classes.

About 80 percent of the titles listed are in Italian, and about half were published before 1900. Titles are listed in three places:

in a classified, or shelflist arrangement; in a chronological arrangement; and in an alphabetical author-title listing. For a further discussion of the Widener Library shelflists see 9.

144. Harvard University. Library. Latin Literature. 610 p. Cambridge, Mass.: distributed by Harvard University Press, 1979 (LC 79-9985). (Widener Library Shelflist v. 59)

Two classes of the Widener Library shelflist are listed here. The L class provides for ancient Latin literature, including anthologies of literature and works by and about individual authors regardless of subject. The ML class provides for medieval and modern Latin belles-lettres. Over half of the 18,600 titles are in Latin, and a majority of the titles were published before 1900. All of the works were cataloged before July, 1976, when the Widener Library switched to the Library of Congress classification system.

For a further discussion of the Widener Library shelflist series see 9.

145. Harvard University. Library. Literature: General and Comparative. 189 p. Cambridge, Mass.: distributed by Harvard University Press, 1968. (Widener Library Shelflist v. 18)

This is another volume in the series of Harvard University's Widener Library shelflists (see 9). This one deals with literature in general, rather than literature of specific languages or countries, and with comparative literature, including the art of literature, histories of comparative literature, anthologies that cover a wide variety of literature, and works on special forms of literature except for drama and folk literature. Generally, literary works themselves are not included, except for those anthologies mentioned above. Literature of all the world is covered, but the emphasis is on European literature.

Of the 5,000 titles listed here, about 2,800 are in English, followed in number by German, French, Spanish, and Italian.

The arrangement is a classified one, according to Widener Library's own classification scheme, with an author-title index, and a chronological listing by date of publication.

146. Harvard University. Library. Slavic History and Literatures. 4 vols. Cambridge, Mass.: distributed by Harvard University Press, 1971 (LC 69-10588). (Widener Library Shelflist v. 28-31)

The Harvard University Slavic collections rank in the United States second only to those of the Library of Congress. In 1971 Harvard had approximately 500,000 volumes (250,000 titles) in the Slavic languages or dealing with the history and literature of the Slavic countries. Approximately 115,000 titles are included in these volumes. The geographic area covered is the U.S.S.R. and its component states (except the Baltic states and Armenia), and Poland, Czechoslovakia, Yugoslavia, and Bulgaria.

The catalog is in three parts: the first is a classified arrangement; the second a chronological listing; and the third a listing by author and title. Three classes of the Widener Library shelflist are arranged here: Pslav, which contains periodicals dealing with general Slavic history and with general Russian history; Slav Doc, which contains government documents; and Slav, which includes nearly all books pertaining to Slavic history and literatures. History is defined as political history, including foreign relations, government and administration, geography and travel, civilization, religious affairs, economic and social conditions, and peoples. Literature is defined to include literary history, anthologies, and works by and about individual authors.

Works are mostly in Russian, followed in number by Polish, English, and other Slavic and Western languages. Authors and titles are transliterated.

This catalog supersedes volume four of the Widener Library shelflists, Russian History Since 1917, and volume three, Twentieth Century Russian Literature.

London. University. Warburg Institute. Catalog of the Warburg Institute Library. 12 vols. Boston: G. K. Hall, 1967. (see 264)

New York (City). Public Library. Research Libraries. Catalog of the Theatre and Drama Collections. 51 vols. Boston: G. K. Hall, 1967-76. (see 304)

147. New York (City). Public Library. Slavonic Division. Dictionary Catalog of the Slavonic Collection. Second edition, revised and enlarged. 44 vols. Boston: G. K. Hall, 1974 (LC 77-150773). Supplemented by Bibliographic Guide to Soviet and East European Studies: 1978- . Boston: G. K. Hall, 1979- .

The Slavonic Division Catalog lists all materials in The New York Public Research Libraries in Slavic or Baltic languages irrespective of subject, and all materials, in any language, about the Baltic and Slavic regions. It "ranks as a major depository of Baltic and Slavic materials in the Western Hemisphere" [Introduction]. The collection is strongest in belles-lettres, linguistics, social sciences, folklore, government publications, translations of Balto-Slavic literature into English, serials, and periodicals. There has been a recent emphasis on economics, and science and technology.

This is a dictionary catalog, with 724,000 entries representing 194,000 volumes of materials cataloged through 1971, when The New York Public Library adopted Anglo-American Cataloging Rules and Library of Congress subject headings. The subject headings used here are the library's own, but there are numerous _see_ and _see-also_ references. There are many analytical entries for periodical articles in Balto-Slavonic and Western languages.

73 percent of the cards are in the Cyrillic alphabet; 62 percent are in Russian, 12 percent in Polish, and the rest in other Slavonic and Baltic languages.

148. Pennsylvania. University. Library. _Catalog of the Programmschriften Collection._ 377 p. Boston: G. K. Hall, 1961 (LC 61-66457).

This is the catalog of a collection of _Programmschriften_, scholarly papers that were appended to the annual statistical reports of most Gymnasien in German-speaking countries of Europe from 1850 to 1918. The University of Pennsylvania acquired this collection of 16, 555 of these pamphlets in 1954 and has cataloged and indexed about one-third of them, now listed in this catalog. These are the _Programmschriften_ dealing with the humanities and with the history of science. Emphasis is on classical and Germanic history and literature. Most of the essays are in German.

The catalog is in two parts: an author catalog and a subject index. Usually one, but sometimes two subject index terms have been assigned to each essay. The index terms are in English and many are the names of individuals whose lives or works have been discussed in the essays.

149. United States. Library of Congress. Catalog Publication Division. _The Slavic Cyrillic Union Catalog of Pre-1956 Imprints._ 174 sheets of microfiche. Totowa, N.J.: Rowman and Littlefield, 1980 (LC 80-80218).

The Slavic Union Catalog was organized at the Library of Congress in 1934 to provide information on the locations of works in Slavic languages. In 1952 the Library began work on the Cyrillic Union Catalog project to provide subject headings for titles in the Slavic Union Catalog. The project was completed in 1956 and the results published in microcard by Readex Microprint in 1963 (see 150). Titles continued to be added to the Slavic Union Catalog but were also being included in _The National Union Catalog_ (see 13). To avoid duplication of effort, it was decided to limit the Slavic Union Catalog to pre-1956 imprints, of which many more had been reported since the close of the Cyrillic Union Catalog project in 1956.

This present publication, now called _The Slavic Cyrillic Union Catalog_, contains 399, 086 cards for works of Slavic materials published in the Cyrillic alphabet with imprint dates of 1955 and earlier. The Library of Congress accounts for about 25 percent of the locations reported to the catalog; 220 North American libraries for the other 75 percent.

Listed in the catalog are books, pamphlets, maps, atlases, and 16, 500 periodicals and other serials. Works are in Russian,

Church Slavic, Byelorussian, Ukrainian, Bulgarian, Serbian, and Macedonian.

Unlike the earlier published Cyrillic Union Catalog, which was in three parts--authors, titles, and subjects--this catalog lists works largely under their main entry, with added entries and cross-references, and is arranged alphabetically by the romanized form of the entry. The rest of the card is in the Cyrillic alphabet, except for added notes and tracings, which are in English.

The Library of Congress printed cards in the Slavic Cyrillic Union Catalog were prepared in accordance with A. L. A. Cataloging Rules for Author and Title Entries or Anglo-American Cataloging Rules (1967 edition). Main entries for titles not represented by LC printed cards have not been edited for uniformity with Library of Congress practices.

All entries include symbols for the libraries owning the title. Beginning with 1980 the Register of Additional Locations, which provides locations for titles listed in The National Union Catalog, will also include new locations for SCUC titles.

The microfiche catalog is accompanied by a guide in paper reproducing the introductory material on the microfiche. This includes a history of the Slavic Union Catalog, transliteration tables, and a list of the symbols for the participating libraries, which are the same as those used in The National Union Catalog.

150. United States. Library of Congress. Cyrillic Bibliographic Project. Cyrillic Union Catalog in Three Parts. 1,244 microcards. New York: Readex Microprint, 1963.

The Library of Congress began maintaining a Slavic Union Catalog in 1934. This catalog listed, by author, publications in the Cyrillic alphabet owned by the Library of Congress and 184 other American libraries. In 1952 a project was initiated to develop title and subject entries for the works in the Slavic Union Catalog. Thirteen major research libraries agreed to provide subject entries for Slavic works in their collections. The project was ended in 1956, and the resulting author, title, and subject catalog was reproduced in microprint in 1963 as the Cyrillic Union Catalog in Three Parts.

The Cyrillic Union Catalog lists 178,226 titles in over 708,000 cards. It includes all of the monographic holdings of the Library of Congress as of March, 1956 in Russian, Byelorussian, Ukrainian, Bulgarian, and Serbian, and the major portion of the collections of those libraries in the United States with significant Slavic holdings. The Library of Congress contributed 106,149 entries; The New York Public Library, 39,877 entries; Columbia University, 17,865 entries; the Hoover Institution on War, Revolution, and Peace, 16,760; Harvard University, 16,617; and Yale University, 11,538.

This is a divided catalog in three parts. Part I, Authors and Added Entries, has 202,400 catalog cards listed on 399 opaque microcards. Part II, Titles, contains a card for every work in the catalog and has been fully edited to eliminate duplication; it is contained in 321 opaque microcards. Part III, Subjects, arranges the entries under Library of Congress subject headings; there are 327,500 catalog cards in 524 opaque microcards. Belles-lettres are listed under form headings for entries in fiction, drama, poetry, etc.

All entries have been completely transliterated and the alphabetical arrangement is according to the order of the Roman alphabet. In addition, an English translation of most of the titles has been provided.

The microcard catalog is accompanied by a paper guide explaining the history and organization of the catalog. Later entries to the union catalog for pre-1956 imprints may be found in the Slavic Cyrillic Union Catalog (see 149).

151. Vienna. Universität. Bibliothek. Katalog der Bestände auf dem Gebiet der slawischen Philologie einschliesslich der Belletristik. Zusammengestellt von Otto Peschl. (Catalog of Holdings in Slavonic Philology Including Belles-Lettres. Compiled by Otto Peschl). 456 p. Boston: G. K. Hall, 1972 (LC 72-3797).

This is a selection of titles in Slavonic philology taken from the author catalog of the University Library of Vienna. It includes works in the field of Slavic linguistics and literatures in all languages, and belles-lettres by Slavic authors both in the original language and in translations. There are more than 30,000 entries representing about 20,000 books, textbooks, and theses.

The library follows the old Austrian cataloging rules and Prussian Instructions. The arrangement is alphabetical by name of author. All titles are transliterated from the Cyrillic according to "international scientific transcription."

152. Yale University. Library. Yale Collection of German Literature. German Baroque Literature: A Catalogue of the Collection in the Yale University Library. By Curt von Faber du Faur. 2 vols. New Haven, Conn.: Yale University Press, 1958-1969.

This is a catalog of first editions of literary works of the German Baroque period, from 1575 to 1740. The collection was begun by Curt von Faber du Faur in 1912 and became part of Yale University Library in 1944. Only literary works are included, but the term has been interpreted in a liberal sense.

Included in the catalog is a lengthy introduction to the literature of the Baroque period by von Faber du Faur. The catalog itself is conceived as a didactic tool; it is divided into chapters based on different aspects of the Baroque period, each with an introductory overview of that aspect. Some of these chapters are based on temporal distinctions, such as "The Middle of the Century"; some on form distinctions, such as "Religious Poetry" or "Jokebooks, Short Stories, Anecdotes"; and some on subject distinctions, such as "Literature on Magic." Included at the end are indexes of authors, composers, and illustrators.

The entries are very detailed in their descriptive cataloging, and annotations are often included. Works by an individual are usually preceded by a few paragraphs describing his life and his contributions. The first volume of the catalog contains around 1,900 entries. The second volume lists new additions to the collection in the same arrangement as the original work.

This Baroque literature collection has been microfilmed by Research Publications, Inc. of New Haven, Connecticut, which has also filmed a complementary collection, the Jantz Collection of German Baroque Literature, and published its catalog (see 137).

12. ENGLISH AND AMERICAN LITERATURE

Several of the most important libraries of English and American literature have published their catalogs, which are described in this chapter. English literature and culture of the sixteenth through the eighteenth century is explored in depth in the collections of the Folger Shakespeare Library in Washington, D. C. (159) and the William Andrews Clark Memorial Library of the University of California at Berkeley (156). The Folger Library's collections are centered on Shakespeare and his times and emphasize the sixteenth and seventeenth centuries, while the Clark Library focuses on Dryden's England and the seventeenth and eighteenth centuries. The Folger Library's catalog has the advantage of more consistently thorough cataloging.

The Folger Library has also published separately a Catalog of the Shakespeare Collection (160), which is that part of its complete published catalog that deals with Shakespeare. It does not have as many entries as the catalog of the Birmingham Shakespeare Library (153), which is replete with analytical entries for articles in periodicals and books, and which is an extraordinarily complete bibliography on Shakespeare.

The field of American literature is served by two collections of literary works, the Harris Collection of Brown University (155) and The New York Public Library's Berg Collection (164), which emphasizes rare first editions and manuscripts. Neither catalog includes much literary criticism.

The widest coverage of English and American literature is provided by two parts of Harvard University's Widener Library shelflist, American Literature (161) and English Literature (162). Both of these include literary criticism as well as literary works of all periods.

153. Birmingham Shakespeare Library. A Shakespeare Bibliography; the Catalogue of the Birmingham Shakespeare Library, Birmingham Public Libraries. New edition. 7 vols. London: Mansell, 1971 (LC 71-873519).

The Birmingham Shakespeare Library was begun in the 1860's. It was envisioned, and to a large extent has become, a library to contain "every edition and every translation of Shakespeare; all the commentators, good, bad and indifferent; in short, every book connected with the life and works of our great poet," as George Dawson, president of the Birmingham Shakespeare Club, stated in 1861 [Introduction, p. ix]. By 1970 the Library had close to 44,000 volumes. The catalog contains many, many analytics for journals, transactions, and articles in books, as well as entries for playbills, lectures, and other ephemera. Publication dates range from the seventeenth century to the present, and there are works in the 85 languages into which Shakespeare has been translated. All of this makes this catalog "the largest, most comprehensive Shakespeare bibliography ever to be assembled" [Introduction, p. xiv].

The catalog is in two parts: volumes one to three contain pre-1932 accessions in a guard book catalog, and volumes four to seven contain post-1932 accessions in a card catalog. Both catalogs are arranged by language. Within language the entries are divided into editions of Shakespeare and Shakespeariana. In the pre-1932 catalog the Shakespeariana sections are arranged by author. The post-1932 catalog has both author and subject entries, interfiled, and there are subject cross-references, making this catalog much easier to use. However, the Introduction should be consulted for an explanation of the peculiarities of the catalog, as well as for an interesting history of the library and of Shakespearean publishing.

154. Boston. Public Library. A Catalog of the Defoe Collection in the Boston Public Library. 200 p. Boston: G. K. Hall, 1966 (LC 68-5152).

This is a catalog of rare books and pamphlets by the English novelist and pamphleteer Daniel Defoe. It is primarily based on a collection of the writings of Defoe assembled by William Peterfield Trent (1862-1939) and purchased by the Boston Public Library in 1929, but includes other works of Defoe in the library. The library holds 360 titles of works by Defoe in about 900 different editions, which are described here in 1,900 cards. The arrangement is by title of work, and the descriptive cataloging is often very extensive. Imprint dates range from the late seventeenth century to the early nineteenth century.

155. Brown University. Library. Dictionary Catalog of the Harris Collection of American Poetry and Plays, Brown University Library, Providence, Rhode Island. 13 vols. Boston: G. K. Hall, 1972 (LC 75-184497). First Supplement. 3 vols., 1977.

The Harris Collection contains more than 150,000 printed books and pamphlets by American and Canadian authors, listed in 321,000 cards. The acquisitions policy "is based on the thesis that every volume of American and Canadian verse and every play with a similar origin is potentially useful to the scholar" [Introduction]. Included are anthologies of poetry, plays and songs; gift books and annuals; ballads; college and other literary magazines; folk music; hymnals, with and without music; minstrelsies; operas; pageants; Phi Beta Kappa poems; plays; psalm books; and songsters, which preserve in verse and music many aspects of American patriotism, history, and customs. Recent works include off-Broadway plays and underground poets of the sixties, often printed on mimeographed paper. In general, critical and biographical works about poets and playwrights are not collected except for four major poets--T. S. Eliot, Edgar Allan Poe, Ezra Pound, and Walt Whitman--by or about whom anything available has been collected. Also included in the catalog are about 4,000 volumes of Latin American poetry and plays, although since the 1950's works by only Mexican authors have been added. Broadsides, manuscripts, and sheet music are not included in the catalog.

The Supplement, which contains material cataloged 1972-1976, consists mostly of poetry from small presses and a significant collection of Yiddish poetry, plays, and music.

This is a dictionary catalog. Form headings, such as "Canadian poetry" or "Yiddish drama," are included, but by no means list all of the works of that type in the collection. Full cataloging based on Library of Congress practices is now the rule for the collection, but in the past cataloging was less complete. There are liberal analytics for parts of books and articles in journals written by authors whose works are collected in depth.

The collection was begun by Judge Albert Gorton Greene (Brown 1820) as a collection of American poetry, and after his death was acquired by Caleb Fiske Harris (Brown 1838), who added American songsters and drama to the collection. After Mr. Harris's death the collection was acquired by his cousin, Senator Henry Bowen Anthony (Brown 1833), who bequeathed the collection to the library of Brown University.

156. California. University. University at Los Angeles. William Andrews Clark Memorial Library. Dictionary Catalog of the William Andrews Clark Memorial Library. 15 vols. Boston: G. K. Hall, 1974 (LC 74-174417).

The Clark Library was founded by William Andrews Clark, Jr. and bequeathed to UCLA in 1934 as a memorial to his father, Montana Senator William A. Clark. By the time of publication of the catalog, the collection had 70,000 volumes and over 5,000 manuscripts on English culture of the seventeenth and eighteenth centuries, and on certain aspects of nineteenth-century English literature and modern fine painting. The prime focus of the library is on the life and thought of Dryden's England. It has what is widely considered to be the finest centralized collection of English books published from 1640 to 1750. It also contains one of the greatest collections on Oscar Wilde, and has strong holdings of ballad operas and librettos. The manuscript holdings of the library are not included in the catalog.

The level of cataloging has varied over time. Some works in the catalog are represented by only a main entry, while others have added title and subject entries. See and see-also references are provided for names and subjects. There are analytical entries for commendatory verses, prologues, and epilogues when the authors are identifiable. Library of Congress subject headings are used with some modifications, and the Library of Congress classification system is also used. Works are mostly in English, although other European languages are represented, and dates of publication range from the seventeenth to the twentieth century.

157. Cornell University. Libraries. The Cornell Wordsworth Collection; A Catalogue of Books and Manuscripts Presented to the University by Mr. Victor Emanuel, Cornell 1919. Compiled by George Harris Healey. 458 p. Ithaca, New York: Cornell University Press, 1957 (LC 58-1430).

The Wordsworth Collection was started by Mrs. Cynthia Morgan St. John of Ithaca in the late 1870's. It was later acquired by Mr. Victor Emanuel and presented by him to Cornell University. Both Cornell and Mr. Emanuel continued to add to the collection, and by the time of publication of the catalog the collection totaled 3, 500 pieces. The catalog is in ten different parts, including books published by Wordsworth before his death; editions after his death; works published by Wordsworth in periodicals; works about Wordsworth; works about Coleridge; works about the Lake District; and manuscripts (now numbering about one-third of the collection). Each section is arranged chronologically. There is also an index by author and title, with fascinating entries under "Wordsworth, William," such as "editors of," "illustrators of," and "parodies and imitations of." There are many analytics for articles in journals and pages in books where references are made to Wordsworth. Dates range from 1793 to 1955, and almost all the titles are in English.

158. Folger Shakespeare Library, Washington, D. C. Catalog of Manuscripts of the Folger Shakespeare Library. 3 vols. Boston: G. K. Hall, 1971 (ISBN 0-8161-0888-9).

This is a dictionary catalog of the manuscript holdings of the Folger Shakespeare Library. The catalog of published material is described elsewhere (see 159). There are main entries, added entries, and subject entries in one alphabet. Many collections have been completely analyzed, with added entries for correspondents.

The aim of the Folger Library is "to throw light on the history of England and of English culture in the sixteenth and seventeenth centuries, and, in the case of the theatre and the drama, in the eighteenth and nineteenth centuries as well" [Introduction]. The chief strength of the manuscript collection is in its theatrical and dramatic manuscripts. There are manuscript copies of plays, documents of particular theatres, promptbooks, letters of actors and actresses, and musical scores. Also included are family papers--

letters, wills, diaries, medical and cookery recipes, sermons, and religious works.

159. Folger Shakespeare Library, Washington, D.C. Catalog of Printed Books of the Folger Shakespeare Library. 28 vols. Boston: G. K. Hall, 1970 (ISBN 0-8161-0887-0). First Supplement. 3 vols., 1976.

This is a major collection on English culture and history, revolving around Shakespeare, his work, and his times. It covers the reigns of the Tudors and Stuarts in England (sixteenth and seventeenth centuries) and the works of Continental authors of the same period. English works discuss religious controversies, military science, exploration and trade, the conduct of life, and music, and include sermons, law books, treatises on agriculture, literary works, and historical and political tracts. The Continental collection is strong in the Reformation and Counter Reformation, humanistic thought, political history, and exploration. Other special strengths of the collection are in the drama and theatre, and in their practitioners: Shakespeare--the Folger houses one of the largest collection of editions of his works, translations, and criticism (see 160)--and other dramatists from the Elizabethan period through the mid-eighteenth century, and Continental playwrights, especially of Italy. The collection ranges in time from medieval and classical materials to the eighteenth century.

This is a dictionary catalog with main entries, added entries, and subject cards interfiled. Titles, editors, and translators are included. American Library Association cataloging rules are followed, and Library of Congress subject headings are used with some modifications. Form headings are also used--under the heading "Sermons" are listed approximately 110 pages of sermons available in the library. Especially useful in this catalog is the excellent subject indexing of rare books, many of which are available as part of commercially published microform collections, such as University Microfilms' collection of Early English Books 1475-1640, that have not been analytically cataloged.

There are two appendices at the end of this catalog. The first lists the periodical collection, with information on which issues are held. The second is a chronological catalog of French and other foreign-language pamphlets.

160. Folger Shakespeare Library, Washington, D.C. Catalog of the Shakespeare Collection. 2 vols. Boston: G. K. Hall, 1972 (LC 72-6446).

This catalog represents the Shakespeare section of the Folger Library's Catalog of Printed Books (see 159). The first volume contains editions of works by Shakespeare, including collected works, works in translation, selections, and separate plays. Listed here are most of the important editions of four centuries, plus significant translations into approximately 50 languages. For the sixteenth and seventeenth centuries, about 90 percent of the known editions of Shakespeare are represented here.

The second volume contains works about Shakespeare arranged into 15 major subject subdivisions, as well as title entries where Shakespeare is the first word of the title.

There are no added entries for editors, translators, or names of series, but in most cases one may locate a particular edition in the catalog by checking the tables of contents of the volumes for the categories in which the edition is likely to be found.

161. Harvard University. Library. American Literature. 2 vols. Cambridge, Mass.: distributed by Harvard University Press, 1970 (LC 69-11163). (Widener Library Shelflist v. 26-27)

In the classification scheme used in the Widener Library of Harvard University, American literature is divided into five classes. The AL class contains works by and about authors whose careers started before 1900. The ALA class contains works by and about twentieth-century authors whose careers started before 1950. The ALB class contains works by and about twentieth-century authors whose careers started after 1950. PZ and PZB are used for popular and minor fiction of the twentieth century written in English by authors of the United States and the British Isles. Also included are literary histories and anthologies. An American author is defined as an author of the continental United States who wrote or writes in English. Histories of American drama and theatre are not included in this catalog.

There are about 50,000 books and periodicals listed here in the AL, ALA, and ALB classes, and an additional 8,000 books in PZ and PZB.

Following the classified arrangement, works are listed alphabetically by author and title and then chronologically by date of publication. Works cataloged in the PZ and PZB classes are included in the alphabetical and chronological lists, but the classified arrangement for those classes is not reproduced.

For further information on the Widener Library shelflists see 9.

Harvard University. Library. Canadian History and Literature. 411 p. Cambridge, Mass.: Harvard Univ. Pr., 1968. (see 133)

162. Harvard University. Library. English Literature. 4 vols. Cambridge, Mass.: distributed by Harvard University Press, 1971 (LC 74-128717). (Widener Library Shelflist v. 35-38)

This part of Harvard University's Widener Library shelflist contains all literary history, all anthologies of literature, and all works by and about English authors. The section for literary history and anthologies includes worldwide literature written in English and the literature written in English by natives of the British Isles. The sections on individual authors include only works by and about natives of the British Isles. Books related to the literature of other English-speaking countries are cataloged in different classes. Also classed elsewhere are histories of the English drama and theatre. Included in these volumes are two classes, PZ and PZB, which contain popular and minor fiction of the twentieth century written in English by authors of the United States and Great Britain.

The catalog is in three parts: the first is the classified arrangement; the second is a chronological listing by date of publication; and the third is an alphabetical arrangement by author and title. The PZ and PZB classes are included only in the chronological and alphabetical listings. Approximately 112,000 books, pamphlets, and periodicals are listed.

163. Keats-Shelley Memorial, Rome. Catalog of Books and Manuscripts at the Keats-Shelley Memorial House in Rome. 667 p. Boston: G. K. Hall, 1969 (LC 75-20400).

This is the catalog of the library of the Keats-Shelley Memorial House in Rome. The building is the house where Keats died in 1821. It was opened as a museum and library commemorating the poets Keats, Shelley, Byron, and Leigh Hunt. At the time of publication of the catalog, the library had 7,500 volumes, including original editions, significant translations, and works of biography and criticism of and about the poets. Also included in the library are diaries and journals of foreign travellers to Italy in the nineteenth century. Its manuscript collection consists of approximately 375 letters, personal papers, and works of art about Keats, Shelley, Byron, and associates.

The catalog is in two parts. There is an author catalog, with some added entries under the names of editors and the like, and a manuscript catalog. There is no subject catalog or any way to find specific criticism of one of the poets. Included in the author catalog are many analytical entries for articles in periodicals.

164. New York (City). Public Library. Berg Collection. Dictionary Catalog of the Henry W. and Albert A. Berg Collection of English and American Literature. 5 vols. Boston: G. K. Hall, 1969 (LC 75-21408). First Supplement. 757 p., 1975.

The Berg Collection is a celebrated library of first editions, manuscripts, letters, rare books, typescripts with annotations, and similar material relating to the work of some of America's and England's finest writers. The emphasis is on writers of the nineteenth and twentieth centuries, including Washington Irving, Nathaniel Hawthorne, Ralph Waldo Emerson, Henry David Thoreau, Walt Whitman, James Russell Lowell, Robert Lowell, Gertrude Stein, John Steinbeck, Eugene O'Neill, T. S. Eliot, Arnold Bennett, Joseph Conrad, George Gissing, Thomas Hardy, John Masefield, Bernard Shaw, Virginia Woolf, Charles Dickens, Robert Browning, William Makepeace Thackeray, Lewis Carroll, Rudyard Kipling, and many lesser known writers.

The collection contains 20,000 printed items and 50,000 manuscripts. Manuscript and archival materials are given item-by-item cataloging. The arrangement is by name of author--first, works by him; then, works about him; then manuscripts.

There are two interesting appendices. The first, Correspondents, is a catalog of letters arranged by name of person to whom the letter is addressed, with occasional added entries for persons referred to. The second, Provenance, lists individuals associated with a particular copy of an author's book; they are usually the owners.

165. San Francisco. Public Library. Schmulowitz Collection. <u>Catalog of the Schmulowitz Collection of Wit and Humor (SCOWAH)</u>. 370 p. San Francisco, 1962. <u>Supplement One</u>. 1977.

As the title indicates, this is a collection of works of and about wit and humor; cartoons are also included. Nat Schmulowitz was a prominent San Francisco attorney, whose first contribution--93 volumes of wit and humor--to the San Francisco Public Library was in 1947. By October, 1961, the collection consisted of more than 11,200 volumes in more than 35 languages and dialects. The supplement lists 3,100 additional titles acquired from 1961 to 1974. Books, pamphlets, and periodicals are all included.

This is a main-entry catalog arranged by language. English, the major part of the catalog, is first, followed by a brief section of periodicals, followed by books in foreign languages. Entries are brief, with only author, title, publisher, place and date of publication, size, and binding included.

166. Scholes, Robert E. <u>The Cornell Joyce Collection, a Catalogue</u>. 225 p. <u>Ithaca, N.Y.: Cornell University Press, 1961</u> (LC 61-16669).

This is a collection of manuscripts, letters, and papers by or relating to James Joyce. The catalog is in several sections. The first part lists 63 manuscripts of works of James Joyce. The second contains over 300 letters, postcards, and telegrams from Joyce. The third lists almost 1,000 letters to Joyce or relating to Joyce from his relatives, friends, business associates, and literary associates. The last section contains miscellany. The manuscripts and the letters of Joyce are arranged in chronological order. Other letters are arranged by the name of the writer and then chronologically. All entries for letters contain the salutation and a quote--often quite a tantalizing one--from the first sentence. The period covered is from 1898 to the 1930's.

167. Wright, R. Glenn, compiler. Author Bibliography of English Language Fiction in the Library of Congress Through 1950. 8 vols. Boston: G. K. Hall, 1973 (LC 74-188840).

This is a bibliography of authors writing in English who published their first volume of prose fiction before 1950. It is compiled from the PZ3 shelflist of the Library of Congress and has about 120,000 entries.

The bibliography is arranged by the nationality of the author and within the nationality alphabetically by the author's name. The geographical areas are Australia, Canada, East and Southeast Asia, Europe, Latin America, New Zealand, South Africa, United Kingdom (including Ireland), and United States. The compilers have worked to establish the nationalities of the authors and to identify the real names of pseudonymous authors. There are cross-references from pseudonyms to real names. A detailed introduction to the bibliography explains the filing arrangement. There is a separate section for authors whose nationalities are unknown.

Also included are several interesting indexes. There is an index to pseudonyms in three sections, each arranged by nationality. The first lists the pseudonym with a reference to the real name, the second lists the real name with a reference to the pseudonym, and the third lists pseudonyms for which real names could not be determined.

The last volume of the bibliography lists translations into English. The first part of this list is arranged by the name of the author and the second by the name of the translator.

168. Wright, R. Glenn, compiler. Chronological Bibliography of English Language Fiction in the Library of Congress Through 1950. 8 vols. Boston: G. K. Hall, 1974 (LC 75-305442).

This is a bibliography of authors writing in English who published their first volume of prose fiction before 1950. It is compiled from the PZ3 shelflist of the Library of Congress and contains more than 130,000 entries.

The arrangement is by nationality of author; then, within country, chronological by date of publication; and then alphabetical by author's name. There are cross-references from variants of titles or editions.

There are eight indexes that provide access to the entries by joint author, pseudonyms, translators, and the like.

For a fuller description see the Author Bibliography of English Language Fiction in the Library of Congress (167).

169. Wright, R. Glenn, compiler. Title Bibliography of English Language Fiction in the Library of Congress Through 1950. 9 vols. Boston: G. K. Hall, 1976 (LC 76-378924).

This is a bibliography of authors writing in English who published their first volume of prose fiction before 1950. It is compiled from entries in the PZ3 shelflist of the Library of Congress and contains more than 130,000 entries.

The cards are arranged by nationality of author and, within nationality, alphabetically by title of book. There are cross-references from variant titles. This work will probably be most useful as an index to English language fiction in the National Union Catalog. Its chief drawback is that the titles are broken down by nationality of author, and if the reader does not know the author of a work he is also unlikely to know the author's nationality.

There are several indexes by joint authors, pseudonyms, translations, and the like.

13. SPAIN, PORTUGAL, LATIN AMERICA, AND THE CARIBBEAN

The history and literature of Mexico, Central America, South America and most of the Caribbean is so associated with that of Spain and Portugal as to necessitate consideration of these areas as a group. And most of the Latin American collections are not limited to history or literature but cover all aspects of that area.

The largest collection of material on Latin America is found in Germany. The Ibero-Amerikanisches Institut in Berlin has published only its subject catalog (170), yet this alone runs to 30 volumes. It is not an easy catalog to use, but it is remarkable for its analytical entries for articles in periodicals, books, and encyclopedias and its detailed subject indexing of people and places.

The largest published Latin American collection catalog in the United States is that of the University of Texas at Austin (189), which is a dictionary catalog of authors, titles, and subjects, following standard Library of Congress practices.

170. Berlin. Ibero-Amerikanisches Institut. Schlagwortkatalog des Ibero-Amerikanischen Instituts, Preussischer Kulturbesitz in Berlin (Subject Catalog of the Ibero-American Institute, Prussian Cultural Heritage Foundation in Berlin). 30 vols. Boston: G. K. Hall, 1977 (LC 78-337931).

The Latin American Institute was founded in 1930 when the Argentine scholar Ernesto Quesada donated his library of 80,000 volumes to the state of Prussia. In 1962, the Latin American Institute was incorporated into the Prussian Cultural Heritage Foundation. The institute is the largest in Europe to collect Spanish, Portuguese, and Latin American library materials on a multidisciplinary basis. The collections of ethnology and archaeology of Latin America are especially noteworthy. The catalog covers 480,000 volumes and the contents of 2,000 periodicals. There are many analytical entries for articles in periodicals, in books, and in encyclopedias.

This is a subject catalog in four parts: volumes 1-19 are a general subject catalog; volumes 19-23 are a geographical catalog; volumes 23-24 are a section of place names; and volumes 24-30 are a biographical section. In the General Catalog the subjects are listed in alphabetical order, and generally subdivided by country.

In the Geographical Section the arrangement is by region or country, subdivided by smaller area and/or subject. The Place Name section is arranged by name of country followed by town or city. The Catalog of Persons is arranged by country and within country by profession.

All of the subject and geographical headings are in German but there are numerous indexes to aid the English- or Spanish-speaking user. At the end of volume 30 there are five indexes: 1) the Schlagwortverzeichnis, an authority list in German of the subject headings used, with many see and see-also references; 2) List of Subject Headings: English-German, a list in English of subjects with their German equivalents (however, many of the German equivalents are not actually used as headings in the catalog, and the Schlagwortverzeichnis should be checked first to find the correct heading); 3) Registro Alfabético De Materias (Español-Alemán), a Spanish-German version of the above; 4) Geographical Names (English Version); and 5) Nombres Geográficos (Version Española). There is also an index of place names at the end of the Place Names section to indicate in which country that place is located; this index is all in German. Finally, at the end of the Catalog of Persons there is an index arranged alphabetically by name of individual to point to the correct country and profession under which works about that individual are cataloged. There is no author index for this catalog.

Works are mostly from the mid-twentieth century and are in Spanish and Portuguese, although German, French, and other European languages may also be found.

In short, this is a very complex catalog, but there are many indexes to help the user and the wealth of material, particularly the analytical entries, should repay the effort for the scholar in the field.

Biblioteca Nacional de Antropología e Historia, Mexico. Catálogos de la Biblioteca Nacional de Antropología e Historia. 10 vols. Boston: G. K. Hall, 1972. (see 59)

171. Boston. Public Library. Ticknor Collection. Catalogue of the Spanish Library and of the Portuguese Books Bequeathed by George Ticknor to the Boston Public Library, Together with the Collection of Spanish and Portuguese Literature in the General Library. By James Lyman Whitney. 550 p. Boston: Printed by Order of the Trustees, 1879. Reprinted with an appendix. Boston: G. K. Hall, 1970 (LC 70-23957).

This is a dictionary catalog of rare books, pamphlets, and manuscripts written in Spanish and Portuguese. For the most part, imprints are from the eighteenth and nineteenth centuries, and the works are concerned with the history and literature of Spain, Portugal, and Latin America, although there are some scientific works. There are analytics for works in series and collected works.

Author, title, and subject entries are filed in one alphabet with see and see-also references for subjects and authors. Subject headings are in English. Under some subjects and authors there are detailed notes with bibliographical references.

At the end of the volume there is an appendix of works added since the 1879 edition, in the form of a short-title list. This is in three parts, for works on Spain, on Portugal, and on Latin America.

172. Canal Zone. Library-Museum, Balboa Heights. Subject Catalog of the Special Panama Collection of the Canal Zone Library-Museum; The History of the Isthmus of Panama as It Applies to Interoceanic Transportation. 381 p. Boston: G. K. Hall, 1964 (LC 64-55255).

________. Supplement, 1964-1968. 141 leaves. Panama: Xerox Corp., 1968.

The Canal Zone Library-Museum was established nine days after the official opening of the Panama Canal in 1914. The collection covers the history of the Isthmus of Panama, early surveys of the area, proposed canal projects, the planning and construction of the canal, projects for improving the canal, and local life and conditions.

At the time of publication of the catalog, the collection contained approximately 10,000 items. Included in the catalog are maps; charts; pamphlets; microfilms of newspapers; documents; monographs; government publications, especially Congressional hearings; and manuscripts; as well as many analytics for magazine and newspaper articles.

The catalog is a subject catalog with approximately 7,000 cards arranged under about 500 different subject headings. Library of Congress subject headings are used, with some modifications that are discussed in the Preface. There is no author or title index to the catalog.

Material dates from the nineteenth and early twentieth century and is mostly in English, although works in Spanish and French are also represented. This is a very specialized and rather fascinating collection.

173. Florida. University, Gainesville. Libraries. Catalog of the Latin American Collection. 13 vols. Boston: G. K. Hall, 1973 (LC 73-175215). First Supplement. 7 vols., 1979.

This dictionary catalog lists 120,000 books, pamphlets, periodicals, and government documents, plus 9,000 units of microfilm. It is strongest in the geographic regions of Brazil and the Caribbean, with an especially fine collection on the West Indies. Aided by grants from the Ford and Rockefeller Foundations, among others, and by the Farmington Plan, the University of Florida libraries have sought out material in Latin America and have microfilmed

West Indian newspapers since the 1950's, as well as major collections located in the West Indies and elsewhere. The emphasis has been on the social sciences and humanities. There is a particularly fine collection of government documents, and holdings include 2,896 reels of film comprising the General Records of the U.S. Department of State, including Consular Despatches, Decimal File, Diplomatic Despatches, and Notes from Foreign Legations, all pertaining to Latin America.

Library of Congress subject headings are used without modification and there are no subject cross-references, although there are cross-references for names. There are no analytical entries. Works are mostly in Spanish, but also in English, Portuguese, and other languages.

174. Gillett, Theresa. Catalog of Luso-Brazilian Material in the University of New Mexico Libraries. Compiled by Theresa Gillett and Helen McIntyre. 961 p. Metuchen, N.J.: Scarecrow Press, 1970 (LC 70-10189).

This is not a separate library or a separate collection in the University of New Mexico libraries but rather a compilation of their material on Portugal and Brazil. It includes material in the Portuguese language, material published in Portugal, Brazil, or any of the present Portuguese dependencies, and material about Portugal, Brazil, or the Portuguese dependencies. It is especially strong in history and literature.

The arrangement is by broad subject and, within subject, alphabetical by author. There is a table of contents listing the subjects covered, and also an author index. Books (some of them rare), pamphlets, periodicals, and microforms are all listed. Library of Congress catalogs are used as the authority for Portuguese personal names.

175. Harvard University. Library. Latin America and Latin American Periodicals. 2 vols. Cambridge, Mass.: distributed by Harvard University Press, 1966 (LC 67-1722). (Widener Library Shelflist v. 5-6)

This volume of the Widener Library shelflist covers the SA classification, which contains the history, civilization, government, general geography and travel, general economic and social conditions, religion, and peoples of the West Indies, Mexico, Central America, and South America. The arrangement is by classification number with an author-title index and a chronological index. Also included here is the SAP classification, which contains general periodicals published in Latin America as well as periodicals dealing with the general history and civilization of Latin America. However, periodicals containing only scholarly studies on the literature of Latin America are classed in the Philol classification and appear in volume 15 of the Widener Library shelflists (see 11), and periodicals containing only literary texts are in the SAL classification and appear in volume 21 of the Widener Library shelflists (see 176). Approximately 1,600 periodical titles are listed in the SAP class and 25,500 titles in the SA class. About half of the works are in Spanish, followed in number by English, Portuguese, and French.

For a further discussion of the Widener Library shelflists see 9.

176. Harvard University. Library. Latin American Literature. 498 p. Cambridge, Mass.: distributed by Harvard University Press, 1969 (LC 68-31060). (Widener Library Shelflist v. 21)

Included in this 21st volume of the Widener Library shelflist series is Harvard's SAL class, containing literary works--poetry, drama, fiction, essays, etc.--by Latin American authors, and writings about these authors and their works. Literary histories and anthologies are also included. Periodicals containing only literary texts are classed in the SAL class, but those which contain a mixture of scholarly studies and texts or only literary studies are classified elsewhere and do not appear in this volume.

The classified arrangement is by language and then by country within language. Within each country the order is general works and anthologies first, followed by individual authors arranged alphabetically. Following the classified arrangement, there is a listing of the works alphabetically by author and title, and then a chronological arrangement. 17,000 titles are listed here, 13,000 of them in Spanish.

For a further discussion of the Widener Library shelflists see 9.

177. Harvard University. Library. Spanish History and Literature. 771 p. Cambridge, Mass.: distributed by Harvard University Press, 1972 (LC 72-75827). (Widener Library Shelflist v. 41)

This volume of the Widener Library shelflist contains works relating to the history and literature of Spain. History is defined to include civilization, government and administration, religious affairs, social life and customs, and geography and description of Spain and the Iberian peninsula as a whole. Economic aspects of Spain are classified elsewhere. Literature includes literary histories, anthologies, and works by and about individual authors. The Cervantes collection is outstanding.[18] Not included in this volume are works on Spain's present or former colonies. Periodicals and Spanish government documents are included here, however.

Of the 30,000 titles listed here, over three-fourths are in Spanish. Most of the works date from the twentieth century, but the collection is also quite strong in works from the eighteenth and nineteenth centuries. Following the classified, or shelflist arrangement are a chronological listing and an author-title listing. For a further discussion of the Widener Library shelflists see 9.

178. Hispanic and Luso-Brazilian Councils. Canning House Library. Canning House Library, Hispanic Council, London: Author Catalogue and Subject Catalogue. 4 vols. Boston: G. K. Hall, 1967 (LC 67-7666). First Supplement. 627 p., 1973.

The Canning House Library is devoted to the cultures of Latin America, Portugal, and Spain. The Hispanic Council portion covers all aspects of Spanish and Spanish-American culture, including philosophy, religion, education, history and biography, geography, economics, sociology, current affairs, law, the arts, language and literature, the armed services, bibliography, and the sciences (omitting only highly technical subjects).

There are separate author and subject catalogs. The subject catalog is arranged by Library of Congress classification number. There is no index to the classification nor a detailed outline of it. There are brief descriptions, or headings, next to some of the classification subdivisions, but these dividers are easy to miss, and since there is not even a table of contents to help the user find a specific classification number or a general subject, the subject catalog is almost impossible to use. Each work has only one entry.

Most of the titles are in Spanish or Portuguese, with some in English. There are over 24,000 books in the Hispanic Library.

179. Hispanic and Luso-Brazilian Councils. Canning House Library. Canning House Library, Luso-Brazilian Council, London: Author Catalogue A-Z and Subject Catalogue A-Z. 567 p. Boston: G. K. Hall, 1967 (LC 67-7667). First Supplement. 288 p., 1973.

The Canning House Library is devoted to the cultures of Latin America, Portugal, and Spain. The library of the Luso-Brazilian Council covers all aspects of Portuguese and Brazilian life and culture, including philosophy, religion, education, history and biography, geography, economics, sociology, current affairs, law, the arts, language and literature, the armed services, bibliography, and the sciences (omitting only highly technical subjects).

In this volume are separate author and subject catalogs. The subject catalog is a classified one, arranged by Library of Congress call number. There is no index to or detailed outline of the classification. The headings dividing the different class numbers are easy to miss, and since there is not even a table of contents to provide the page numbers on which different classes, or subjects, may be found, the catalog becomes extremely difficult to use. The volume contains two separate lists of serials: the first lists cultural and bibliographical serials; the second, economic and social serials. Information on holdings is provided for both. The Luso-Brazilian Library contains over 6,000 books, mostly in Portuguese, Spanish, or English.

180. Hispanic Society of America. Printed Books, 1468-1700, in

the Hispanic Society of America. A Listing by Clara Louisa Penney. 614 p. New York: The Society, 1965 (LC 65-22528).

This is a short-title catalog, arranged alphabetically by author, of books printed between 1468 and 1700 found in the Library of the Hispanic Society of America. The library uses the British Museum as the authority for authors' names. There are cross-references from alternate forms of names. There are also added entries for editors, translators, and compilers. Included in the entries are many references to standard reference works and catalogs of Hispanic subjects. Over 2,000 pamphlets are included among the rare books.

For later works found in this library consult the Catalogue of the Library of the Hispanic Society of America (see 181).

181. Hispanic Society of America. Library. Catalogue of the Library. 10 vols. Boston: G. K. Hall, 1962 (LC 62-52682). First Supplement. 4 vols., 1970.

The Hispanic Society of America, located in New York City, was founded in 1904 by Archer M. Huntington, and the library of the society began with Huntington's personal collection. By 1962 this library had over 100,000 volumes. Through the early twentieth century the library collected on the art, literature, and history of all countries where Spanish or Portuguese was spoken. The collection policy is now limited to Spain, Portugal, and what was formerly colonial Hispanic America, including music, social customs, regional costumes, and description and travel in these areas, but excluding Indian subjects. Many rare books and pamphlets are included here, but only those published after 1700; for early imprints there is a separate catalog, Printed Books, 1468-1700 in the Hispanic Society of America (see 180). Also included in the present catalog are some entries for reprints or extracts of journal articles and analytical entries for some works in collections.

Many different classification and descriptive cataloging systems have been used in the library, with the result being many different forms of entry. For many books there is only an author card, although in general this is a dictionary catalog with title and subject entries as well. Library of Congress classification and cataloging is now used, but the library still does its own original and very detailed cataloging. Cross-references are made from all conceivable forms of Hispanic, Portuguese, and Brazilian names, but variant spellings of family names are filed together. With the publication of the First Supplement, a master file of subject headings and subject cross-references was established, but many of the references in the supplement refer only to entries in the 1962 catalog and may appear as blind references in the supplement. Where there have been major changes in the subject heading scheme, such as in the "Paintings" section, all of the cards have been reprinted in the supplement.

182. Institute of Jamaica, Kingston. West India Reference Library. The Catalogue of the West India Reference Library. 6 vols. Millwood, N. Y.: Kraus International Pub., 1980 (LC 76-56698).

The West India Reference Library was founded in 1894 as a section of the Public Library of the Institute of Jamaica. It contains works on the West Indies printed from 1547 to 1975. Books, pamphlets, periodicals, and publications of West Indian governments, especially Jamaica, are included. Coverage is as comprehensive as possible for Jamaica and the English-speaking Caribbean, especially for the subjects of history, description and travel, government, economic and social conditions, and literature. Particular strengths lie in the subjects of slavery and the slave trade, sugar cane, the plantation economy, and African retentions in the culture and life of the West Indies.

The catalog is in two parts: an author-title catalog of three volumes, and a subject catalog, also of three volumes. Library of Congress and Sears subject headings are used with some modifications. There are many see and see-also references in both catalogs. The classification system is Dewey Decimal. Of particular interest are the many analytical entries for articles in selected periodicals.

183. Miami, University of, Coral Gables, Fla. Cuban and Caribbean Library. Catalog of the Cuban and Caribbean Library, University of Miami, Coral Gables, Florida. 6 vols. Boston: G. K. Hall, 1977 (LC 78-301899).

Despite its title, this catalog represents not a separate Cuban and Caribbean Library but cards on the subject of Cuba and the Caribbean pulled from the main library catalog. Included are cards for books whose subject headings or titles indicated their content is within the catalog's scope; books by known authors important to the Caribbean; and books on Cuban, Dominican, and Puerto Rican literature, history, art, music, etc. that were identified by their Library of Congress classification number in the shelflist.

Library of Congress subject headings are used and most of the cards are LC printed cards. There are no listings for periodicals or government documents, but there are analytics for individual titles in the library's microform collections.

The catalog covers the geographical area of Cuba and the rest of the Greater and Lesser Antilles, the Guyanas, Venezuela, Colombia, and Central America except El Salvador. Titles are mostly in Spanish and English.

New York (City). Public Library. Reference Dept. Dictionary Catalog of the History of the Americas. 28 vols. Boston: G. K. Hall, 1961. (see 111)

184. Newberry Library, Chicago. A Catalog of the William B.

Greenlee Collection of Portuguese History and Literature and the Portuguese Materials in the Newberry Library. Compiled by Doris Varner Welsh. 342 p. Chicago: Newberry Library, 1953 (LC 53-6595).

William Brooks Greenlee was a businessman and scholar of Portuguese history and culture. He donated his collection to the Newberry Library in 1937 but continued to add to it until his death in 1953. The subject matter of the collection he founded is the history and culture of Portugal and its colonies, especially Brazil. His particular interest was Portuguese seafarers and explorers.

This catalog includes materials from the Newberry Library's Ayer Collection of Americana and American Indians, as well as from the general Newberry Library collection, that relate to Portugal or Portuguese colonies.

The catalog is arranged as a classified subject catalog with an author index. Entries are very brief--just main entry; shortened title; name of editor, translator, or compiler; imprint; and pagination. Most of the works are in Portuguese.

For more recent additions to this collection, and the catalog in dictionary form see 185.

185. Newberry Library, Chicago. A Catalogue of the Greenlee Collection, the Newberry Library, Chicago. 2 vols. Boston: G. K. Hall, 1970 (LC 70-166464).

William Brooks Greenlee was a businessman and scholar of Portuguese history and culture. He donated his book collection to the Newberry Library in 1937 but continued to add to it until his death in 1953. The subject matter of the collection he founded is the history and culture of Portugal and its colonies, especially Brazil. His particular interest was Portuguese seafarers and explorers. Works in this catalog are mostly in Portuguese and range in imprint date from the seventeenth century to the 1960's.

This is a dictionary catalog of authors, titles, and subjects. Library of Congress subject headings are used. There are some analytical entries for series, journal articles, and a few books.

In contrast to the 1953 catalog of the Greenlee Collection (see 184) this catalog does not list materials on Portugal or things Portuguese held in the Newberry Library outside of the Greenlee Collection, as the earlier catalog does. It contains more recent additions to the collection, and is in a different form (the earlier catalog is a classified one).

186. Oliveira Lima Library. Catalog of the Oliveira Lima Library, The Catholic University of America. 2 vols. Boston: G. K. Hall, 1970 (LC 73-24857).

This collection was founded in 1916 by Manoel de Oliveira Lima, the well-known historian. By 1970 there were almost 50,000 volumes in the library, now part of the Catholic University in Washington, D. C., not all of which are represented in the 32,000 cards of the catalog.

The focus of the collection is on the Luso-Brazilian world, particularly Portuguese and Brazilian history and literature, and the history and ethnography of present and former Portuguese territories or spheres of influence. The collection on Brazil is especially strong, with its holdings of diplomatic papers, parliamentary and ministerial records, serials, and newspapers. For Portugal, the major emphasis is on the Age of Discovery, the Restoration, the War of the Spanish Succession, the Enlightenment, the Peninsular War, Liberalism, and diplomatic and ecclesiastical history. The library also collects works on the Portuguese in Africa, India, and the Far East, and there is a small section on Spain and the Spanish-American War.

This is primarily an author catalog. Recently some subject, title, and added entries have been included. Older entries may list authors under more than one form of their name, with no cross-references between the forms. There are five appendices listing the pamphlet and periodical collections, and some manuscript and photographic collections. Most of the works are in Portuguese and Spanish.

187. Pan American Union. Columbus Memorial Library. Index to Latin American Periodical Literature, 1929-1960. 8 vols. Boston: G. K. Hall, 1962 (LC 63-590). Supplements: 1961-1965. 2 vols., 1968. 1966-1970. 2 vols., 1980.

The Pan American Union is the secretariat of the Organization of American States. Its library in Washington, D. C., the Columbus Memorial Library, maintains this catalog, which is actually an index to periodical articles in more than 3,000 different periodicals, mostly of Latin American origin. Also included is material published in the official gazettes of Latin American countries, such as decrees, laws, regulations, and resolutions. Library of Congress subject headings are used, and there are cross-references. Before 1951, only subject entries were made; after 1951, author and secondary entries were included.

Subjects indexed are in the economic, political, governmental, social, and cultural fields. However, articles selected for indexing in the Indice General de Publicaciones Latinoamericanas; Humanidades y Ciencias Sociales (Index to Latin American Periodicals; Humanities and Social Sciences), which began in 1963, are not included in the supplements. The main set has about 250,000 entries for articles from over 3,000 periodicals, but only about 1,600 titles--those periodicals indexed from 1950 to 1960--are included in the catalog's List of Periodicals Indexed.

188. Peru. Biblioteca Nacional, Lima. Catálogo de Autores de la Colección Peruana (Author Catalog of the Peruvian Collection, National Library of Peru). 6 vols. Boston: G. K. Hall, 1979 (LC 79-109143).

The National Library of Peru was created by General José de San Martín on August 28, 1821, one month after the proclamation of Peruvian independence, but it was destroyed by fire in 1943 and had to be reconstructed. "The catalog includes catalog cards for Peruvian imprints and for publications about Peru from 1553 through 1977 which are found in the National Library" [Preface]. Works focus on the economic, social, and technological development of Peru, primarily literature, history, geography, Indians, medicine and science, business, and sociology. Included are books, pamphlets, serials, maps, and music in Spanish, English, French, other European languages, and Peruvian Indian dialects.

This is a main-entry catalog with some cross-references to correct headings. The classification system used is based on the Dewey Decimal system, adapted by the library. Anglo-American cataloging rules are followed. Volume six contains separate catalogs of about 10,000 periodicals and 1,300 maps and plans.

189. Texas. University at Austin. Library. Latin American Collection. Catalog of the Latin American Collection. 31 vols. Boston: G. K. Hall, 1969 (LC 70-10540). First Supplement. 5 vols., 1971. Second Supplement. 3 vols., 1973. Third Supplement. 8 vols., 1975. Fourth Supplement. 3 vols., 1977. Further supplemented by Bibliographic Guide to Latin American Studies: 1978- . Boston: G. K. Hall, 1979- .

This is a major Latin American collection, which acquires Latin American material in all disciplines, particularly anthropology, economics, education, geography, government, history, law, literature, philology, philosophy, religion, and pure and applied sciences and technology. The original emphasis of the collection was on Mexico, and its greatest strength is still in this area; its weakest area is probably in its holdings on the Caribbean.

The original 31 volumes listed 175,000 printed books, pamphlets, periodicals, and microfilms, as well as newspapers published before 1890. Also included are government documents from the United States and some Latin American countries, and doctoral dissertations from the United States and Latin America, particularly Mexico. Works are primarily in Spanish and Portuguese, with English and other Western European languages also represented.

This is a dictionary catalog. Subject headings are from the Library of Congress's list. There are many see and see-also references. There is no indexing of journal articles, but there are analytics for many monographic series.

The fourth supplement bears the new name of the collection: the Nettie Lee Benson Latin American Collection.

190. Tulane University of Louisiana. Latin American Library. Catalog of the Latin American Library of the Tulane University Library, New Orleans. 9 vols. Boston: G. K. Hall, 1970 (LC 74-26732). First Supplement.

2 vols., 1973. Second Supplement. 2 vols., 1975. Third Supplement. 2 vols., 1978.

Until 1962 this library was known as the Library of the Middle American Research Institute, and it is still strongest in the areas of Mexico, Central America, and the Caribbean. Under the Farmington Plan the library was assigned responsibility for collecting materials concerning all countries of Central America between Panama and Mexico, except for Costa Rica. The library collects in all areas of Latin America and in all subjects except pure science, medicine, and literature, but material on literature found in other libraries of Tulane University is included in the published catalogs. The subject emphasis is on anthropology, archaeology, and history.

By the time the Third Supplement was published, the Latin American Library had about 101,000 titles in its collections. These, and 12,000 literature titles in Tulane University Library's Humanities Division, appear in the printed catalogs. Newspapers, manuscripts, and maps are not included in the catalogs, but books, journals, microforms, pamphlets, and United States and Latin American government documents are.

The catalog is in dictionary form and uses Library of Congress subject headings. There are some analytical entries for journals and series. Works are mostly in Spanish, English, and Portuguese.

191. United States. Library of Congress. Catalog of Brazilian Acquisitions of the Library of Congress, 1964-1974. Compiled by William V. Jackson. 751 p. Boston: G. K. Hall, 1977 (LC 77-363609).

This represents Professor William V. Jackson's collection of 15,000 Library of Congress catalog cards for material relating to Brazil or published in Brazil and acquired by the Library of Congress from 1964 to 1974. The catalog is particularly strong in history, literature, and the social sciences. Most of the titles are in Portuguese, but English and other Western European languages are also included. The material listed ranges from monographs to serials, pamphlets, government documents, and papers presented at conferences.

The catalog is arranged by Library of Congress classification number, hence items appear only once in the catalog. There is a table of contents providing the page numbers where the broad classes begin. There is also an author index that includes title and corporate main entries, and a specific subject index, which provides references to a specific class or range of class numbers. Also included is a separate section of Unclassified Law, separated because the Library of Congress law classification was incomplete at the time of publication. Most of the laws and publications of the Brazilian Congress and ministries are listed here.

United States. Library of Congress. Hispanic Law Division. Index to Latin American Legislation. 2 vols. Boston: G. K. Hall, 1961. (see 351)

192. Universidad de Buenos Aires. Argentine Bibliography: A Union Catalog of Argentine Holdings in the Libraries of the University of Buenos Aires. (Bibliografía Argentina: Catálogo de Materiales Argentinos en las Bibliotecas de la Universidad de Buenos Aires). 7 vols. Boston: G. K. Hall, 1980 (ISBN 0-8161-0317-8).

The Instituto Bibliotecológico was founded in 1943 as the coordinating body for the University of Buenos Aires libraries. One of its responsibilities was the compilation of a union catalog for the university. Simultaneously it began another catalog of duplicate cards for Argentine printed books. Included in this present catalog, which grew out of that project, are works printed in Argentina and the works of Argentine authors printed abroad, in the scientific, technical, and humanistic areas. It is a union catalog of the books and pamphlets found in 17 central and 56 departmental libraries of the University of Buenos Aires' Faculties, Schools, and Institutes.

The catalog contains 110,000 cards cataloged in accordance with Apostolic Vatican Library Rules and filed according to American Library Association filing rules. It is a main-entry catalog with many cross-references from alternate forms of names. Almost all the works are in Spanish.

14. THE MIDDLE EAST

Middle Eastern studies in the United States and Europe have until recently focused mostly on the ancient history of the area as one of the cradles of civilization, and on the literature and religion of the region. With the growing importance of the Middle East in international politics, some of this emphasis is changing, but the library collections that have been built up over the years still reflect the older viewpoints.

The Catalog of the Oriental Institute Library of the University of Chicago (193) and The New York Public Library's Dictionary Catalog of the Oriental Collection (197) represent distinguished collections on the ancient Near East and the literature, languages, and religions of the Middle East. Both are dictionary catalogs containing significant numbers of analytical entries for periodical articles, and both contain works in Western and Middle Eastern languages. The New York Public Library catalog is the larger of the two, but it includes material about the Far East as well as the Middle East. A third catalog of importance for the history, religion, and literature of the area is Harvard's Catalogue of Arabic, Persian, and Ottoman Turkish Books (194) which, as its title indicates, contains no Western-language books.

Other catalogs of works in the languages of the area are the Hoover Institution catalogs of works in Arabic (198) and in Turkish and Persian (199). Unlike the catalogs mentioned above, these emphasize the political, economic, and social affairs of the countries of the Middle East. For works in Western languages on present-day affairs of the Middle East, consult the catalog of the Western languages collection of the Hoover Institution (93).

Additional catalogs with significant collections on this part of the world may be found in the index.

193. Chicago. University. Oriental Institute. Library. Catalog of the Oriental Institute Library, University of Chicago. 16 vols. Boston: G. K. Hall, 1970 (LC 77-166463). First Supplement: Catalog of the Middle Eastern Collection, University of Chicago. 962 p., 1977.

The Oriental Institute Library was founded in 1919 and became a department of the University of Chicago Library in the early 1940's.

It is "probably the finest library in the United States for the study of the ancient Near East and Medieval Islam," aiming "to collect all useful printed material on every aspect of the Near East" [Preface]. The original catalog is a dictionary catalog covering 50,000 volumes and 220 current periodical titles in the areas of art, literature, philology, history, science, and religion. Regions included are ancient Mesopotamia, Egypt, Palestine, Anatolia, and Iran. The collection is especially rich in Assyriology, Egyptology, and Islam (including Arabic, Persian, and Turkish texts and translations).

Works date from the sixteenth century to the present and are in both European and Near Eastern languages. Authority cards are included for almost all Arab, Persian, and Turkish authors. The catalog is replete with analytics, including book reviews, and long runs of some series are completely analyzed. Library of Congress subject headings are used, with modifications and additions made by the library.

The supplement to the catalog is almost exclusively a main-entry catalog.

194. Harvard University. Library. Catalogue of Arabic, Persian, and Ottoman Turkish Books. 5 vols. Cambridge, Mass.: distributed by Harvard University Press, 1968 (LC 68-29108).

Harvard University has one of the largest Middle Eastern collections in the country. Volumes one to three of this catalog are a dictionary catalog of authors, titles, and personal subjects representing 30,000 volumes in Arabic. Volume four contains two catalogs: the first is an author, title, and personal subject catalog of 5,500 titles in Persian; the second is an author, title, and personal subject catalog of about 4,000 Turkish books. There is no transliteration. Volume five of the catalog is a Topical Subject Catalogue arranged alphabetically by English-language subject headings. The subject headings are drawn from the Harvard List of Subject Headings. Only works cataloged since 1961 appear in the topical catalog.

Harvard collects in a wide spectrum of Islamic and Middle Eastern studies from pre-Islamic classical antiquity to the present, including history, literature, philosophy, and religion. The collection is especially strong in language and literature. Titles in this catalog include works in Widener Library, the Law School Library, the Countway Library of Medicine, the Andover-Harvard Theological Library, and the Houghton Library. The catalog reflects the growth of Middle Eastern studies at Harvard, which was slow through the mid-1950's but then spurted with the establishment of the Center for Middle Eastern Studies in 1954, and then the inclusion of the United Arab Republic in the P.L. 480 Program in 1962.

Jerusalem. Ecole biblique et archéologique française. Bibliothèque. Catalogue de la bibliothèque de l'Ecole biblique et archéologique française. 13 vols. Boston: G. K. Hall, 1975. (see 263)

195. London. University. School of Oriental and African Studies. Library. Index Islamicus, 1906-1955; A Catalogue of Articles on Islamic Subjects in Periodicals and Other Collective Publications. 897 p. London: Mansell, 1972. Supplements: 1956-1960. 316 p. Cambridge: Heffer, 1962. 1961-1965. 342 p. Cambridge: Heffer, 1967. 1966-1970. 384 p. London: Mansell, 1972. 1971-1975. 429 p. London: Mansell, 1978. (Annual supplements, cumulated every five years).

This catalog, maintained by the University of London School of Oriental and African Studies, indexes articles in periodicals, Festschriften, other collective works, and congresses. The original volume has 26,000 entries from 12,000 volumes of 510 periodical titles, 120 Festschriften, and 70 volumes of congress proceedings. Works are in all European languages, including Russian.

The index covers the whole field of Islamic studies, excluding only pure science and technology. The periodicals indexed are those concerned with Islamic, Christian Oriental, and Jewish studies; Byzantine, Spanish, and Slavic studies; theology, philosophy, law, history of science, history, geography, anthropology, archaeology, linguistics, philology, education, and other social sciences. The arrangement of the index is by subject; an author index is included.

196. London. University. School of Oriental and African Studies. Library. Library Catalogue. 28 vols. Boston: G. K. Hall, 1963 (LC 64-5766). First Supplement. 16 vols., 1968. Second Supplement. 16 vols., 1973. Third Supplement. 19 vols., 1979.

The University of London School of Oriental and African Studies exists "to further research in, and to extend the study and knowledge of, the languages of Eastern and African peoples, Ancient and Modern, and the Literature, History, Religion, Law, Customs and Art of those peoples" [Introduction]. The areas of the world that are covered by the school and its library are Africa, Asia, and Oceania.

The catalog is in three parts: author (main entry), title, and subject. In the author catalog, the entry "Series" has detailed lists of individual titles in the monographic series owned by the library, and the entry "Periodical Publications" lists the journals owned. In the subject catalog, material is classified by region (Africa, Middle East, etc.) and within region by country or language (if the language is Asian, African, or Oriental) and then by subject. The subject catalog is rather difficult to use, as there are few cross-references and no guide to the subjects or to the form of the name of each country. Up until 1973 the library used British Museum cataloging rules, but in that year it changed to the use of Anglo-American Cataloging Rules.

In addition to the three main catalogs, there is a separate list of manuscripts and microfilms, and there are also separate catalogs of works in Chinese and Japanese. The main catalog contains the library's holdings in all other languages, including 2,500 Asian, African, and Oceanic tongues.

With the publication of the third supplement, the number of volumes in the library stood at a half million.

197. New York (City). Public Library. Reference Department. Dictionary Catalog of the Oriental Collection. 16 vols. Boston: G. K. Hall, 1960 (LC 60-51081). First Supplement. 8 vols., 1976.

The catalog of the Oriental Collection, including the supplement, contains references to 107,000 volumes in the Oriental Division of The New York Public Library and to material relating to the Orient in other divisions of the library. Works are in 100 languages of the East and in Western languages as well. The Orient is defined to include the Near or Middle East, including North Africa, and the Far East. The collection is especially strong in the ancient Near East (Egypt, Mesopotamia, etc.); Arabic language and literature; India; the languages, literatures, and civilizations of Iran, Armenia, Georgia, Turkey, Central Asia, Southeast Asia, China, and Japan; missionaries; Islam, Buddhism, and other religions of the East; Sanskrit; Korea; and Malaya. This is a very good historical collection; works date from the eighteenth century to the 1970's.

This is a dictionary catalog of main and added entries, form and subject entries. The arrangement is alphabetical by letters of the Roman alphabet. The library uses its own system of subject headings, and these headings, along with the cataloging methods in general, have varied greatly over the life of the catalog. There are many cross-references included. Also listed are approximately 15,000 cards for indexed periodical articles.

The supplement includes materials added to the collection from 1961 to 1971, when The New York Public Library closed its catalog and adopted Anglo-American Cataloging Rules and Library of Congress subject headings. More recent acquisitions are listed in the Dictionary Catalog of the Research Libraries (see 16).

198. Stanford University. Hoover Institution on War, Revolution, and Peace. The Library Catalogs of the Hoover Institution on War, Revolution, and Peace, Stanford University: Catalog of the Arabic Collection. 902 p. Boston: G. K. Hall, 1969 (LC 75-17738).

This is the catalog of the Arabic-language holdings of the library of the Hoover Institution on War, Revolution, and Peace. It includes all Arabic-language materials at Stanford University. All subjects are covered, but the emphasis is on the political, economic, and social affairs of the Arab countries of the Middle East and North Africa. Books, government documents, society publications, periodicals, and newspapers are all listed.

This is, in general, a dictionary catalog of authors, titles, subjects, translators, and editors. There are separate lists for uncataloged material, government documents, serials, and newspapers, which requires making several searches to locate a given item. Most of the cards for the cataloged books were prepared by the Hoover Institution, and give, in romanized form, the author's name, the title transliterated according to the Library of Congress system, the translation of the title, the place of publication, publisher, date, number of pages, and size of the volume. The forms of Arabic names, however, sometimes differ from Library of Congress practice and may appear in one way in the uncataloged material section and another way in the main catalog, which can be very confusing.[19] Library of Congress subject headings are used.

For a fuller description of the Hoover Institution on War, Revolution, and Peace see 93.

199. Stanford University. Hoover Institution on War, Revolution, and Peace. The Library Catalogs of the Hoover Institution on War, Revolution, and Peace: Catalogs of the Turkish and Persian Collections. 670 p. Boston: G. K. Hall, 1969 (LC 70-17557).

As the Hoover Institution Library is the only depository for Turkish and Persian materials at Stanford University, all subjects are included, but the emphasis is on the political, economic, and social affairs of the nineteenth and twentieth centuries. Books, government documents, society publications, serials and newspapers, and rare books in Turkish or Persian are included in two separate catalogs. Western-language material on Turkey and Iran is included in the Catalog of the Western Language Collections of the Hoover Institution on War, Revolution, and Peace (see 93).

The Turkish catalog is divided into different sections for books, uncataloged materials, special collections, government documents, society publications, and serials and newspapers. The Persian catalog and the main Turkish catalog of books are both dictionary catalogs of authors, titles, subjects, translators, and editors. Library of Congress subject headings are used. All cards in the Turkish collection were prepared by the Hoover Institution and are in the Latin script now used in Turkey. Translations of Turkish titles into English are included. The Persian catalog also gives the translation of the title into English and provides the author and title in the Arabic script as well as in transliterated form.

200. Utah. University. Middle East Center. Library. Aziz S. Atiya Library. Arabic Collection. 841 p. Salt Lake City, Utah: University of Utah Press, 1968. Supplement One. 470 p., 1971.

Middle East studies at the University of Utah is relatively young; the program began in 1959. This is the catalog of the Arabic collection of the Middle East Center Library. The emphasis is on humanities--history, literature, languages and dictionaries, rhetoric, philosophy, theology, culture, and politics. Generally, modern science and technology is not included. The collection was originally gathered in Egypt and is probably still strongest in works from and about that country. Included are many old and rare first editions, periodicals, and monographs.

The catalog is arranged by the very general subject categories of the Library of Congress classification. Within these categories the arrangement is alphabetical by transliterated authors and titles.

15. EASTERN AND SOUTHERN ASIA

Most of the major libraries of works in Chinese, Japanese, and Korean in the United States have published their catalogs. These include the Far Eastern Languages Catalog of the Library of Congress (216), the catalogs of the East Asiatic Library of the University of California at Berkeley (201), the catalogs of the Far Eastern Library of the University of Chicago (202), the Catalogs of the Asia Library of the University of Michigan (208), and the catalogs of the Chinese collection (213) and of the Japanese collection (214) of the Hoover Institution. The University of Michigan and the Hoover Institution collections are particularly strong in works on contemporary Chinese and Japanese affairs; the Library of Congress aims to collect comprehensively on all aspects of Far Eastern life; and the Universities of Chicago and of California emphasize language and literature studies.

Works in Western languages on China, Japan, and Korea may be found in the catalogs (described in other chapters) of The New York Public Library's Oriental Collection (197) and the University of London School of Oriental and African Studies (196), which also have significant numbers of works in East Asian languages, and in the Western languages catalog of the Hoover Institution (93), which is particularly strong in contemporary Asian affairs.

The South and Southeast Asian library catalogs that have been published contain, for the most part, works in Western languages. The two largest, the catalogs of the India Office Library (206) and of the Ames Library of the University of Minnesota (209), are chiefly concerned with the dominant country of the area, India, and with British rule over that country. The most useful catalog for the countries of Southeast Asia is the Library of Congress's Southeast Asia Subject Catalog (217), which emphasizes subject cataloging of periodical articles.

Asian Development Bank. Library. Subject Catalog of Books. 4 vols. The Bank, 1974. (see 352)

201. California. University. Library. East Asiatic Library. Author-Title Catalog. 13 vols. Boston: G. K. Hall, 1968 (LC 68-3142). First Supplement. 2 vols., 1973.

______. Subject Catalog. 6 vols. Boston: G. K. Hall, 1968 (LC 68-7266). First Supplement. 2 vols., 1973.

This is a catalog of Chinese, Japanese, and Korean language monographs and periodicals in the East Asiatic Library of the University of California at Berkeley. The library originally concentrated on collecting in the areas of the language, literature, history, and art of the East. It now also collects in the social sciences, and is building up the collections in the natural and applied sciences. Greatest strengths are in music, fine arts, archaeology, biography and genealogy, and local gazetteers.[20] Exchange agreements with institutions in China, Korea, and Japan have swelled the number of current periodical titles to more than 1,700. The East Asiatic Library became a separate library at Berkeley in 1947; most of the titles are of twentieth-century origin.

The Author-Title Catalog is divided by language. Chinese characters are not transliterated but are arranged according to the sequence of "radicals" in Mathews' Chinese-English Dictionary. Chinese entries are followed by Japanese Kana and Korean han'gŭl characters. There is a Table of Contents at the beginning of each volume and there are cross-references to help guide the user. At the end of the Author-Title Catalog is an alphabetical supplement with works in languages other than Japanese, Chinese, or Korean; entries that have been romanized; and entries under "form" headings, such as "China. Laws, statutes, etc."

The supplement to the Author-Title Catalog, however, is arranged alphabetically by the romanized name of the author, or, if there is no author, by the romanized title. There are no cross-references.

The Subject Catalog is arranged by Library of Congress subject headings in English.

202. Chicago. University. Library. Far Eastern Library. Author-Title Catalog of the Chinese Collection. 8 vols. Boston: G. K. Hall, 1973 (LC 74-152782). First Supplement. 4 vols., 1980.

______. Author-Title Catalog of the Japanese Collection. 4 vols. Boston: G. K. Hall, 1973 (LC 74-152781). First Supplement. 4 vols., 1980.

______. Classified Catalog and Subject Index of the Chinese and Japanese Collections. 6 vols. Boston: G. K. Hall, 1973 (LC 74-152780). First Supplement. 4 vols., 1980.

The Far Eastern Library of the University of Chicago was founded in 1936. The initial collection was compiled in China with an emphasis on basic reference tools, learned journals, and research materials for the study of Chinese literature, history, and institutions, especially of the ancient period. At the time of publication of the 1973 catalog, the library contained approximately 265,000 volumes, including 200,000 in Chinese, 60,000 in Japanese, and

5,000 in Korean, Manchu, Mongol, and Tibetan. There are also 5,000 reels or boxes of microtext, 6,000 pamphlets in vertical files, and approximately 1,000 current periodicals. The catalog is divided into three separate parts.

The Author-Title Catalog of the Chinese Collection consists of author, title, and personal subject cards. The cards are arranged in alphabetical order of the romanized entries; the Wade-Giles system of romanization is used. Cards for books cataloged before 1958 follow the format of Harvard-Yenching printed cards. After 1958, Library of Congress and American Library Association cataloging rules were followed, and later the 1967 Anglo-American cataloging code was used. The Chinese collection is especially strong in classics, philosophy, archaeology, history, local gazetteers, histories of institutions, classical philology, literature, fine arts, ts'ung shu, bibliographies, and general reference works. Its collection of classics and classical philology is the strongest outside of the Far East. The library is also rich in materials for the study of ancient and pre-modern China, and is becoming stronger in the social sciences and the literature of contemporary China.

The Japanese collection has, for the most part, been developed only since 1958. It is especially strong in Japanese language, literature, history, biography, customs and folklore, thought and religion, fine arts, Sinology, bibliography, reference works, and learned journals. There is a notable selection of Japanese works in Chinese studies. The catalog is arranged by romanized entries according to Kenkyusha's New Japanese-English Dictionary, 1967 edition. Cataloging follows Anglo-American cataloging rules. All large sets have been analyzed.

The Classified Catalog and Subject Index is arranged according to the Harvard-Yenching classification system. Main headings and subheadings are provided for the different classes. There is an alphabetical index to the scheme, the entries in which are based on Library of Congress subject headings. In the index are see references but no see-also references. There is also a three-page list of the main classes in the Harvard-Yenching classification system, in English and in Chinese. Works in Korean and Manchu are included in the classified arrangement.

203. Cornell University. Libraries. Southeast Asia Catalog. 7 vols. Boston: G. K. Hall, 1976 (LC 76-362237).

Cornell's Southeast Asia Program was begun in 1950 with the receipt of a Rockefeller Foundation grant. Later, Cornell acquired the responsibility for collecting in Southeast Asia under the Farmington Plan. The result is "one of the largest collections of books, periodicals, newspapers, maps, and microforms in the world on Southeast Asia."[21] Southeast Asia is defined as the countries of Burma, Cambodia (Kampuchea), Indonesia, Laos, Malaysia, Singapore, Brunei, the Philippines, Portuguese Timor (now part of Indonesia), Thailand, and Vietnam. The library collects materials both about and from these countries. Its holdings are strongest for Indonesia (both vernacular and Western-language publications),

Vietnam (both Vietnamese and French publications), and the Philippines (mostly Western-language material).

The catalog is arranged by type of material--Western Language Monographs, Vernacular Monographs, Serials, Newspapers, and Maps--and within each type of material by country, and then alphabetically by main entry. There is only one entry per item. The library uses Library of Congress classification and often Library of Congress printed cards. The Serials Catalog, which is included, lists which issues are held.

The library was named the John M. Echols Collection in 1967, in honor of this scholar's contribution to the field and to the library.

204. Harvard University. Library. China, Japan, and Korea. 494 p. Cambridge, Mass.: distributed by Harvard University Press, 1968 (LC 68-14151). (Widener Library Shelflist v. 14)

This is a classified arrangement (by Harvard's own classification scheme) of works in the Widener Library on Japan, Korea, and China. It includes works in Western languages on the history, civilization, government, geography, description, economic and social life and customs, religion, and peoples of the three countries; as well as works in Western languages on Japanese, Chinese, and Korean literature and philosophy, and translations of Japanese, Chinese, and Korean literary works.

15,300 volumes and pamphlets are listed here, most of them in English. Works date from the sixteenth to the twentieth centuries, but the majority were published in the twentieth century. In addition to the classified arrangement, there is a listing by author and title, and one by imprint date.

For a further discussion of the Widener Library shelflists see 9.

205. Harvard University. Library. Southern Asia: Afghanistan, Bhutan, Burma, Cambodia, Ceylon, India, Laos, Malaya, Nepal, Pakistan, Sikkim, Singapore, Thailand, Vietnam. 543 p. Cambridge, Mass.: distributed by Harvard University Press, 1968 (LC 68-15927). (Widener Library Shelflist v. 19)

Included in this catalog are works on the history, civilization, government, geography and travel, religious affairs, and peoples of Afghanistan, Bhutan, Burma, Cambodia (Kampuchea), Ceylon (Sri Lanka), India, Laos, Malaya (Malaysia), Nepal, Pakistan, Sikkim (now part of India), Singapore, Thailand, and Vietnam. For some of the countries, economic history is also included. Not included here is the literature of Southern Asia.

This volume is part of the Widener Library shelflist series (see 9) and the first part lists the works in shelflist, or call number order. This is followed by an author-title list, and finally a chronological arrangement. There are about 10,000 titles listed in this catalog, all of them in Western languages and about 85 percent of them in English. Most of the imprint dates are of this century.

206. India Office Library. Catalogue of European Printed Books, India Office Library. 10 vols. Boston: G. K. Hall, 1964 (LC 73-180814).

The India Office Library was originally founded in 1801 as the Library of the Honourable East India Company. It came under the newly-created India Office in 1858 on the transfer of the East India Company's powers and possessions to the crown. In 1947, as a result of Indian independence, its jurisdiction was obtained by the Secretary of State for Commonwealth Relations.

"The scope of the library may best be defined as covering Indology: it aims to acquire all significant works, wherever published and in whatever language, bearing on the environment, history, life, and civilization of the peoples of the Indo-Pakistan subcontinent and of neighboring countries of related culture such as Afghanistan, Tibet, Ceylon, Burma, and Malaysia."[22] Throughout its history the library has had two functions: to serve as a library of official reference and to serve as a learned library for the use of Orientalists. The library is especially strong in geology and geography, archaeology and history, linguistics and literature, religion and philosophy, art, anthropology, sociology, politics, and economics. This catalog lists works in European languages only, particularly English. Pamphlets and government documents are included, but manuscripts are listed in a separate catalog (see 207).

The catalog is arranged in several parts. Pre-1937 acquisitions are listed in a sheaf catalog arranged by author (volumes one to two). Works from 1937 and after are in a separate catalog divided into an author catalog (volumes three to six) and a subject catalog (volumes seven to nine). Library of Congress subject headings are used in the subject catalog but are modified extensively by the library. The last volume of the catalog is a periodicals catalog, listing more than 2,700 serial publications in European languages, arranged by title with many cross-references from alternate titles.

207. India Office Library. Index of Post-1937 European Manuscript Accessions. 156 p. Boston: G. K. Hall, 1964 (LC 74-166559).

Most of the manuscripts included here are the private papers of persons who held high office under the British in India; for example: Presidents of the Board of Control, Secretaries of State for India, Viceroys, and Governors-General of India. There are also papers of members of the Council of India and of prominent Indian civilians, as well as various minutes, notes, reports, private journals, and other miscellaneous papers. Entries for microform copies of manuscripts that are in the possession of other libraries are also included.

A main-entry card describes each manuscript collection and each separately acquired individual manuscript. There are also entries under personal name for individuals whose correspondence is included in a collection.

For a further description of the India Office Library see 206.

London. University. School of Oriental and African Studies. Library. Library Catalogue. 28 vols. Boston: G. K. Hall, 1963. (see 196)

208. Michigan. University. Asia Library. Catalogs of the Asia Library, the University of Michigan, Ann Arbor. 25 vols. Boston: G. K. Hall, 1978 (LC 78-108964).

This is a catalog of the works in Chinese, Japanese, and Korean that comprise the Asia Library of the University of Michigan. The University of Michigan began offering Chinese and Japanese language courses in the 1930's, and the Army established its Far East languages training school at Michigan during the Second World War. A Center for Japanese Studies was established in 1947, and a Center for Chinese Studies in 1961. By 1976, holdings of the Asia Library were more than 300,000 volumes and 18,000 reels of microfilm. The Chinese collection accounted for 161,929 volumes and 12,828 reels of film, and the Japanese collection for 137,276 volumes and 5,453 reels of film.

The Chinese and Japanese catalogs are separate, but both are dictionary catalogs with authors, titles, and subjects interfiled in one alphabetical sequence. Chinese authors and titles are romanized using the modified Wade-Giles system; Japanese using the modified Hepburn system; and Korean using the McCune-Reischauer system. Library of Congress subject headings are used with some modifications, along with the Library of Congress classification. Anglo-American cataloging rules are followed.

The Chinese collection (volumes 1-13) is strong in political and economic developments in China after 1949, including the complete microfilm files on China compiled by the Union Research Institute, and the classified files on the Cultural Revolution compiled by the Contemporary China Research Institute. Other strengths include local histories, literary works of eminent Ming personalities, literature of the 1930's, and rare books on microfilm.

The Japanese collection (v. 14-25) is strong in history, literature, and the social sciences, particularly local history, legislation, education, and statistical compilations. Special collections include the Pacific War and Occupation Collection, the Harley Harris Bartlett Collection of Botanical Works, documents from the archives of the Ikeda family of Okayama, scripts of Japanese drama, Japanese Foreign Office Archives from 1868-1945 (on 1,531 reels of microfilm), and Japanese works on China. The Japanese catalog also includes works on Korea.

209. Minnesota. University. Library. Ames Library of South Asia. Catalog of the Ames Library of South Asia, University of Minnesota. 16 vols. Boston: G. K. Hall, 1980 (ISBN 0-8161-0275-9).

The Ames Library of South Asia is a collection of material in the social sciences and humanities on the countries of India, Pakistan, Nepal, Bhutan, Sikkim, Sri Lanka, Bangladesh, Afghanistan, and Burma and, to a lesser extent, Tibet and other neighboring countries of the Indian peninsula, and the islands Mauritius and Reunion in the Indian Ocean. The core of the collection is nineteenth-century British Indian history, but there are works on political science, economics, sociology, geography, and ancient Hindu law and medicine for both historic and prehistoric periods.

The collection was begun in 1908 by Charles Lesley Ames, a Minnesota businessman, after he read a book on the Indian Mutiny that stimulated his interest in India. His collection was physically transferred to the University of Minnesota in 1961, at which time it numbered 25,000 volumes or 80,000 individual items. Under the PL 480 program the University of Minnesota subsequently received published material from India and Pakistan, and later from Nepal and Ceylon (now Sri Lanka). In addition, the South Asia Historical Atlas Project, which produced A Historical Atlas of South Asia in 1978, was based at the University of Minnesota from 1966 to 1977 and recommended many valuable purchases. In 1967 a Federally funded South Asia Center was established on the campus, resulting in further growth of the Ames Library. By 1979, the library had over 90,000 volumes.

Included in the collection, and listed in the catalog, are books, periodicals, manuscripts, rare books, microforms, pamphlets, British Information Center publications, documents, vertical file materials, lithographs, and three small collections of material in the languages of the area. Most of the titles are in English, but other European languages are included, as are works in Bengali, Hindi, Urdu, Persian, and Punjabi.

This is a dictionary catalog of authors, titles, and subjects. Library of Congress subject headings are used with some slight modifications. Library of Congress, Dewey, and other classification systems are used, and cataloging practices have varied over time. There are some cross-references for names.

New York (City). Public Library. Reference Dept. Dictionary Catalog of the Oriental Collection. 16 vols. Boston: G. K. Hall, 1960. (see 197)

210. Newberry Library, Chicago. A Catalogue of Printed Materials Relating to the Philippine Islands 1519-1900, in the Newberry Library. Compiled by Doris Varner Welsh. 179 p. Chicago, 1959 (LC 58-11546).

The major part of this collection on the Philippines was acquired by a purchase of Edward E. Ayer after the victory in 1898 of Admiral Dewey at Manila Bay. Listed in the catalog are 1,900 titles arranged as a classified checklist, with an index by name of author (personal or corporate), translator, editor, compiler, etc. The classification is broken down into six major headings: General References, Political History, Ecclesiastical History, Economic History, Social and Cultural History (including ethnology and natural history), and Local History. Most of the entries include brief annotations describing the contents of the work or pointing out unusual features. There are a few analytics for journal articles and parts of books, and microforms and some Philippine government documents are included. Works are mostly in Spanish.

Titles listed here are also included in the later Dictionary Catalog of the Edward E. Ayer Collection of Americana and American Indians (see 64).

211. Rochester, N. Y. University. East Asian Library. Catalog of the East Asian Collection, East Asian Library, East Asian Language and Area Center, University of Rochester. 592 p. Rochester, N. Y., 1968 (LC 70-4645). Supplement. 364 p., 1970. Second Supplement. 509 p., 1974.

The East Asian Library was established at the University of Rochester in 1965. With the Second Supplement the catalog contains materials published through October, 1973. By then the library's collection totalled nearly 40,000 volumes, primarily in Chinese and Japanese. Included are works on the history, language, literature, and philosophy of East Asia, as well as basic reference books. Books, current periodicals, and newspapers are included.

The catalog is in several parts. The first part is a classified subject catalog arranged by Library of Congress classification and divided into two subdivisions--first, Chinese works, and second, Japanese works. The second part of the catalog contains an author list of the Chinese collection and then an author list of the Japanese collection. The third part contains current periodicals and newspapers, again in separate lists for works in Chinese and in Japanese. Selected works on China and Japan written in English are also included.

212. Singapore (City). University. Library. Catalogue of the Singapore/Malaysia Collection. 757 p. Boston: G. K. Hall, 1968 (LC 73-180960).

This is a catalog of works about Malaysia and Singapore. It is especially strong in source material on the development of the Malayan States, Singapore, and Bornean regions (excluding Brunei and Indonesian Borneo) from their founding to the period of colonial government to independence and after. Only legal and medical literature is excluded.

Much of the source material consists of microfilms of public records, government documents, rare serials, newspapers, and manuscripts. There are also over 1,000 theses submitted to universities and colleges abroad dealing with Singapore or Malaysia, or submitted to the Universities of Singapore and Malaysia. Also included are press clippings, company reports, pamphlets, current journals, and directories. There are analytics for book chapters, special issues of journals, reprint serials, and individual conference papers; however, in the classified portion of the catalog, these analytical entries are classed with the title in which they appear, limiting the usefulness of the analytical entries. Works are principally in English, but much of the material was published in Singapore or Malaysia.

This is actually two catalogs in one volume. The first catalog is a main-entry catalog. The second is a classified catalog arranged by Library of Congress classification system, modified to suit the needs of the collection. The use of the LC classification is rather interesting here, since most of the LC classes are used but the catalog deals only with Singapore and Malaysia; the LC classification thus becomes a sort of sub-classification for these areas. A detailed outline of the classification as used by the collection is provided. Microfilmed items and press clippings are only broadly classified; they are arranged alphabetically at the head of each broad subject division.

The catalog has 17,000 cards representing about 7,500 cataloged items.

213. Stanford University. Hoover Institution on War, Revolution, and Peace. The Library Catalogs of the Hoover Institution on War, Revolution, and Peace, Stanford University: Catalog of the Chinese Collection. 13 vols. Boston: G. K. Hall, 1969 (LC 78-15916). First Supplement. 2 vols., 1972. Second Supplement. 2 vols., 1977.

This collection is generally recognized as the strongest collection on modern China in the Western world. It is particularly strong in the social and political sciences, but it is also a general Chinese-language library. Included are books, pamphlets, government documents, institutional reports, archival material, ephemera, and periodicals. Only materials in Chinese are listed here; Western-language material on China is included in the Catalog of the Western Language Collections of the Hoover Institution (see 93).

This is a dictionary catalog. Almost all material is fully cataloged, including subject entries. Library of Congress subject headings are used with some modifications. The classification system used is the Harvard-Yenching system, with some changes. All titles and authors appear in both the original and romanized forms.

214. Stanford University. Hoover Institution on War, Revolution, and Peace. The Library Catalogs of the Hoover Institution on War, Revolution, and Peace: Catalog of the Japanese Collection. 7 vols. Boston: G. K. Hall,

1969 (LC 76-14771). First Supplement. 567 p., 1972. Second Supplement. 729 p., 1977.

This is one of the most extensive collections on modern Japan in the United States. It is especially strong in politics, economics, social conditions, and modern history, and has recently expanded its holdings of instructional and research materials on language, literature, religion, and art. There are also many books in Japanese about China. Books, pamphlets, periodicals, government documents, and many Japanese wartime publications are listed, all in the Japanese language. Western-language material about Japan is included in the Catalog of the Western Language Collections of the Hoover Institution on War, Revolution, and Peace (see 93).

This is a dictionary catalog. Library of Congress subject headings are used. The material is classified according to the modified Nippon Decimal Classification used by the National Diet Library of Japan. Almost all authors and titles are shown in both the original and the romanized forms.

215. Union Catalogue of Asian Publications 1965-1970. Edited by David E. Hall, compiled under the auspices of the Orientalists' Group, Standing Conference of National and University Libraries, sponsored by and edited at the School of Oriental and African Studies, University of London. 4 vols. London: Mansell, 1971 (LC 72-180434). 1971 Supplement. 1973.

This is a union catalog of works published in Asia and acquired by British libraries since 1965. The original catalog does not include accessions of the University of London's School of Oriental and African Studies, which publishes its own catalog (see 196), or of the Bodleian Library, Oxford. The supplement, however, does include entries for these libraries. Symbols for the owning libraries are supplied.

Included are works in all languages published in Asia outside the Soviet Union, and those in non-European scripts published in North and Northeast Africa, in all subjects except pure science. Monographs, reports, yearbooks, government documents, and microforms are all listed. Titles date mostly from 1960 to 1970, but some were published before that date.

This is a main-entry catalog. The editor has standardized the spelling of names, and followed the romanization practices of the Library of the School of Oriental and African Studies. The Anglo-American cataloging code is used with some modifications.

216. United States. Library of Congress. Far Eastern Division. Far Eastern Languages Catalog. 22 vols. Boston: G. K. Hall, 1972 (LC 72-5364).

This catalog represents works located in the Orientalia Division (now the Asian Division) of the Reference Department, as well as works in the Far Eastern Law Division of the Law Library of the Library of Congress. There are about 55,000 titles in Chinese, the same number in Japanese, and 11,000 titles in Korean, and these 121,000 works are represented in the catalog by about 332,000 cards.

While the Library of Congress aims to collect comprehensively in all subjects in Far Eastern languages, the collection is particularly strong in the humanities, social sciences, and law, with secondary strengths in scientific and technical works. The Korean collection's specialties are history, literature, economics, politics, law, and science, while the Chinese collection is best known for works on communism, law, history, archaeology, literature, and for its technical handbooks.

This is a dictionary catalog of authors, titles, and subjects. Either American Library Association (1949) or Anglo-American (1967) cataloging rules are used, along with Library of Congress subject headings and the Library of Congress classification. Chinese characters are romanized using the Wade-Giles system; Japanese characters are romanized with the modified Hepburn system; and McCune-Reischauer is used for Korean.

In 1958 the Library of Congress decided on a uniform set of descriptive cataloging rules for works in Chinese, Japanese, and Korean. Works cataloged before 1958 are not listed here or in the National Union Catalog.

217. United States. Library of Congress. Orientalia Division. Southeast Asia Subject Catalog. 6 vols. Boston: G. K. Hall, 1972 (LC 72-5257).

This is not an official catalog of the Library of Congress, but a catalog maintained for 25 years by the Southeast Asia section of the Orientalia Division (now the Asian Division). "It is essentially a subject catalog of bibliographic citations to books, pamphlets, journal articles, theses, microforms, and other materials dealing with Southeast Asia and written primarily in Western languages" [Introduction].

The countries defined as part of Southeast Asia and covered in the catalog are Brunei, Burma, Cambodia, Indonesia, Laos, Malaysia, the Philippines, Portuguese Timor (now part of Indonesia), Sabah and Sarawak (now part of Malaysia), Singapore, Thailand, and North and South Vietnam (now unified). All aspects of these countries are indexed, including economics, anthropology and sociology, politics, education, geography, history, health and medicine, language and literature, music and arts, religion and philosophy, natural sciences, and technology.

The catalog is arranged with a general section first, and then by country. Entries for each country are divided into a maximum of 41 different subjects, some of which are further subdivided. Most of the material is in English, with material in French a close second, and the dates of the items are, in the main, 1943-1969. Most of the entries are analytics from approximately 350 serials, and there are occasional annotations. The catalog has more than 76,000 cards.

218. Yale University. Library. Southeast Asia Collection. Checklist of Southeast Asian Serials, Southeast Asia Collection, Yale University Library. 320 p. Boston: G. K. Hall, 1968 (LC 76-31500).

Yale University began collecting material on Southeast Asia in 1899 and established its Southeast Asia Studies program in 1947. This catalog lists all serial titles in the Yale University Library published in the countries of Southeast Asia (Burma, Thailand, Laos, Cambodia, Philippines, Malaysia, Brunei, Singapore, and Indonesia), as well as those published in other countries that concern Southeast Asia. Over 3,800 serials are listed, including government publications and society publications. Also included are monograph and pamphlet series, for which a listing by author and title is provided.

The arrangement is by main entry. There is an index by country, with subject subdivisions. Most of the titles are of twentieth-century origin, and are in Romance, Germanic, Slavic, and Southeast Asian languages.

16. HAWAII AND THE PACIFIC

These catalogs are bibliographies of the exploration, history, anthropology, geology, and natural history of the continents and islands of the Pacific Ocean. The most comprehensive for the region as a whole is the Dictionary Catalog of Printed Books of the Mitchell Library in Sydney, Australia (223).

219. Bernice Pauahi Bishop Museum, Honolulu. Library. Dictionary Catalog of the Library. 9 vols. Boston: G. K. Hall, 1964 (LC 65-2405). First Supplement. 676 p., 1967. Second Supplement. 239 p., 1969.

The Bernice P. Bishop Museum Library specializes in the anthropology and natural history of the Pacific, emphasizing cultural anthropology, archaeology, botany, marine biology, malacology, geology, entomology, music, linguistics, astronomy, and bibliography. The First Supplement reflects improved zoological holdings, especially in entomology. The Second Supplement consists of the catalog of the Fuller Collection, purchased in 1963, of 2, 500 volumes on the exploration and history of the Pacific. Holdings in the original catalog include accounts of early Pacific voyages, texts in Pacific languages, manuscripts, maps, photographs, U. S. government publications, and documents of governments in the Pacific. It is particularly rich in analytics for many scholarly journals, local newspapers, Pacific regional magazines, and some books.

Subject headings used are modifications of Library of Congress headings. Works are mostly in English, with the exceptions being some European language publications and the Pacific texts mentioned above.

The Museum was named after a direct descendant of the monarch Kamehama I, Bernice Pauahi, who refused the Hawaiian throne to marry Charles Reed Bishop, the founder of the first bank in Hawaii. The Bishops planned the Museum to preserve the Hawaiian heritage, and it was begun after Bernice Pauahi's death in 1884.

220. California. University of California-Santa Cruz. University Library. Catalog of the South Pacific Collection. 722 p. Santa Cruz, Calif.: University Library, University of California, Santa Cruz, 1978 (LC 79-620747).

When the University of California at Santa Cruz was founded in the early 1960's, it was decided that the South Pacific would be an area of specialization; it was also decided that the library would use a computer-produced book catalog. The catalog described here consists of all the South Pacific material culled from the database of the library's collection. South Pacific is defined to include Polynesia, Melanesia, Micronesia, Australia, and New Zealand. Excluded are Western New Guinea, the Philippines, and Southeast Asia. The collection covers political, cultural, scientific, and economic development, and includes books, series, and government publications of South Pacific countries.

The catalog is in two parts: an Author-Title-Series Catalog, and a Subject Catalog. In the Author-Title-Series Catalog, main entries have full bibliographic information, including tracings; added entries give the title, call number, and a reference to the main entry. Library of Congress classification and subject headings are used. The catalog has approximately 8,500 titles, mostly in English, and mostly twentieth-century imprints.

221. Hawaii. University, Honolulu. Hawaiian Collection. Dictionary Catalog. 4 vols. Boston: G. K. Hall, 1963 (LC 65-22).

The Hawaiian Collection of the University of Hawaii's Sinclair Library was begun in 1908 and became a separate collection in 1927. It is probably the world's largest collection on Hawaii, with holdings (as of 1963) of 20,000 cataloged books and pamphlets. The library collects in all subjects as they relate to Hawaii, including its history, natural resources, agriculture, education, culture, geology, etc. Among the holdings are many accounts of early voyages and travels.

The University of Hawaii has been an official depository of Hawaiian government publications since 1915, and they are fully cataloged. There are analytics for University of Hawaii graduate theses and for all of the university's published series, including those of the Hawaii Agricultural Experiment Station and of the Cooperative Extension Service. Bishop Museum publications and Hawaiian Historical Society publications are also analyzed, as are some Hawaiian periodicals that are not indexed in any standard periodical indexes.

Library of Congress subject headings are used, together with supplementary headings developed for the collection. There are many see and see-also references.

London. University. School of Oriental and African Studies. Library. Library Catalogue. 28 vols. Boston: G. K. Hall, 1963. (see 196)

222. Nieves M. Flores Memorial Library. Union Catalog of the Guam Public Library, Guam and Pacific Area Materials:

Collections of the Guam Public Library and the Micronesian Area Research Center. Prepared by the staff of the Nieves M. Flores Memorial Library. 464 p. Agana, Guam: Nieves M. Flores Memorial Library, 1974 (LC 76-621252).

This is a union catalog of the special collections of the Nieves M. Flores Memorial Library, Guam Public Library, and the Micronesian Area Research Center of the University of Guam. The subject matter is the Pacific area in general and Guam in particular. Included are many government publications and research reports, as well as books.

This is a main-entry catalog. Each entry has full bibliographic information, including tracings. Both Library of Congress and the Dewey Decimal classifications are used. The catalog lists approximately 4,000 titles, most of them in English.

223. Sydney. Public Library of New South Wales. Mitchell Library. Dictionary Catalog of Printed Books. 38 vols. Boston: G. K. Hall, 1968 (ISBN 0-8161-0790-4). First Supplement. 837 p., 1970.

David Scott Mitchell was a book collector who first collected English literature, and then turned to collecting comprehensively the documentary record of Australia and the surrounding region. In 1907 he bequeathed his entire collection to the Public Library of New South Wales, the "national" library of the state. By July, 1967, the Mitchell Library contained 227,000 printed books, 16,700 volumes of manuscripts, 7,700 microfilm reels, and 53,000 maps. Generally, maps, pictures, and portraits are not included in the printed catalog.

The principal subject matter of the Mitchell Library is Australia and the adjacent region, extending from the Philippines and Hawaii to the Antarctic, and from Easter Island to Sumatra. The emphasis is on Australia, New Zealand, and the Pacific Islands, including their history, geography, natural history, and anthropology. The rich holdings on anthropology and the native peoples of the area are illustrated by the fact that there are 136 pages of entries on the Maoris, and 143 pages of entries on Australian aborigines.

This is a dictionary catalog compiled under the cataloging rules of the Public Library of New South Wales. Many of the entries are handwritten, and the quality of the cataloging is uneven. The library uses its own subject headings, and there are many cross-references. The collection is classified by the Dewey Classification, 12th edition, with special expansions and adaptations for Australia. There are many analytical entries for articles in periodicals and essays and chapters in books.

Works were published from the fifteenth century to the 1960's and are mostly in English.

17. AFRICAN AND BLACK STUDIES

This chapter describes library collections on Blacks in Africa and in the Americas. Most of the catalogs, in fact, list titles by or about Blacks irrespective of nationality.

The largest collection described here is the Jesse E. Moorland Collection of Negro Life and History (236), which contains works by and about people of African descent around the world. The Arthur B. Spingarn Collection of Negro Authors (235), now part of the Moorland-Spingarn Foundation, lists works by Black authors on any subject in any language. The Schomburg Collection of The New York Public Library (242) is very similar to the Moorland Collection, but cataloging practices here have emphasized detailed subject cataloging, and more subject entries are provided for each title than may be found in most catalogs.

Periodical indexing of works by and about Blacks is provided by two published library catalogs. Post-1950 articles are indexed by the work now titled Index to Periodical Articles By and About Blacks (238); the indexing is done at the Hallie Q. Brown Library of Central State University in Wilberforce, Ohio. A catalog of pre-1940 periodical articles and books in Chicago libraries (228) was compiled as a WPA project and housed in the Vivian G. Harsh Collection of Afro-American History and Literature. This published catalog is probably the best source for finding periodical articles about Blacks published before 1940.

A particularly interesting and unusual catalog of Black studies is the Catalog of the Old Slave Mart Museum and Library (243), which lists (besides books) periodicals, documents, slides, photographs, and realia--mostly with very detailed cataloging information provided.

Also listed in this chapter are catalogs solely on Africa, the most important being the Catalog of the Melville J. Herskovits Library (241), an author-title catalog, and the Classified Catalog of the Africa Section of the Musée de l'homme, in Paris (244).

224. Amistad Research Center. Author and Added Entry Catalog of the American Missionary Association Archives. 3 vols. Westport, Conn.: Greenwood Pub. Corp., 1970 (LC 72-104397).

The Amistad Research Center in New Orleans "is a historical research library devoted to the collection and use of primary source materials on the history of America's ethnic minorities, with particular emphasis on Afro-Americans, American Indians, and immigrant groups."[23] Among its collections are the archives of the American Missionary Association. The Association was founded in 1846. Its aim was the abolition of slavery by peaceful means, and after the Civil War it worked to establish schools among American Blacks in the South. These archives related primarily to the abolitionist movement, conditions in the South, schools for freedmen, denominational rivalries, and criticism of the war and reconstructionist policies of the government. Members of the Association also acted as missionaries to Indians and to Chinese immigrants in California.

This is a catalog of manuscript items. Letters of members of the Association predominate, but account books, reports, and essays are also included. The catalog lists 105,000 of the 250,000 items that have been processed by the Amistad Research Center; there are 350,000 items in the collection. The entries are arranged by author of the item in question, with some cross-references by subject. The period covered is, in the main, 1839-1882.

225. Atlanta University. Trevor-Arnett Library. Black Culture Collection Catalog: United States Section; the Black Experience in America since the 17th Century. 3 vols. Wooster, Ohio: Micro Photo Div., Bell and Howell, 1974.

This is a catalog of 6,000 titles which are a part of the Negro Collection in the Trevor-Arnett Library at Atlanta University and are available as a microfilm collection from Bell and Howell. The Negro Collection grew from the 10,000 items, purchased by Atlanta University in 1946, that were collected by the Black bibliophile Henry P. Slaughter. Emphasis is on Black studies, especially the study of Blacks in the United States. Included in the catalog is the Tuttle pamphlet collection, which focuses on the anti-slavery movement in the United States and the British Commonwealth. Books, reports of societies, speeches, Atlanta University master's theses, and Atlanta University publications can all be found in the catalog. Emphasis is on the nineteenth century, but many twentieth-century works are also included.

The catalog is in three parts. Volume one is an Author Catalog that includes joint authors, editors, illustrators, corporate authors, and title main entries. The main-entry cards give full bibliographic information, including tracings. Volume two, the Title Catalog, lists the title and main entry only, and serves primarily as a title index to volume one. Volume three, Subjects, gives full bibliographic information but omits the tracings. Works are cataloged according to Anglo-American Cataloging Rules and Library of Congress practice. Library of Congress subject headings are used. Works about individuals are included in the Subject

Catalog. There are many see and see-also references in both the Author and Subject Catalogs.

226. Boston University. Libraries. Catalog of African Government Documents. Third edition, revised and enlarged, 679 p. Boston: G. K. Hall, 1976 (LC 77-362336).

The African documents collection was begun in 1953 when the Boston University African Studies Program was started. The catalog includes government documents of the different countries of Africa, arranged by country according to a modification of the Library of Congress classification J700-J881 for African states. There is an alphabetical index of countries included. Also found in the catalog are British government documents and publications of pan-African organizations, of the United Nations, and of other international bodies. The documents are in English and French. 13,000 titles are listed, many of them serials.

227. Chicago. Public Library. Vivian G. Harsh Collection. The Dictionary Catalog of the Vivian G. Harsh Collection of Afro-American History and Literature, The Chicago Public Library. 4 vols. Boston: G. K. Hall, 1978 (ISBN 0-8161-0252-X).

The Afro-American Collection was begun in 1932 by Vivian G. Harsh, for whom it was later named. It covers all phases of Afro-American life and culture and some areas of Africana. The collection is especially strong in religion, sociology, politics and education, art, music, literature and drama, biography, Afro-American and Afro-Caribbean history, and Chicago Afro-American history. Included in the catalog and the collection is the Charlemae Hill Rollins Collection of Children's Literature.

The first three volumes of the catalog and most of the fourth volume are a catalog of books, listing over 20,000 titles. This is a dictionary catalog of authors, titles, and subjects. Library of Congress subject headings are used, as are both Library of Congress and Dewey classification systems.

The fourth volume of the catalog includes several separate catalogs or indexes. First is a Biographical Index, arranged by the subject of the biography. This contains references to pages in books where biographical information about the individual appears. Some of the entries have annotations. About 350 individuals are included. Second are indexes to records of the U. S. Committee on Fair Employment Practice (1943-1946), available in the library on microfilm. There is a separate catalog of The Heritage Press Archives, which consist of original manuscripts by 33 leading Afro-American poets who published works in the London-based Heritage Poetry Series during the 1960's. Also included is a catalog of the Illinois Writers Project Collection. Finally, there are separate catalogs of recordings, of cassettes, and of periodical titles.

228. The Chicago Afro-American Union Analytic Catalog: An Index to Materials on the Afro-American in the Principal Libraries of Chicago, Housed in the Vivian G. Harsh Collection of Afro-American History and Literature at the George Cleveland Hall Branch of the Chicago Public Library. 5 vols. Boston: G. K. Hall, 1972 (LC 75-315725).

The Chicago Afro-American Union Analytic Catalog began as a WPA project aimed "to develop a definitive bibliography of Afro-American literature in the United States from early times to 1940, using the resources, excluding newspapers, found in the principal libraries of Chicago" [Introduction]. As such, it is a dictionary catalog containing more than 75,000 entries for books, speeches, pamphlets, yearbooks, agency reports, theses, and articles in more than 1,000 foreign and domestic periodicals, from the late 1800's to 1940. Most entries include annotations. Book reviews are arranged by the book's author under the heading "Book Reviews," as well as after both the main entry and the title entry for the book.

The catalog covers every element of Afro-American life, excluding works about Africa. The chief drawback to this remarkable index lies in the fact that the subject headings were locally developed and are poorly controlled, with no list of subject headings, and no cross-references. But the information made available by this catalog is certainly worth the effort involved in locating the correct subject heading.

229. Detroit. Public Library. E. Azalia Hackley Collection. Catalog of the E. Azalia Hackley Memorial Collection of Negro Music, Dance, and Drama. 510 p. Boston: G. K. Hall, 1979 (ISBN 0-8161-0299-6).

This collection was established in 1943 through the efforts of the Detroit Musicians Association, local chapter of the National Association of Negro Musicians, and was later named to honor Madame E. Azalia Hackley, a Detroit musician who was a teacher, singer, choral director, and humanitarian with particular interest in providing opportunities for talented Black musicians. The collection originally emphasized Negro folksongs, especially spirituals, and the accomplishments of Black concert artists, but it now includes the whole field of Black music, particularly jazz and blues, as well as Blacks in dance and drama.

In 1979 the collection included 2,000 books, 1,600 scores, 2,050 pieces of sheet music, 2,200 recordings, 1,350 vertical file folders, and 2,000 pamphlets. The recordings and some of the vertical file materials are not listed in this catalog of approximately 12,000 cards. The catalog is in four parts. Part I, the catalog of books of music scores, is a dictionary catalog of author, title, and subject entries, with full cataloging information for both books and music. Following this are separate shelf lists of books and of music. Part II is an Historic Sheet Music Index, an alphabetically arranged composer-title index to sheet music by Black composers.

The composer cards provide full publishing information. Part III, Broadsides and Posters, is an alphabetical listing of these materials by performing artist, title of the production, and/or sponsoring organization. The main entry includes content, dates, form, and other characteristics. Part IV is an index of photographs arranged first by name of individual performer and second by title of production, with many cross-references.

Works are mostly in English, but some material in French, Spanish, and other foreign languages is included.

230. Dinstel, Marion. List of French Doctoral Dissertations on Africa, 1884-1961. With indexes by Mary Darrah Herrick. 336 p. Boston: G. K. Hall, 1966 (LC 68-367).

This is a catalog maintained at the African Document Center of Boston University Libraries. However, items included in it are not necessarily in the Boston University Libraries. Items listed here are, as the title states, doctoral dissertations, in French, on the subject of Africa. The arrangement is by country or area in Africa, and then alphabetically by author. There is an author index and a very broad subject index. The list was compiled by Marion Dinstel from the following:

Ministère de l'Education Nationale. Direction des Bibliothèques de France. Catalogue des Thèses de Doctorat Soutenues Devant les Universités Françaises.

French Cultural Service of New York. French Doctoral Theses. Sciences, 1951-53. (French bibliographical digest series in various subjects, Series III, No. 1) Dec., 1955.

231. Fisk University, Nashville. Library. Dictionary Catalog of the Negro Collection of the Fisk University Library, Nashville, Tennessee. 6 vols. Boston: G. K. Hall, 1974 (LC 75-304596).

Fisk University was founded in 1866 for "the education and training of young men and women irrespective of color" [Introduction]. Its library began collecting materials about Blacks in 1929. During the 1930's, Arthur A. Schomburg, whose personal collection formed the nucleus of The New York Public Library's Schomburg Center for Research in Black Culture (see 242), was curator of the Negro Collection.

The catalog includes 35,000 volumes and pamphlets on Blacks in America, Africa, and the West Indies. Listed are rare books, cataloged microforms, journals, recordings, Fisk University masters' theses, theses from other universities, and some African and West Indian government documents. There are no analytical entries for books or journals, and the material is primarily in English.

This is a dictionary catalog, using Library of Congress

subject headings. However, when LC-printed cards are used, the library will sometimes add subject headings to those the Library of Congress has assigned. Older material is cataloged in the Dewey Decimal classification and newer material in the Library of Congress classification.

232. Freetown, Sierra Leone. Fourah Bay College. Library. Catalog of the Sierra Leone Collection, Fourah Bay College Library, University of Sierra Leone. 411 p. Boston: G. K. Hall, 1979 (LC 78-25759).

Fourah Bay College was founded in 1827 and joined with Njala University College in 1966 to form the University of Sierra Leone. The Sierra Leone Collection was established as a separate collection in 1964. Included in it is material by Sierra Leoneans and about Sierra Leone, namely books, seminar papers, periodicals, newspapers, and unpublished materials such as missionary journals and account books. There are many analytical entries for articles in selected periodicals and for periodical reprints.

The catalog is arranged by subjects, which are listed in the Table of Contents, and by author within each subject. See-also references link subjects, and an author index is included. Generally there is only one entry for each item. The classification system that the library uses is Dewey Decimal. Works are mostly in English but also in French, Portuguese, Dutch, Spanish, German, Arabic, and African languages. Titles of periodicals and newspapers held are listed separately at the end of the catalog.

233. Hampton Institute, Hampton, Va. Collis P. Huntington Memorial Library. Dictionary Catalog of the George Foster Peabody Collection of Negro Literature and History. 2 vols. Westport, Conn.: Greenwood, 1972.

This is a collection of 15,000 items "by and about the black man," including 11,500 monographs and more than 1,700 pamphlets and documents on slavery and reconstruction in the United States. Photographs, vertical file materials, phonograph records, and paintings are not included in the catalog. The emphasis of the collection is on the nineteenth century, particularly the American Civil War, and works are primarily in English. Library of Congress subject headings are used in this dictionary catalog.

234. Harvard University. Library. African History and Literatures. 600 p. Cambridge, Mass.: distributed by Harvard University Press, 1971 (LC 70-128716). (Widener Library Shelflist v. 34)

Like the other volumes making up the series of Widener Library shelflists, this catalog is in three parts: a classified arrangement by call number, a chronological arrangement, and an author-title listing. In this case the classes covered are the Afr class and the Afr Doc class. The Afr class was originally published as volume two of the Widener Library shelflist but has increased in size by one-third in five years and now totals about 18, 800 titles, while Afr Doc contains about 1, 200 documents.

The Afr class includes works on history, civilization and government, general geography and travel, general social and economic conditions, literature, religious affairs, and the various peoples of the continent of Africa. However, not included are works on the ancient period in North Africa, works on some specific aspects of social and economic conditions (such as crime and agriculture), Afrikaans literature, literatures in the Semitic and Hamitic languages of North Africa, and African literature cataloged before 1960.

About half of the entries are in English, with a large number in French, followed by German and other languages, mostly European.

For more information about the Widener Library shelflists, see 9.

235. Howard University. Washington, D. C. Library. Dictionary Catalog of the Arthur B. Spingarn Collection of Negro Authors. 2 vols. Boston: G. K. Hall, 1970 (LC 72-187159).

The basis of this library is the collection of Arthur Barnett Spingarn, a New York attorney, who at first collected works by Black authors to prove to his friends the intellectual capacity of Blacks, and then became a collector of whatever he could find written by Blacks in any language and on any subject. His collection was acquired by Howard University in 1946 but was added to by Spingarn until 1968. It is now part of the Moorland-Spingarn Research Center (see 236).

The collection contains books, pamphlets, bound volumes and single issues of periodicals, and ephemera, such as programs, invitations, mimeographed speeches, and letters. There are hundreds of analytics for journal articles and for essays in books. Most of the works are on concerns of Blacks, but the subject matter is not limited to this. Of particular interest are early Afro-American writings, slave narratives, and Caribbean, Afro-Cuban, and Afro-Brazilian literature.[24]

This is a dictionary catalog, in which Library of Congress subject headings are used, with some additions. There are many added entries for Black illustrators, translators, editors, and compilers. There is also a separate music catalog at the end.

236. Howard University, Washington, D. C. Library. Moorland Foundation. Dictionary Catalog of the Jesse E. Moorland Collection of Negro Life and History, Howard University, Washington, D. C. 9 vols. Boston: G. K. Hall, 1970 (LC 72-195773). First Supplement. 3 vols., 1976.

Howard University was incorporated in 1867. Its library grew as a result of several major donations, including that of Dr. Jesse Edward Moorland, who donated his private library in 1914 and continued to contribute material until his death in 1940. As of 1970 the library had 105,000 cataloged and indexed items by and about people of African descent around the world. In 1973 the Moorland-Spingarn Collection (see also 235) was re-organized as the Moorland-Spingarn Research Center, made independent of the University Library system, and expanded to include an Archives and Museum, the Ralph J. Bunche Oral History Collection, and the Black Press Archives, which are not included, however, in the published catalogs. "The Moorland-Spingarn Research Center is recognized as one of the largest and most comprehensive repositories in the world for the collection, preservation, and dissemination of historical materials documenting from antiquity to the present the history and culture of Black people in Africa, Europe, the Caribbean and the U.S."[25]

The primary strength of this collection is Black life in America, although its holdings of material on African studies are being developed. It has a large anti-slavery collection, and is also especially rich in works of Afro-American and African scholars, statesmen, poets, and novelists, and in autobiographical and biographical works. It has one of the finest collections of Black newspapers and magazines from the early nineteenth century to the present. Included in the catalog are books, pamphlets, journal articles, speeches in newspapers, plays, and sheet music. Manuscripts, phonograph records, tapes, microforms, and vertical file materials are not included. Works are primarily in English.

This is a dictionary catalog, and Library of Congress subject headings are used without modification. Volume nine of the 1970 catalog contains three separate indexes: 1) an index to the names of African periodicals by titles and by subjects; 2) an index to the names of Black American periodicals, also by title and by subject, with many editors being treated as subjects; and 3) an index to brief biographies (generally one or two pages) appearing in books and periodicals.

237. Ibadan, Nigeria. University. Library. Africana Catalogue of the Ibadan University Library, Ibadan, Nigeria. 2 vols. Boston: G. K. Hall, 1973 (LC 73-180196).

The Africana Catalogue is an author catalog, with some title entries, and as such is most useful for locating copies of known works about Africa. The collection includes rare books; pamphlets, including church and political pamphlets; missionary magazines; newspapers; government documents; microfilms; theses; and unpublished manuscripts. There are occasional analytical entries for series and for reprinted journal articles. The library holds the private libraries of Dr. Henry Carr, a Nigerian educator and churchman, and Herbert Macaulay, "the Father of Nigerian Nationalism." Since 1950, the library has received copies of everything published in Nigeria. The vast majority of the works listed in the catalog are in English. The classification system used is the Bliss Bibliographic Classification.

The library will provide photocopies and microfilm copies for inter-library loan purposes.

238. Index to Selected Periodicals Received in the Hallie Q. Brown Library; Decennial Cumulation, 1950-1959. Edited by Charlotte W. Lytle. 501 p. Boston: G. K. Hall, 1961 (ISBN 0-8161-0503-0).

Index to Periodical Articles By and About Negroes; Cumulated 1960-1970. Compiled by the staffs of the Hallie Q. Brown Memorial Library, Central State University, Wilberforce, Ohio and the Schomburg Collection, The New York Public Library. 606 p. Boston: G. K. Hall, 1971 (ISBN 0-8161-0847-1).

Index to Periodical Articles By and About Negroes, 1971. Compiled by the staff of the Hallie Q. Brown Memorial Library, Central State University, Wilberforce, Ohio. 543 p. Boston: G. K. Hall, 1973 (ISBN 0-8161-0869-2). Annual, 1972.

Index to Periodical Articles By and About Blacks, 1973- . Boston: G. K. Hall.

These indexes have undergone some changes in title and in indexing organizations (for ten years the Schomburg Collection of The New York Public Library joined the Hallie Q. Brown Library in producing the index) but the content has remained the same. They are indexes to periodical articles by and about Blacks. Popular periodicals aimed at Black audiences, such as Ebony and Jet, as well as scholarly journals devoted to Black studies, such as the Journal of Negro History, are indexed. An attempt is made to index journals not covered elsewhere. Some journal titles are indexed selectively, others comprehensively.

Subject strengths include women, pan-Africanism, education, medicine, music, theatre, slavery, civil rights, segregation, and discrimination.

The index includes, in one alphabet, authors, subjects, and some titles of creative works. Library of Congress subject headings are used. Reviews and obituaries are given extensive coverage; book reviews are listed under "Book Reviews," movie reviews under "Motion Picture Reviews," etc. There are many cross-references. Since 1971 the index has been produced by computer, and the coverage has expanded. Unfortunately, the computer type is all capitals and is rather unsightly and difficult to read.

239. International African Institute. Library. Cumulative Bibliography of African Studies: Author Catalogue. 2 vols. Boston: G. K. Hall, 1973 (LC 74-154305).

________. Cumulative Bibliography of African Studies: Classified Catalogue. 3 vols. Boston: G. K. Hall, 1973 (LC 74-154303).

This catalog is essentially a card index that was compiled in the Library of the International African Institute in London. Most of the entries are for books and articles that were listed in the quarterly bibliography published in the journal Africa, 1929-1970, and in the International African Bibliography, 1971-72. Also included are works in the Institute's small library and those gleaned from other published bibliographies. Whole runs of some journals have been indexed. Most of the works appeared in this century and are in English and other Western languages, although some works in African languages are included.

The subject matter is tropical Africa south of the Sahara, with an emphasis on human studies in general and anthropology and linguistics in particular.

The catalog is in two parts. The Author Catalogue, in two volumes, includes added entries for joint authors and biographies, and also indexes book reviews. The Classified Catalogue, in three volumes, is arranged into eight geographical regions, with further subdividions by area and country. The tables of contents at the beginning of each volume list the geographic arrangement. Within each geographic area the arrangement is alphabetical by broad subject. At the end of volume three there is an index to the subject headings used, with cross-references. Also listed in this index are names of different African ethnic groups with a reference to the geographic area each is listed under. The catalog has been edited from time to time to attempt conformity with Anglo-American cataloging rules. Entries appear in both the Author and Classified Catalogues, and sometimes in more than one section of the Classified Catalogue.

240. Lincoln University. Vail Memorial Library. Catalog of the Special Negro and African Collection, Vail Memorial Library, Lincoln University, Pennsylvania. 2 vols. Lincoln, Pa., 1970.

Included in this catalog are 8,300 titles on all aspects of the Black experience, including slavery and the slave trade; missionary and colonizing efforts; anthropological and sociological studies of Black societies; and history, literature, language, art, music, dance, religion, psychology, science, and the civil rights struggle. Many rare books and first editions are listed, but vertical file material and photographs are omitted from the catalog.

The catalog is in three parts. Volume one contains an author catalog and a title catalog. Volume two is the subject catalog, which contains 6,000 subject headings taken from the Library of Congress list of subject headings and from those used in the Schomburg collection (see 242), with some local modifications. Each entry provides only brief bibliographical information--chiefly author, title, publisher and date of publication, and Library of Congress classification number.

The library is now known as the Langston Hughes Memorial Library.

London. University. School of Oriental and African Studies. Library. Library Catalogue. 28 vols. Boston: G. K. Hall, 1963. (see 196)

241. Melville J. Herskovits Library of African Studies. Catalog of the Melville J. Herskovits Library of African Studies, Northwestern University Library (Evanston, Illinois) and Africana in Selected Libraries. 8 vols. Boston: G. K. Hall, 1972 (LC 73-151178). First Supplement. 6 vols., 1978.

This is primarily an author-title catalog, useful for locating known materials. The Herskovits Library attempts to obtain all publications from sub-Saharan or tropical Africa, and purchases only selectively from South Africa and from northern Africa. The catalog covers all aspects of Africa, including African literature. African government documents and official publications of colonial governments, rare books, microforms, periodicals, pamphlets, and ephemera are all included. The catalog includes items from the Joint Acquisitions List of Africana (JALA) and gives locations for those items which the Herskovits Library does not own. The supplement is in two parts: volumes one to four list works to be found in the Herskovits Library, and volumes five to six are those reported in the Joint Acquisitions List.

242. New York (City). Public Library. Schomburg Collection of Negro Literature and History. Dictionary Catalog of the Schomburg Collection of Negro Literature and History. 9 vols. Boston: G. K. Hall, 1962 (LC 66-1573). First Supplement. 2 vols., 1967. Second Supplement. 4 vols., 1972. Supplement 1974. 580 p., 1976. Further supplemented by Bibliographic Guide to Black Studies: 1975- . Boston: G. K. Hall, 1976- .

The basis of the Schomburg Collection (now called the Schomburg Center for Research in Black Culture) was the private library of Arthur A. Schomburg, a Puerto Rican of African descent, whose goal was to find all the evidence he could that the "Negro had a long and honorable past." As of 1962, the Schomburg Collection had more than 36,000 bound volumes, more than half of which concerned Africa. The First Supplement listed another 7,000 titles, and the Second Supplement 15,000 more. The specialization of the library is the literature, history, and art of all peoples of African descent. It is thus not limited to Blacks in the United States, but is world-wide in scope. Works are in English, French, German, Spanish, and other languages.

This is a dictionary catalog that uses Library of Congress

subject headings supplemented by the library's own. When LC-printed cards are used, subject headings are often added to those the Library of Congress has assigned; one of the library's major objectives is to provide good subject access to the collection. Included in the catalog are British and United States government documents, some state documents, rare books, pamphlets, local (New York City) and Southern newspapers, microfilm, sheet music, and records. Manuscripts, photographs, and vertical file materials are not included in the catalog and, unlike the other catalogs of The New York Public Library, journals are not analyzed.

243. Old Slave Mart Museum and Library. Catalog of the Old Slave Mart Museum and Library, Charleston, South Carolina. 2 vols. Boston: G. K. Hall, 1978 (LC 78-104755).

The Old Slave Mart Museum collection was begun in the 1930's by Miriam B. Wilson, who came to Charleston, South Carolina on a visit from her home in Ohio and stayed to collect information and material on Charleston history and the Negro heritage. She was especially interested in collecting slave handicrafts and comparing them with African handicrafts. Besides the handicrafts, the collection came to include field notes, card files, photographs, and similar material on Black history, the slave trade, South Carolina history, civil rights, and twentieth-century Black artists.

The cataloging of the collection was for the most part completed in a year and a half under a Federal grant, and the resulting catalog is consistent in its practices, and contains generous tracings and cross-references. There are actually ten separate catalogs for 1) books and pamphlets; 2) periodicals; 3) documents; 4) maps; 5) realia; 6) vertical files and ephemera; 7) audio-visual materials; 8) slides; 9) photographs; and 10) flatwork (pictorial materials). Some of the catalogs are in dictionary form and some are divided. The subject headings are in some cases based on Library of Congress headings and in some cases on Miriam B. Wilson's own subject headings, depending upon the needs of the material. Some of the cataloging is incredibly detailed; for example, the slide catalog lists not collections of slides but individual transparencies, with information on the subject of the slide and its source.

Of particular interest is the catalog of realia, which describes museum artifacts, including toys, tools, clothing, musical instruments, etc.

244. Paris. Musée de l'homme. Bibliothèque. Catalogue systématique de la section Afrique (Classified Catalog of the Africa Section). 2 vols. Boston: G. K. Hall, 1970 (LC 72-15420).

The Musée de l'homme was established in 1877, but its library did not begin to function effectively until 1931. At the time of publication of the catalog the library consisted of approximately 180,000 volumes. The Africa section, of which this is the catalog, contains approximately 8,000 books and periodicals.

This is a classified catalog arranged by the Library of Congress classification system, as modified by the library of the Musée de l'homme. Since this is a catalog on Africa, most of the material falls into the DT class, with an additional section on African prehistory in GN. The library is particularly rich in ethnographic material, and there is a special category, DT15, that contains ethnographic accounts of various ethnic and tribal groups, arranged alphabetically by name of the group. This category includes journal articles and pamphlets, and there are some cross-references to help find the correct form of the group's name. Arrangement of the rest of the DT class is primarily by country, and within country as follows: periodicals, bibliography, linguistics, general works, description and travel, archaeology, ethnology (further subdivided into subjects), history, local history and description, and last, a separate section for pamphlets. Many items are given two classification numbers to enable them to appear in more than one section of the catalog.

Material is primarily in French, although there is an abundance of English-language publications.

245. Philadelphia. Library Company. Afro-Americana, 1553-1906: Author Catalog of the Library Company of Philadelphia and the Historical Society of Pennsylvania. 714 p. Boston: G. K. Hall, 1973 (LC 73-15908).

The Library Company of Philadelphia was founded in 1731 and the Historical Society of Pennsylvania in 1824. The combined value of their collections in Afro-Americana was discovered during a joint exhibition of books on "Negro History, 1553-1903," and as a result of that exhibition and with grants from the Ford Foundation and the Pennsylvania Abolition Society, this catalog was prepared.

The subject matter of the collection is Blacks, slavery and the anti-slavery movement, African exploration, and works written by Blacks, which are preceded by an asterisk in the test. Books, pamphlets, broadsides, and manuscripts are included, but not maps, prints, or government documents.

The catalog is in three sections: 1) Books and Pamphlets, with 11,466 entries; 2) Manuscripts, with 4,952 entries; and 3) Broadsides, with 180 entries. Each section is alphabetically arranged by author. The section on books and pamphlets has its own subject index of very broad subjects.

246. Texas Southern University. Library. Catalogue: Heartman Negro Collection, Texas Southern University. 325 p. Houston, Texas: Texas Southern University, 1956 (Its Library News Notes, v. 5, no. 12).

This collection was purchased during the early years of Texas Southern University from Mr. Charles Heartman, a book dealer.

It is "perhaps the largest and most important collection on the Negro to be found in the Southwestern section of the United States" [Introduction]. The collection has 15,000 items, including 6,000 books, 5,000 pamphlets, newspapers, broadsides, maps, and other items. However, only about 5,000 items appear in this catalog. The emphasis is on the background and development of Black people, principally in the United States, but also around the world. Works date from 1600 to 1955, but were printed mostly in the late nineteenth or early twentieth century.

The catalog is arranged by the Dewey Decimal classification system. Entries are brief and give only author, title, publisher, and date of publication.

247. United States. Library of Congress. African Section. Africa South of the Sahara: Index to Periodical Literature, 1900-1970. 4 vols. Boston: G. K. Hall, 1971 (LC 74-170939). First Supplement. 591 p., 1973.

The African Section of the Library of Congress was established in 1960, and is now part of the African and Middle Eastern Division. This is its catalog of journal articles on Africa. It contains entries from several major indexes interfiled with citations prepared by the Library of Congress and by international organizations. Among these organizations are the Centre d'Analyse et de Recherche Documentaires pour l'Afrique Noire (CARDAN), Paris; the Centre International de Documentation Economique et Sociale Africaine (CIDESA), Brussels; and the Fondation Nationale des Sciences Politiques, Paris. The catalog's Introduction emphasizes that it should be used as a supplement to, rather than a substitute for, standard periodical indexes.

The emphasis of the catalog is on international relations, arts, anthropology and ethnology, language and linguistics, economics, politics, and history of sub-Saharan Africa. Most of the citations are for articles published in scholarly journals in Africa, Asia, Europe, and North America, but citations to essays and papers delivered at international conferences are included. Titles are in Western European languages, and most of the items were published after 1960.

The arrangement is by geographic region of Africa and by subject within region. Each volume has a table of contents in the front consisting of an alphabetical list of the subject headings. There is a literary index at the end of the fourth volume with references to 3,000 African literary works. The First Supplement includes an author index and a list of the names of ethnic groups used in both the original catalog and the supplement.

248. University of Rhodesia. Library. Catalogue of the C. M. Doke Collection on African Languages in the Library of the University of Rhodesia. 546 p. Boston: G. K. Hall, 1972 (LC 72-2074).

This catalog contains the records of the collection of books of C. M. Doke, a distinguished professor of Bantu languages. More than 3,000 books, pamphlets, and manuscripts on and in African languages are described in approximately 7,000 cards.

The catalog is in two parts. The author section contains main entries, title entries, added entries, and cross-references. The subject section is arranged by the Library of Congress classification system; the call numbers represented are chiefly PL8000-8844, which is the classification for African languages and literature.

The University of Rhodesia is now named the University of Zimbabwe; it is located in Salisbury, Zimbabwe.

18. WOMEN'S STUDIES

These three catalogs on the history of women and the women's movement represent fascinating collections of books, periodicals and periodical articles, and documentary materials. Each of the three catalogs uses unique classification and cataloging systems, and none are particularly easy to use. Of the three, the Schlesinger Library catalog (249) is probably the least complicated, since most of the monographic material is listed in a dictionary catalog that uses Library of Congress subject headings. The collection focuses on the history of women in America.

The Sophia Smith Collection (251) is the largest, and while its emphasis is also on the history of women in the United States, its coverage is international. The subject headings take some getting used to, but the effort is worthwhile.

The Catalogue of the Library of the International Archive for the Women's Movement in Amsterdam (250) is the most truly cosmopolitan of the three catalogs, but its subject catalog is extraordinarily difficult to use.

249. Arthur and Elizabeth Schlesinger Library on the History of Women in America. The Manuscript Inventories and the Catalogs of Manuscripts, Books and Pictures. 3 vols. Boston: G. K. Hall, 1973 (LC 74-176020).

This is the catalog of a major collection of source material on the history of women in America, maintained at Radcliffe College, Cambridge, Massachusetts. The collection grew from a 1943 donation by Maud Wood Park of the papers of approximately 100 suffrage leaders, plus books, pamphlets, banners, pictures, and memorabilia. It was later built upon by Arthur M. Schlesinger. The library is devoted to the history of women in America, but running throughout the catalogs is an emphasis on a variety of social issues: the anti-slavery movement, temperance, prison reform, settlement houses, and the work of organized charities.

These three volumes contain six separate catalogs: the Book Catalog, the Etiquette Catalog, the Periodicals Catalog, the Manuscript Catalog, the Manuscript Inventories, and the Picture Catalog.

The Book Catalog, in volumes one and two, is a dictionary catalog of books, pamphlets, reports, and some reprints of journal articles. Standard Library of Congress subject headings are used, but most of the cataloging is original and there is a tendency towards using broad headings, such as "Anthropology" or "Business." There are many see and see-also references.

The library has a cookbook collection, which is included in the Book Catalog, and an etiquette collection, which has its own separate main-entry catalog in volume two.

Holdings of many full runs of periodicals--including recent ones of the women's movement--underground papers, and newsletters are listed in the separate Periodicals Catalog, in volume two.

Included in the Manuscript Catalog are the papers of women pioneers in the "men's professions" of medicine, law, government administration, social service, and higher education. The Manuscript Catalog has cards for manuscripts, microfilms, and tapes. There is a main-entry card for each manuscript collection, plus cards for individuals mentioned in the collection; i.e., there are entries for all famous individuals and for all individuals represented by sizable numbers of documents in a collection. There are also subject cards indicating which manuscript collections have information on those subjects.

The Manuscript Inventories are arranged by name of manuscript collection, and list in some detail the contents of each collection. There are 200 major collections, many smaller collections about individual women, and 31 archives of important women's organizations. The Manuscript Inventories, the Manuscript Catalog, and a separate Picture Catalog make up the third volume of this set.

In general, the period covered by the library's collections is the nineteenth and twentieth centuries, and works are mostly in English.

250. Internationaal Archief voor de Vrouwenbeweging. Catalogue of the Library of the International Archives for the Women's Movement, Amsterdam. 3 vols. Boston: G. K. Hall, 1980 (ISBN 0-8161-0287-2).

The International Archive of the Women's Movement was founded in 1935 by prominent individuals in the Dutch women's movement "to collect and keep all material that was published both nationally and internationally pertaining to the women's movement, ... to facilitate the study and promote the knowledge of the history of the women's movement, and to document discrimination against women" [Preface]. Included as part of the study of women's lives and the women's movement are such subjects as marriage, family life, art, rape, and women's organizations. Most of the works are twentieth-century imprints, including a significant amount of material from the early years of the century. Titles are mostly in Dutch, German, or English.

This catalog lists the book collection of the archive, including pamphlets, leaflets, essays, and conference papers. There are some analytics for articles in books and papers appearing in conference proceedings.

The catalog is in two sections. First is an author catalog,

listing works under the name of the author or joint author (for up to three joint authors), or under title for anonymous works or works with more than three authors. The second part is a classified, or systematic catalog. The classification system was developed by the library and is a simple and logical one, but the classified catalog is almost impossible to use. Outlines of the classification are provided in both English and Dutch, along with the decimal classification numbers, but the classification numbers do not appear on the catalog cards themselves. Nor do the numbers or the subjects appear as running headings on each page of the classified catalog. Nor, finally, does the outline of the classification system indicate on what page a particular subject begins. It is extraordinarily difficult, therefore, to move from the outline of the classification to the entries for a particular subject. There is also a subject index to the classification in both Dutch and English, arranged alphabetically only by the Dutch terms. This index does not refer you to the classification numbers used for a particular subject, but only to the exact term used for that subject in the outline of the classification system. The index has little relationship to the catalog itself.

The material listed in the catalog is quite interesting; it is a pity it is so hard to use the subject approach to it.

251. Sophia Smith Collection. Catalogs of the Sophia Smith Collection, Women's History Archive, Smith College, Northampton, Massachusetts. 7 vols. Boston: G. K. Hall, 1975 (LC 76-358485).

The Sophia Smith Collection is an internationally known facility for women's studies located at Smith College. The emphasis is on the history of women in the United States, but material on women all over the world is included. It contains thousands of retrospective and contemporary manuscripts; about 85,000 books and pamphlets; periodicals; theses; and photographs. Included are manuscripts and records of Margaret Sanger, Elizabeth Cutter Morrow, Agnes de Mille, the Planned Parenthood Federation of America, the Y. W. C. A., and the Canadian-American Women's Association.

The catalog is in several parts: an author catalog, a subject catalog, a manuscript catalog, and a photograph catalog. The library uses its own cataloging and classification systems. The subject headings are also the library's own, and although some are quite straightforward (works on women in other countries are found simply listed under the name of the country), others may require some imagination to find, such as "Primitive society, women in," particularly since there are few cross-references. Women authors are listed in the subject catalog under "Authors."

There are very extensive analytics for journals from the early 1900's to the early 1960's. Entries for journal articles may appear in two places. First, in the author catalog, under the name of an individual journal, will be found entries for articles about women that have appeared in that journal. Second, in the subject catalog, journal articles are cataloged under appropriate subject headings and treated like books. There are also some very detailed analytics for books; some are as specific as a reference to a topic covered in one or two pages of a book.

The Manuscript Catalog is not very accurately named, as it includes newspaper clippings, papers delivered at meetings, journal articles, and pamphlets, as well as the expected letters and papers of individuals. The catalog of photographs is included in the seventh volume with the Manuscript Catalog.

19. JUDAIC AND HEBRAIC STUDIES

The catalogs of the libraries of Jewish studies include works in Western languages and in Hebrew. In many cases Hebrew titles on all subjects, not just on Jews and Judaism, are included in these catalogs. The two largest comprehensive catalogs of Judaic and Hebraic studies are the Dictionary Catalog of the Klau Library of the Hebrew Union College-Jewish Institute of Religion (255) and the Dictionary Catalog of the Jewish Collection of The New York Public Library (256). Both include analytical entries for articles in periodicals. The Klau Library catalog is the larger but also the older of the two, and it emphasizes Judaic studies, while The New York Public Library collection includes works in Hebrew on all subjects, as well as works in all languages on Jews and Judaism.

252. Harvard University. Library. Catalogue of Hebrew Books. 6 vols. Cambridge, Mass.: distributed by Harvard University Press, 1968 (LC 68-22416). Supplement I. 3 vols., 1972.

The Judaica collection at Harvard has become the leading university research collection in its field in the United States, and one of the world's major resources. In 1968 the Hebrew collection numbered around 40,000 titles. Subject strengths are Hebrew rabbinic literature; Biblical, Talmudic, and liturgical texts; Jewish history and culture in the Diaspora and in Israel; Jews in Western Europe; Jews in Eastern Europe, especially Holocaust literature and Zionism; and materials on modern Israel. Included in the catalog are books, periodicals, and Israeli government documents.

There have been many changes in cataloging practices over the years, but about 40 percent of the cards were added after the Hebrew Division of the library was established in 1962 and represent the highest standards of cataloging. Many other cards have been revised. Volumes one to four of the 1968 catalog are a dictionary catalog of author headings, selected subject headings, and main entries for anonymous classics, with headings in Latin characters. Volumes five and six are a separate catalog of distinctive titles arranged according to the Hebrew alphabet. Cataloging is done in accordance with American Library Association and Library of Congress cataloging rules, with some exceptions. The transliteration scheme is ALA's. The classification scheme is Harvard's own, and the subject headings are from Harvard College Library's List of Subjects Used in the Public Catalogue.

The supplement lists 13,000 additional titles in three volumes. The first volume is a classified catalog arranged according to the Harvard classification, a schedule of which is reproduced at the beginning of the volume. The second volume is a catalog of authors and selected subjects--mainly personal name and corporate name subjects. Volume three is a catalog of titles.

253. Harvard University. Library. Judaica. 302 p. Cambridge, Mass.: distributed by Harvard University Press, 1971 (LC 78-179663). (Widener Library Shelflist v. 39)

Harvard University's collection of Judaica, as of 1971, numbered about 100,000 volumes--40,000 in Hebrew, 10,000 in Yiddish, and the remainder in other languages. The catalog of the books in Hebrew has been published separately (see 252). Here are listed about 9,000 titles, half of which are in English, 2,500 in German, and the rest in the common European languages. All are cataloged in Harvard's Jud and PJud classes.

The Jud class includes works on Judaism, the history of the Jews, and Jewish literature. The PJud class includes periodicals relating to Jewish history, culture, religion, literature, etc. Like the other volumes in this series, this catalog is in three parts: a classified arrangement, a chronological listing, and an author-title listing. For more information on the Widener Library shelflists see 9.

254. Hebrew Union College-Jewish Institute of Religion. American Jewish Archives. Manuscript Catalog of the American Jewish Archives, Cincinnati. 4 vols. Boston: G. K. Hall, 1971 (LC 79-173374). First Supplement. 908 p., 1978.

"The American Jewish Archives is a national institution dedicated to the preservation of documents which illuminate the history of the Jews in the Western Hemisphere.... [It] preserves and catalogues sources relating to virtually every phase of American Jewish culture and civilization" [Introduction]. The documents collected include letters, memoirs, genealogies, and organizational records, some dating back to the seventeenth and eighteenth centuries, as well as the papers of distinguished individuals and institutions, and of synagogues. The archives also collects "nearprints"--mimeographed and multilithed materials, announcements, news releases, annual reports, advertisements, throwaways, broadsides, and newspaper and magazine clippings. The archives also tries to collect all M.A. and Ph.D. theses on American Jews.

All items are cataloged by author, title, geographic provenance, and content, with many cross-references. There are some references to materials in other libraries. The last volume of the catalog is an appendix with separate catalogs of materials in four major collections of the Archives.

The American Jewish Archives was established in 1947 and by 1971 had 4,000,000 pages of documents.

255. Hebrew Union Catalog-Jewish Institute of Religion. Library. Dictionary Catalog of the Klau Library, Cincinnati. 32 vols. Boston: G. K. Hall, 1964 (LC 65-1601).

This is a dictionary catalog of authors, titles, and subjects, but until 1958 title entries were made only for books in Hebrew characters, which are listed in a separate Hebrew title catalog (volumes 28-32). Hebrew books are also interfiled in the main catalog by author and subject. Library of Congress subject headings are used, but some subject headings differ considerably from those used by the Library of Congress. There are some cross-references.

The main subjects of this catalog are Jews and Judaism, the Bible, and the ancient Near East. Special strengths are in Jewish music, fifteenth- and sixteenth-century Judaica and Hebraica, and Spinoza. In this catalog one will find, for example, 200 pages of entries on Spinoza, which contain about 4, 200 cards, including many analytical entries for articles in periodicals, yearbooks, and encyclopedias; and several hundred pages of entries under "United States" that are subdivided geographically and topically, and which list the library's holdings on Jews in the United States. About 200, 000 items are listed in this catalog, mostly in Hebrew, German, or English.

256. New York (City). Public Library. Reference Department. Dictionary Catalog of the Jewish Collection. 14 vols. Boston: G. K. Hall, 1960 (LC 60-3398). First Supplement. 8 vols., 1975.

This is the catalog of one of the five major libraries of Jewish studies in the world. With the supplement, the catalog represents approximately 140, 000 volumes, including works in the Jewish Division and materials on Jews and Judaism in other divisions of The New York Public Library. The collection is strong in biography, bibliography, and other reference works; history of the Jews; Bible commentaries; archaeology of Palestine; medieval and modern rabbinic, philosophic, and Kabbalistic texts; social studies; and belles lettres. In general, the aim of the Jewish Division is to collect materials about Jews and Judaism in any language and materials in Hebrew, Yiddish, and Ladino (Judeo-Spanish) on all subjects.

This is a dictionary catalog, and Hebrew, Yiddish, and Ladino subject and author entries are interfiled with other entries; the Introduction explains the filing rules. Hebrew and Ladino title entries are listed separately in their own alphabetical arrangements in the last volumes of the catalog. The subject headings used are New York Public's own. These headings started as an alphabetico-classed system, but since 1925 the tendency has been towards the use of Library of Congress headings. See and see-also references are included. There are analytics for books and periodicals. The supplement includes material cataloged through the end of 1971, when the library switched to Anglo-American Cataloging Rules. Subsequently cataloged items are included in the computer-produced Dictionary Catalog of the Research Libraries (see 16).

257. United States. Library of Congress. Hebraic Section. Hebraic Title Catalog. 25 vols. Washington, D. C.: Library of Congress Photoduplication Service, 1968.

This catalog lists 39,000 works by title in Hebrew alphabetic order in two sequences. Volumes 1-18 list Hebrew titles, and volumes 19-25 list Yiddish titles. Approximately two-thirds of the titles are from the Library of Congress's own collection, and one-third from libraries throughout the country.

This catalog was offered for sale by the Library of Congress on microfilm or various paper stock and has been cut and bound in different ways by different libraries.[26]

20. PHILOSOPHY AND RELIGION

The most unusual catalog in this group is that of the Warburg Institute Library (264), a bibliography of works concerned with symbols of classical antiquity in contemporary culture that covers the whole range of the history of ideas, including philosophy, religion, history, and art. The catalog is a shelflist, and each work is listed only once, thereby limiting its usefulness. The other important shelflist in this chapter is the Shelf List of the Union Theological Seminary Library in New York City (267), which is also available arranged alphabetically by main entry, and is concerned with theology and religion, particularly Christianity.

The major dictionary catalog of philosophy is the Catalog of the Hoose Library of Philosophy of the University of Southern California (265).

Most of the other catalogs listed here specialize in one particular aspect of religious studies, such as missionaries (266), ecumenicalism (272), or the Bible and the Holy Land (263).

258. Cashel, Ire. (Diocese). Library. Catalogue of the Cashel Diocesan Library, County Tipperary, Republic of Ireland. 635 p. Boston: G. K. Hall, 1973 (LC 73-12758).

The Cashel Diocesan Library was founded in Ireland in the eighteenth century principally for the use of the clergy of the Church of England. The holdings come primarily from the collecting activities of Archbishop Theophilus Bolton of Cashel and Archbishop William King of Dublin. The result of their work is a collection of rare books, incunabula, and manuscripts primarily from the seventeenth and eighteenth centuries, although the oldest item was produced in 1473.

Most of the works are in Latin and about half are on theology. The rest cover a variety of other subjects.

The catalog is in five parts: 1) an Author Catalogue; 2) Appendix of Manuscripts; 3) Index of Early Printers (up to and including 1510 A. D.); 4) Index to Listing of Seventeenth-Century Periodicals (arranged alphabetically by title); 5) Listing of Seventeenth-Century Periodicals (arranged chronologically).

259. Cornell University. Libraries. Witchcraft: Catalogue of the Witchcraft Collection in the Cornell University

Library. Edited by Martha J. Crowe. 644 p. Millwood, N.Y.: Kraus Thomson Organization, 1977 (LC 76-41552).

"The Witchcraft Collection in Cornell University Library is a research collection of historical and scholarly materials pertaining to the phenomenon of witchcraft in Europe and North America. The main topics included are demonic possession, theological and legal disputations, witchcraft trials, and torture" [Preface, vii]. This has been called the most important collection on witchcraft in the world. Works date from the fifteenth to the twentieth century and are in many Western European languages, especially Latin. It is primarily a collection of rare books.

In the catalog, in one alphabet, are found main entries, added entries for title, editor, translator, etc., and subject entries referring to persons and their works. There is a topical subject index at the end of the volume, but it covers only major subjects such as "Demonology" and "Trials" or witchcraft in different countries, and provides only the page numbers (often long lists of page numbers) of the relevant entries after the subject term. There is a 50-page introduction to the collection by Rossell Hope Robbins that discusses the history of the Witchcraft Collection at Cornell and the study of witchcraft in general, and is available as a separately published work.

260. Graduate Theological Union. Library. Union Catalog of the Graduate Theological Union Library. 15 vols. Berkeley, Calif., 1972.

This is a union catalog formed from the holdings of the Graduate Theological Union Library as well as from affiliated and independent seminary libraries in the San Francisco Bay area, plus the canon law collection of the University of California Law School and the religious materials of the Stanford Library. Christian theology and religion are the main subjects of the catalog, but there are also significant collections on all of the world's religions.

However, there are no subject entries; this is a main-entry catalog with some title added entries. There are many cross-references to the correct form of names, and attempts have been made to see that the form of the main entry corresponds to that used by the Library of Congress.

Books, doctoral dissertations, and some pamphlets are listed; periodicals are not, except for some annuals. Most of the titles were published in the twentieth century, although some are much older. The major languages included are English and Latin, along with other Western and Middle Eastern languages.

261. Harvard University. Library. Philosophy and Psychology. 2 vols. Cambridge, Mass.: distributed by Harvard University Press, 1973 (LC 72-83389). (Widener Library Shelflist v. 42-43)

This section of Harvard's Widener Library shelflist includes nearly all works in Widener relating to philosophy, including metaphysics, cosmology, ontology and epistemology, logic, esthetics, philosophy of religion, and ethics, as well as psychology. The Kant collection is outstanding.[27] Over 56,000 titles are listed, about half of them in English, a quarter in German, and the rest in French, Italian, and other languages. While imprint dates are predominantly of the twentieth century, the collection is strong in nineteenth-century titles as well. The classified, or shelflist, arrangement is followed by a chronological listing, and then by an author and title list. For further information on the Widener Library shelflists see 9.

262. Institut des études augustiniennes. Fichier Augustinien (Augustine Bibliography). 4 vols. Boston: G. K. Hall, 1972 (ISBN 0-8161-0947-8).

The Institut des Etudes Augustiniennes in Paris was founded in 1943 as a source of library information and bibliographic documentation of publications relating to Saint Aurelius Augustine. The catalog is in two parts. The first is an author catalog (Fichier-Auteurs) divided into texts by St. Augustine and studies about him. The second part is a subject catalog (Fichier-Matières) divided into general subjects and subdivisions, and containing works by and about Saint Augustine and his doctrines. There are many analytics for parts of books and collections and for articles in periodicals. Works date from the sixteenth to the twentieth century and are mostly in Italian, Latin, French, or German.

263. Jerusalem. Ecole biblique et archéologique française. Bibliothèque. Catalogue de la Bibliothèque de l'Ecole biblique et archéologique française (Catalog of the Library of the French Biblical and Archeological School, Jerusalem, Israel). 13 vols. Boston: G. K. Hall, 1975 (LC 76-452906).

The Library of the French Biblical and Archeological School was founded in 1890 and by the time of publication of its catalog held over 50,000 volumes. Special strengths of the library include the Old and New Testament, Judaism, Christian antiquity, papyrology, linguistics, epigraphy, numismatics, archaeology, Assyriology, Egyptology, geography, Oriental history, and Biblical theory. It also contains all significant material on Qumran and the Dead Sea Scrolls. The library receives more than 300 journals, and each article in a journal receives the same cataloging treatment as a book.

This is a dictionary catalog. The subject headings are in French and were developed by the library. There is no list of, or guide to, the subject headings, and there are no cross-references, making the locating of material on a particular subject quite difficult at times. Works are listed in chronological order under the subject heading. All books of the Bible are treated as separate subjects, as are various Dead Sea Scrolls, with subheadings by chapter and verse.

Titles were published mostly in the nineteenth and twentieth centuries and are in all major European languages.

This can be a difficult catalog for the average student to use, but it should be quite rewarding for the scholar.

264. London. University. Warburg Institute. Catalog of the Warburg Institute Library. Second edition, revised and enlarged. 12 vols. Boston: G. K. Hall, 1967 (LC 68-4522). First Supplement. 676 p., 1971.

"The Warburg Institute is concerned with the study of the survival and revival of classical antiquity in the thought, literature, art and institutions of European civilization" [Introduction]. It studies what antiquity signified in different contexts and different epochs. The study of symbols is of major importance, and the library also includes material relevant to preclassical or tribal civilizations. Its published catalog has been called by one scholar "the best bibliography on the history of ideas known to me."[28]

Aby Warburg began the library in Hamburg in the late nineteenth century. The Warburg Institute was established in 1921, moved to London in 1934, and became part of the University of London in 1944.

The catalog itself is actually a shelflist, and each work is listed only once. It is arranged in four main divisions--Social Patterns and History; Religion, Magic and Science, Philosophy; Literature; and Art and Archaeology--with different subdivisions. The first volume gives a subject outline of the catalog, and in each volume there is an alphabetical index to the subject divisions and a detailed table of contents for that volume. The subjects emphasized are art, history, religion, anthropology, sociology, psychology, archaeology, and antiquity.

There are many analytics for series, articles in journals, and some book chapters. Works are in Western European languages, predominantly German.

265. Los Angeles. University of Southern California. School of Philosophy. Hoose Library of Philosophy. Catalog of the Hoose Library of Philosophy. 6 vols. Boston: G. K. Hall, 1968 (ISBN 0-8161-0816-2).

This catalog represents 37,000 volumes and 100 periodical titles on Western European philosophy. Special strengths of the collection are in metaphysics, epistemology, logic, ethics, value theory, the philosophy of religion, and classical philosophy. There is comprehensive coverage of the periods of Enlightenment and Romanticism and extensive holdings on European philosophy in the eighteenth century, especially in Germany. Other strengths include personalism, phenomenology, and Latin American philosophy.

This is a dictionary catalog of authors, titles, and subjects that "follows standard practices." Library of Congress subject headings are used along with LC printed cards. There are see and some see-also references for names and subjects. The Dewey Decimal classification is used.

Works are in various Western European languages and were published mostly in the nineteenth and twentieth centuries. Microforms are included, as are manuscripts, some dating from the thirteenth century.

266. New York (City). Missionary Research Library. Dictionary Catalog of the Missionary Research Library, New York. 17 vols. Boston: G. K. Hall, 1968 (LC 74-169177).

The Missionary Research Library was founded in 1914 by the Foreign Missions Conference of North America. It is currently housed as a separate library in the Union Theological Seminary in New York. The library collects works on missions and missionaries all over the world--in particular, the theory and practice of missions; history of missionary societies; biographies of missionaries and individuals in the countries to which they have gone; studies of peoples in those countries, including their political, economic, social, and religious life; books on the younger churches and their literature; international relations; ideologies, etc. During much of the nineteenth century, missions furnished the primary point of contact between the United States and countries of Asia, Africa, and South America, making early mission reports of interest to historians and anthropologists. The emphasis of the collection is on Protestant missions outside of the United States, but there is also material on missions from Europe, on Roman Catholic missions, and on work among the American Indians.

The library contains more than 100,000 cataloged items in the form of books, periodicals, pamphlets, reports, and archives. These are listed in 273,000 entries in the catalog, interfiled by author, title, and subject. There are also analytical entries for articles in periodicals and parts of books entered under the subject, and under the author's name if the author is significant. The library uses its own subject headings. The emphasis is on geographical headings to bring together material about an area. There are few cross-references. A variety of classification systems are used.

The library currently receives about 800 missionary magazines and has extensive files of nineteenth-century magazines. Volume 17 lists the holdings of periodicals and of reports of various missions, churches, hospitals, etc. These reports are also listed in the main catalog.

267. New York (City). Union Theological Seminary. Library. Alphabetical Arrangement of Main Entries from the Shelf List; Union Theological Seminary Library, New York City. 10 vols. Boston: G. K. Hall, 1960 (LC 75-313282).

________. The Shelf List of the Union Theological Seminary Library in New York City; in Classification Order. 10 vols. Boston: G. K. Hall, 1960 (LC 61-4932).

The Union Theological Seminary Library is a strong historical collection of theology and religion, with its emphasis on Christianity. It is richest in works on the Bible, sacred music, church history, missions, and ecumenics. Books, pamphlets, theses, and periodicals are all included in about 190,000 entries in the shelflist. Works are in English and other Western European languages.

The alphabetically arranged catalog is just as its title says: an alphabetical arrangement of main entries. There are no cross-references and no added entries.

The Shelf List is arranged according to the library's own classification system, which is a theological classification. There is no outline of the classification system provided nor is there an alphabetical subject index to the classification. However, the classification scheme has been published separately as: Classification of the Library of Union Theological Seminary in the City of New York; prepared by Julia Petee, with additions and corrections 1939-December 1966; edited by Ruth C. Eisenhart (New York: Union Theological Seminary, 1967). Without this guide, the catalog in shelflist form is really unusable; with it, the catalog becomes an excellent bibliography for theology.

268. New York. Union Theological Seminary. Library. Catalogue of the McAlpin Collection of British History and Theology. Compiled and edited by Charles Ripley Gillett. 5 vols. New York, 1927-30 (LC 29-29688).

________. Catalogue of the McAlpin Collection of British History and Theology in the Union Theological Seminary Library, New York City: Acquisitions 1924-1978. 427 p. Boston: G. K. Hall, 1979 (ISBN 0-8161-0292-9).

The McAlpin Collection is named after David Hunter McAlpin, who originally provided the funds to purchase a collection of books on English deism. The collection now contains over 18,000 books and pamphlets on British history and theology that bear imprint dates from 1501 to 1700. It has outstanding coverage of political, theological, and ecclesiastical conflicts of the mid-seventeenth century.

The original catalog, published from 1927 to 1930, lists 15,000 books and pamphlets arranged chronologically by year of publication and, within each year, alphabetically by author. The descriptive cataloging is very detailed. The last volume is an index in a straight alphabetical arrangement, in which are names of persons listed on title pages (not only authors) and titles of anonymous works. Author's names are given in full, if known, with their dates and a statement as to the author's position, occupation, or other characteristics. The index has many cross-references from names of persons to the actual author and title of the books concerned.

The supplement to the catalog, published in 1979, lists approximately 3,000 books and pamphlets acquired since the original catalog was published. This catalog is in two parts. The first part is a dictionary catalog of authors, titles, and subjects--subjects being mostly persons or books. The second part of the catalog is arranged chronologically. Entries often have references to numbers in "Wing"[29] or "STC."[30]

269. Pontifical Institute of Mediaeval Studies. Library. Dictionary Catalogue of the Library of the Pontifical Institute of Mediaeval Studies, Toronto, Canada. 5 vols. Boston: G. K. Hall, 1972 (LC 74-152760). First Supplement. 641 p., 1979.

The Pontifical Institute of Mediaeval Studies is a separate, independent unit of St. Michael's College of the University of Toronto. It was founded in 1929. The subject matter of the library is the Middle Ages, with a focus on art history, Byzantine studies, canon and civil law, church history, patristics, philosophy, theology, and vernacular literature.

The library holds 40,000 volumes of monographs and periodicals containing primary and secondary sources. Other holdings include early printed works and facsimile manuscripts dating back to the ninth century. Titles are in English, Latin, Italian, and other Western European languages, but English dominates.

This is a dictionary catalog of authors, titles, and subjects. Library of Congress subject headings and the Library of Congress classification system are used, except for some areas such as Catholic theology, law, and church history. In volume five there is a separate catalog of manuscripts on microfilm.

270. Rowe, Kenneth E., editor. Methodist Union Catalog, Pre-1976 Imprints. v. 1- Metuchen, N.J.: Scarecrow Press, 1975- (LC 75-33190).

This is a union list of the cataloged holdings on Methodists in more than 200 libraries in the United States, Canada, Great Britain, and several other European countries. It includes publications by and about Methodists from their beginnings at Oxford in 1729 to the present. There are works on Methodist history, biography, doctrine, polity, missions, education, and sermons. Books, pamphlets, and theses are listed in the catalog; manuscripts, periodicals, and other serials are not. Only works printed in the Latin alphabet are included; most of them date from the nineteenth century to 1975.

This is an author catalog, with only one entry per title. Library locations are included in the entries. All entries have been edited for consistency according to Anglo-American Cataloging Rules, North American text, 1967 edition. It is projected that the catalog will total 20 volumes, and subject, title, and added-entry indexes are planned.

271. Williams Library, London. Early Nonconformity, 1566-1800: A Catalogue of Books in Dr. Williams's Library, London. 12 vols. Boston: G. K. Hall, 1968.

Dr. Daniel Williams (c. 1643-1717) was a Presbyterian minister in Ireland and later in London. He left his fortune for charitable purposes and his books for a public library. The Williams Library was opened in 1729 and by 1968 had 112,000 volumes.

This is the catalog of the collection of books and pamphlets in the Williams Library that were printed in and are concerned with the early period of English Nonconformity. The books were printed between 1566 and 1800, mostly in England, but there are also related works from Scotland, Ireland, Wales, and New England. Included here are the works, whether theological or not, of nonconformist divines; works by laymen where relevant; works of Anglican and Roman Catholic writers where relevant; and works of a general historical or philosophical nature that bear on nonconformity. Books of a purely devotional, catechetical, or Biblical nature are not included, nor are the library's numerous works by Continental reformers and Huguenot and Dutch reformers, except where translated or published in England.

The catalog is in three parts. The Author Catalogue (five volumes) includes, besides the authors of books, analytical entries for the authors of items--individual letters, postscripts, sermons, and the like--appearing in books. There are also entries for individuals held to be the authors of anonymous or pseudonymous works, and added entries for editors, translators, and other individuals. The library uses its own subject headings in the Subject Catalogue (five volumes), and there are many see and see-also references for aid. Finally, there is a Chronological Catalogue (2 volumes), arranged by date of publication.

272. World Council of Churches. Library. Classified Catalog of the Ecumenical Movement. 2 vols. Boston: G. K. Hall, 1972 (LC 73-155601).

This catalog lists only the ecumenical collection (about 11,000 titles) of the World Council of Churches in Geneva, Switzerland. "The main strength and usefulness of this catalog lies in the fact that it lists and describes the most complete collection of literature on the ecumenical movement in the twentieth century. It contains full documentation on the several organs of the movement since 1910. It contains, in a reclassification made within the last seven years, a full collection of theological monographs related to the ecumenical movement, and this in all foreign languages" [Introduction]. Also included are works of importance to ecumenism published during the period 1500-1900 or dealing with that period; works on the history of ecumenical movements in the early twentieth century; complete World Council of Churches documentation; works on ecumenical movements in all countries; works dealing with Christian unity, and the like.

This is a classified catalog arranged according to a decimal classification system devised by the library. An outline of the classification and detailed tables of the classification are provided. The catalog lists printed books, pamphlets, and serial holdings. There is a substantial number of analytics for periodical articles. Archival material is not included. The catalog contains an alphabetical index of names, which includes authors, added entries, and writers of articles in periodicals.

21. ART AND ARCHITECTURE

In the fields of art, published library catalogs have long been known to provide some of the best bibliographies and periodical indexes. The major published catalog of art history is that of the Metropolitan Museum of Art in New York (289), now in its second edition, in 48 volumes. Second to this is The New York Public Library's Dictionary Catalog of Art and Architecture (291).

Focusing on architecture are two distinguished collections, those of the Avery Architectural Library of Columbia University (280) and Harvard University's Graduate School of Design Library (286). Both of these libraries index periodical articles in addition to books; the Graduate School of Design Library in the past included them in its dictionary catalog, while the Avery Library publishes its catalog of periodical articles as the Avery Index to Architectural Periodicals (278).

Other indexes to art periodicals are provided by the Chicago Art Institute's Index to Art Periodicals (277) and the Catalogue d'articles de périodiques, arts décoratifs et beaux-arts, Bibliothèque Forney, Paris (295), the latter specializing in the applied arts.

The subject catalog of the Bibliothèque Forney (297) also focuses on the applied, or decorative arts, as do the catalog of the library of the Winterthur Museum (287) and the catalog of the Victoria and Albert Museum (299), which additionally includes works on the arts in general.

The art of film is included in many of these catalogs on art, particularly in the catalog of the library of the Museum of Modern Art (290), the Catalogue of the Book Library of the British Film Institute (275), and Motion Pictures: A Catalog of Books, Periodicals, Screenplays, Television Scripts, and Production Stills of the University of California at Los Angeles (276).

273. Archives of American Art. The Card Catalog of the Manuscript Collections of the Archives of American Art. 10 vols. Wilmington, Del.: Scholarly Resources, 1981 (LC 80-53039).

The Archives of American Art began as part of the library of the Detroit Institute of Arts in 1954. It is now a bureau of the Smithsonian Institution, with its main processing center in Washington, D. C., and four other centers in Detroit, New York, Boston, and San Francisco. The Archives collects records and documents of American artists and art institutions. It does not attempt to acquire all of the original documents, but rather to microfilm all records--those it owns and those that are still in private hands or in the keeping of other institutions. Copies of these microfilms are available at each of the five Archives offices and through interlibrary loan. The documents consist of letters, exhibition catalogs, photographs, business records, etc.

At the time of publication of the catalog the Archives owned, in originals or microfilms, 5,000 collections with a total of six million items. Cataloging practices have varied over time and with availability of funds. Some collections are described only briefly, with a sentence or a paragraph describing the entire collection. Others have been given analytical cataloging, with lists of some of the items in the collection, and with added entries for some of the individuals or subjects discussed by the collection or its individual items. Most of the entries are for names of individuals or institutions, although there are some subject entries. The depth of cataloging can be ascertained from the fact that the 5,000 separate collections are described in over 40,000 catalog cards.

The catalog of the Archives of American Art collection of exhibition catalogs has been published separately (see 274).

274. Archives of American Art. Collection of Exhibition Catalogs; the Archives of American Art. 851 p. Boston: G. K. Hall, 1979 (LC 79-107465).

The Archives of American Art was established in Detroit in 1954 to encourage research and publication in American art. It collects documentary sources to further this aim. In the mid-1960's F. Ivor D. Avellino conducted a survey of museums, libraries, and historical societies to record and film their exhibition catalogs of American art. Those filmed and those later found in the Archives' own holdings form the basis of this catalog.

The catalog is arranged in one alphabet with entries for the name of the exhibiting institution (commercial gallery, museum, or art society), and the name of the artist or artists involved (if no more than three were exhibited). Entries include the exhibition date and the microfilm number of the catalog. All the catalogs are available on microfilm for consultation at the Archives' regional centers or through interlibrary loan. Dates of the catalogs range from the early nineteenth century through the mid-1960's. Approximately 15,000 catalogs are listed, filling nearly 200 rolls of microfilm.

In 1970 the Archives of American Art became a bureau of the Smithsonian Institution. There are centers in Detroit, Washington, D. C., New York, Boston, and San Francisco. The catalog of the rest of the archival collections has been published separately (see 273).

275. British Film Institute, London. Library. Catalogue of the Book Library of the British Film Institute, London, England. 3 vols. Boston: G. K. Hall, 1975 (ISBN 0-8161-0004-7).

This is a very valuable and detailed bibliography of film (i. e., motion pictures) and, to some extent, of television and the mass media in general. Included in it are books, pamphlets, and published and unpublished screenplays. More than 20, 000 titles are cataloged, including over 4, 000 film scripts.

The catalog is in four parts: Author, Title, Subject, and Script Catalogues. The Author Catalogue contains the most detailed cataloging for material acquired before 1971, and there are many items in the Author Catalogue that cannot be found in the Title or Subject Catalogues.

The Subject Catalogue has two very useful separate catalogs of personalities (individuals) and of films. Both of these consist mainly of analytical entries for essays or chapters in books dealing with an individual or film. The rest of the Subject Catalogue is a classified catalog based on the Universal Decimal Classification; an outline of the classification scheme is provided along with a subject index to the classification. Books may be assigned two different classification numbers in order that they may appear in more than one place in the catalog. Often, a book will be assigned one number and chapters from the book will be assigned different classification numbers depending on the subject of the chapter. There is detailed analytical cataloging of books throughout the catalog.

The Script Catalogue includes screenplays, shooting scripts, and translations prepared for National Film Theatre screenings, as well as published scripts, and has analytical entries for script collections.

Works are mostly in English, but titles in French, Italian, German and other languages are included.

276. California. University. University at Los Angeles. Library. Motion Pictures: A Catalog of Books, Periodicals, Screenplays, Television Scripts and Production Stills/ Theatre Arts Library, University of California, Los Angeles. Second edition, revised and expanded. 775 p. Boston: G. K. Hall, 1976.

The title of this catalog is a full description of its contents. It is arranged in five parts, according to the type of material. The first part, Books, Periodicals, and Journals, is a main-entry catalog of published material on film, including published screenplays entered under the name of the screenwriter.

The second part, Published Screenplays, includes screenplays published individually, in anthologies, and in the periodical L'avant-scene du cinema. The screenplays are entered under the title of the film, and there are cross-references from the English title to the original title for foreign-language films.

The third part, Unpublished Screenplays, lists 6,000 American, British, and foreign-language screenplays by the release title of the film. Entries include the release date, the name of the screenwriter, and often the director, the producer, and other information.

Television Scripts, the fourth part, includes more than 3,000 television scripts entered under the name of the television series. Information given for each script may include the titles of individual episodes, the producer, the director, the network, the dates the series ran, etc.

The fifth part, Production Stills, is a list of the collection of still photographs from individual films, arranged by name of film and giving country of origin, production company and/or distributor, release date of the film, and some indication of what types of supplementary material, such as posters or slides, are available.

277. Chicago. Art Institute. Ryerson Library. Index to Art Periodicals. 11 vols. Boston: G. K. Hall, 1962 (LC 62-6346). First Supplement. 573 p., 1975.

The Index to Art Periodicals was begun by the Art Institute of Chicago in 1907. When the Wilson Art Index appeared in 1929 the Art Institute shifted its emphasis to items not covered by Art Index, especially museum bulletins and foreign periodicals. The List of Periodicals Indexed has approximately 350 periodicals of the nineteenth and twentieth centuries and gives the dates they are indexed and whether and when the Art Index began indexing them or stopped indexing them.

This is a subject index only; there are no author entries. Subject headings are "not standard," and several differences between the headings used and Library of Congress headings are pointed out in the Preface. There are many see and see-also references, and individuals are included as subjects. The First Supplement includes indexing from 1961 through October, 1974, but also includes entries for older periodicals and issues newly acquired, as well as retrospective indexing of titles added to the coverage of Art Index in 1969.

278. Columbia University. Libraries. Avery Architectural Library. Avery Index to Architectural Periodicals. Second edition, revised and enlarged. 15 vols. Boston: G. K. Hall, 1973 (LC 74-152756). First Supplement. 823 p., 1975. Second Supplement. 882 p., 1977. Third Supplement. 705 p., 1979.

The Avery Architectural Library was established in 1890, and this catalog of periodical articles was begun in 1934. Most of the indexing postdates that year, but crucial American and some British publications have been indexed in their entirety. This is considered the major index in the field of architecture, covering architecture in its widest sense, including architectural aspects of archaeology, of the decorative arts, of interior design, and of city planning and housing.

The subject headings used here are the library's own, and are the same as those used in the Catalog of the Avery Memorial Architectural Library (see 280), with some additional, specialized headings added. The Preface goes into some detail on the use of the subject headings. Architects are indexed whenever they are mentioned in an article.

There is a list of periodicals indexed provided in the first volume, and this includes all major architectural magazines published in the United States, Great Britain and the British Commonwealth, and most available South American, French, Swiss, German, Italian, Spanish, Belgian, Dutch, and Scandinavian periodicals, and Japanese periodicals with English summaries.

The second edition of the Avery Index includes the entire first edition plus its seven supplement, and contains additions and corrections later made to those entries. New periodicals have been added and some retrospective indexing has also been done.

279. Columbia University. Libraries. Avery Architectural Library. Avery Obituary Index of Architects. Second edition. 530 p. Boston: G. K. Hall, 1980 (ISBN 0-8161-1068-9).

This is a catalog maintained at the Avery Library of Columbia University. As its title indicates, it is an index to obituaries, mainly of architects, but also of art historians, archaeologists, and city planners. Artists were included until 1960. The arrangement is alphabetical by name of the individual. For each entry the year of death is given as well as, where available, the year of birth, along with a reference to the periodical in which the obituary appeared.

The index was begun in 1934 but the four crucial American architectural periodicals, the American Architect, Architectural Forum, Architectural Record, and Progressive Architecture, have been indexed to their founding. The British Journal of the Royal Institute of British Architects and its predecessor, Transaction, are back-indexed to 1865. Major French and German periodicals are also retrospectively indexed. Also indexed are newspapers, primarily The New York Times. At present, all major architectural journals of the Western world are scanned for obituary information.

A major problem with this index is the fact that many references are simply to the Avery Library's own "Newspaper Obituary File" without specifying what newspaper or on which date the obituary appeared. However, the library will provide reproductions of the clippings upon request.

The new edition of the Avery Obituary Index contains over 17,000 entries for obituaries in over 500 periodicals. It is a unique source for biographical information on architects and those in related professions.

280. Columbia University. Libraries. Avery Architectural Library.

<u>Catalog of the Avery Memorial Architectural Library of Columbia University.</u> Second edition, enlarged. 19 vols. Boston: G. K. Hall, 1968 (LC 76-358000). <u>First Supplement.</u> 4 vols., 1973. <u>Second Supplement.</u> 4 vols., 1975. <u>Third Supplement.</u> 3 vols., 1977. <u>Fourth Supplement.</u> 3 vols., 1979.

The Avery Memorial Architectural Library is considered to be the most extensive architectural library in the Western world. During the life of the Farmington Plan the Avery Library received all current architectural books from Western Europe. The collection focuses, of course, on architecture, from prehistoric archaeology to city planning and modern architectural technology. Also included are the decorative arts (furniture design, mural painting, vase painting, stained glass, metal work, costume, mosaics, etc.), landscape architecture, urban renewal, and urban design. The intention is to provide comprehensive coverage of the field.

This is a dictionary catalog of authors, subjects, and selected titles. Library of Congress subject headings are used with certain modifications that are explained in the Introduction.

This is also a union catalog of all art and architecture books in the Columbia system, including approximately 80,000 volumes of books and periodicals in Avery itself, and about 35,000 volumes in the Fine Arts Library (mostly on sculpture, painting, and the graphic arts), plus other small holdings. The first three supplements add another 55,000 titles. Among the holdings the catalog lists are rare books, drawings, and sales catalogs.

Under the terms of Samuel Putnam Avery's will, the collection is for reference use only, and no interlibrary loans are made. However, the library will provide photocopies or make microfilm copies.

281. Dumbarton Oaks. <u>Dictionary Catalogue of the Byzantine Collection of the Dumbarton Oaks Research Library.</u> 12 vols. Boston: G. K. Hall, 1975 (LC 75-314103).

The Dumbarton Oaks Research Library in Washington, D.C. serves the Center for Byzantine Studies, which is part of Harvard University. "The present aim of the library is to collect, as completely as possible, all relevant material on Byzantine and medieval civilizations.... It has become the finest library in the United States in its subject area" [Introduction]. Its subject area includes the late Graeco-Roman world, the world of early and medieval Islam and of the Orthodox Slavs, and the disciplines of epigraphy, numismatics, palaeography, and papyrology. The collection is especially strong in Byzantine art and archaeology, but it also covers all aspects of Byzantine culture, including political, social, and economic history, church history and liturgy, and canon and civil law.

At the time of publication of the catalog, the library housed some 84,000 volumes, including 800 currently received periodicals, museum catalogs, United States and foreign government documents, and important editions of literary and historical texts and documents.

Titles were published mostly in the nineteenth and twentieth centuries, and are in English and various modern European languages, as well as Latin, Greek, Coptic, Syriac, Arabic, Persian, Turkish, Georgian, Armenian, and Old Slavonic.

This is a dictionary catalog with entries filed according to ALA Rules for Filing Catalog Cards, second edition, 1968. There are main, subject, and added entries. The library uses Library of Congress subject headings, and often uses Library of Congress printed cards, but in many cases will add subject headings to those the Library of Congress has assigned. There are some analytics for works in series and some entries for article extracts.

282. Florence. Kunsthistorisches Institut. Katalog des Kunsthistorischen Instituts in Florenz (Catalog of the Institute for the History of Art, Florence, Italy). 9 vols. Boston: G. K. Hall, 1964 (LC 65-8839). Erster Nachtragsband (First Supplement). 2 vols., 1968. Zweiter Nachtragsband (Second Supplement). 2 vols., 1972. Dritter Nachtragsband (Third Supplement). 2 vols., 1976.

The Kunsthistorisches Institut in Florenz was formed in 1888, a time when foreign scholars were gathering in Florence to study Italian art. Now maintained by a supporting society (Verein zur Erhaltung des Kunsthistorischen Instituts in Florenz) and by the German government, the Institute aims to collect as completely as possible the materials needed for the study of the history of Italian art. All the arts are included: painting, sculpture, the graphic arts, architecture, and the decorative arts from early Christian times to the present. Arts of other countries are included only as they relate to Italian art. Included in the library are monographs, catalogs, and the publications of various societies.

This is an author catalog. Entries are handwritten in the original catalog and in all supplements. Catalogs of collections, auctions, and exhibitions are entered under the name of the city, with cross-references from the name of the owner.

The original catalog contains entries for approximately 60,000 volumes. The first supplement adds another 15,000 titles. The second supplement adds 14,000 new titles, concentrating on Venice and the Veneto, and the number of periodical titles increases to 1,220. The third supplement adds 15,000 additional titles and 440 new periodicals.

283. Freer Gallery of Art, Washington, D.C. Library. Dictionary Catalog of the Library of the Freer Gallery of Art, Smithsonian Institution, Washington, D.C. 6 vols. Boston: G. K. Hall, 1967 (ISBN 0-8161-0799-8).

The Freer Gallery of Art and its library specialize in the art of the Far East, India, and the Near East, as well as in the nineteenth-century American art of James Whistler and his contemporaries. The catalog lists 40,000 books, pamphlets, and periodicals, as well as letters and documents of James McNeill Whistler. There are many analytics for periodical articles.

The catalog is in two sections: volumes one to four cover works in Western languages; volumes five to six cover Asian languages. The author and title entries in the Asian language catalog are romanized. Both sections are dictionary catalogs with author, title, and subject entries. The books in Western languages are classified in the Dewey Decimal classification; those in Asian languages are classed with the Chinese Decimal classification. Library of Congress subject headings are used.

284. Harvard University. Berenson Library. Catalogues of the Berenson Library of the Harvard University Center for Italian Renaissance Studies at Villa I Tatti, Florence, Italy. 4 vols. Boston: G. K. Hall, 1972 (LC 76-352697).

Bernard Berenson, the art historian and critic, acquired Villa I Tatti, near Florence, in 1900. When he died in 1959 he left the villa with its art collection and library to Harvard University. At that time the library had about 50,000 volumes and 150,000 photographs. By the time of publication of this catalog there were more than 70,000 volumes. The nucleus of the library is the collection of books and photographs on Italian painting of the late Middle Ages and the Renaissance. Berenson also collected on classical and Near Eastern archaeology; medieval illuminated manuscripts; comparative religion, literature, and philosophy; and modern history (many biographies and memoirs can be found in the collection). The emphasis of the library now is on Renaissance art, history, and literature. Works are mostly in Italian, German, English, and French, and were published in the nineteenth and twentieth centuries. The collection also includes the Gordon and Elizabeth Morrill Library of Renaissance music.

Most of the catalog was compiled while the library was in private hands and reflects the idiosyncracies of different cataloging styles. The Author Catalogue has been completely reproduced in two volumes. Entries tend to be brief--consisting of author, title, imprint, and size. There are many cross-references to the correct forms of names.

The Subject Catalogue consists of many different catalogs, not all of which have been reproduced for the published catalog. Volume one of the Subject Catalogue contains the following separate listings: History; Church History, Theology, Hagiography; Archaeology; Painting; Drawing, Graphic Art; Architecture; Sculpture; Iconography; Topographical; Biography of Artists; Exhibition Catalogue. Volume two of the Subject Catalogue contains: Catalogue of Galleries; Catalogues of Private Collections; Manuscript; Manuscript, Topographical; Catalogues of Libraries; Music Catalogue; Periodicals; Cards of Sales by Owners; Lists of Sales by Dealers and Countries. Most of these catalogs consist of see references to the author cards in the Author Catalogue. However, each separate catalog of the Subject Catalogue has its own arrangement.

For example, the Topographical Catalogue, consisting of references to works about places, is arranged by name of country (not in alphabetical order), and within country, alphabetically by city; and the Music Catalogue appears to be a shelflist, but the classification system is neither named nor explained. The Introduction does not elucidate the mysteries of the Subject Catalogue. The result is that while the Author Catalogue may be of great help in finding a known work, only the most patient scholar will be able to wrest any information from the Subject Catalogue.

285. Harvard University. Fine Arts Library. Catalogue of the Harvard University Fine Arts Library, the Fogg Art Museum. 15 vols. Boston: G. K. Hall, 1971 (LC 72-179505). First Supplement. 3 vols., 1975.

In 1963 the Fine Arts Library was formed when the art collection in Harvard's Widener Library was merged with that in the Fogg Art Museum, which dates from 1895. This catalog includes those collections plus the art collections of other Harvard libraries: Widener's collection of classical archaeology and the book arts; the Peabody Museum Library's collection of prehistoric, pre-Columbian, Oceanic, and other ethnic arts; the historical portion of the Graduate School of Design Library; and the holdings of the Department of Printing and Graphic Arts in the Houghton Library. The Fine Arts Library itself has exhaustive collections of the literature of master drawings, Romanesque sculpture, Italian primitives, and Dutch seventeenth-century art. Also collected in depth are works about American art, the history of still photography, the history of film, decorative arts, restoration and conservation of art and, in general, the history of Western art of all periods.

This is a dictionary catalog of authors, added entries, and subjects. Library of Congress subject headings are used with some modifications; when Library of Congress printed cards are used the subject headings assigned by the Library of Congress are often added to or changed. Several different classification systems have been used by the library; none of them is Library of Congress. At the end of June, 1974, the collection numbered 144,159 volumes, including 935 currently received periodical titles. Pamphlets, ephemera, photographs, and slides are not included in the catalog.

Volume fifteen of the Catalogue constitutes a separate catalog of main entries for 20,000 auction sales catalogs. The arrangement is by name of dealer. However, added entries for the sales catalogs are included in the main catalog.

286. Harvard University. Graduate School of Design. Library. Catalogue of the Library of the Graduate School of Design, Harvard University. 44 vols. Boston: G. K. Hall, 1968 (LC 73-169433). First Supplement. 2 vols., 1970. Second Supplement. 5 vols., 1974.

Frances L. Loeb Library. Catalogue of the Library of the

Graduate School of Design, Frances Loeb Library, Harvard University, Third Supplement. 3 vols. Boston: G. K. Hall, 1979 (LC 79-120193).

Two separate libraries at Harvard University--the Library of Architecture, and the Library of Landscape Architecture and City Planning--were united in 1956 in one library within the Graduate School of Design. Collection building in the major subjects of interest--architecture, landscape architecture, and city and regional planning--dates back to the early 1900's. Beginning with the second supplement there is expanded coverage of behavioral and social sciences, pollution, conservation and preservation, community development, and computer applications.

The original catalog indexes 140, 000 volumes of books, pamphlets, periodicals, theses, and reports. Periodicals are listed both under the name of the periodical and under the heading "Periodicals." The third supplement includes full cataloging records for all Comprehensive Planning Assistance Reports produced in the six New England states, in New York City, and in Washington, D. C.

Perhaps the most important aspect of this catalog is its analytics. It is particularly rich in analytical entries for periodical articles. After 1963, the library did not often analyze journals appearing in Art Index, but foreign periodicals, and periodicals on urban planning, regional science, and landscape architecture are indexed by as many subjects as are appropriate, by author, and by designer. There are also some analytics for chapters in books. Beginning with the First Supplement, entries for periodical articles are in a separate dictionary catalog within the supplement.

The Graduate School of Design catalog is a dictionary catalog of authors, titles, and subjects. Subject indexing has been emphasized and there are many see and see-also references, which are particularly helpful because the library uses its own subject headings. Several different classification systems have been used at different times in the two libraries. The Third Supplement contains material cataloged through June, 1978; beginning with July, 1978 the library will use Library of Congress subject headings and the Library of Congress classification, and will catalog using OCLC.

287. Henry Francis du Pont Winterthur Museum. Libraries. The Winterthur Museum Collection of Printed Books and Periodicals. 9 vols. Wilmington, Del.: Scholarly Resources, 1974 (LC 73-88753).

The late Henry Francis du Pont established the Winterthur Museum to house his collection of art made or used by the citizens of the United States from 1600 to 1840. The collection emphasizes American-made furniture, metalwork, and prints, as well as imported materials such as British prints, ceramics, and textiles. Subsidiary collections include paintings, sculpture, architectural interiors, drawings, and maps. The library supports the work of the curators of the collection, as well as a graduate program for the study of the arts of early America.

The strengths of the library, therefore, are in early American visual arts, or "material culture," with a superior collection of antique books from the sixteenth to the twentieth centuries. Its collections of world-wide importance include those of English architectural books, English pattern books and trade catalogs, and American architecture books. It also maintains a strong collection of secondary sources on the decorative arts such as glass, ceramics, metals, and woodwork, and on American sculpture and architecture. In addition, the library houses books relating to Winterthur's collection of American art and to early American culture in general, such as early American works on manners and customs (sports, eating, social structure, marriage, birth and death, games, etc.), geography and maps, technology of individual crafts, early travel books, and heraldry.

The catalog is in several parts. Volumes one to seven are a general dictionary catalog of authors, titles, and subjects. Library of Congress subject headings are used, as well as the Library of Congress classification, with some modifications. Library of Congress printed cards are often used. Books and pamphlets are both listed, along with many analytics for articles in periodicals. These analytical entries are usually only subject entries, and range in date from the 1800's to the 1960's.

Volume eight and part of volume nine constitute a rare book catalog in dictionary form. The rest of volume nine contains two other catalogs: an auction catalog and the catalog of the Edward Deming Andrews Memorial Shaker Collection.

288. International Federation of Film Archives. Union Catalogue of Books and Periodicals Published Before 1914 (Catalogue collectif des livres et périodiques publiés avant 1914 en possession des cinémathèques membres de la Fédération internationale des archives du film). 89 leaves. Bruxelles: Cinémathèque Royale de Belgique, Palais des Beaux-Arts, 1967 (LC 68-139644).

This is a union catalog of works, in 24 libraries from almost as many countries, that have any relationship with the cinema--provided they were published before 1914. Included are books on physics and optics, manufacturers' catalogs of instruments, books on Chinese shadows, magazines devoted to magic lanterns, as well as books on photography, electricity, etc. Entries are arranged chronologically by date of publication, beginning with the earliest entry, dated 1646. Each entry gives the author, title, publisher, place of publication, and number of pages in a book, or number of issues held for a periodical. There are separate indexes of authors and titles. Most of the works are in French, German, Italian, or English.

289. New York (City). Metropolitan Museum of Art. Library. Library Catalog of the Metropolitan Museum of Art,

New York. Second edition, revised and enlarged. 48 vols. Boston: G. K. Hall, 1980 (LC 80-113258).

This new edition of the Library Catalog of the Metropolitan Museum of Art supersedes the earlier (1960) catalog and its seven supplements. The library is widely regarded as the leading art history research library in the Western Hemisphere, covering five thousand years of art and archaeology from the days of ancient Egypt to the contemporary period. Its special strengths are in art history, painting, sculpture, archaeology, decorative arts, arms and armor, and architecture. The library was established in 1880 and one hundred years later had 220,000 volumes, which are represented in this catalog by about one million cards.

This is a dictionary catalog of authors, titles, and subjects. The library uses its own classification system but tends to follow Library of Congress subject headings. An attempt is made to provide very thorough subject indexing, however, and even when using LC printed cards the library often adds subject headings. With this new edition cards have been extensively revised to achieve uniformity of headings. There are many cross-references.

Volumes 46-48 are a separate catalog of sales catalogs. In addition, the main catalog lists many exhibition catalogs, rare books, early works in art history, art periodicals, and reports and journals of learned societies. Before the appearance of Art Index, in 1930, the library did extensive indexing of journal articles, and continues selectively indexing journals still.

290. New York (City). Museum of Modern Art. Library. Catalog of the Library of the Museum of Modern Art, New York City. 14 vols. Boston: G. K. Hall, 1976 (LC 76-383620).

The Library of the Museum of Modern Art was founded in 1932. At the time of publication of the catalog, the collection numbered approximately 30,000 bound volumes and about 700 periodical titles--probably the most extensive documentation devoted exclusively to modern art in this country, and perhaps in the world. The emphasis is on Western European and American art, particularly the visual arts: painting and sculpture, drawings and prints, architecture and design, photography, and film.

This is a dictionary catalog of authors, titles, and subjects. Almost all of the cataloging is original, and Library of Congress practice and American Library Association cataloging rules have not been strictly followed. The classification system used is the library's own but is based on the Dewey Decimal classification. The subject headings are also the library's own but are very similar to Library of Congress headings. Extensive subject analysis is emphasized and there are many see and see-also references. There are analytics for articles in periodicals that are not included in Art Index or the Répertoire d'art et d'archéologie, and for some articles in books. Generally these analytics appear only as subject entries. Major exhibition catalogs are cataloged as extensively as books; minor ones are given abbreviated cataloging. In volume 14 there is a separate catalog of periodicals and of the Latin American Archives, which consist of exhibition catalogs and of artists' files.

Most of the titles were published from the 1930's to the present, and are in English and other European languages, except Slavic languages.

291. New York (City). Public Library. Art and Architecture Division. Dictionary Catalog of the Art and Architecture Division. 30 vols. Boston: G. K. Hall, 1975 (ISBN 0-8161-1157-X). Supplement 1974. 556 p., 1976. Further supplemented by Bibliographic Guide to Art and Architecture: 1975- . Boston: G. K. Hall, 1976- .

The Art and Architecture Division is one of the oldest parts of the Research Libraries of The New York Public Library. It originated in 1839, ten years before the founding of the Astor Library, which was one of the three major precursors of The New York Public Library.

Included in this catalog are entries for works about art that are located in the Division and those found elsewhere in the general collections of The New York Public Library. The subjects covered here are painting, drawing, sculpture, and the history and design aspects of architecture and the applied arts from prehistoric to contemporary times. Subjects that will not be found in any depth in this catalog, mostly because they are covered in other catalogs of The New York Public Library, are prints; archaeology; book arts; city planning; materials, techniques, and specifications of architecture; photography; pre-Columbian and American Indian art; numismatics; engraved gems; techniques and manufacture of the applied arts; arms and armor; military costume and fortifications; and theatrical costume and architecture.

Rare books, local histories, exhibition catalogs, and some government documents are all included. All languages are represented in the catalog, including Oriental languages and those using Cyrillic and Hebrew characters. There are many analytics for articles in periodicals and works in series.

This is a dictionary catalog containing works from the earliest times to the end of 1971, when The New York Public Library adopted Anglo-American Cataloging Rules and Library of Congress subject headings, and instituted a computer-produced, dictionary catalog for the entire Research Libraries system (see 16). In the Dictionary Catalog of the Art and Architecture Division all the cataloging is original, and The New York Public Library's own subject headings are used. These headings were originally based on the alphabetico-classed system developed at Harvard during the nineteenth century. Although the tendency since 1925 has been toward adoption of Library of Congress subject headings, there is still a prevalence of very general subjects subdivided by place or smaller topic.

292. New York (City). Public Library. Prints Division. Dictionary Catalog of the Prints Division. 5 vols. Boston: G. K. Hall, 1975 (LC 75-332052).

This is not a catalog of individual prints but rather a catalog of books and book-like materials (including pamphlets, clipping files, and other ephemera) on prints and print-making. There are extensive analytical entries for articles in periodicals and collections. The division is particularly strong in historical and technical works on print-making, both Western and Oriental; book illustration; biographies of print-makers and catalogs of their works; bibliographies, handbooks, and periodicals devoted exclusively to prints; illustrated books containing original graphic works; scrapbooks on prominent American cartoonists; and clipping files. Entries that refer to the clipping files merely indicate that such a file exists, but do not identify the content or the source of the clippings. Works are in Western and Eastern European languages.

This is a dictionary catalog of works added to the collection up to July, 1975. Since 1972 new books have been cataloged using Anglo-American Cataloging Rules and Library of Congress subject headings. Before that date the library used its own subject headings and cataloging rules.

The Prints Division was established as a separate department in The New York Public Library with a gift of nearly 19,000 prints from Samuel Putnam Avery.

293. New York University. Institute of Fine Arts. Conservation Center. Library Catalog of the Conservation Center of the Institute of Fine Arts. 934 p. Boston: G. K. Hall, 1980 (ISBN 0-8161-0303-8).

The Conservation Center was founded in 1959 as a division of New York University's Institute of Fine Arts. The Library is "considered the most comprehensive collection in support of the study and practice of conservation of works of art" [Introduction]. The collection is particularly well developed in such topics as the properties of materials (pigments, glass, ivory, metals, minerals) and provides extensive coverage of both historical and contemporary techniques and construction of artistic works. Of special interest are several hundred eighteenth- and nineteenth-century artists' manuals and chemical formularies.

The library has more than 6,500 volumes, including books, serials, and an outstanding collection of conference papers. The catalog itself is in two parts: an Author-Title Catalog, and a Subject Catalog. The Subject Catalog uses Library of Congress subject headings and contains many cross-references. Works are in English and various other European languages.

294. Ottawa. National Gallery of Canada. Library. Catalogue of the Library of the National Gallery of Canada. 8 vols. Boston: G. K. Hall, 1973 (LC 74-166203).

The National Gallery of Canada began collecting books around 1910 but did not employ its first librarian until 1956, when the Gallery already had a working library of some 5,000 volumes. At the time of publication of this catalog there were over 38,000 fully cataloged volumes and 1,000 serial titles.

The emphasis of the collection is on Canadian art, from the religious art of French Canada three centuries ago to the contemporary art scene. The library is also strong in works on Western European painting and sculpture and is improving its collection on the decorative arts, modern American art, and photography.

This is a dictionary catalog of authors, titles, added entries, and subjects. The library, in general, follows Library of Congress practices and American Library Association cataloging rules, but makes numerous exceptions. The Library of Congress classification and subject headings are used with some modifications. Subject headings in French are included, with cross-references to the heading in English. There are many <u>see</u> and <u>see-also</u> references. Most of the cataloging is original. Holdings are given for most periodicals.

One of the interesting features of this catalog is the subject heading "Artists, Canadian--Individual," under which is listed 375 pages of <u>see</u> references to the names of individual Canadian artists, arranged alphabetically by the name of the artist. In effect, this provides a nearly complete list of the major and minor artists of Canada.

Works are in most Western European languages and include many exhibition catalogs (especially for Canadiana), Canadian government publications, and some theses. The availability of archival material for individual artists is indicated by a card with the name of the individual, the fact that he is a Canadian artist, his date of birth, and the note "Documentation."

295. Paris. Bibliothèque Forney. <u>Catalogue d'articles de périodiques, arts décoratifs et beaux-arts, Bibliothèque Forney, Paris</u> (Catalog of Periodical Articles, Decorative and Fine Arts). 4 vols. Boston: G. K. Hall, 1972 (LC 72-221666).

The Bibliothèque Forney was founded in 1866 with a bequest made to the City of Paris by Aimé Samuel Forney, a Parisian industrialist, to stimulate the artisans of the Faubourg Sainte-Antoine by providing them with free literature. The subject matter of the library, and of this index, is the decorative arts, especially interior decoration such as furniture, woodworking, wallpaper, curtains, and wrought iron.

This catalog is actually an index to articles in 1,350 periodicals. From 1919 to 1950 only particularly relevant articles were selected for indexing. Since 1950, periodical holdings have been systematically cataloged. Volume one has a list of the periodicals indexed. Subject headings are in French; there are many cross-references (<u>voir</u> and <u>voir-aussi</u>). Individuals are included as subjects. Most of the articles indexed are in French.

This catalog supplements the Répertoire d'Art et Archéologie and the Art Index, which accord only a small place to the decorative arts.

296. Paris. Bibliothèque Forney. Catalogue des catalogues de ventes d'art, Bibliothèque Forney, Paris (Catalog of the Catalogs of Sales of Art). 2 vols. Boston: G. K. Hall, 1972 (LC 72-226228).

Listed in this catalog are approximately 14,000 catalogs of art sales, most of them illustrated, dating from 1859 to 1971. Most of the titles are in French, but English and other European languages are also included. Additions to the collection have come from gifts from individuals and from such organizations as the Sotheby Galleries of London, the Parke-Bernet Galleries of New York, and trade union committees of the appraisers. The catalog is arranged in three parts: 1) alphabetically by name of collector; 2) chronologically by date of auction; and 3) alphabetically by place of auction. "Since 1950, entries have followed international rules" [Preface].

297. Paris. Bibliothèque Forney. Catalogue matières: arts-décoratifs, beaux-arts, métiers, techniques. 4 vols. Paris: Société des amis de la Bibliothèque Forney, 1970-1974 (LC 75-574191). Supplement. 1979- (to be completed in 2 vols.).

This is a subject catalog of material on the decorative arts, including interior decoration--wall and floor coverings, furniture, lights, ironwork; and also related subjects--goldwork, medallions, ceramics, ivories, etc. Also included are works on clothing, theatre decoration, and parlor games. Subject headings are in French, with many cross-references, also in French. Most of the titles are in French, although the library has been collecting on a worldwide basis since 1945. The main catalog represents 100,000 volumes and 1,347 periodical titles.

For the Bibliothèque Forney's index to periodical articles, see 295. For its catalog of sales catalogs, see 296.

298. Paris. Université. Bibliothèque d'art et d'archéologie (Fondation Jacques Doucet). Catalogue général: périodiques. 224 p. Nendeln: Kraus-Thomson Organization, 1972.

This is the main-entry catalog of periodicals in the art library of the University of Paris. Information indicating which issues are held is included. Titles have mainly nineteenth- and twentieth-century imprint dates and are in French, German, and other Western European languages.

299. Victoria and Albert Museum, South Kensington. National Art Library. National Art Library Catalogue, Victoria and Albert Museum, London, England. 10 vols. Boston: G. K. Hall, 1972 (LC 73-153208).

_______. Catalogue of Exhibition Catalogues. 623 p. Boston: G. K. Hall, 1972.

The Library of the Victoria and Albert Museum had its beginnings in 1837 and became the National Art Library in 1868. The focus of the catalog is on fine arts and design in the applied arts, including architecture, sculpture, painting, graphic arts, ornament, textiles, costumes, ceramics, glass, woodwork, furniture, metalwork, jewelry, illuminated manuscripts, and book arts. The library "probably has no equal in the fields of decorative and applied arts."[31]

This is a main-entry catalog only. The cataloging rules are based on the cataloging code of the British Museum Library (now the British Library, see 3). There are some added entries in the form of references to main entries. The tenth volume is an author catalog of pre-1890 titles. In total, the catalog contains over 300,000 entries.

The separate Catalogue of Exhibition Catalogues lists over 50,000 catalogs of art exhibitions held during the past century and a half. It is arranged first geographically and then by organizing institution. It is "the only catalogue of its size which provides a key to this important area of art research."[32]

300. Whitney Museum of American Art, New York. Library. Catalog of the Library of the Whitney Museum of American Art, New York, New York. 2 vols. Boston: G. K. Hall, 1979 (ISBN 0-8161-0288-0).

The Whitney Museum of American Art was founded in 1930 by Gertrude Vanderbilt Whitney, whose personal library formed the basis of the museum's library. By the time of publication of the catalog, the collection totalled over 10,000 books and exhibition catalogs. The subject of the library's collection is American art, especially twentieth-century American painting, sculpture, drawing, and graphics, but also included is Colonial and nineteenth-century American art, folk art, and photography.

This is a dictionary catalog that conforms in general to American Library Association and Library of Congress cataloging principles, with certain modifications. For example, in cataloging exhibition catalogs, there are additional entries made for artists in group shows. Not all exhibition catalogs in the library are included in the published catalog, however. The catalog is about 75 percent Library of Congress printed cards and 25 percent cards from original cataloging. Library of Congress subject headings and classification schedules are used.

22. THE PERFORMING ARTS

The performing arts are those that involve public performance, such as music, dance, and drama. The most important published catalogs of music collections are those of the Library of Congress (307), the Boston Public Library (301), and The New York Public Library (303). The Library of Congress's catalog of music includes recordings of music, unlike the other two mentioned, but also unlike the other two it is an author listing with a subject index, and not a dictionary catalog. A most useful and interesting catalog of music recordings is the Catalog of Sound Recordings of the Eastman School of Music's Sibley Music Library (306), which provides analytical indexing of all works contained on each record or tape in the collection.

The foremost dance collection in the United States is in The New York Public Library's Performing Arts Research Center, which has published its Dictionary Catalog of multimedia materials (302). The New York Public Library is also responsible for the publication of the 51-volume Catalog of the Theatre and Drama Collections (304), an unparalleled listing of drama and works on the theatre.

Catalogs emphasizing collections on the art of film may be found in chapter 21, "Art and Architecture."

301. Boston. Public Library. Dictionary Catalog of the Music Collection. 20 vols. Boston: G. K. Hall, 1972 (LC 72-182384). First Supplement. 4 vols., 1976.

Boston Public Library's Music Collection "covers all important writings on all aspects of music study during the past four hundred years or more" [Preface]. The collection began with a gift from Allen A. Brown in 1894. It covers all aspects of music study but its emphasis is on Western classical music history and criticism, theory and composition, and biography. Included in the catalog are monographs, early printed works, scores, and manuscripts. Not included are the library's special listing of sheet music, its sound recordings, and some of its archival materials.

This is a dictionary catalog with author, title, subject, and added entries. There are analytics for some works in collections and in series. Generally, Library of Congress subject headings are used, but the word "Music" is usually ignored if it is the first part of the heading; e.g., "Music--History and Criticism" becomes

"History." Three different classification systems have been used in the collection; the most recent is Library of Congress. Most of the works have imprint dates from the nineteenth or twentieth century, although some titles are considerably older. The collection is very strong in material in Western European languages, with foreign language material outnumbering English language works.

Detroit. Public Library. E. Azalia Hackley Collection. Catalog of the E. Azalia Hackley Memorial Collection of Negro Music, Dance, and Drama. 510 p. Boston: G. K. Hall, 1979. (see 229)

302. New York (City). Public Library. Dance Collection. Dictionary Catalog of the Dance Collection: A List of Authors, Titles, and Subjects of Multi-media Materials in the Dance Collection of the Performing Arts Research Center of the New York Public Library. 10 vols. New York: New York Public Library, distributed by G. K. Hall, 1974 (LC 74-81726). Supplemented by Bibliographic Guide to Dance: 1975- . Boston: G. K. Hall, 1976- .

The aim of the Dance Collection is to preserve records of every aspect--historical, theatrical, or economic--of every kind of dance, whether modern, ballet, expressionistic, social, theatrical, variety, folk, or burlesque. Toward this end the collection has accumulated 26,000 books; 6,000 libretti; 600 original drawings; 4,000 woodcuts, engravings, and lithographs; 150,000 photographs; 1,800,000 feet of film; 500,000 manuscripts and letters; and 1,500 oral history tapes. About five-eighths of the holdings are represented in the catalog. Also included in the catalog are extensive analytics for books and journals. The collection is international in scope, with great strengths in the history of American dance, and in English, Russian, and Italian ballet, and Asian dance.

The library uses its own list of 8,000 subject headings. There are many see and see-also references, as well as scope notes for some subject headings. Many entries have been given extensive annotations.

This fascinating and unique multimedia collection is located in the Performing Arts Research Center at Lincoln Center for the Performing Arts.

303. New York (City). Public Library. Reference Department. Dictionary Catalog of the Music Collection. 33 vols. Boston: G. K. Hall, 1964 (LC 66-503). Cumulative Supplement, 1964-1971. 10 vols., 1973. Supplement 1974. 559 p., 1976. Further supplement by Bibliographic Guide to Music: 1975- . Boston: G. K. Hall, 1976- .

The Music Collection covers all musical subjects and is one of the great music collections of the world. Its special strengths are folk songs, eighteenth- and nineteenth-century libretti, full scores of operas, complete works, historical editions, Beethoven, Americana, American music, periodicals, vocal music, literature on the voice, programs, and record catalogs.

This is a dictionary catalog of authors, titles, and subjects. The Music Collection uses its own subject headings (New York Public Library. Reference Dept. Music Subject Headings. 2nd ed., enlarged. Boston: G. K. Hall, 1966), and there are many see and see-also references. There are extensive analytics for books, series, and journals. Works can be found in most Western European languages.

The Music Collection is now located in the Performing Arts Research Center at Lincoln Center for the Performing Arts.

304. New York (City). Public Library. Research Libraries. Catalog of the Theatre and Drama Collections. 51 vols. Boston: G. K. Hall, 1967-76 (LC 68-5330). First Supplement. 3 vols., 1973 (supplements Parts I and II). Supplement 1974 to Parts I and II. 276 p., 1976. Further supplemented by Bibliographic Guide to Theatre Arts: 1975- . Boston: G. K. Hall, 1976- .

Part I: Drama Collection. 12 vols., 1967

The Catalog of the Theatre and Drama Collections is in three parts. This first part, the Drama Collection, is a collection of more than 120,000 plays written in Western languages or translated into Western languages. There are entries for volumes containing single dramatic works or collected plays of a single author, dramas appearing in anthologies or periodicals, and phonorecords of plays or readings from plays. Not included are entries for volumes containing plays of two or more authors, children's plays, Christmas plays, or moralities.

The Drama Collection catalog is itself in two parts. The first part is a listing by author, or by title for anonymous works. It is a main-entry only catalog. The second part is a subject listing by cultural origin. Here works may have more than one entry: under the original language and under the language of translation. Sample headings from this catalog include: "Drama, English--Bibliography," "Drama, English--Chinese authors," "Drama, English--Translations from Finnish," and "Drama, English--Translations into German."

Part II: Theatre Collection. 9 vols., 1967

At The New York Public Library, theatre is given a broad meaning; within the scope of this catalog are stage, cinema, radio, television, carnivals, nightclub performances, the circus, vaudeville, marionettes, and magic. All aspects of these arts are covered. For example, works on the stage include materials on stage history, production techniques, acting, theatre criticism, individual theatres, and biography. No published plays are included in this part of the catalog, but typescripts, promptbooks, and working scripts of movies, television, and radio are. There are also analytics for selected articles in periodicals.

This is a dictionary catalog of authors, titles, and subjects. Subject headings are the library's own, but there are no subject cross-references in the catalog. However, a separate list of Theatre Subject Headings Authorized for Use in the Catalog of the Theatre Collection (Boston: G. K. Hall, 1966) has been published. These headings are very specific and were developed especially for the Theatre Collection. They differ considerably from Library of Congress subject headings.

Part III: Non-Book Collection. 30 vols., 1976

The Non-Book Collection contains such things as programs, production photographs, portraits, reviews, press clippings, and scrapbooks, as well as page analytics of periodicals and monographs. The subject matter is entertainment, from live theatre to amusement parks. The emphasis is on production rather than the literary aspects of a work.

There are entries in the catalog under names of individual personalities, names of plays and other productions, and subjects such as "Theatres." The "Theatres" entries, which are subdivided geographically, are especially interesting and often give exact citations to books or periodicals where photographs or architectural reviews of a particular theatre may be found. Entries for individual productions often give the author, the stars, where the work was produced (city and theatre), and sometimes the date when and publication where a review appeared. However, often the only notation is "Clippings." There are cross-references from alternate titles of productions.

Works date from the eighteenth century to the present, and are generally in English. The last volume of the catalog contains a listing of materials with donor-imposed restrictions.

305. Newberry Library, Chicago. Bibliographical Inventory to the Early Music in the Newberry Library, Chicago, Illinois. Edited by D. W. Krummel. 587 p. Boston: G. K. Hall, 1976 (LC 77-351972).

The Newberry Library has one of the most important music collections in the United States. It is particularly rich in Renaissance music, early theory, and Americana. This catalog includes works published before 1861, about 10 percent of the collection. It lists manuscripts, sheet music (except most of the American sheet music), and works about music.

The arrangement is a classified one, based on the country and the time period. Within each division the arrangement is chronological, geographical, or by publisher, depending on what was thought to be most useful to the music historian. There are two indexes: 1) Index to Composers, Editors and Other Musical Subjects, and 2) Index to Printers, Engravers, Artists, Copyists, and Publishers.

306. Sibley Music Library. Catalog of Sound Recordings: The University of Rochester, Eastman School of Music, Rochester, New York. 14 vols. Boston: G. K. Hall, 1977 (LC 78-307798).

The Sibley Music Library was begun with a gift from Hiram W. Sibley in 1904; its record collection began in the 1930's. "Today the Sibley Music Library is the nation's largest collegiate music library" [Introduction].

This catalog represents 25,000 of the library's long-playing disc and tape recordings in over 200,000 cards. There are analytics for each bibliographically independent work recorded on a disc or tape, either in the form of added entries or as separate main entries. This is a dictionary catalog of authors and titles; the only subject entries are for "Medieval Music" and "Renaissance Music." Performers, series, and titles of works appear as added entries. Anglo-American cataloging rules are followed.

The majority of the recordings are of Western classical music.

307. United States. Library of Congress. Library of Congress Catalog: Music and Phonorecords; A Cumulative List of Works Represented by Library of Congress Printed Cards. Washington, 1953-1972 (LC 53-60012). Semiannual with annual and quinquennial cumulations:

_______. 1953-1957 (v. 27 of The National Union Catalog, 1953-1957). 1049 p. Ann Arbor, Mich.: J. W. Edwards, 1958.

_______. 1958-1962 (v. 51-52 of The National Union Catalog, 1958-1962). 2 vols. New York: Rowman and Littlefield, 1963.

_______. 1963-1967. 5 vols. Ann Arbor, Mich.: J. W. Edwards, 1969.

_______. 1968-1972. 5 vols. Ann Arbor, Mich.: J. W. Edwards, 1973.

_______. Library of Congress Catalog: Music, Books on Music, and Sound Recordings. Washington, 1973- (LC 74-64051). Semiannual with annual and quinquennial cumulations:

________. 1973-1977. 8 vols. New York: Rowman and Littlefield, 1978.

This Library of Congress catalog includes music scores, sheet music, libretti, and books about music and musicians, as well as sound recordings of all kinds, not only of music. It has been published since 1953; works from before that date may be found in The National Union Catalog: Pre-1956 Imprints (see 13). Still included in the ongoing National Union Catalog is literature about music, libretti, and music textbooks, but the NUC does not include sound recordings, sheet music, or music scores.

Until 1973 Library of Congress Catalog: Music and Phonorecords contained only LC printed cards. After that date, however, titles cataloged by libraries in the following universities have also been included: University of Toronto, Stanford University, University of Chicago, University of Illinois Music Library, Harvard University Edna Kuhn Loeb Music Library, University of North Carolina at Chapel Hill, Bowling Green State University, Oberlin College, and Ohio State University.

Included in all cumulations of the catalog is a subject index based on Library of Congress subject headings. In the last cumulation this index refers to LC printed cards only, and does not include the titles cataloged by the contributing libraries.

308. Vaughan Williams Memorial Library. The Vaughan Williams Memorial Library Catalogue of the English Folk Dance and Song Society: Acquisitions to the Library of Books, Pamphlets, Periodicals, Sheet Music and Manuscripts, from Its Inception to 1971. 769 p. London: Mansell, 1973 (LC 74-165155).

This collection had its origin when Cecil Sharp left his library to the English Folk Dance Society in 1924. This society merged in 1932 with the English Folk Song Society. When the society's president, Ralph Vaughan Williams, died in 1958, the library was named in his memory and funds were collected to expand it further. At the time of the catalog's publication, the library contained 7,000 books, pamphlets, and periodicals, plus tape recordings, records, and other materials not included in this catalog. Manuscripts and sheet music are listed in the catalog. The emphasis of the collection is on folk music, especially on the folk songs and folk dances of the British Isles.

The catalog is in two parts. The Subject Catalogue is a classified catalog based loosely on the Library of Congress classification. There is a short Subject Index arranged alphabetically by subject with reference to the appropriate classification number. The Author Catalogue is arranged alphabetically by author's name or title if there is no author. Entries are brief, providing the author, title, publisher, date, and place of publication, and occasionally an indication that there are illustrations or a bibliography. Both the Subject and Author Catalogues contain many entries for articles in periodicals.

The Vaughan Williams Memorial Library is in London, England.

23. GENERAL SOCIAL SCIENCE AND SOCIOLOGY

Included in this chapter are those catalogs that relate to the social sciences in general and to sociology and its special subdisciplines in particular. They are an especially interesting and heterogeneous group.

Of the catalogs treating the social sciences in general, the two most important are A London Bibliography of the Social Sciences (318) and the Bibliographie courante d'articles de périodiques postérieur à 1944 sur les problèmes politiques, économiques, et sociaux (310). The former is the well-known catalog of the British Library of Political and Economic Science, which has become, in essence, an annual bibliography of the social sciences. The latter, less well-known, is a catalog of periodical articles maintained by the Centre de Documentation Contemporaire of the Fondation Nationale des Sciences Politique in Paris, which indexes articles concerned with contemporary political, social, and economic affairs.

The Dictionary Catalog of the Whitney M. Young, Jr. Memorial Library of Social Work (313) of Columbia University is a very significant addition to the bibliography of social work. Related to social work are catalogs on the problems of the blind--Dictionary Catalog of the M. C. Migel Memorial Library, American Foundation for the Blind (309)--and of the deaf--Dictionary Catalog on Deafness and the Deaf of Gallaudet College in Washington, D. C. (315).

Three catalogs on criminology have been published. The largest, but most difficult to use, is The Library Catalogue of the Radzinowicz Library of Cambridge University (311). The Catalog of the Police Library of the Los Angeles Public Library (319) is an easy-to-use dictionary catalog, more oriented towards police science in the United States and more useful than the catalogs of the United States Law Enforcement Assistance Administration (321).

Also included here are catalogs on linguistics (312), gerontology (314), communications (317), and population (320).

309. American Foundation for the Blind. M. C. Migel Library. Dictionary Catalog of the M. C. Migel Memorial Library, American Foundation for the Blind. 2 vols. Boston: G. K. Hall, 1966 (ISBN 0-8161-0705-X).

"The American Foundation for the Blind is a national nonprofit agency whose purpose is to help those handicapped by blindness achieve the fullest possible development and utilization of their capacities and the maximum integration into the social, cultural and economic life of the community" [Introduction]. The foundation, located in New York City, began to assemble a library in the late 1920's, and by 1966 it had 25,000 volumes of monographs, serials, pamphlets, dissertations, and Federal, state, and local government publications, all dealing with the blind and different aspects of blindness.

This is a good historical collection. Most of the titles date from the early twentieth century, but some go back as far as the seventeenth century. Most of the titles are in English, but other Western languages are also collected. This is not a catalog of books in Braille.

This dictionary catalog has 23,000 cards for authors, titles, and subjects. The classification system used is a modification of the Library of Congress classification. Subject headings tend to be very specific; the word <u>blind</u> is normally not used since the whole library is about blindness. Thus, the subject heading "Dreams" is really about dreams of the blind. Exceptions are headings like "Blind authors," under which is listed works by writers who are blind, and "Blind in literature," under which is listed fiction about blind people. Many of these latter entries are stories in magazines. The library does a great deal of analytical indexing of articles in magazines and pages in books that deal with specific aspects of blindness.

Some of the other subjects covered here are the education of blind children, Braille, guide dogs, perception, the war-blinded, and the deaf-blind.

310. <u>Bibliographie courante d'articles de périodiques postérieur à 1944 sur les problèmes politiques, économiques, et sociaux</u> (Index to Post-1944 Periodical Articles on Political, Economic and Social Problems). 17 vols. Boston: G. K. Hall, 1968 (LC 70-409780). <u>First Supplement.</u> 2 vols., 1969. <u>Second Supplement.</u> 2 vols., 1970. <u>Third Supplement.</u> 2 vols., 1971. <u>Fourth Supplement.</u> 2 vols., 1972. <u>Fifth Supplement.</u> 2 vols., 1973. <u>Sixth Supplement.</u> 2 vols., 1974. <u>Seventh Supplement.</u> 2 vols., 1976. <u>Eighth Supplement.</u> 2 vols., 1977. <u>Ninth Supplement.</u> 2 vols., 1978. <u>Tenth Supplement.</u> 2 vols., 1979.

This is a catalog of periodical articles maintained by the Centre de Documentation Contemporaire of the Fondation Nationale des Sciences Politique in Paris. The foundation was created in 1945 to insure the diffusion and advancement of the political, social, and economic sciences in France and abroad. The Center for Contemporary Documentation indexes articles concerned with contemporary political, financial, and social phenomena, rather than historical articles or those containing purely theoretical contributions. In this it is similar to the Public Affairs Information Service Bulletin, but only periodical articles are indexed, and the coverage is world-wide and extends to thousands of journals. In 1967 the Center was receiving over 3,000 major French and foreign periodicals; 1,720 of them were analyzed at least partially, and over 20,000 articles a year were indexed. In 1976 approximately 27,650 articles were analyzed from 2,245 periodicals. Periodicals whose contents are not analyzed are given an entry for the periodical as a whole.

The arrangement is a classified one. The original breakdown is geographic by name of country; then, in a decimal classification, there is division by subject: internal administration, foreign affairs and defense, education and culture, social questions, economy, etc. The first volume of the index provides a detailed breakdown of the classification in French, with some English introductory material. There is also a French index to the classification system. Each article is given only one classification number, except in certain instances of relations between countries. Volume one also has a list of journals indexed, in their abbreviated form. Each supplement also contains the list of periodicals indexed in that supplement and an updated outline of the classification scheme.

311. Cambridge. University. Radzinowicz Library. The Library Catalogue of the Radzinowicz Library. 6 vols. Boston: G. K. Hall, 1979 (ISBN 0-8161-0242-2).

This is the catalog of the library of the Institute of Criminology at the University of Cambridge. The institute was established in 1959 as a research and teaching department within the Faculty of Law of the University. The library was named after Sir Leon Radzinowicz, the first director of the institute. The library collects materials in criminology on a world-wide basis and in many languages, although most titles in the catalog are in English. Related subjects covered in the collection include law, sociology, social administration, forensic psychology and psychiatry, philosophy, and history.

Listed in the catalog are 19,000 monographs, 9,500 pamphlets and offprints, and 192 current periodicals, as well as numerous official publications of the United Kingdom. Not included are the library's collection of statistics, annual reports, microforms, and ephemera. However, there are many analytics for periodical articles and for individual items from conference proceedings and edited collections, some with annotations.

The catalog is in four parts: 1) an Author Catalogue, which includes the names of persons as subjects and the names of defendants in trials, as well as the titles of United Kingdom documents; 2) a Periodicals Catalogue, containing many cross-references from sponsoring organizations to the names of journals; 3) a Classified Catalogue, arranged according to the first edition of the Bliss Classification System, adapted to the library; and 4) a brief Alphabetical Subject Index to the classification system. There is, unfortunately, no overall outline or guide to the classification system. The subject index, while helpful, is too brief to be an adequate guide, and the Bliss Classification can be very confusing in its use of both upper and lower case letters, plus numbers.

312. Center for Applied Linguistics. Library. Dictionary Catalog of the Library of the Center for Applied Linguistics, Washington, D. C. 4 vols. Boston: G. K. Hall, 1974 (LC 75-301806).

The principal aims of the Center for Applied Linguistics are: "1) to apply the results of linguistic research to practical language problems; 2) to promote cooperation between linguistics and other disciplines concerned with language problems; 3) to encourage incorporation of the findings of linguistic science into the American educational system." The library thus specializes in language and linguistics, especially in: the teaching of English as a second language; Arabic language and literature; Russian; bilingual education; the teaching of African and Asian languages in the United States; and American Indian language education policy.

Included in the collection are manuscripts and unpublished works contributed by the authors and working papers of linguistics departments and societies. There are analytics for these working papers and for various series. The library uses the Library of Congress classification system and Library of Congress subject headings with some modifications.

313. Columbia University. Libraries. School of Social Work Library. Dictionary Catalog of the Whitney M. Young, Jr. Memorial Library of Social Work, Columbia University, New York. 10 vols. Boston: G. K. Hall, 1980 (ISBN 0-8161-0307-0).

"The School of Social Work Library at Columbia University is the largest single library in the country supporting professional social work education" [Introduction]. The collection dates from 1882, when the New York Charity Organization Society formed a library. In time, the collection came to incorporate the holdings of the libraries of the Charity Organization Society, the New York State Charities Aid, the Association for Improving the Condition of the Poor, the Russell Sage Foundation, the New York School of Philanthropy, and the New York School of Social Work, the predecessor of the School of Social Work at Columbia University. In 1975 the library was named in honor of Whitney M. Young, Jr., the late civil rights and social work leader.

The catalog contains over 170,000 cards representing over 60,000 volumes of books; monographic serials; more than 1,000 periodicals; municipal, state, and Federal documents; doctoral dissertations and masters' essays in social work; and standard reference works. The library is particularly strong in the publications of the voluntary social welfare agencies, such as the Child Welfare League of America and the Family Service Association of America. It has an excellent historical collection of such publications and of nineteenth- and early twentieth-century government reports on the state of the poor in the United States and Great Britain. Very few foreign language titles are acquired.

The library collects material in the following areas: 1)

history and philosophy of social welfare with special emphasis on social work; 2) social services, including services to families and children, day care, and legal services; 3) community organization; 4) social policy development and administration; 5) health and mental health; 6) aging; 7) social security; 8) corrections and court services, including probation, parole, and diversionary treatment; 9) alcoholism and drug addiction; 10) industrial social welfare and manpower; 11) urban education; 12) intergroup relations; and 13) social and physical rehabilitation.

The catalog itself is divided into three parts. The bulk of the catalog (volumes one to eight) is a dictionary catalog of monographs and serials from traditional publishing sources. Library of Congress subject headings are used and there are many see references from alternate forms of subject headings and of names. Also included are many analytical entries for articles in periodicals and in books, particularly for the first half of the twentieth century. The quality of the cataloging has varied with time and has also depended upon the practices of the library that first cataloged the book; some of the material is listed with only the briefest of bibliographical information.

Volume nine, the Agency Catalog, includes "quasi-cataloged" material from voluntary and public social welfare agencies, including conferences and workshop proceedings, position papers, reports, and training and case documents. The arrangement is alphabetical by issuing agency, and under the name of each agency are listed all the reports of that agency owned by the library. The size of the Agency Catalog is deceiving. There are over 10,000 cards in the volume but most cards list from four to seven reports, so that the total number of agency reports owned by the library must be well over 50,000. Duplicate copies of the reports owned by the library are part of the circulating collection and are listed in the dictionary catalog.

Volume ten of the catalog is a Projects Catalog of over 5,000 uncataloged masters' essays and reports of other special projects produced by students at the New York School of Social Work from 1932 to 1963 and the Columbia University School of Social Work from 1963 to 1974. It is a divided catalog of subjects, authors' names, and sponsoring agencies.

314. Ethel Percy Andrus Gerontology Center. Library. Catalogs of the Ethel Percy Andrus Gerontology Center, University of Southern California, Los Angeles. 2 vols. Boston: G. K. Hall, 1976 (LC 77-350910).

The Andrus Gerontology Center is active in research on aging, practical community work with the aged, and the education of professional personnel in the field of gerontology. The library supports all three functions. It was started as an office collection in 1966, and ten years later its catalog listed 5,500 titles including monographs, research reports, conference proceedings, state and Federal documents, publications of agencies, proceedings of colloquia and symposia, and a collection of microfilmed doctoral dissertations on aging. The primary emphasis of the collection is on social gerontology, but also included are materials in psychology, sociology, social work, biology, physiology, architecture, environmental planning, geriatric nursing, housing, and health care, all related to aging. Most of the imprint dates are post-1960, and most of the works are in English.

This is a divided catalog. The first volume is an author-title catalog; the second volume is a subject catalog. The library uses modifications of the Library of Congress classification system and subject headings. All of the cataloging is original.

315. Gallaudet College, Washington, D. C. Edward Miner Gallaudet Memorial Library. Dictionary Catalog on Deafness and the Deaf. 2 vols. Boston: G. K. Hall, 1970 (ISBN 0-8161-0877-3).

Gallaudet College is the world's only liberal arts college specifically for the deaf. The specialty of the library is, obviously, information on deafness and the deaf. Most of the works listed in this catalog are of twentieth-century origin, but there is an historical collection of works from 1546 to 1900. The core of this collection, known as the Baker Collection, consists of 500 works that have been microfilmed and made available for purchase.

The catalog of the Gallaudet Library is a dictionary catalog. Library of Congress subject headings are used but extensively modified. The library uses its own classification system. Included in the catalog are entries for books, reprints, reports of research, proceedings of conferences, periodicals, annual reports of schools for the deaf, pamphlets, and theses from Gallaudet and other colleges. There are many analytical entries for reprints of journal articles and for chapters in books.

316. Harvard University. Library. Sociology. 2 vols. Cambridge, Mass.: distributed by Harvard University Press, 1973 (LC 72-83391). (Widener Library Shelflist v. 45-46)

Included in these volumes are 49, 000 titles representing most of Harvard University's collection in sociology. This includes sociological history and theory, social groups and institutions, social problems and social reform, and social psychology. Also listed are works on specific social groups or issues: socialism, labor, charity and welfare, crime, alcoholism, women, marriage, family, youth and the aged, societies, and clubs. Works treating the social sciences collectively are also listed here, but works on general social conditions and social policy in different parts of the world are included in the volumes of the Widener shelflist that cover the various history classes.

Titles are listed in three places: first, there is a classified, or shelflist arrangement; second is a chronological listing; and third, an author-title listing. The majority of the titles here are in English, with substantial holdings in German, some in French, and with other languages represented. For further information on the Widener Library shelflists see 9.

317. Illinois. University at Urbana-Champaign. Library. Catalog of the Communications Library. 3 vols. Boston: G. K. Hall, 1975 (ISBN 0-8161-1174-X).

The University of Illinois' Communications Library is "probably the largest collection of English-language books on the subject assembled as a single unit" [Introduction]. The collection was begun in 1933 as a reading room, but by the time of publication of the catalog it had 12,500 monographs and 400 serials and periodicals, as well as a rich pamphlet collection. Subjects included in the library are mass communications; communication theory; advertising; freedom of the press; popular culture; mass media, including newspapers, television, radio, cable television, magazines, and book publishing; graphic arts, especially the history of photography, works of photographers, and typography; copyright; public opinion; and language and linguistics. Coverage is international, but works are in English only.

This is a dictionary catalog of authors, titles, and subjects. The library uses Library of Congress subject headings and the Dewey Decimal classification. About half of the cards are Library of Congress printed cards; the rest represent original cataloging. There are some see references for names, but no cross-references at all for subjects. Most of the works were published in the third quarter of the twentieth century.

318. A London Bibliography of the Social Sciences. 4 vols. London: Mansell, 1929- (LC 31-9970). First Supplement (1929-1931). v. 5, 1934. Second Supplement (1931-1936). v. 6, 1937. Third Supplement (1936-1950). v. 7-9, 1955. Fourth Supplement (1950-1955). v. 10-11, 1958. Fifth Supplement (1955-1962). v. 12-14, 1966. Sixth Supplement (1962-1968). v. 15-21, 1970. Seventh Supplement (1969-1972). v. 22-28, 1973. Eighth Supplement (1972-1973). v. 29-31, 1975. Ninth Supplement (1974). v. 32, 1975. Tenth Supplement (1975). v. 33, 1976. Eleventh Supplement (1976). v. 34, 1977.

This work was originally conceived as the subject catalog of the Library of Political and Economic Science at the London School of Economics. The original compilation, representing some 600,000 items, and the First Supplement actually included holdings of this library (now called the British Library of Political and Economic Science) as well as holdings in the social sciences from the Edward Fry Library of International Law, the Goldsmiths' Library of Economic Literature (see also 360), the National Institute of International Affairs, and the Royal Statistical Society, and some special collections from three other libraries. The bulk of the entries, however, are from the London School of Economics, and subsequent supplements include holdings only from the British Library of Political and Economic Science and from the Edward Fry Library of International Law. In general, all aspects of the social sciences are covered, and materials include books, pamphlets, government documents, dissertations, and pamphlets.

This is a subject catalog. Library of Congress subject headings are used with some modifications. The Sixth Supplement lists all the subject headings used in alphabetical order; later supplements list the subject headings arranged by broad topic. Under the topic "Biography" in these lists may be found the names of individuals about whom biographies appear in the supplement. Early volumes have extensive cross-references; later ones abandon these in favor of the lists of subject headings just mentioned. There are author indexes for volumes one to six.

The bibliographic information provided for each title tends to be quite brief, although later volumes have more extensive information.

The initial compilation and the first six supplements were originally published by the London School of Economics itself.

319. Los Angeles. Public Library. Municipal Reference Library. Catalog of the Police Library of the Los Angeles Public Library. 2 vols. Boston: G. K. Hall, 1972 (LC 73-158794). First Supplement. 2 vols., 1980.

Listed in the original catalog are 35,000 cards for books, magazine articles, pamphlets, annual and statistical reports from major city, county, and state law enforcement agencies, reports and studies of commissions, conference proceedings, seminar papers, and theses. These are arranged in a dictionary catalog of authors, titles, and subjects. Library of Congress subject headings are used, augmented by police science and criminology technical terms. The classification system used is Dewey Decimal.

As its title indicates, the major subject of this catalog is police science. It is strongest in criminology, scientific investigation, crime and criminals, riots, violence, and police history. Other strengths include traffic, censorship, juvenile delinquency, drugs, guns, jails and prisons, alcoholism, probation and correction, vice and gambling, police administration, planning, police research and development, training, the administration of justice, and crime prevention.

Of particular interest in this catalog are the analytics for police science and criminology journals and for articles on police science in popular periodicals, since criminology indexes date back only to 1961. This catalog lists periodical articles from well before that date and would act as a useful addition for later periods as well. The supplement continues the analytical indexing of periodicals and includes many pre-1970 titles. Also indexed are parts of books relating to police.

320. Population Council, New York. Library. Catalogue of the

Population Council Library, New York. 3 vols. Boston: G. K. Hall, 1979 (ISBN 0-8161-0278-3).

The Population Council was established in 1952 as an independent, nonprofit organization conducting multidisciplinary research in the broad field of population. It now has "one of the most extensive population library collections in existence" [Introduction], with 10,000 books; pamphlets; documents of the United Nations, the United States, and other governments; theses; considerable report literature; and unpublished materials. The library collects in the fields of population policy, development, social change, women's and family studies, birth control and family planning, and demography.

The catalog is divided into an Author/Title Catalog (volumes one and two), which includes added entries; and a Subject Catalog (volume three). Modified Library of Congress subject headings are used, and most of the collection is classified using the Library of Congress classification system, although other systems are also used for selected types of materials (e. g., UN documents, theses). All items are fully cataloged. The library underwent a two-year reorganization beginning in 1974, the intent of which was to insure good bibliographic citations and accurate subject headings.

Most of the material is in English, although other European languages are included, and the collection contains works on all countries of the world. Most of the works are current, generally having been published in the 1970's.

321. United States. Law Enforcement Assistance Administration. Library Book Catalog. 4 vols. Washington, D. C.: for sale by Government Printing Office, 1972. Supplement. 4 vols., December, 1974. Supplement. 3 vols. December, 1975.

This is the consolidated catalog of the libraries of the Law Enforcement Assistance Administration, the Federal Bureau of Prisons, and the Bureau of Narcotics and Dangerous Drugs. The 1974 supplement also includes the holdings of the National Criminal Justice Reference Service (NCJRS), an international clearinghouse of the Law Enforcement Assistance Administration for criminal justice reference and information dissemination.

The catalog is a divided one, and each volume is actually a separate catalog. There is an Author Catalog, a Title Catalog, a Subject Catalog, and a Periodicals Catalog. The library tries to conform to Library of Congress practices, including LC subject headings and call numbers, with some modifications. The 1974 and 1975 subject supplements include lists of the subject headings used. Entries are brief, consisting only of author, title, call number, place and date of publication, publisher, and a symbol for the holding library.

The catalog with its supplements contains well over 10,000 books and documents in law enforcement, criminology, penology, and police science.

24. PSYCHOLOGY

Although this chapter is titled "Psychology," there is, in fact, no one general catalog of psychology in it. Rather, libraries devoted to particular aspects of psychology or psychiatry have published their catalogs. These include the catalog of the library of the Analytical Psychology Club (322); the Catalog of the Menninger Clinic Library (326), devoted to research in psychiatry; and the fascinating monograph (325) and periodical literature (324) catalogs of the Institute for Sex Research.

322. Analytical Psychology Club, New York. Kristine Mann Library. Catalog of the Kristine Mann Library of the Analytical Psychology Club of New York, Inc. 2 vols. Boston: G. K. Hall, 1978 (ISBN 0-8161-0085-3).

The Kristine Mann Library of the Analytical Psychology Club of New York was established in 1945 and named in honor of a founding member of the club. The emphasis of the library is on analytical psychology, especially works by and about Carl Gustav Jung. Holdings of the library include approximately 6,000 volumes, file clippings, unpublished papers and some tapes of club lectures. There is thorough coverage of publications of the Analytical Psychology Club of New York, the C. G. Jung Foundation of New York, the Jung Institute in Zurich, and other analytical psychology institutes. There are many analytics for articles in journals and in books, and detailed analytical entries for proceedings.

The catalog is in two parts: volume one is an author/title catalog, and volume two is a subject catalog. Subject headings are based on Library of Congress headings, amplified and adapted to the vocabulary of analytical psychology. The classification system is the library's own. All of the cataloging is original, and there are many see and see-also references. The library is open to visitors but, as of the time of publication of the catalog, it had no facilities for interlibrary loan or photocopying.

323. Geneva. University. Catalogue des Archives Jean Piaget, Université de Genève, Suisse. (Catalog of the Jean Piaget Archives, University of Geneva, Switzerland). 384 p. Boston: G. K. Hall, 1975 (ISBN 0-8161-1184-7).

Most of the material in this catalog has been collected in the University of Geneva's Piaget Archives, which were set up, as Piaget himself states in the Foreword, because he has never been able to keep his published works together, "having written far too much, thinking only of whatever happened to be in hand or was in gestation at the time, and quickly losing interest in books and articles once they were finished." This catalog is, in effect, a major bibliography of and on Jean Piaget and his work in psychology. It is arranged in three parts. Part One is a bibliography of publications by Jean Piaget arranged by type of publication; e.g., monographs, serial publications, articles, chapters, lectures, reports, etc. Part Two lists the works of Jean Piaget's collaborators. Part Three, which is arranged by country, contains works about Piaget and Genevan psychology, consisting mainly of periodical articles. Part Three contains indexes by author and keyword, and lists periodicals and conference proceedings referred to in Part Three.

Works by Piaget in this catalog total approximately 1,500 manuscripts, books, articles, prefaces, commentaries, and responses. Works about Piaget total approximately 940 references to articles published in periodicals and in conference proceedings. Works are primarily in French and English, and cover the period 1907-1974.

Harvard University. Library. Philosophy and Psychology. 2 vols. Cambridge, Mass.: Harvard Univ. Pr., 1973. (see 261)

324. Institute for Sex Research. Library. Catalog of Periodical Literature in the Social and Behavioral Sciences Section, Library of the Institute for Sex Research, Indiana University; Including Supplement to Monographs, 1973-1975. 4 vols. Boston: G. K. Hall, 1976 (ISBN 0-8161-0041-1).

Included in this catalog are over 14,000 articles in periodicals, reprints of journal articles, and papers, plus about 1,000 new monograph titles that supplement the Catalog of the Social and Behavioral Sciences, Monograph Section (see 325). The subject of the collection is sexual behavior and sex research.

This is a dictionary catalog of authors, titles, and subjects. Anglo-American cataloging rules are followed. The subject headings used here are completely different from those used in the Catalog of Monographs. They were developed by the library and are reproduced in Sexual Nomenclature: A Thesaurus (Boston: G. K. Hall, 1976), which is a hierarchical, interdisciplinary vocabulary for indexing material in the field of sex research. The Introduction to the Catalog of Periodical Literature advises using the Thesaurus when doing a thorough search of the catalog, but in fact the catalogers have been so generous with cross-references and guide cards that reference to the Thesaurus is not absolutely necessary. The guide cards list broader terms, narrower terms, and related terms. There are also references to subjects found in the Catalog of the Social and Behavioral Sciences, Monograph Section.

325. Institute for Sex Research. Library. Catalog of the Social and Behavioral Sciences, Monograph Section, of the Library of the Institute for Sex Research, Indiana University, Bloomington, Indiana. 4 vols. Boston: G. K. Hall, 1975 (LC 75-310797).

The Institute for Sex Research was founded by Dr. Alfred C. Kinsey in 1947. By 1975 its library contained more than 30,000 volumes, making it "one of the greatest and most extensive collections on sexual behavior."[33] Included are histories of early sex education and material on marriage, abortion, contraception, women's rights, sex ethics, religion, sex laws, venereal disease, prostitution, and contemporary research in sex behavior and attitudes. The library maintains an erotica collection which is not listed in the catalog.

This is the monograph catalog of the library; there are entries for books as well as essays in or chapters in books. It is a dictionary catalog using Anglo-American cataloging rules and its own classification system. Subject headings were developed by the library but are similar to Library of Congress headings. They are completely different from those subject headings used in the library's Catalog of Periodical Literature (see 324), which also supplements this monograph catalog. There are many subject and author cross-references.

Books listed here are from all historical periods, but the emphasis is on the nineteenth and twentieth centuries. Material cataloged only through September, 1973 is included. Works are mostly in English and other Western languages.

326. Menninger Clinic, Topeka, Kansas. Library. Catalog of the Menninger Clinic Library, the Menninger Foundation, Topeka, Kansas. 4 vols. Boston: G. K. Hall, 1971 (ISBN 0-8161-0961-3). First Supplement: Catalog of the Professional Library of the Menninger Foundation--First Supplement. 2 vols., 1978.

The Menninger Foundation is a non-profit institution concerned with treatment, education, prevention, and research in psychiatry. The library dates back to 1930, and covers all aspects of psychiatry and psychology, including neurology, psychoanalysis, mental health administration, pastoral counseling, theology, sociology, behavioral sciences, social work, nursing, law, psychophysiology, psychopharmacology, anthropology, penology, art, literature, and adjunctive therapy. The original catalog represents 30,000 volumes, including 400 current journals; the supplement records 6,500 additional volumes added from 1972 to June, 1977.

The catalog is in two parts: volumes one to three are an author-title catalog; volume four is a subject catalog. National Library of Medicine subject headings are used, and the classification system is a combination of Library of Congress and NLM. There are author analytics for publications appearing in books of Menninger Foundation staff members, and author analytics for all writings of members of the Menninger family. The supplement includes author analytics for all publications written by the professional staff while they were employed at the Foundation, including book reviews, correspondence, and interviews, as well as scholarly papers.

Works are mostly in English and generally date from 1950 on.

327. North East London Polytechnic. The Psychology Readings Catalogue of the North East London Polytechnic, London, England. 2 vols. Boston: G. K. Hall, 1976 (ISBN 0-8161-1179-0).

This is a catalog of 24,000 analytical entries, filed alphabetically by author, for books of multiple authorship--books of readings, symposia, conference proceedings, annual meetings, annual reviews, festschriften, and similar compilations--in the field of psychology. It acts as a sort of Essay and General Literature Index for psychology.

Only first authors are indexed; there are cross-references from second authors. Most of the essays had been published elsewhere before they were reprinted in collections, and the entries give the original sources as well as the bibliographic information for the collections in which they now appear. There is a list of the books analyzed at the end of the second volume. In addition, in the second volume is a list of topics with the names of the psychologists writing about them. This serves as a subject index to the catalog and also as a helpful guide for students wanting to know who the important "names" are in a field.

North East Polytechnic was formed by the merging of three colleges in London: Barking, Newham, and Waltham Forest. The result was one of the largest psychology departments in the country.

328. Reiss-Davis Child Study Center. Research Library. Catalog of the Research Library of the Reiss-Davis Child Study Center, Los Angeles, California. 2 vols. Boston: G. K. Hall, 1978 (ISBN 0-8161-0086-1).

This library was founded in 1950 soon after the Reiss-Davis Clinic (later Reiss-Davis Child Study Center) was founded. By 1978 it had 12,000 bound volumes, 200 serial publications, 400 audio tapes, 25 films, and approximately 5,000 pamphlets, reprints, and reports. Only the books are included in the published catalog.

The subject matter of the collection is child study, including child psychiatry, child psychology, child psychoanalysis, psychiatric social work with children and their families, child welfare, special education, and learning disabilities. Most of the works were published in the 1960's and 1970's, when the field began expanding greatly.

This is a dictionary catalog. Subject headings are a combination of Library of Congress headings, medical headings from the National Library of Medicine, and some locally derived headings. There are many see and see-also references. The Library of Congress classification system is used.

329. Society for Psychical Research, London. Library. Catalogue of the Library of the Society for Psychical Research, London, England. 341 p., Boston: G. K. Hall, 1976 (LC 76-358758).

The Society for Psychical Research was founded in 1882 and began its library shortly thereafter. By 1957 it had about 8,000 books. "It is generally acknowledged to be the greatest psychical research library in the world" [Introduction]. Included are works on telepathy and all forms of paranormal cognition, mediumship, psychology, philosophy, mysticism, and hypnotism.

The catalog is in two parts: a title catalog and an author catalog. Entries are brief, consisting only of author, title, publisher, date and place of publication. The library uses its own classification system.

Most of the works are monographs, but there are some entries for conference proceedings. Titles generally bear imprint dates from the nineteenth and twentieth centuries, although some were printed as early as 1595. They are mostly in English, with other Western European languages also represented.

330. Tavistock Joint Library. Catalogue of the Tavistock Joint Library, London, England. 2 vols. Boston: G. K. Hall, 1975 (ISBN 0-8161-1167-7).

The Tavistock Clinic was begun after the First World War. The library serves both the Clinic and the Tavistock Institute of Human Relations, which are oriented towards research and teaching in psychology, psychiatry, psychoanalysis, sociology, and the study of organizations. The library is particularly rich in holdings on group psychotherapy, and on experimental and sociological works on the family and other small groups.

The catalog is an author catalog of 10,000 books, 5,500 pamphlets and offprints, and photocopies of periodical articles. There are many analytics for essays in books, and for journal articles. In fact, most of the entries seem to be analytics. There is a list of periodicals currently received at the beginning of the first volume.

25. EDUCATION AND CHILDREN'S BOOKS

The foremost published catalog of works on education is the Dictionary Catalog of the Teachers College Library (333) of Columbia University. It is, however, a collection biased towards the study of education in the United States; for information on education around the world the Catalogue of the Comparative Education Library (335) of the University of London may be more valuable.

Similarly, the catalogs of the International Youth Library (336) list children's books published in all countries, providing access to them by name of author and of illustrator, by title, by subject, and by country of publication. The Dictionary Catalog of the Children's Collection in the General Library, Boston Public Library (331) lists collections of children's books that are mostly in English and were selected for children in Boston to borrow and read.

331. Boston. Public Library. Dictionary Catalog of the Children's Collection in the General Library, Boston Public Library. 5 vols. Cambridge, Mass.: Produced for the Trustees of the Boston Public Library by General Microfilm Co., 1974.

This is a dictionary catalog representing about 40,000 volumes of 20,000 titles that formed the circulating collection of the Children's Room in the Central Library of the Boston Public Library as of December, 1973. Books have been selected to meet the needs of children up to the age of 13. Books for young adult readers are listed in the Young Adult Catalog of the Boston Public Library (see 332).

Subject entries used in the library have evolved from unique Boston Public Library practices to the use of Sears headings and most recently to Library of Congress subject headings. All three systems are represented in the catalog. See and see-also references have been added to aid the user. The library's classification system has changed from a system based upon Cutter to the Dewey classification to the Library of Congress classification, and the catalog again contains a mixture of these three systems.

Non-print material is not included in the catalog, nor are some older, rare juvenile books. Foreign language material, however, is included.

332. Boston. Public Library. Young Adult Catalog of the Boston Public Library. 2 vols. Boston: G. K. Hall, 1972 (ISBN 0-8161-1028-X).

This is a dictionary catalog of 6,000 titles selected for teen-aged, or young adult, readers. Out-of-print material is not generally included nor are periodicals, recordings, and other non-print materials. The collection includes material reviewed by young adult readers themselves, by professionals working with young adults, as well as by professional librarians.

Material is cataloged in the Library of Congress classification.

333. Columbia University. Teachers College. Library. Dictionary Catalog of the Teachers College Library. 36 vols. Boston: G. K. Hall, 1970 (LC 72-13958). First Supplement. 5 vols., 1971. Second Supplement. 2 vols., 1973. Third Supplement. 10 vols., 1977. Further supplemented by Bibliographic Guide to Education: 1978- . Boston: G. K. Hall, 1979- .

Teachers College is a graduate school designed for "advanced studies in the practice of education, for study of the philosophical and theoretical bases for practice, and for the advancement of knowledge of both theory and practice" [Introduction]. The library is designed to meet the needs of the graduate students and faculty. Its collections are comprehensive in the fields of psychology, particularly applied psychology; educational administration; the history and philosophy of education; guidance; special education; higher education; adult education; speech pathology and audiology; health education; nursing education; home and family life; curriculum and teaching; educational technology; recreation; international and comparative education; and the teaching of particular subjects such as mathematics, art, science, business, music, social sciences, languages, physical education, and speech.

The original catalog lists over 400,000 books as well as current and backfiles of periodicals, and audiovisual materials. Original documents, historical and contemporary textbooks, and administrative reports of school systems are all collected. Works are mostly in English, but all European and many non-European languages are included.

This is a dictionary catalog of authors, titles, and subjects. The subject headings used in the catalog were developed from List of Educational Subject Headings, by Belle L. Vogelein (Columbus, Ohio, 1928), Subject Headings in Education by Clyde Pettus (New York, 1938) and, more recently, from Library of Congress Subject Headings. The Library of Congress classification system was adopted in 1968.

334. Harvard University. Library. Education and Education Periodicals. 2 vols. Cambridge, Mass.: distributed by

Harvard University Press, 1968 (LC 68-15925). (Widener Library Shelflist v. 16-17)

This is a classified arrangement of about 30,000 monographs and 1,800 periodicals on education. Included are general treatises on education, works on special types of education and special types of schools, works on the theory and methods of teaching and the training of teachers, and histories of education. Not to be found here are histories, reports, and catalogs of individual schools, colleges, and universities; the historic textbook collection; or the holdings of Harvard's Graduate School of Education Library.

About two-thirds of the titles listed are in English and most works were published in the nineteenth and twentieth centuries. In addition to the classified arrangement, there is a listing by author and title, and a chronological listing.

For more information on the Widener Library shelflists see 9.

335. London. University. Institute of Education. Library. Catalogue of the Comparative Education Library, University of London, Institute of Education. 6 vols. Boston: G. K. Hall, 1971 (LC 70-17337). First Supplement. 3 vols., 1974.

This library was formed by the merger of two collections: Comparative Education and Education in Tropical Areas. The library contains books, pamphlets, and government documents on history, sociology, anthropology, religion, demography, geography and, of course, education. There is also a valuable collection of annual reports. Included are some analytical entries for journals and collections.

The catalog is in three parts: an author-title catalog, a subject catalog, and a regional catalog. The author-title catalog includes subject entries for persons and corporate bodies. The subject catalog uses the library's own subject headings, subdivided by country or region. The regional catalog is subdivided by subject. There is some duplication of entries between the subject and the regional catalogs, but both catalogs should be checked for information about a particular subject in a particular country. Special emphasis is on countries of the British Commonwealth.

The library began using modified Anglo-American Cataloging Rules in 1969, and the supplement reflects the changes.

336. Munich. Internationale Jugendbibliothek (International Youth Library). Alphabetischer Katalog (Alphabetical Catalog). 5 vols. Boston: G. K. Hall, 1968 (ISBN 0-8161-0759-9).

_______. Illustratorenkatalog (Catalog of Illustrators). 3 vols. Boston: G. K. Hall, 1968 (ISBN 0-8161-0109-4).

_______. Länderkatalog (Languages Section Catalog). 4 vols. Boston: G. K. Hall, 1968 (LC 70-6878).

________. Systematischer Katalog (Classified Catalog). 2 vols. Boston: G. K. Hall, 1968 (ISBN 0-8161-0108-6).

________. Titelkatalog (Title Catalog). 4 vols. Boston: G. K. Hall (ISBN 0-8161-0111-6).

The International Youth Library attempts to acquire books for children and youth in all languages from all over the world. It was established in 1948 and supported by grants from private citizens, the German Federal Republic, the Free State of Bavaria, the City of Munich, UNESCO, and the Rockefeller Foundation. It receives free donations from publishers of their latest books displayed in an annual exhibition. The library also collects works about children's books. The books were published mostly in the 1950's and 1960's.

The catalog of the Internationale Jugendbibliothek is in five parts. The Alphabetischer Katalog is arranged alphabetically by author, or sometimes by title. There are cross-references to the correct form of an author's name, and some added entries. The Illustratorenkatalog is arranged alphabetically by the name of the illustrator of the book. The Länderkatalog is arranged alphabetically by name of country of publication and within country by author. The Systematischer Katalog is arranged in order by Dewey Decimal classification. The first volume contains both a summary of the main classes and an alphabetical index to the classification, in German. The Titelkatalog is arranged alphabetically by title of book. The library uses Prussian cataloging rules and the new German "book of rules" (Regelwerk).

337. New York (City). Public Library. The Branch Libraries: Children's Catalog. New York: New York Public Library, 1973- .

This is a computer-produced book catalog of children's books in the Branch Libraries system of The New York Public Library cataloged since June, 1972. Included are works in the Central Children's Room of the Donnell Library Center, including a broad collection of children's books in foreign languages and on phonodiscs and cassettes; the special collections of children's materials in the performing arts (theatre, drama, music, dance, puppetry, and the circus) maintained at the Performing Arts Research Center; and the collection of materials on the Black experience at the Countee Cullen branch; as well as material cataloged for the general circulating collections of the branch libraries in Manhattan, The Bronx, and Staten Island.

The catalog is divided into three parts. The Names Catalog includes names of persons, institutions, and organizations, and lists works both by and about them. The main entries have complete bibliographic information and include brief annotations describing the subject content of the book. The Titles Catalog and the Subjects Catalog have briefer entries, except where the title is the main entry for the book.

New additions to the collection are listed in supplements, but the catalog is cumulated and reissued regularly.

United States. Department of Health, Education and Welfare. Library. <u>Author/Title and Subject Catalogs of the Department Library.</u> 49 vols. Boston: G. K. Hall, 1965. (see 349)

338. United States. Library of Congress. Rare Book Division. <u>Children's Books in the Rare Book Division of the Library of Congress.</u> 2 vols. Totowa, N.J.: Rowman and Littlefield, 1975 (LC 75-9605).

Described here is a separate special collection of approximately 15,000 volumes selected by the Rare Book Division from the Library of Congress's immense collection of children's books, plus another 1,000 children's books in the Rare Book Division that are not part of the Children's Books Section. These are mostly nineteenth-century books, but each year some new children's books are selected to be placed in the Rare Book Division. Books published up to 1973 are listed here. Most of the titles are of American origin, but there are some British and Continental books and some American editions of foreign authors.

The catalog is in two parts. The first volume is an author catalog, arranged alphabetically by the author's name or the title if there is no author. The second volume is a chronological catalog.

26. GOVERNMENT, PUBLIC ADMINISTRATION, AND LAW

The published catalogs of collections on government and law are numerous and large. Some of the largest are the catalogs of government libraries, like the libraries of the United States Departments of Health, Education, and Welfare (349) and of Housing and Urban Development (350). The Catalogues of the United Kingdom Department of the Environment Library (342) are similar to the HUD catalog in their emphasis on housing and land use planning.

Government is an object of study in universities as well as in government itself, and the Institute of Governmental Studies at the University of California at Berkeley has developed a significant collection of works about government and of documents published by governments, and has listed them in its Subject Catalog (339). Publications of the United States and foreign governments are the content of the Catalog of Government Publications in the Research Libraries of The New York Public Library (346), a 40-volume catalog that requires some care to use.

Several large law libraries have published their catalogs. The largest general catalog is the Dictionary Catalog of the Columbia University Law Library (340), which includes works on international law but stresses law of the United States and Great Britain. Catalogs on international law are Harvard University's Catalog of International Law and Relations (343), the largest, and the Catalogue of the Library of the Institute of Advanced Legal Studies, University of London (345).

Bibliographie courante d'articles de périodiques postérieur à 1944 sur les problèmes politiques, économiques, et sociaux. 17 vols. Boston: G. K. Hall, 1968. (see 310)

339\. California. University. Institute of Governmental Studies. Subject Catalog of the Institute of Governmental Studies Library, University of California, Berkeley. 26 vols. Boston: G. K. Hall, 1970 (LC 73-152341). First Supplement. 5 vols., 1978.

The Institute of Governmental Studies at the University of California at Berkeley began as the Bureau of Public Administration in 1921, but the library dates from a collection started by the Department of

Economics in 1918. The collection now has approximately 320,000 cataloged items. Collection development centers on the study of government in the United States, including: administration; finance; taxation and budgeting; public personnel; city, county, state, and regional planning; criminology and police administration; metropolitan problems; welfare; minority groups; transportation and traffic; elections and voting; public health; and school administration.

Included in the catalog are pamphlets, periodicals, government documents, and some books published in English in the twentieth century. There are also analytical entries for articles from 285 currently published periodicals and from about the same number of defunct titles. The first volume contains a list of the titles analyzed.

This is a subject catalog that uses more than 2,000 locally developed subject headings (the authority list is provided in volume one). There are no author or title entries, but the subject headings have in some cases been used as corporate author headings: e.g., United States government publications are listed under "Federal departments," subdivided by corporate author, and California state government publications are listed under "State government California," though items listed in either place can also be found under other pertinent subject headings. Publications of non-public agencies may be found by consulting an authority list in volume twelve, which gives the subject heading assigned to that agency, although the agency's publications will also be found under subjects relevant to each title.

The supplement no longer follows this practice of using subject headings as quasi-main entries.

California. University. Water Resources Center. Archives. Dictionary Catalog of the Water Resources Center Archives. 5 vols. Boston: G. K. Hall, 1970. (see 394)

340. Columbia University. Libraries. Law Library. Dictionary Catalog of the Columbia University Law Library. 28 vols. Boston: G. K. Hall, 1969 (LC 73-5252). First Supplement. 7 vols., 1973. Second Supplement. 4 vols., 1977.

Founded in 1859, this is one of the greatest law libraries in the United States. As of July, 1967, the collection included 470,000 volumes and about 700 periodicals. Although especially rich in the legal literature of the United States and the British Commonwealth, the library has a large collection of foreign law, including Roman and medieval law, legal literature of various European countries, African law, and a complete set of the laws and decisions of the Russian Imperial and Provisional governments and those of the Soviet government that are available. Also included are many U.S. and foreign theses.

In this dictionary catalog, Library of Congress subject headings are often used, but are supplemented extensively by the

Library's own subject headings: "each foreign legal system is represented by a semi-classified section under the name of the legal system for that group" [Introduction]. Some items are also given topical headings; e.g., in the classified arrangement a work may be listed under "French law--Contracts," but that same work may also be found under "Contracts--France." Three different classification systems are used: for Anglo-American law there is a simple topical division; for international law the Library of Congress JX class is used; and for foreign law the Schiller Foreign Law Classification is used.

The Introduction to the Second Supplement states that the Columbia Law Library has begun conforming to the Library of Congress forms of personal and corporate entries, and that the Second Supplement is the last supplement.

341. Evanston, Ill. Transportation Center at Northwestern University. Library. Catalog of the Transportation Center Library, Northwestern University. 12 vols. Boston: G. K. Hall, 1972.

The Transportation Center Library is concerned with all aspects of transportation, including management, operations, planning, economics, regulation, and impact of all modes of transport, as well as the linking of different kinds of transport, their physical distribution, and traffic safety. Socio-economic and operational aspects are emphasized, and the collection in transport technology is limited to material about system-wide innovations. The library is especially strong in operations research, systems analysis, and other analytical applications. It also maintains collections in traffic-law enforcement and police patrol, personnel administration, and manpower allocation. Material on both domestic and foreign transportation is included.

The catalog contains 204,000 references to 80,000 books and reports and 52,000 journal articles. Most of the entries are for journal articles or consultant reports, proceedings of conferences, and for some dissertations. The library's collection of annual reports for transportation companies is not included in the catalog.

This is a divided catalog. The Author/Title Catalog, which is in three volumes, has personal author and title entries for books, and corporate author, sponsoring agency, and selected title entries for report literature. It contains no entries for periodical articles, conference papers or pamphlets.

The Subject Catalog has entries for all publications, including periodical articles and analytics for conference proceedings. It is divided into two parts: a pre-1965 catalog and a post-1964 catalog. The dividing moment occurred apparently when a change in subject headings took place. The pre-1965 catalog has many see and see-also references. The later catalog has none. Instead, there are three separate indexes in the last volume to act as a guide to the subject headings. The first, a geographic index, is arranged alphabetically by geographic name and indicates which subject headings contain that geographic subdivision. The second is a commodity index. The third is a subject index that lists the subject headings together with cross-references in the form of broader terms, related terms, and narrower terms. The subject headings were developed by the staff of the Transportation Center.

Foreign Relations Library. Catalog of the Foreign Relations Library. 9 vols. Boston: G. K. Hall, 1969. (see 88)

342. Great Britain. Dept. of the Environment. Library. Catalogues of the United Kingdom Department of the Environment Library. 15 vols. Boston: G. K. Hall, 1977 (ISBN 0-8161-0066-7).

The Department of the Environment was formed in 1970 from a merger of the Ministry of Housing and Local Government, the Ministry of Transport, and the Ministry of Public Buildings and Works. The library was formed from the libraries of the first two. Its collections date back to the nineteenth century and reflect the responsibilities of the ministries and now the department, including: environmental health, housing, local government, transportation (including shipping and aviation), regional and land use planning, protection of the environment, air, water, and noise pollution, and historic preservation.

The 250,000 volumes in the library include monographs, Census publications, Parliamentary and other government publications, pamphlets (which are a major part of the collection), reports, and 2,500 periodical titles.

There are four separate catalogs included in this publication. The first is an author catalog of books, pamphlets, and monographs, including government publications, reports, and other kinds of published and semi-published material. There are analytical entries for collected papers and reports, and for papers delivered at seminars. The second is a classified catalog of the same material arranged by Library of Congress classification number.

The third catalog is an author catalog of periodical articles. The fourth is a classified catalog of periodical articles, arranged by Library of Congress classification and within class by date. Abstracts are included.

There is a subject index to the Library of Congress classification included. The cataloging standards are based on the Anglo-American Code of 1908. Included in all the catalogs are many added entries and cross-references for additional authors, editors, organizations, etc. In the classified catalogs, works may be listed under more than one classification number, sometimes as a see reference to another number.

343. Harvard University. Law School. Library. Catalog of International Law and Relations. Edited by Margaret Moody. 20 vols. Cambridge, Mass. (distributed by Oceana Publications, Dobbs Ferry, N.Y.), 1965-67 (LC 65-23603).

The subject of this catalog is international law and international relations. The basis of the collection was the library of the Spanish diplomat, the Marquis de Olivart. The catalog includes books, pamphlets, many publications of the United Nations and of foreign countries, original documents of international disputes and arbitrations, papers of meetings and conferences, periodicals, laws, and treaties. There are some analytics for works in series.

This is a dictionary catalog of authors, titles, and subjects. The library uses its own classification system and, apparently, its own subject headings. Titles were published mostly in the nineteenth and twentieth centuries and are in most Western European languages.

344. Harvard University. Library. Government. 263 p. Cambridge, Mass.: distributed by Harvard University Press, 1969 (LC 68-8886). (Widener Library Shelflist v. 22)

This is a classified arrangement of works in Harvard University's Widener Library on the history and theory of political science and the theory of the state; as well as general and comparative works on constitutional law and on the government and administration of countries, of local political divisions, and of colonies. Also included are works on civil law. Works that are found in Harvard's Law Library or in the Littauer Library of the Kennedy School of Government are not included in this catalog, nor are government publications.

Following the classified, or shelflist arrangement, works are listed alphabetically by author and title, and then chronologically by date of publication. Approximately 7,000 titles are listed, of which 3,800 are in English, 1,000 in German, 800 in French, and the rest in various, mostly Western European languages.

For further information on the Widener Library shelflists see 9.

345. London. University. Institute of Advanced Legal Studies. Library. Catalogue of the Library of the Institute of Advanced Legal Studies, University of London. 6 vols. Boston: G. K. Hall, 1978 (ISBN 0-8161-0099-3).

The Institute of Advanced Legal Studies was established at the University of London in 1947. The library collects works on law in all jurisdictions and all branches of law except Oriental laws and East European legal literature in Eastern European languages. It is especially strong in English law, the law of the rest of the British Isles, law of members and ex-members of the British Commonwealth (except India), law of the United States, European Community Law and the law of countries of Western Europe, public international law, comparative law, and jurisprudence. The library is currently building its collection of Latin American law.

Works have mostly twentieth-century imprint dates and are in English as well as other European languages. The library holds approximately 130,000 volumes, two-thirds of which are serials--series of legislation, treaty collections, law reports, law reviews, etc. There are also many British and European dissertations.

The catalog is in two main parts. Volumes one to three are a name catalog containing entries for individual and corporate authors. Conferences, law reviews, and law reports are listed here under their titles. Legislation and government publications are entered under the name of the jurisdiction. Monograph series are listed under the name of the series and there are subject entries for individuals and institutions.

Volumes four to six are a subject catalog. Volume four contains a list of the subject headings used, which were developed by the library. There are liberal see and see-also references in the subject headings list and in the body of the catalog.

In addition, there are four small auxiliary catalogs: 1) a list of United Kingdom command papers arranged in numerical order; 2) a catalog of University of London legal theses, in order of acquisition; 3) a catalog of theses from non-British universities, by country and date; and 4) a subject catalog of works on librarianship. These items are also listed in the main catalogs.

346. New York (City). Public Library. Research Libraries. Catalog of Government Publications in the Research Libraries. 40 vols. Boston: G. K. Hall, 1972 (LC 74-171015). Supplement 1974. 2 vols., 1976. Further supplemented by Bibliographic Guide to Government Publications--U. S.: 1975- . Boston: G. K. Hall, 1976- , and Bibliographic Guide to Government Publications--Foreign: 1975- . Boston: G. K. Hall, 1976- .

This is the catalog of the government documents collection located in the Economic and Public Affairs Division of the Research Libraries of The New York Public Library. The catalog contains 581,000 cards for government publications of the United States and its foreign political jurisdictions, U. S. state and local governments, and American colonial and territorial governments, as well as documents of foreign governments and provinces. Holdings are strongest for the United States, Great Britain and its related states, the Scandinavian countries, and Western Europe. The documents include official gazettes, parliamentary debates and papers, session laws, correspondence on foreign relations, treaties, statistical annuals and reports, and journals and monographs. The earliest holdings are from the eighteenth century.

The organization of the catalog is unusual, and the Introduction must be consulted before using the catalog. Generally, the arrangement is alphabetical by political jurisdiction (country, state, city, etc.) and within the jurisdiction by agency. Under each agency, serial publications are arranged alphabetically, and monographs chronologically. There are no subject entries or added entries for personal authors. There are title entries for government periodicals only since 1930.

347. Philadelphia. Free Library. Hampton L. Carson Collection.

Catalog of the Hampton L. Carson Collection Illustrative of the Growth of the Common Law, in the Free Library of Philadelphia. 2 vols. Boston: G. K. Hall, 1962 (LC 62-53509).

The Carson Collection is a collection of works on the common law in Britain and America, including historical, biographical, and social studies of the growth of the law from the thirteenth to the twentieth century, with emphasis on the sixteenth and seventeenth centuries. Titles are mostly in English, with some Latin and other Western European languages included. Many of the works are very rare.

Among the approximately 10,000 titles included are yearbooks, abridgements, records, statutes, reports, trials, and editions of the treatises of Glanville, Bracton, Littleton, Coke, Hale, and Blackstone, plus books about the law. There are over 100 manuscripts, more than 2,000 letters of English and American lawyers, and 10,000 prints of persons and places.

This is a dictionary catalog, compiled over many years and showing evidence of different cataloging practices. There are separate catalogs of manuscripts, prints, bookplates, and letters. Library of Congress subject headings are used.

Royal Institute of International Affairs. Library. Index to Periodical Articles. 2 vols. Boston: G. K. Hall, 1964. (see 92)

348. Seide, Katharine, compiler. The Paul Felix Warburg Union Catalog of Arbitration; A Selective Bibliography and Subject Index of Peaceful Dispute Settlement Procedures. 3 vols. Totowa, N.J.: Rowman and Littlefield, 1974 (LC 74-5266).

This is a union catalog of the holdings of 19 cooperating libraries, mostly law libraries, in the field of arbitration. Many United States and foreign government documents are included, along with publications of international agencies. There are also many analytics for journal articles and conference proceedings. Most of the periodical indexing was done by the Eastman Library of the American Arbitration Association in New York City. A list of journals indexed, with the abbreviations used for them, is provided.

The catalog is in two parts. Volume one is a catalog arranged by main entry, which is usually a personal or corporate author, but is sometimes a title. Volumes two and three are arranged into four broad subject categories--Commercial Arbitration, International Commercial Arbitration, International Public Arbitration, and Labor Arbitration--subdivided alphabetically by more specific subjects. These specific subject headings are listed at the beginning of each section with many see and see-also references.

Works are in English and other Western European languages and were published up to early 1972.

United States. Bureau of the Census. Library. Catalogs of the Bureau of the Census Library. 20 vols. Boston: G. K. Hall, 1976. (see 361)

349. United States. Department of Health, Education, and Welfare. Library. Author/Title Catalog of the Department Library. 29 vols. Boston: G. K. Hall, 1965 (ISBN 0-8161-0717-3). First Supplement. 7 vols., 1973.

________. Subject Catalog of the Department Library. 20 vols. Boston: G. K. Hall, 1965 (ISBN 0-8161-0234-X). First Supplement. 4 vols., 1973.

The United States Department of Health, Education, and Welfare was created in 1943 in a merger of the Office of Education, the Food and Drug Administration, the Public Health Service, the Social Security Administration, the Vocational Rehabilitation Administration, and the Welfare Administration. Many of these agencies had their own libraries, which were merged. Until 1963/64 the library maintained two catalogs, an Education Catalog and a Welfare Catalog, each with its own system of filing and its own subject heading structure. When the two catalogs were merged many inconsistencies were left unreconciled.

The catalogs list books, pamphlets, papers and proceedings of conferences, Federal, state, and local documents, and a few periodical titles. Analytics for journal articles have been removed. The library is especially strong in the fields of education, social welfare, health, medicine, and the social sciences in general. It has an excellent research collection in law and the most complete set of the Departmental and operating agencies' publications in existence.

This is a divided catalog, with the Author/Title Catalog and the Subject Catalog published separately. The total catalog, including the supplements, has well over one million cards. The Author/Title Catalog has cards for personal and corporate authors, joint authors, editors, translators, titles, and series, plus subject cards for works about persons or corporate bodies. Cards are filed according to American Library Association filing rules, and there are many cross-references from alternate forms of headings.

The Subject Catalog uses Library of Congress subject headings with some modifications, as well as headings from Selected List of Subject Headings Used in the Social Security Board Library. Many see and see-also references are included. Titles are classified with the Library of Congress classification system.

350. United States. Department of Housing and Urban Development. Library and Information Division. Dictionary Catalog of the United States Department of Housing and Urban Development, Library and Information Division, Washington, D.C. 19 vols. Boston: G. K. Hall, 1972 (LC 73-152937). First Supplement. 2 vols., 1974. Second Supplement. 2 vols., 1975.

This catalog represents a consolidation of the libraries of the former Federal Housing Administration (founded 1934), the Public Housing Administration (founded 1937), and the Housing and Home Finance Agency (founded 1949). The focus of this collection of 550,000 items is on urban affairs, housing, urban planning, sociology, land use, architecture, mortgage and construction finance, and community development.

Included in the catalog are books, pamphlets, slides, films, microforms, and local, state, Federal, and foreign government documents. Most of the entries are for report-type material; there are few trade publications. Included in this catalog is the only complete index to over 30,000 HUD-sponsored research and planning studies. Also, in the last volumes, there are computer-produced indexes to over 20,000 Comprehensive Planning Reports. There are some analytical entries for periodical articles and works in series, but in general the library's indexing of periodical articles is published in Housing and Planning References, a bi-monthly bibliography of books, documents, journal articles, and reports.

This is a dictionary catalog of authors, titles, and subjects. The classification system used is an adaptation of the Universal Decimal Classification. The subject headings used are listed in the "Urban Vocabulary" at the beginning of the first volume, complete with see, see-also, and see-from references; these cross-references are repeated in the catalog itself. The UDC numbers for particular subjects are also listed in the Urban Vocabulary. Also in volume one is a periodical list in three parts: Titles, Subjects, and Publishers (with addresses).

United States. Department of Labor. Library. United States Department of Labor Library Catalog. 38 vols. Boston: G. K. Hall, 1975. (see 370)

351. United States. Library of Congress. Hispanic Law Division. Index to Latin American Legislation, 1950-1960. 2 vols. Boston: G. K. Hall, 1961 (LC 61-66038). First Supplement, 1961-1965. 2 vols., 1970. Second Supplement. 2 vols., 1973. Third Supplement. 2 vols., 1978.

This catalog was started as a working tool for internal use in the Hispanic Law Division of the Law Library of the Library of Congress. It indexes national legislation appearing in the original gazettes of 20 Latin American republics. This includes both legislative and administrative enactments, as well as matters of general interest, basic codes, and organic laws. Subjects covered include commercial law, taxation, domestic relations, labor law, investment law, plus matters important to a particular country's economy.

The catalog is arranged by country and then subdivided by Library of Congress subject headings with modifications. There are many see and see-also references. Entries give the decree or law number and a brief, one-sentence description (in English) of the content. Also provided is the effect of new legislation or decrees on previous ones--i.e., repeals, amendments, and the like.

27. BUSINESS AND ECONOMICS

The preeminent library of business and business administration is the Baker Library of Harvard University, which has published its Author-Title and Subject Catalogs (355), and collects in economics and economic history, as well as in business and management.

In the field of international economics, the 207 volumes of the catalogs of the Institute for World Economics (359) represent a formidable collection. Included in the catalogs are books, journal articles, government documents, reports of research and commercial organizations, and legal publications. While the format of the catalogs may be unusual to the user of American library catalogs, the wealth of material to be found here is extraordinary.

The focus of this collection is on contemporary economics, as opposed to two famous and complementary collections of economic history: the Goldsmiths' Library of Economic Literature (360) and the Kress Library of Business and Economics (356), both of which are collections of works on economics published before 1850.

352. Asian Development Bank. Library. Subject Catalog of Books in the Asian Development Bank Library. 4 vols. The Bank, 1974 (LC 76-366634).

This is a subject catalog prepared for the staff of the Asian Development Bank. The subject matter is predominantly banking, business and economics, labor, and agriculture, and although the works listed deal with all areas of the world, their emphasis is on Asia.

Each volume has a table of contents listing the subjects covered in that volume. The catalog uses Library of Congress subject headings, with an emphasis on geographic headings. Included are acquisitions from 1967 to 1972; most titles are in English. Only books are listed in the catalog, and there are no analytics. The collection employs the Library of Congress classification.

Bibliographie courante d'articles de périodiques postérieur à 1944 sur les problèmes politiques, économiques, et sociaux. 17 vols. Boston: G. K. Hall, 1968. (see 310)

353. California. University. Giannini Foundation of Agricultural

Economics. Dictionary Catalog of the Giannini Foundation of Agricultural Economics Library. 12 vols. Boston: G. K. Hall, 1971 (ISBN 0-8161-0908-7).

"The Giannini Foundation of Agricultural Economics was established in 1928 to provide for research in agricultural economics, with particular application to problems affecting agriculture in California" [Introduction]. The library was opened in 1930. The subject matter of the collection is, of course, agricultural economics, with emphasis on economic aspects of agricultural labor; land utilization, valuation, and tenure; costs of production, marketing, and transportation of agricultural products; water resources; farm management; agricultural credit, finance, insurance, and taxation; cooperation; rural poverty, population, organizations, and institutions; prices and cost-of-living; food supply; recreation; conservation of natural resources; and food-supply problems of developing countries.

Titles cataloged are mostly in English and published in this century. They include reports and documents from federal, state, regional, and local government agencies, and from associations, societies, research foundations, and businesses; they also include conference proceedings and symposia. Comparatively few titles are commercially published monographs. There are analytics for individual titles in series and for articles in periodicals, particularly from before 1958.

This is a dictionary catalog of authors and subjects. The subject headings are the library's own. Most of the cataloging is original, but the descriptive cataloging is a modification of Library of Congress practices. An effort is made to bring out geographic and commodity subdivisions; there are entries as well under issuing agencies, joint authors, and editors. There are many cross-references to the correct subject headings and forms of entry.

Cornell University. New York State School of Industrial and Labor Relations. Library. Library Catalog. 12 vols. Boston: G. K. Hall, 1967. (see 363)

354. Detroit. Public Library. The Automotive History Collection of the Detroit Public Library: A Simplified Guide to Its Holdings. 2 vols. Boston: G. K. Hall, 1966 (LC 76-357392).

Material in this collection on the automobile ranges from technical manuals to joke books, and includes fiction; books on design and engineering; 50,000 advertising pieces, the earliest from an 1891 catalog and the latest from publications of the 1960's; owner's instruction books; shop manuals; ephemera; and periodicals, both European and American, from the 1890's on. Material is primarily in English, but the collection also includes publications in German, Chinese, Russian, Spanish, Turkish, and other languages.

The catalog is divided into four parts. The first and largest section is a dictionary catalog of books. The second section is a list of periodicals. The third part includes automobile catalogs, manuals, advertising matter, parts books, references to cars in magazines and books, etc., all arranged by name of the automobile. The fourth part consists of other collections of miscellanea.

355. Harvard University. Graduate School of Business Administration. Baker Library. Author-Title Catalog of the Baker Library, Graduate School of Business Administration, Harvard University. 22 vols. Boston: G. K. Hall, 1971 (ISBN 0-8161-0893-5). First Supplement. 2 vols., 1974.

_____. Subject Catalog of the Baker Library, Graduate School of Business Administration, Harvard University. 10 vols. Boston: G. K. Hall, 1971 (LC 70-170935). First Supplement. 827 p., 1974.

The Harvard Business School was founded in 1908. Its library is especially strong in economics, behavioral sciences and mathematics, the theory and practice of business and business management, the theory of organization and administration, business history and biography, and economic history before 1850. Coverage is strongest in American, Canadian, British, and German materials, but there is selective coverage of publications of other countries. Included are books, journals, United States and United Nations publications, financial reports and instrumentalities, and business documents. Corporate records, current journals, and manuscripts are not included.

This is a divided catalog with separate author-title and subject listings. Included in the Author-Title Catalog are main entries for works in the Kress Library of Business and Economics, which consists largely of titles published before 1850 and is especially strong in economic data and theory and in business practices (see 356). The Author-Title Catalog includes added entries and many see and see-also references for alternate forms of names, and uses 1967 Anglo-American cataloging rules for more recent entries.

Similarly, in the Subject Catalog only newer titles are cataloged with Library of Congress subject headings; older ones use Harvard's own subject headings. The library uses its own classification system, which has been described in: A Classification of Business Literature (The Baker Library Classification) (Camden, Conn.: Shoe String Press, 1960).

The Baker Library catalogs were closed at the end of 1970. The new catalogs (represented by the supplement) conform to Anglo-American Cataloging Rules and Library of Congress Subject Headings.

Current periodicals of the Baker Library are listed in a separate publication: Current Periodical Publications in Baker Library, published annually and sold by the library.

356. Harvard University. Graduate School of Business Administration. Baker Library. Kress Library of Business and

Economics. Catalogue; With Data Upon Cognate Items in Other Harvard Libraries. 5 vols. Boston: Baker Library, Harvard Graduate School of Business Administration, 1940-1967 (LC 40-30321).

The Kress Library was named for Claude Washington Kress, a businessman of New York City, who provided the funds for the purchase of much of the material in the library, and for the physical facilities of the library itself, which opened in 1938. The basis of the Kress Library was the collection of Professor Herbert Somerton Foxwell, of Cambridge, England. Professor Foxwell had previously assembled the collection that became the Goldsmiths' Library of the University of London (see 360). These two libraries, the Goldsmiths' Library and the Kress Library, together with the Seligman Collection of Columbia University, are the greatest collections of historical material on business and economics.

The Foxwell collection consisted of 30,000 individual items at the time of its purchase by Harvard University. Over the years it has been supplemented by additional purchases and by the transfer of materials from other Harvard libraries. In addition, the Kress Library printed catalog lists materials in other Harvard libraries on the subjects of business and economics published before 1850.

The arrangement of the catalog is by year, and within each year alphabetical by title. Volume one lists material published through 1776. Volume two is a supplement to volume one, listing new additions to the library. Volume three lists items published from 1777 to 1817. Volume four lists items published from 1818 to 1848. Volume five is a supplement of additions to the library published from 1473 to 1848, and includes all the new additions listed in the second volume. Each volume has an author and title index. The materials listed in the catalog are books and pamphlets, as well as some broadsides, published in Western Europe and North America. As of 1960 these items filled over 30,000 volumes. Main entries for works in the Kress Library are also listed in the later Author-Title Catalog of Harvard University's Baker Library (355).

The catalogs of the library reveal the development of economic ideas and the evolution of economic life and institutions. The emphasis is on the history of commerce, money, banking and public finance, and the economic aspects of agriculture, manufacturing, and transportation. Also of note are the collections of material on Adam Smith and his ideas, on railroads, and on taxation. The library also contains material on political and social history up to 1850.

Research Publications, Inc. is preparing a microfilm collection of the combined holdings of the Goldsmiths' Library and the Kress Library.

357. Harvard University. Library. Economics and Economics Periodicals. 2 vols. Cambridge, Mass.: distributed by Harvard University Press, 1970 (LC 69-10587). (Widener Library Shelflist v. 23-24)

This is a classified, or shelflist arrangement of the books and periodicals in Harvard University's Widener Library on economics. These include works on economic theory, economic history, and economic conditions, as well as on transportation and communication, commerce and finance, and on more specialized aspects of economics such as demography, corporations, and taxation. Not included in this catalog are most books in Widener Library on labor and cooperation and on public works, or the statistical publications of national governments. Also not listed here are the holdings of the Graduate School of Business Administration's Baker Library, which have been published elsewhere (see 355), or the holdings of the Law School Library, or those of the Littauer Library of the Kennedy School of Government.

The classified arrangement is followed by a listing of the same books arranged alphabetically by author and title, and then chronologically by date of publication. Over 67,000 books and periodicals are listed in this catalog, over half of them in English.

For further information on the Widener Library shelflists, see 9.

358. Institute of Chartered Accountants in England and Wales, London. Library. Historical Accounting Literature: A Catalogue of the Collection of Early Works on Book-Keeping and Accounting in the Library of the Institute of Chartered Accountants in England and Wales, Together with a Bibliography of Literature on the Subject Published Before 1750 and Not in the Institute Library. Compiled by Geoffrey Paul. 386 p. London: Mansell, 1975 (LC 75-328383).

Included here are 3,000 entries for 2,500 works on accounting and bookkeeping, published from the late fifteenth century to the early twentieth century. The bulk of the titles are from the nineteenth century. Works are in English, Italian, German, Dutch, French, Spanish, Portuguese, Danish, Hungarian, Rumanian, Greek, Slavonic languages, and Japanese. The bulk of the material is arranged by language group and, within language, chronologically. There are supplementary bibliographies of related subjects, and indexes by author and illustrator. At the beginning of the volume is a long introductory essay, "Four Centuries of Books on Book-Keeping and Accounting," by Basil S. Yamey.

359. Kiel. Universität. Institut für Weltwirtschaft. Bibliothek. Behördenkatalog. (Catalog of Administrative Authorities, Library of the Institute for World Economics, Kiel). 10 vols. Boston: G. K. Hall, 1967 (LC 76-457628).

________. Körperschaftenkatalog (Catalog of Corporations). 13 vols. Boston: G. K. Hall, 1967 (LC 76-457636).

________. Personenkatalog (Bibliographical and Biographical

Catalog of Persons). 30 vols. Boston: G. K. Hall, 1966 (LC 72-213362).

_______. Regionenkatalog (Regional Catalog). 52 vols. Boston: G. K. Hall, 1967 (LC 67-9425).

_______. Sachkatalog (Subject Catalog). 83 vols. Boston: G. K. Hall, 1968 (ISBN 0-8161-0192-2).

_______. Standortskartei der Periodika (Shelf List of Periodical Holdings). 6 vols. Boston: G. K. Hall, 1968 (LC 76-457624).

_______. Titelkatalog (Title Catalog). 13 vols. Boston: G. K. Hall, 1968 (LC 76-457617).

The Institute for World Economics was founded at the University of Kiel in 1914. As its name suggests, it is concerned with economic development on an international basis. Besides economics, the library collects extensively on geography, history and politics, law and administration, culture, and sociology. Monographs, periodicals, government publications, reports of organizations, statistical material, legal publications and gazettes, reports of banks and other commercial firms, and reports of social and cultural institutions are all collected. Materials acquired outside of the book trade account for 60 to 70 percent of the library's holdings. Titles are in all Western European languages and are mostly of this century.

The library believes in cataloging in depth and does extensive analytical cataloging of books and periodicals. Since 1935, articles in periodicals and collective works have been cataloged as extensively as monographs. Maps, bibliographies, and statistics within a book or article may also be cataloged as separate entities, as may chapters, or even pages in monographs.

The library's catalog has been issued in seven distinct parts, which will be described here in alphabetical order.

The Behördenkatalog, or Catalog of Administrative Authorities, is a listing of the publications of official agencies. For the most part these are government agencies, so this functions as a catalog of government publications. Also included are some university publications. The arrangement is by geographical political unit and, within units, alphabetical by name of agency. There are cross-references both to the correct name of an agency as used in this catalog, and also to entries in other catalogs of the library.

The Körperschaftenkatalog (Catalog of Corporations) includes publications of private and public corporations, institutions, foundations, learned societies, congresses, conferences, international associations, universities, etc. It includes works about these organizations as well as by them, including periodical articles. The arrangement is alphabetical by name of organization, and there are many cross-references to the correct form of the name.

The Personenkatalog (Bibliographical and Biographical Catalog of Persons) is basically an author catalog of personal authors only. Also included are translators, editors, preface writers, etc., and works about individuals. Official publications that have been authored by individuals are included, as are analytical entries for articles in periodicals or parts of books.

The Regionenkatalog (Regional Catalog) includes works about regions, i.e., countries, continents, localities, etc. All material about geographic areas smaller than a country is listed under the name of the country. Within the geographic area, entries are subdivided by subject, and listed chronologically within the subject. The geographic names and the subject headings are in German. Works may be assigned more than one geographic heading.

The Sachkatalog, or Subject Catalog, is arranged alphabetically by subjects, which are subdivided geographically. The subject headings are in German. There is a Register, or Subject Index, in a separate volume that acts as a guide to the Sachkatalog. It contains a list of the German subject headings with cross-references and subheadings. It also contains an English-German index to the subject headings, which does not include the cross-references or the subdivisions, but does allow the English-speaking user to locate the correct subject headings in German.

The Standortskartei der Periodika, or Shelf List of Periodical Holdings, is a listing of serial titles and holdings arranged by a call number system. Yearbooks, periodicals, and newspapers are listed separately. Within each type of publication the arrangement is by size. Serials are also listed in the other catalogs, but here complete information is provided on title changes, editors, issuing agencies, etc. There is no title index to the catalog, and it can only be used in conjunction with the other catalogs of the Institute, particularly the Titelkatalog.

The Titelkatalog (Title Catalog) lists the titles of yearbooks, periodicals, newspapers, collected works, series, and anonymous writings. The arrangement is alphabetical by the first word that is not an article or a running number.

360. London. University. Goldsmiths' Company Library of Economic Literature. Catalogue of the Goldsmiths' Library of Economic Literature. Compiled by Margaret Canney and David Knott. 2 vols. London: Cambridge University Press, 1970-1975 (LC 70-121364).

This historical collection of economic literature was formed by Professor Herbert S. Foxwell, who sold it to the Worshipful Company of Goldsmiths in 1903. The Company then gave it to the University of London. Professor Foxwell later developed another, similar collection that became the Kress Library of Harvard University (see 356).

Listed in the Catalogue of the Goldsmiths' Library are 60,000 printed books and pamphlets, 400 manuscripts, and 350 autograph letters, dating from the fifteenth century to 1850. The arrangement is chronological by year. Within each year entries are arranged under fourteen standard subjects, and within each subject the arrangement is alphabetical by author. Volume one lists books published before 1801, and volume two, books published from 1801 to 1850. A third volume, to contain periodicals, manuscripts, and an index, has not been published.

Entries are fairly brief, usually consisting of author, title (sometimes abbreviated), pagination, and sometimes place of publication and publisher. Also included are references to standard descriptive bibliographies. There are cross-references from the earliest edition of a work to later ones.

The catalog includes a great deal that is of interest on political science, history, and sociology, in addition, of course, to its main emphasis on economic history, and there are special collections on slavery, transport, temperance, and city guilds and companies. Works are mostly in English, but also in other European languages.

Royal Institute of International Affairs. Library. Index to Periodical Articles. 2 vols. Boston: G. K. Hall, 1964. (see 92)

361. United States. Bureau of the Census. Library. Catalogs of the Bureau of the Census Library, Washington, D. C. 20 vols. Boston: G. K. Hall, 1976 (LC 77-355426). First Supplement. 5 vols., 1979.

The Bureau of the Census Library was established in 1952 and includes holdings of books, periodicals, reports, maps, microforms, and many government publications. There are also many analytical entries for articles in journals. The emphasis of the collection is on statistics of agriculture, business, construction, economics, foreign trade, governments, housing, industry, population, and transportation, and on statistical methodology of urban studies, as well as data processing. In most cases the material is of current, rather than historical interest.

This is a dictionary catalog. American Library Association filing rules are followed and there are many see and see-also references. The library uses its own subject headings and the Glidden-Marchus Library Classification for Public Administration Materials.

Several special collections are included in this catalog. The U. S. Census Collection, included in the main catalog, is archival in scope, and is made up of publications issued by the Bureau of the Census and its predecessors, beginning in 1790. It also includes reports based on surveys conducted by the Bureau, and papers prepared by Census staff members. The Foreign and International Statistics Collection, also included in the main catalog, has censuses, statistical yearbooks, and statistical bulletins from approximately 100 countries in nearly 40 languages.

The State and Local Documents Collection, listed separately in volume 20, is a computer printout of 11,500 serial titles issued by state and local governments, arranged alphabetically by state. The emphasis is on financial and other government activities. The

EDP-Micrographics Collection is a computer science collection listed in its own dictionary catalog at the end of volume 19. It includes periodicals, technical reports, and current monographs.

362. Washington, D. C. Joint Library of the International Monetary Fund and the International Bank for Reconstruction and Development. Economics and Finance: Index to Periodical Articles, 1947-1971. 4 vols. Boston: G. K. Hall, 1972 (LC 75-156075). First Supplement, 1972-1973-1974. 425 p., 1976. Second Supplement, 1975-1976-1977. 419 p., 1979.

The Joint Bank-Fund Library in Washington, D. C. was established in 1946 to serve the International Monetary Fund and the International Bank for Reconstruction and Development (the World Bank), both agencies of the United Nations. This index was begun by the library in 1947 as a monthly current-awareness list to keep the staff of the Bank and the Fund aware of currently acquired literature.

Economic journals and weeklies, bank bulletins, government periodicals, proceedings, and yearbooks are indexed. Works may be in English, French, Spanish, German, Italian, Portuguese, Dutch, or Scandinavian languages. Non-English titles are translated into English.

The main subject of the index is descriptive economics and theory, including money and banking, fiscal policy, taxation, international finance, international commerce, commodities, and the economic aspects of such subjects as agriculture, education, and transportation.

The index is in a classified arrangement in three parts. Part A, Theoretical and Descriptive Economics, is broken down into eight broad areas, such as economic theory, wages and prices, etc. Within these broad areas the arrangement is chronological by year and then alphabetical by subject. Part B is divided into the six specific subjects of capital markets, capital movements, Eurodollars, exchange rates, gold, and taxation. Within each specific subject the arrangement is alphabetical by author. The bulk of the index (volumes two to four) is Part C, the geographical arrangement. Countries or geographic regions are subdivided by subject or by date. Articles may appear in more than one country or subject section.

This index can be very difficult to use because the categories tend to be very broad, with hundreds of entries arranged alphabetically or chronologically. It is probably most useful for finding information on smaller countries for which little information is available, and which may not be included in standard periodical indexes.

28. LABOR

Library collections on labor range from collections on labor-management relations to collections on the history of radical labor and socialist movements. The former is represented by the catalog of the library of the New York State School of Industrial and Labor Relations at Cornell University (363); the latter by the catalogs of the Tamiment Institute Library (369) and the library of the International Institute for Social History (365).

The most substantial catalog on labor, however, is the United States Department of Labor Library Catalog (370), in 38 volumes, describing a library of over 535,000 volumes on all aspects of labor and economic conditions that affect workers.

Most of the catalogs dealing with labor include references to periodical articles, but the major source for these are the cumulative editions of International Labour Documentation (366-367), an index to journal articles, some books, and International Labor Office publications.

363. Cornell University. New York State School of Industrial and Labor Relations. Library. Library Catalog of the Martin P. Catherwood Library of the New York State School of Industrial and Labor Relations. 12 vols. Boston: G. K. Hall, 1967 (LC 72-185999). Cumulated Supplement. 9 vols., 1976. First Supplement to the Cumulation. 897 p., 1977. Second Supplement to the Cumulation. 2 vols., 1978. Third Supplement to the Cumulation. 2 vols., 1979.

The focus of this collection is on labor-management relations, human relations in industry, personnel, social insurance and employee welfare, labor economics, labor union organization and administration, labor history, and international labor conditions and problems. Included are books, pamphlets, U. S. government publications, International Labor Organization series (analyzed), and original source material from the Labor Management Documentation Center. Periodical titles are not included. However, there are author and subject analytics for selected articles in periodicals since 1952, and for works in such series as the U. S. Bureau of Labor Statistics Reports and Bulletins.

This is a dictionary catalog which uses Library of Congress

subject headings plus A Standard List of Subject Headings in Industrial Relations, which is a publication of the Committee of University Industrial Relations Librarians. There are many see and see-also references. The original 12 volumes include entries for 78,000 cataloged volumes and a selection of the library's 80,000 pamphlets. The Cumulated Supplement includes entries in the first seven supplements to the original catalog plus 10,000 additional entries.

364. Fondazione Giangiacomo Feltrinelli, Milan. Biblioteca. Catalogo dei Periodici della Biblioteca (Catalog of Periodicals in the Library). 3 vols. Nendeln: KTO Press, 1977 (ISBN 3-262-00001-9).

This is a catalog of periodical titles, including both the "informative" press and political and cultural periodicals. The subject strength of this library is socialism in Europe, including the history of workers' and socialist movements, from the eighteenth century to the present, especially national and international movements, the history of the proletariat, and the history of the Italian workers' movement.

The arrangement of the catalog is alphabetical by title of periodical. Information given for each entry includes the subtitle, the dates of publication, and some information on the library's holdings of the title. Periodicals date from the nineteenth and twentieth century and are mostly in Italian, with many holdings in other Western and non-Western languages.

365. International Institute for Social History. Alphabetical Catalog of the Books and Pamphlets of the International Institite of Social History, Amsterdam (Alfabetische Catalogus van de Boeken en Brochures van het Internationaal Instituut voor Sociale Geschiedenis). 12 vols. Boston: G. K. Hall, 1970 (ISBN 0-8161-0807-2). First Supplement. 2 vols., 1974. Second Supplement. 3 vols., 1979.

With 350,000 volumes this is one of the largest specialized libraries on social and labor history. The Institute was founded in 1935 to preserve traces of social history, with much of the material being brought out of Nazi Germany.[34] It includes special collections on the Paris Commune, on anarchism, on early German socialism, on American communistic colonies in the nineteenth century, and on radical and social ideas and movements in England, Scotland, and Ireland from 1600 to 1860. Books, pamphlets, and some reproductions of journal articles are included.

This is a main-entry catalog, but there are no entries for corporate bodies. Title main entries are entered under the first noun in the nominative case. While there are no subject entries, there is access to works about individuals in the form of see references from the individual's name to the main entry for works about that person.

Titles are mostly in Western European languages, particularly German.

366. International Labour Office. Library. Subject Index to International Labour Documentation, 1957-1964. 2 vols. Boston: G. K. Hall, 1968 (ISBN 0-8161-0785-8).

The Library of the Central Labour Office began issuing a Daily Reference List of journal articles received by the library in 1949. In 1957 the library began keeping a cumulative record, on cards, of the articles appearing on the list, which had been renamed International Labour Documentation in 1954. This catalog represents that card index maintained from 1957 to 1964, after which a new system of document analysis was introduced (see 367). The catalog contains references to over 14,500 journal articles from 3,000 of the most important periodicals received by the library.

The arrangement is alphabetical by subject, subdivided by country or geographical region, and then arranged chronologically. Library of Congress subject headings are used. There is a list of those subject headings at the beginning of volume one. There is also a list of the journals indexed.

Subjects covered include industrial relations, social security, industrial hygiene and safety, cooperation, and agriculture. Titles are in Western European languages or Russian.

367. International Labour Office. Library. International Labour Documentation: Cumulative Edition, 1965-1969. 8 vols. Boston: G. K. Hall, 1970 (ISBN 0-8161-0902-8).

________. International Labour Documentation: Cumulative Edition, 1970-1971. 2 vols. Boston: G. K. Hall, 1972 (ISBN 0-8161-0940-2).

________. International Labour Documentation: Cumulative Edition, 1972-1976. 5 vols. Boston: G. K. Hall, 1978 (ISBN 0-8161-1091-3).

This is a computer-produced compilation of the weekly current awareness bulletin of the library of the International Labour Office in Geneva. The bulletin, International Labour Documentation, lists new books, journal articles, major ILO publications, and other technical documents acquired by the library. The major subjects covered here are industrial relations, manpower planning, educational planning, vocational training, and problems of economic and social development in the Third World.

The major part of these catalogs, the Master Index, is arranged by sequential abstract number, and most entries have short abstracts in English. Each abstract contains a number of words that act as subject descriptors for that entry. The subject index to each compilation lists each entry under its subject descriptors and other key words or phrases; each heading is subdivided geographically. There are an average of eight descriptors per item. Also included are an author index, which consists of the author's last name and the number of the abstract, and a geographic index, which lists developing countries only, and is arranged alphabetically by country and subdivided alphabetically by subject descriptor. In the later cumulative editions the subject and geographic indexes have been combined, so that in one index you can find countries subdivided by subjects or subjects subdivided geographically.

For earlier acquisitions by the library of the International Labour Office see its Subject Index to International Labour Documentation, 1957-1964 (366).

368. Marx Memorial Library. Catalogue of the Marx Memorial Library, London. 3 vols. Boston: G. K. Hall, 1979 (LC 80-100463).

The library was founded in 1933 as the Marx Memorial Library and Workers School, to commemorate the 50th anniversary of the death of Karl Marx. It contains items on Marxism and radical social movements; works by and about Marx, Lenin, and other leaders of Marxist thought; and pamphlets on the workers movement. Works are mostly in English, but also in German, Italian, Spanish, and Russian. Besides the many pamphlets and the books, there are considerable archival material, journals, and much ephemera.

The catalog was mostly put together by volunteers and uses a unique cataloging and classification system. The arrangement is in several parts. Volume one is a book catalog in three parts: 1) an author catalog of English-language books; 2) a catalog of reference books; 3) a catalog of foreign-language books, arranged by language and then alphabetically by author. Volume two contains: 1) a subject catalog of books in a classified arrangement; 2) catalogs of special collections, including the Williamson Collection on the history of the American Labour Movement and the Bernal Peace Collection, which themselves include journals, periodicals, newspapers, and documents. Volume three is a catalog of the pamphlet collection, arranged partly by title and partly by author. It is absolutely necessary to read the Introduction to understand the contents and arrangement of the catalog; there are no cross-references or other aids. Many of the cards are handwritten, although quite clear.

369. New York University. Tamiment Institute Library. Catalog of the Tamiment Institute Library of New York University. 4 vols. Boston: G. K. Hall, 1980 (ISBN 0-8161-0358-5).

"The Tamiment Institute Library is a unique center for scholarly research in American labor history, workers' education movements, socialism, communism, anarchism, and American radicalism" [Preface]. The library was originally the Library of the Rand School of Social Sciences, which was founded in 1906 as a school for workers and socialists. The Rand School closed in 1956, and the library was taken over by the Tamiment Institute, which gave it to New York University in 1963.

Reflecting the time period that the Rand School was in operation, the library's holdings date mainly from the late nineteenth and early-to-mid-twentieth centuries. Listed in the catalog are about 10,000 cataloged books and at least that number of cataloged pamphlets, many of them in microfilm. Its periodical holdings encompass all of the major titles and many of the minor titles of the American socialist and left-wing press from the second half of the nineteenth century to the present; 400 of the titles are currently received. Also listed in the catalog are 65 manuscript collections. The material listed is primarily in English, with many German titles as well.

Cataloging follows Library of Congress practices. The catalog itself is divided into several parts. First, there is a catalog of books, divided into an author catalog and a shelflist arranged by the Library of Congress classification. There is a separate pamphlet catalog, also in two parts: an author-title catalog in one alphabet, and a subject catalog, arranged by Library of Congress subject headings. Serials and manuscripts are listed separately.

Also included in the Tamiment Library Catalog are two periodical indexes. The first is an index to the International Socialist Review, the most substantial of the Socialist Party's publications, from 1900 to February, 1918. The second is an index to Mother Earth, 1906-1917, an anarchist literary and political monthly edited by Alexander Berkman and Emma Goldman.

Seide, Katharine. The Paul Felix Warburg Union Catalog of Arbitration. 3 vols. Totowa, N.J.: Rowman and Littlefield, 1974. (see 348)

370. United States. Department of Labor. Library. United States Department of Labor Library Catalog. 38 vols. Boston: G. K. Hall, 1975 (ISBN 0-8161-1165-0).

The catalog of the U.S. Department of Labor Library represents over 535,000 volumes on all matters relating to labor and to economic conditions that affect workers. Specifically, this includes the history of the labor movement; labor economics and labor relations; arbitration, conciliation, and mediation; labor laws; employment and unemployment; labor force and labor market; unemployment insurance; workman's compensation; apprenticeship and training; wages and hours; working conditions; women's employment; industrial hygiene and safety; wholesale and retail prices; cost of living; productivity; and other related subjects. Coverage is worldwide in scope, but the emphasis is on the United States.

The catalog includes books, periodicals, reports, microforms, and cassettes. There are extensive coverage of labor union publications--primarily proceedings, constitutions, and journals--and long runs of reports from state labor departments.

Of course, holdings of United States government documents, particularly documents of the Department of Labor, are voluminous; "U. S." as a corporate entry takes up more than three volumes, and entries under "U. S. Bureau of Labor Statistics" run for almost 200 pages.

Until 1960 analytics for periodicals and books were used extensively. Recently, analytics have been recommenced for many journals, Congressional hearings, and other special material.

This is a dictionary catalog. Library of Congress subject headings and classification are used, and there are many cross-references.

29. SPORTS AND HOBBIES

The development of a library devoted to physical education and leisure studies signifies the importance that leisure time now assumes in the lives of many people in the United States and the Western world. Yet while the Dictionary Catalog of the Applied Life Studies Library (376) may be the only catalog covering sports and leisure studies in general, other catalogs exist that list works on individual sports or hobbies.

The Racquet and Tennis Club of New York has published its catalog on tennis and related sports (377), and the Alpine Association Library has produced a six-volume divided catalog on mountain-climbing and hiking in high mountains, particularly the Alps (375). More sedentary hobbies of chess (373), stamp-collecting (374), and coin-collecting (371-372) are also represented by published catalogs.

371. American Numismatic Association. Library. Library Catalogue of the American Numismatic Association. Second edition. 768 p. Colorado Springs, Colo.: The Association, 1977 (LC 77-93078).

The American Numismatic Association was founded in 1891 and now has the world's largest circulating library on numismatics. The library contains 6,000 books, 5,000 periodical volumes, and 5,000 auction catalogs. Members of the association may borrow by mail; the library will also make photocopies. Subjects included in the collection are coins, coin collecting, medals and tokens, currency, and money in general.

This is a classified catalog arranged by the library's own classification system, which is listed in detail at the beginning of the volume. There are separate author and subject indexes, and the subject index has numerous see-also references. There are separate listings of periodicals and of auction catalogs. Titles bear mostly twentieth-century publishing dates and are in English and other Western European languages. There are analytics for works in series and some entries for journal article reprints.

372. American Numismatic Society. Library. Dictionary Catalogue of the Library of the American Numismatic Society. 6 vols. Boston: G. K. Hall, 1962 (LC 76-356280).

_______. Auction Catalogue of the Library of the American Numismatic Society. 731 p. Boston: G. K. Hall, 1962 (76-356267).

_______. First Supplement: Dictionary and Auction Catalogues 1962-1967. 819 p., 1967. Second Supplement. 824 p., 1973. Third Supplement. 2 vols., 1978.

The function of the American Numismatic Society in New York is given as "the collection and preservation of coins and medals, with an investigation into their history, and other subjects connected therewith" [Introduction]. To that end it has amassed the most comprehensive numismatic library in America. The main catalog lists 50,000 items in approximately 125,000 entries. Included are books, periodicals, pamphlets, auction catalogs, fixed price lists, microfilm, and unpublished manuscripts.

This is a dictionary catalog, using the library's own subject headings. The majority of the entries appear to be analytics; there are analytical entries for articles in every significant numismatic periodical from 1930, and many from before, plus entries for numismatic articles in non-numismatic periodicals, as well as articles in books.

The Auction Catalogue is in two parts: American and Foreign. It is arranged by dealer, with entries listed chronologically under each dealer. There are added entries for collector or collections when known.

373. Cleveland. Public Library. John G. White Dept. Catalog of the Chess Collection (Including Checkers). 2 vols. Boston: G. K. Hall, 1964.

This collection is part of the John G. White Department of Folklore, Orientalia, and Chess of the Cleveland Public Library. The department originated as the personal library of John Griswold White, who served for many years as President and member of the Board of Trustees of the Cleveland Public Library. The subjects covered here are chess and checkers exclusively; this is considered to be the largest chess collection in the world. The aim is to collect every edition of every work on chess and all important literary works that make significant references to chess. At the time of publication of the catalog, 15,000 such items had been collected.

Volume one of the catalog is an author catalog. Volume two contains separate subject catalogs of chess and of checkers. The headings are all "Chess" (or "Checkers") subdivided by subject and then by geographic area. The subject headings are the library's own. The classification system used is the Dewey Decimal, with modifications. The collection includes periodicals, many rare books, and nearly 1,000 manuscripts in many languages, dating from the fifteenth century to the present. There are analytical entries for articles in periodicals and for parts of books.

374. Collectors Club, New York. Library. Philately: A Catalog of the Collectors Club Library, New York City. 682 p. Boston: G. K. Hall, 1974 (LC 74-987).

The subject of this catalog is philately (stamp-collecting) and the history of postal stamps and postal services. Included are pamphlets, books, stamp catalogs, rare books, and auction and exhibition catalogs, dating from 1574 to the 1970's, in English and other European languages. The catalog is in several parts: an Author Catalog, Subject Catalog, Title Catalog, and Periodicals Catalog. The Subject Catalog is arranged, in general, alphabetically by country, with some topical headings. The Periodicals Catalog includes information indicating which issues are held. There are analytics for many articles in specialized journals.

375. Deutscher Alpenverein. Alpenvereinsbücherei, Munich. Kataloge der Alpenvereins Bücherei, München: Autorenkatalog (Catalogs of the Alpine Association Library: Author Catalog). 3 vols. Boston: G. K. Hall, 1970 (LC 76-464262).

_______. Kataloge der Alpenvereins Bücherei: Sachkatalog (Catalogs of the Alpine Association Library: Subject Catalog). 3 vols. Boston: G. K. Hall, 1970 (ISBN 0-8161-0101-9).

The Alpine Association Library was founded in 1901 with an endowment of the Asian researcher, Dr. Willi Rickmer Rickmers. At the time of reproduction of the catalog, the library had approximately 24,000 volumes plus about 2,000 maps, but the maps are not included in the catalog. This is a specialized library on mountain-climbing and hiking in high mountain chains, especially the Alps. It also covers geography, geology, botany, zoology, and map-reading.

The Author Catalog is based on modified Prussian Library Regulations and includes a keyword index interfiled with the author entries; the result is close to an author-title catalog. The Subject Catalog is arranged alphabetically by subject headings in German, with geographical headings being emphasized. Most of the titles are in German, but other European languages are included.

376. Illinois. University at Urbana-Champaign. Applied Life Studies Library. Dictionary Catalog of the Applied Life Studies Library (formerly Physical Education Library) University of Illinois at Urbana-Champaign. 4 vols. Boston: G. K. Hall, 1977 (LC 77-360766).

This collection began in 1949 as the Physical Education Library, with 4,000 books. By the time of the catalog's publication the collection had grown to 17,000 books and microfilms. In addition to books, the library collects Federal, state, and World Health

Organization documents, performance programs, and University of Illinois masters' and doctoral theses. The subject headings used are Library of Congress's, and the classification system is the Dewey Decimal.

The library has two main areas of specialty. The first, physical education, covers biomechanics, growth and motor development, physical therapy, all aspects of sport, and elementary and secondary physical education. The second major field is leisure studies, including outdoor recreation, planning, municipal park administration, outdoor education, theories of play, and therapeutic recreation. Other subjects of interest are health and safety education, including public health, epidemiology, drug and alcohol abuse education, sex education, human ecology, personal hygiene, traffic safety, driver education, and first aid; and dance, including dance history, ballet, contemporary dance, folk and ethnic dance, choreography, notation, and dance therapy.

Most of the titles date from the 1950's to 1977 and are in English.

377. Racquet and Tennis Club, New York. Library. <u>A Dictionary Catalogue of the Library of Sports in the Racquet and Tennis Club, with Special Collections on Tennis, Lawn Tennis, and Early American Sport, New York.</u> 2 vols. <u>Boston: G. K. Hall, 1970 (LC 78-166482).</u>

The Library of Sports in the Racquet and Tennis Club covers all sports, but the major emphasis is on what the library broadly construes as bat-and-ball and related games. Among all the sports included are hunting, mountaineering, yachting, fishing, horsemanship, baseball, billiards, golf, hockey, ancient games, and early American sports, and recent sports like sky-diving and scuba diving. The collection is most comprehensive in tennis and lawn tennis. Imprint dates range from the fifteenth century to the 1960's and titles are mostly in English. Many rare books are included in the library. At the time of publication of the catalog, the library had over 14,300 volumes, represented by some 34,500 cards.

This is a dictionary catalog of authors and subjects. The list of subject headings used is in the beginning of volume one, complete with <u>see</u> and <u>see-also</u> references. In the catalog itself entries are brief--only the author, title, place and date of publication, size, and sometimes publisher are provided. There are some analytics for newspaper articles and articles in books.

30. GENERAL SCIENCE, PHYSICAL SCIENCES, AND TECHNOLOGY

Collected in this chapter are catalogs on science and the history of science in general, and catalogs that deal with the physical sciences and technology. The most significant of the catalogs on general science are the Author-Title and Subject Catalogs of the John Crerar Library (380), one of the largest public science libraries in the United States. Unfortunately, the catalogs' usefulness is somewhat limited by their age and lack of supplements. They are, however, a tremendous resource for research in the history of science, as are the catalogs of the University of Oklahoma History of Science Collections (382), the Edgar Fahs Smith Memorial Collection in the History of Chemistry (383), and the Union Catalogue of Scientific Libraries in the University of Cambridge: Books Published Before 1801 (385).

The standard catalog of engineering is that of the Engineering Societies Library (381), a classified subject catalog. In the more specific fields of mining and mining engineering, the Colorado School of Mines has published its Subject Catalog (378). Also described in this chapter are catalogs of atmospheric sciences (379) and of astronomy (387).

One of the most useful catalogs is the Union Catalogue of Scientific Libraries in the University of Cambridge: Scientific Conference Proceedings (386), which provides an extremely good index to scientific conference proceedings published from 1644 to 1972.

American Geographical Society of New York. Dept. of Exploration and Field Research. Catalogs of the Glaciology Collection. 3 vols. Boston: G. K. Hall, 1971. (see 32)

378. Arthur Lakes Library. Subject Catalog of the Arthur Lakes Library of the Colorado School of Mines, Golden, Colorado. 6 vols. Boston: G. K. Hall, 1977 (LC 77-377323).

The Colorado School of Mines was founded in 1870 and is the second oldest mining school in the United States and the largest mining school in the world. The library contains about 130,000 volumes, including 1,800 current periodical titles and 1,850 theses, as well as books, research reports, proceedings of professional societies, periodicals, and government publications of the United States and Canada.

The major concern of the library is mines and mining, but this includes the engineering of chemical and petroleum refining, chemistry and geochemistry, geology and geological engineering, geophysics, mathematics, metallurgical engineering, mineral economics, mining engineering, petroleum engineering, and physics. Energy and the environment are more recent concerns of the library.

This is a subject catalog only. The library uses the Library of Congress classification system and Library of Congress subject headings, and, when possible, Library of Congress catalog cards. Volume six contains a separate catalog of doctoral, masters', and senior theses of the Colorado School of Mines.

Items date from the mid-nineteenth century to the 1970's and are mostly in English, German, French, and Russian.

379. Environmental Science Information Center. Library and Information Services Division. Catalog of the Atmospheric Sciences Collection in the Library and Information Services Division, Environmental Data and Information Service, National Oceanic and Atmospheric Administration. 24 vols. Boston: G. K. Hall, 1978 (LC 78-109415). (Vol. 1-20: Acquisitions 1890-August, 1971; Vol. 21-24: Acquisitions September, 1971-1974)

This collection was originally constituted in 1890 as the library in the weather service of the Signal Office, United States Army. Later it became the Weather Bureau Library in the Department of Agriculture and then in the Department of Commerce. It is now part of the National Oceanic and Atmospheric Administration. Subjects covered include the atmospheric and oceanic sciences, particularly meteorology, climatology, hydrology, physical oceanography, and air chemistry. Material in most European languages, including a great deal in Russian, is collected, in the form of books, government documents, research reports, theses, periodicals, pamphlets, and conference proceedings. There are analytics for works in series and for some conference proceedings.

This is a dictionary catalog of authors, titles, and subjects. The subject headings are based on those of the Library of Congress. In 1940 the library began using the meteorological expansion of the Universal Decimal Classification for meteorological material and the Dewey Decimal Classification for non-meteorological material. In 1971 the library adopted the Library of Congress Classification, closed its catalog, and started a new one. Hence, volumes 1-20 of this catalog cover acquisitions from 1890 to August, 1971, and volumes 21-24 cover September, 1971-1974. The latter catalog manifests considerable overlap with NOAA's own published catalog, Book Catalog of the Library and Information Services Division (see 396), which contains material cataloged April, 1972-December, 1975 in atmospheric and oceanographic sciences.

Interafrican Committee for Hydraulic Studies. Documentation Center. Catalog du Centre de documentation, Comité interafricain d'études hydrauliques, Ouagadougou, Haute-Volta. 2 vols. Boston: G. K. Hall, 1977. (see 399)

380. John Crerar Library, Chicago. Author-Title Catalog. 35 vols. Boston: G. K. Hall, 1967 (LC 67-7669).

________. Classified Subject Catalog. 42 vols. Boston: G. K. Hall, 1967 (LC 68-1635).

The John Crerar Library was founded in Chicago in 1895 as a public reference library of scientific, technical, and medical literature. The library houses more than 1,100,000 volumes of current and historical materials in the pure and applied sciences; it is very strong in nineteenth-century materials. Included in the catalogs are books, periodicals, pamphlets, reports, and papers delivered at meetings. There are a few analytical entries for works in series and for some articles in older periodicals.

The Author-Title Catalog has approximately 563,000 cards. It is actually a main-entry catalog with many added entries. Mostly works are entered under their titles only if the title is the main entry. The catalog is in general accordance with Anglo-American cataloging rules. Most of the cards represent original cataloging.

The Subject Catalog is a classified catalog arranged according to the Dewey Decimal Classification, with some local expansions and revisions of the tables. Books are classified under the most specific class possible. There is a subject index to the classification (volume 42 of the Classified Subject Catalog), which itself contains about 40,000 entries. The subject terms are taken from the terminology of science and from subject heading lists issued by the Library of Congress, the National Library of Medicine, and the Defense Documentation Center. The index refers you to one or more (usually several) classification numbers for different aspects of that subject. There are a few cross-references in the index.

381. New York. Engineering Societies Library. Classed Subject Catalog. 12 vols. Boston: G. K. Hall, 1963 (LC 64-6834). First Supplement. 564 p., 1964. Second Supplement. 536 p., 1965. Third Supplement. 610 p., 1966. Fourth Supplement. 422 p., 1967. Fifth Supplement. 521 p., 1968. Sixth Supplement. 606 p., 1970. Seventh Supplement. 615 p., 1971. Eighth Supplement. 591 p., 1972. Ninth Supplement. 548 p., 1973. Tenth Supplement. 411 p., 1974. Further supplemented by: Bibliographic Guide to Technology: 1975- . Boston: G. K. Hall, 1976- .

________. Index to the Classed Subject Catalog. 356 p. Boston: G. K. Hall, 1963.

The Engineering Societies Library is "one of the largest, most comprehensive engineering libraries in the world."[35] It was started circa 1913 when three national engineering societies combined their libraries. By 1963 it was supported by more than a dozen engineering societies and had 185,000 volumes. The library is maintained for the practicing engineer and for graduate engineering students. Its emphasis is on engineering and related physical sciences, namely: chemical, civil, electrical and electronic, marine and naval, illuminating, industrial, and mechanical engineering; aerospace sciences; rockets and missiles; nuclear technology; metallurgy and metallography; welding; mining; shipbuilding; petroleum technology; computers and instrumentation; engineering materials; geology; geophysics; the history of technology; and engineering as a profession. Works take the form of books, journals, abstracts, catalogs, bibliographies, films, government reports, unpublished manuscripts, and conference proceedings.

This is a classified catalog, arranged by a somewhat modified Universal Decimal Classification. Works may have more than one entry; commonly they have two, but they may have up to thirty. There is a separate alphabetical Index to the Classed Subject Catalog, but there is no outline of the classification system. Each supplement includes its own index with new terms added during the period of the supplement.

The proliferation of uncumulated supplements limits this catalog's usefulness as a retrospective bibliography.

382. Oklahoma. University. Library. The Catalogue of the History of Science Collections of the University of Oklahoma Libraries. Compiled by Duane H. D. Roller and Marcia M. Goodman. 2 vols. London: Mansell, 1976 (LC 76-381954).

This collection was established through the efforts of Everette Lee DeGolyer, who began donating rare books in the history of science to the University of Oklahoma in 1949. The present catalog of 39,000 entries represents 40,000 printed volumes and 10,000 volumes in microform. Imprint dates of works range from the sixteenth to the twentieth century and are in all Western European languages. Ephemera, dissertations, and some manuscripts are included.

This is basically a main-entry catalog with subject entries for individuals. There are no topical subject entries. Many cross-references from alternate forms of names are included.

383. Pennsylvania. University. Edgar Fahs Smith Memorial Library. Catalog of the Edgar Fahs Smith Memorial Collection in the History of Chemistry. 524 p. Boston: G. K. Hall, 1960 (LC 61-4162).

This collection on the history of chemistry and on chemists and their work was assembled by Edgar Fahs Smith, Professor of

Chemistry and Provost of the University of Pennsylvania. It was given to the University of Pennsylvania on Prof. Smith's death in 1927, and after it was endowed by his widow the collection continued to expand. As part of its main subject interest, the collection is strong in alchemy, early medicine, metallurgy, mineralogy, pharmacy, and pyrotechnics.[36]

Much of the catalog consists of rare books, manuscripts, and prints, mostly from the eighteenth and nineteenth centuries. Titles are primarily in German, English, French, and Russian.

This is an author-title catalog. Entries are arranged alphabetically under personal authors; names of institutions, societies, and other agencies; and titles of anonymous works and works of collaboration. There are analytical entries for parts of books, individual items in pamphlet collections, reprints, and Festschriften.

384. Princeton University. Plasma Physics Laboratory. Library. Dictionary Catalog of the Princeton University Plasma Physics Laboratory Library. 4 vols. Boston: G. K. Hall, 1970 (LC 72-179161). First Supplement. 874 p., 1973.

The Plasma Physics Laboratory began with a program in fusion research in 1952. Its library now includes 13,000 volumes on basic plasma physics, astrophysics, and space physics, as well as fusion research. Listed in the catalog are books, journals, technical reports, microfiche of all reports on controlled thermonuclear fusion issued by the U.S. Atomic Energy Commission, and translations of articles. Most entries include abstracts, which are written in the same language as the article. Most of the titles are in English, although all European languages are included. There are analytical entries for chapters in composite works, for selected symposia and serials, for 15,000 journal articles, and for reports, reprints, and books. Most of the material is in the form of journal articles or technical reports.

This is a dictionary catalog with entries under author, issuing agency, report number, and subject. The library uses 80 subject headings, which are listed in volume one, as well as its own classification system. Also in volume one is a list of journals subscribed to by the library.

The supplement includes, in a separate section, catalog cards of the Fusion Power Library, which has over 1,000 books, symposia, reports, and reprints related to electric power, energy, and reactor studies.

385. Union Catalogue of Scientific Libraries in the University of Cambridge: Books Published Before 1801. Compiled at the Scientific Periodicals Library, University of Cambridge. Microfiche, 9 sheets. London: Mansell, 1977.

This catalog lists 5,000-6,000 scientific books that were published between 1478 and 1801, and that are held in 25 different libraries at Cambridge University. Included are original copies of rare books as well as facsimiles and reprints. Titles are in English and other European languages.

The catalog is in two parts. The first part is an alphabetically arranged list of the books by author, editor, or title. The second is arranged chronologically by date of publication and provides only the briefest of information: date, author, and short title. Anglo-American Cataloging Rules (1967 edition) is followed, but the Introduction states that the cataloging has been done for scientists, not bibliophiles. The locations of holding libraries are given.

386. Union Catalogue of Scientific Libraries in the University of Cambridge: Scientific Conference Proceedings, 1644-1972. Compiled at the Scientific Periodicals Library, University of Cambridge. 2 vols. London: Mansell, 1975 (LC 76-357440).

This is a computer-produced union catalog of the published proceedings of conferences owned by 40 scientific research libraries at the University of Cambridge. The conferences include symposia, lecture meetings, summer institutes, and the like. Most of the proceedings were published after 1950 in English and other Western European languages. All branches of science are covered, including biology, geography and geology, chemistry, physics, mathematics, psychology, and medicine.

Generally, Anglo-American Cataloging Rules (1967 edition) is followed. There are entries for the official name of a conference, for the title of its published proceedings, for corporate bodies involved in the conference, for keywords that appear in the title, and for venues, in one alphabetical arrangement. There are no cross-references from alternate forms of names, and no subject headings other than the keywords from the title. Each entry includes sponsoring organization, name of the conference, title of the published proceedings, place and date of publication, publisher, editors, number of pages (in most cases), and the holding library at Cambridge. There are entries for conference proceedings that appeared as part of the memoirs or transactions of societies.

The great value of this catalog is in the large number of entries for each symposium--there are 25,000 entries for 6,000 conferences--since conferences can be notoriously difficult to locate in most card catalogs. The entries under the place of the conference are particularly helpful.

United States. Geological Survey. Library. Catalog of the United States Geological Survey Library. 25 vols. Boston: G. K. Hall, 1964. (see 405)

387. United States. Naval Observatory. Library. Catalog of the Naval Observatory Library, Washington, D.C. 6 vols. Boston: G. K. Hall, 1976 (LC 76-383099).

The Naval Observatory was founded in 1830 as the Depot of Charts and Instruments. The library began circa 1842, and by 1976 had 75,000 volumes, including bound periodicals.

All areas of astronomy are covered, including the latest technical works, textbooks, popular books, bibliographic reference works, observatory publications from all over the world, star catalogs and scientific society publications from the seventeenth and eighteenth centuries, and astronomical journals. Also included are mathematics texts and journals and, to a lesser extent, works on physics, astrophysics, geophysics, celestial mechanics, and navigation. Works are in English and many foreign languages and date mostly from the nineteenth and twentieth centuries. There are analytics for important articles in journals up to the late 1950's.

This is a dictionary catalog. Library of Congress subject headings and the LC classification system are used. There are generous cross-references.

31. NATURAL AND ENVIRONMENTAL SCIENCES

Combined here are catalogs of what can roughly be called the natural and environmental sciences. The lines are becoming harder to draw between disciplines, especially as sciences like ecology and problems like conservation lead practitioners to cross fields looking for solutions to problems. Therefore, natural history, zoology, oceanography, and the resources of the natural environment have all been grouped together in this chapter.

What has been known variously as natural science or natural history--i.e., the description of the works of nature--is represented by the first three catalogs in this chapter. The catalogs of the American Museum of Natural History (389) are perhaps the best sources for finding books and periodical articles in natural history, while the Catalog of the Academy of Natural Sciences of Philadelphia (388) and the Catalog of Books in the American Philosophical Society (390) are both excellent bibliographies of the history of the natural sciences, the latter being especially rich in analytical entries for periodical articles.

The science of zoology is covered in three other catalogs. The two most useful are the Dictionary Catalogue of the Blacker-Wood Library of Zoology and Ornithology (392) and the Catalogue of the Harvard University Museum of Comparative Zoology (398). The Royal Entomological Society of London has also published its catalog (402), but since this is primarily a listing by author's name, those researchers interested in finding works on particular subjects in entomology would probably be better off with one of the other two catalogs.

Several catalogs of works in oceanography have been published. Probably the easiest to use are the Catalogues of the Library of the Marine Biological Association of the United Kingdom (401), which emphasize literature from the United Kingdom and Europe. The Catalog of the Library of the Marine Biological Laboratory and the Woods Hole Oceanographic Institution (400) is an author catalog. However, it is complemented by the Oceanographic Indexes of its periodical holdings prepared by Mary Sears (403). The Catalogs of the Scripps Institution of Oceanography Library (393) are also available, but again are most useful if author or title is already known.

Freshwater biology is also the subject of a publication, the

Catalogues of the Library of the Freshwater Biological Association, United Kingdom (397), a predominantly main-entry catalog of freshwater biology and limnology.

Water as a natural resource, rather than as an ecological environment, is the focus of the catalogs of the Water Resources Center of the University of California at Berkeley (394) and of the Interafrican Committee for Hydraulic Studies (399). The latter specializes in water resources and agricultural land use in West and Central Africa, while the former collects material on water use and control in general, although the emphasis is on the United States, specifically the Western United States.

The only catalog with conservation as its sole province is the Catalog of the Conservation Library of the Denver Public Library (395), a very useful catalog of books, reports, and articles. The United States Department of the Interior Dictionary Catalog (404) includes conservation and all other subjects under the jurisdiction of the department, including mining, land resources, energy, fisheries, Indian tribes, water resources, and outdoor recreation. The catalogs of the U. S. Geological Survey (405) and the Environmental Science Information Center (396) cover geology more specifically, and the latter includes ocean and atmospheric sciences as well. Finally, the Dictionary Catalogue of the Yale Forestry Library (406) focuses on the specific environment of the forest.

388. Academy of Natural Sciences of Philadelphia. Library. Catalog. 16 vols. Boston: G. K. Hall, 1972 (LC 74-171266).

The subject strengths of the library are in the natural sciences, specifically: descriptive and systematic biology, paleontology and stratigraphic geology, entomology, limnology, marine biology, ecology, and animal behavior. As of the time of publication of the catalog, the collection totalled 150, 000 volumes, and 3, 000 periodical titles were being received. The library is known for finely illustrated monographs, complete sets of early journals, long runs of serial publications of scientific societies, and publications of foreign geological surveys. Some United States and foreign government documents are included in the catalog.

The library was founded in 1812. It has 700 items published before 1750 and some items dating back to 1527. The age of the library combined with its excellent collections of early journals make it valuable for those interested in the history of science. From 1947 to 1957 the library was modernized and the collection cataloged using the Library of Congress classification. Library of Congress subject headings are also used, and see and see-also references are included in this dictionary catalog. There are analytics for articles in some series and journals. The library's holdings are in English and all other modern languages.

389. American Museum of Natural History, New York. Library. Research Catalog of the Library of the American Museum of Natural History: Authors. 13 vols. Boston: G. K. Hall, 1977 (LC 77-374031).

________. Research Catalog of the American Museum of Natural History: Classed Catalog. 10 vols. Boston: G. K. Hall, 1978 (ISBN 0-8161-0238-4).

The Library of the American Museum of Natural History is one of the world's leading natural history collections. "Nearly all collections are outstanding for depth of coverage and international range."[37] Subjects covered include anthropology, archaeology, paleontology, entomology, mammalogy, ornithology, ichthyology, malacology, herpetology, minerology, geology, museology, and voyages and travels.

The library is rich in older materials and rare books in its fields of coverage. There are extensive holdings of 17,000 periodical titles, as well as manuscripts, pamphlets, visuals, letters, and publications of museums and governmental and international bodies. Works are in almost all modern European languages and date from the sixteenth century to the mid-1960's, when the library converted to Anglo-American cataloging rules and the Library of Congress classification system and closed its catalogs.

In the Author Catalog are entries for personal, corporate, and joint authors, for compilers, editors, and illustrators, as well as for works about individuals.

The Classed Catalog can be very difficult to use, although it is somewhat easier if the user has a good science background. Volume one contains Subject and Geographic Guides to the catalog. The classification system used to arrange the catalog and the library was the Conspectus Methodicus and Alphabeticus, a scientific classification, which had not been revised since the late 1920's and did not reflect modern systematics--one reason why the classification was abandoned in the mid-1960's in favor of the Library of Congress classification. The Subject Guide lists both common and Latin names of organisms, but is not a complete index to the classification, nor is there an overall outline of the classification provided. Anthropological subjects, in particular, may be difficult to find since their terminology is not as structured as the biological terminology. Subjects usually have geographic subdivisions. Individual items may have entries in several different places depending on the number of subjects covered in the work.

Both catalogs have many analytical entries for journal articles and chapters in books, making them particularly valuable. These analytics, plus the great range and depth of the library's collection, make worthwhile the effort involved in using the catalogs.

390. American Philosophical Society, Philadelphia. Library. Catalog of Books in the American Philosophical Society Library. 28 vols. Westport, Conn.: Greenwood Pub. Corp., 1970 (LC 70-20392).

The emphasis in this collection is not on philosophy as we know it, but on the natural sciences, especially as they relate to American history. There is no fiction, poetry or criticism; little political history; and no archaeology. Strengths of the collection are its materials on Benjamin Franklin, eighteenth-century natural history, Darwinian evolution, genetics, and American Indian linguistics. It also has a major strength in journals important to the history of science.

This is a dictionary catalog, with entries primarily for author and subject, with some titles. Subject headings used are those of the Library of Congress with some modifications; there are cross-references. Pamphlets, United States government documents, and microforms are included in the catalog. Also included, and a major asset of the catalog, are thousands of entries for journal articles and proceedings of societies. Because of these extensive analytics and the focusing of the collecting policy in certain areas, the catalog becomes a series of major bibliographies in certain subjects, such as works by and about Darwin and Darwinism. Entries for items by and about Benjamin Franklin run for 322 pages. Works are mostly in English, but other Western European languages are well represented.

391. American Philosophical Society, Philadelphia. Library. Catalog of Manuscripts in the American Philosophical Society Library. 10 vols. Westport, Conn.: Greenwood, 1970 (LC 77-297105).

The focus of the manuscript collections in the library of the American Philosophical Society is on natural history and on American history. In the field of American history, the collections primarily cover the pre-1800 period, and include the papers of Richard Henry and Arthur Lee, transcripts of early records of the colony of Pennsylvania, the journals of Lewis and Clark (deposited by Thomas Jefferson, a president of the society), and the papers of Benjamin Franklin covering both American history and the history of science.

The library's collection of manuscripts is of great value to anyone interested in the history of science since about 1700. It includes the correspondence of Sir Charles Lyell and Charles Darwin, the papers of Simon Flexner, and the papers of modern geneticists like Charles B. Davenport and George H. Shull. The library also owns microfilm copies of manuscripts held elsewhere. Its collecting policy for the thirty years preceding the publication of its catalog concentrated on the history of science.

This is a dictionary catalog, with entries primarily under personal names, but there are also some topical subjects. Thousands of manuscripts are cataloged individually, rather than as part of collections, and there are entries under the author of an item, the subject of it, and the person addressed if the manuscript is a letter.

Also included in the catalog, at the end of volume nine and in all of volume ten, are the archives of the American Philosophical Society, including reports, letters, and other documents of the society's officers. The arrangement is primarily chronological.

The catalog of printed books of the Library of the American Philosophical Society has been published separately (see 390).

392. Blacker-Wood Library of Zoology and Ornithology. A Dictionary Catalogue of the Blacker-Wood Library of Zoology and Ornithology. 9 vols. Boston: G. K. Hall, 1966 (LC 75-15898).

This library of McGill University specializes in zoology and ornithology, and in natural history in general. It contains nearly 60, 000 volumes, including bound reprints and periodicals. Of the 2, 000 periodical titles held by the library, only 500 are current, making this an important source for historical material. Analytics have been made for articles in some of the older, more important runs of serials, although there are not nearly as many analytical entries as may be found in the catalogs of the American Museum of Natural History (see 389). Also included in the catalog, in an appendix, are original drawings, paintings, and manuscript letters of famous ornithologists.

This is a dictionary catalog with some cross-references. The subject headings used were developed by the library. Works in the catalog were printed mostly in the nineteenth and twentieth centuries, although some rare books may date from the fifteenth century.

393. California. University. Scripps Institution of Oceanography, La Jolla. Library. Catalogs of the Scripps Institution of Oceanography Library: Author-Title Catalog. 7 vols. Boston: G. K. Hall, 1970 (LC 75-15307).

________. Catalogs of the Scripps Institution of Oceanography Library: Subject Catalog. 2 vols. Boston: G. K. Hall, 1970 (LC 79-15308).

________. Catalogs of the Scripps Institution of Oceanography Library: Shelf List. 2 vols. Boston: G. K. Hall, 1970 (LC 73-16140).

________. Catalogs of the Scripps Institution of Oceanography Library: Shelf List of Documents, Reports and Translations Collection. 592 p. Boston: G. K. Hall, 1970 (LC 77-16184).

________. First Supplement: Author-Title Catalog. 3 vols., 1973. Subject Catalog, Shelf List, Shelf List of Documents and Reports. 998 p., 1973.

________. Second Supplement: Author-Title Catalog. 3 vols., 1979. Subject Catalog. 709 p., 1979. Shelf List of Documents and Reports, Shelf List (Monographs, Serials and Reference). 716 p., 1979.

The Scripps Institution of Oceanography was founded in 1903 as the San Diego Marine Biological Association, an independent research station, and became part of the University of California in 1912. The Library houses outstanding collections in physical oceanography, marine biology, and marine technology. It also specializes in atmospheric sciences, fisheries, geology, geophysics, and zoology, and holds a major collection of oceanographic expedition literature. Books, research reports, and government documents are all listed in the catalog, as are analytical entries for certain important monographic series and sets. As of 1970, the library contained about 80,000 bound volumes.

The Author-Title Catalog includes main entries for titles in the University of California at San Diego Science and Engineering Library. The Subject Catalog uses Library of Congress subject headings, and includes see and see-also references.

The Shelf List is arranged by Library of Congress classification number; principally the Q class is represented. The monograph, serial, and reference collections are included, but the reference collection is listed separately. Also included is the microform collection, arranged in accession number order. Most of the microforms are masters' and doctoral theses.

The Documents, Reports, and Translations Collection contains 13,000 items, many on microfilm, forming an assemblage of documents, reports, and translations issued by the Scripps Institution and by other educational, governmental, and industrial institutions in marine research. Since the order of the documents in the shelflist is determined by author notation (letters and numbers representing the first few letters of an author's name), the result is a main-entry list, generally of organizations, with no cross-references. The translations shelflist is separate, and is arranged by accession number. The translations are also listed in the Author-Title Catalog. The translations were apparently done by the Scripps Institution, and most are translations from Russian into English.

394. California. University. Water Resources Center. Archives. Dictionary Catalog of the Water Resources Center Archives, University of California, Berkeley. 5 vols. Boston: G. K. Hall, 1970 (LC 76-20584). First Supplement. 929 p., 1971. Second Supplement. 855 p., 1972. Third Supplement. 2 vols., 1973. Fourth Supplement. 942 p., 1974. Fifth Supplement. 2 vols., 1976. Sixth Supplement. 2 vols., 1978.

The Water Resources Center Archives at the University of California at Berkeley was begun in 1957. The original catalog indexes a collection of approximately 80,000 pieces. The emphasis is on report literature, including technical and scientific reports; municipal, state, regional, and federal government publications; publications of water-related societies and associations; conference proceedings and symposia; and photographs and maps. All of these are concerned with water as a natural resource and its utilization.

Specific subjects covered are: municipal and industrial water uses and problems; flood control; irrigation and reclamation; waste disposal; coastal engineering; sediment transport; water quality; water pollution; water law; and water resources development and management. While the emphasis is on California and the West, coverage is country- and even world-wide, and items date back to the 1890's.

There are analytics for some journal articles, and series are fully analyzed under personal author and subject. This is a dictionary catalog of authors and subjects. The classification scheme and the subject headings were specifically developed for the collection, and special attention is paid to geographic entries.

The supplements reflect a growing concern with public policy aspects of water use, with water pollution, and with water supply. Beginning with the Fourth Supplement there are added entries of titles for all works with distinctive titles.

395. Denver. Public Library. Conservation Library. Catalog of the Conservation Library, Denver Public Library. 6 vols. Boston: G. K. Hall, 1974 (LC 74-189815). First Supplement. 2 vols., 1978.

Established in 1960, this was the first collection covering the broad field of conservation to be housed in a public library. Subjects included are the economic, social, historical, and management aspects of conservation and the environment, as well as fish, wildlife, and pollution. The library is a depository for the United States Forest Service, the U.S. Public Land Law Review Commission, the International Association of Game, Fish, and Conservation Commissioners, the National Wildlife Federation, and the Conservation Foundation.

The first two volumes of this work are a regular dictionary catalog of books with liberal see and see-also references and scope notes. Library of Congress subject headings are used, and there is a list of serials at the end of volume two. Volumes three to six are a Special Indexing File of pamphlets, unpublished reports, manuscripts, reports of Federal and state government agencies, and many analytical entries for journal articles. Again, Library of Congress subject headings are used, but these have been adapted for use with this file, either being made more specific, or inverted to keep similar material together.

396. Environmental Science Information Center. Library and Information Services Division. Book Catalog of the Library and Information Services Division. 3 vols. Rockville, Md.: U.S. Dept. of Commerce, National Oceanic and Atmospheric Administration, Environmental Data Service, Library and Information Services Division, Environmental Science Information Center, 1977 (LC 77-602307).

This is a computer-produced book catalog of material received and cataloged by the Environmental Science Information Center from

April, 1972 to December, 1975. The library used Library of Congress MARC II records and, for part of the project, OCLC. Each entry in the catalog contains different typefaces, and the result is a catalog that is easy to use and to read. 12,670 titles are included, mostly in English. There are many entries for government publications; research reports, especially for work done under government contracts and grants; and United States and foreign doctoral dissertations. Subjects covered include oceanography, geography and geology, astronomy, meteorology, physics (particularly geophysics), climatology, and aquaculture.

The catalog is in three parts. Volume one is a Classification Catalog, or shelflist. It uses the Library of Congress classification and entries have full bibliographic descriptions and include tracings. Volume two consists of separate Author, Title, and Series Catalogs, with only brief entries--author, title, and classification number. Volume three is a Subject Catalog, also providing only brief entries.

Many of the titles included here are also listed in the Catalog of the Atmospheric Sciences Collection in the Library and Information Sciences Division, published by G. K. Hall in 1978 (see 379). That catalog includes material from 1890 to 1974, but its holdings are limited to the atmospheric sciences.

Environmental Science Information Center. Library and Information Services Division. Catalog of the Atmospheric Sciences Collection in the Library and Information Services Division. 24 vols. Boston: G. K. Hall, 1978. (see 379)

397. Freshwater Biological Association. Library. Catalogues of the Library of the Freshwater Biological Association, United Kingdom. 6 vols. Boston: G. K. Hall, 1979 (ISBN 0-8161-0289-9).

The Freshwater Biological Association of the United Kingdom was founded in 1929 to further the study of fresh waters. Subjects covered include all aspects of freshwater biology and limnology, such as physical and chemical factors of the freshwater environment, ecology of lakes and rivers, taxonomy, physiology and ecology of macro- and micro-organisms, including fishes, and the ecological history of lakes by investigation of their sediments.

The major part of the catalog, volumes one to five, is a main-entry catalog of books, monographs, and reprints, together with virtually all papers on fresh water published since 1963 in journals, conference proceedings, and symposia. There are over 110,000 entries, of which 50,000 are for journal reprints, and only 4,000 are for books. Also included are 1,100 periodical titles (of which 550 are currently received) in 10,000 volumes. The second half of volume five is a classified subject catalog of books and major monographs based on the Universal Dewey Decimal Classification.

Volume six contains: a) a subject index of approximately

10,000 limnology papers published in the British Isles between 1957 and 1975; and b) an index to articles by the Freshwater Biological Association's staff from 1931 to 1979. Both are arranged by the FBA's own classification system, explained at the beginning of volume six.

Works are mostly in English, but other Western European languages and some Russian titles are included; Russian titles have been transliterated into English.

The association is located in Ambleside, in Cumbria, England.

398. Harvard University. Museum of Comparative Zoology. Library. Catalogue. 8 vols. Boston: G. K. Hall, 1967 (LC 68-4175). First Supplement. 770 p., 1976.

Subjects covered in this catalog include zoology, paleozoology, and geology relating to paleozoology. There are special collections on geology, travel and exploration, entomology, worms, ornithology, crustacea, and Japanese ornithology. Books, pamphlets, periodicals, and Canadian and U.S. federal and state documents are included.

All important monograph series are analyzed, and there are many entries for articles in periodicals, mostly dating from the 1850's to the 1930's. There are also some entries for individual chapters in books. This is a dictionary catalog of personal and corporate authors, titles, editors, serials, and series. There are no subject entries except for biographies, and for works about institutions, scientific expeditions, and ships used in expeditions. Works are mostly in English and other European languages.

399. Interafrican Committee for Hydraulic Studies. Documentation Center. Catalog du Centre de documentation, Comité interafricain d'études hydrauliques, Ouagadougou, Haute-Volta (Catalog of the Documentation Center, Interafrican Committee for Hydraulic Studies, Ouagadougou, Upper Volta). 2 vols. Boston: G. K. Hall, 1977 (LC 78-374789).

The International Committee for Hydraulic Studies was formed in 1960 to exchange information, conduct technical studies, and provide technical consultation. It has twelve member states: Benin, Cameroon, Chad, Congo, Gabon, Ivory Coast, Mali, Mauritania, Niger, Senegal, Togo, and Upper Volta, and the material in the Documentation Center refers to these countries of West and Central Africa. Included among the 6,800 documents are official publications from African, European, and North American countries; reports from the United Nations and its specialized agencies; documents of African development organizations; studies undertaken by governmental and quasi-governmental organizations and by private consulting firms; and maps and atlases. There are also over 1,300 analytical entries for articles from more than 100 periodicals. The material is about 60 percent in French and 40 percent in English.

All of the documentation is on water resources and agricultural land use in West and Central Africa. Specifically, this includes hydrology (surface water), hydrogeology (ground water), hydraulics, meteorology and climatology, range management, forestry, fisheries, soil science, demography, remote sensing, planning, and national and regional development.

The catalog contains 27,000 cards in an unusual arrangement. The first volume is an author catalog of personal authors with corporate and series added entries. The names of countries and organizations are in French. The second volume is a Geographic Catalog, in three separate sections. The first section is made up of five broad geographic subject headings: Africa, Liptako-Gourma (a region covering parts of Niger, Mali, and Upper Volta), Sahara, Sahel, and West Africa. The second section is arranged by ten-degree square coordinates of longitude and latitude. The third section is arranged by one-degree square coordinates of longitude and latitude. There are maps to clarify the divisions. The second section lists studies of water resources in large areas, such as one or more countries, while the third section lists studies of small areas, such as cities, towns, or small regions. Reports may appear in more than one section if they refer to both large areas and specific parts of those areas.

400. Library of the Marine Biological Laboratory and the Woods Hole Oceanographic Institution. Catalog. 12 vols. Boston: G. K. Hall, 1971 (LC 75-173373).

The Marine Biological Laboratory at Woods Hole, Massachusetts, was established in 1881 as the first biological station in America, and its library was considered important to the institution from the beginning. The Library of the Woods Hole Oceanographic Institute is also a part of the Marine Biological Laboratory Library.

This is an author catalog only. Included are entries for 12,000 books and monographs, 138 expedition reports and, making up the major part of the catalog, entries for nearly 300,000 journal article reprints. The last volume of the catalog is a separate catalog of 4,000 journal titles, representing 140,000 volumes in 35 languages.

The major subject of the catalog is marine biology and oceanography, including: biology, zoology, botany, physiology, microbiology, medicine, physics, chemistry, mathematics, geology, meteorology, geophysics, and fisheries.

Complementing this catalog is an index to the journals collected by the library: Oceanographic Index, by Mary Sears (see 403).

401. Marine Biological Association of the United Kingdom. Library. Catalogues of the Library of the Marine Biological Association of the United Kingdom. 16 vols. Boston: G. K. Hall, 1977 (LC 78-301931).

The Library of the Marine Biological Association of the United Kingdom, in Plymouth, England, contains comprehensive, specialized collections on physical, chemical, and biological oceanography, fisheries, and related subjects. It is particularly strong in its coverage of literature from the United Kingdom and from Europe, and it is known for its thorough coverage of recent journal articles. The library's holdings total 50,000 volumes.

The catalog is in three parts: a main-entry catalog, a subject catalog, and a Subject Index on Marine and Estuarine Pollution. This latter is a classified arrangement of broad subjects--general aspects of water pollution, chemical pollution, biological pollution, and physical pollution--all further subdivided into more specific topics. Most of the entries are analytics for articles in periodicals; many government reports are included.

402. Royal Entomological Society of London. Library. Catalogue of the Library of the Royal Entomological Society of London. 5 vols. Boston: G. K. Hall, 1980 (ISBN 0-8161-0315-1).

The Entomological Society of London was founded in 1833. Its library has become one of the finest entomological libraries in the world, holding a very complete collection of older works on systematics dating from 1609. The library now contains approximately 9,000 monographs and works of reference, 50,000 separates, and holdings of some 600 journals, of which 270 are current. Separates, or authors' separates, are reprints of articles appearing in journals, and the large number of them listed in this catalog makes it, in part, an excellent periodical index.

The library's current acqusitions policy emphasizes the purchase of works of systematic entomology in all languages and those expensive monographs and taxonomic catalogs that are beyond the resources of most individuals.

The catalog is basically an author catalog with a few title and subject entries. In the past, British Museum cataloging rules were followed; now Anglo-American Cataloging Rules have been adopted. The library has attempted to provide extensive cross-references to aid the reader. Books are classified according to a taxonomic classification. Serials are listed separately, but the title of each journal is cross-referenced in the catalog. There are many analytical entries for essays appearing in books.

403. Sears, Mary, compiler. Oceanographic Index: Author Cumulation, 1946-1970. 3 vols. Boston: G. K. Hall, 1971 (LC 78-166466).

_______. Oceanographic Index: Author Cumulation, 1971-1974: Supplement. 756 p. Boston: G. K. Hall, 1976 (LC 76-369794).

_______. Oceanographic Index, Cumulation 1946-1973--

Marine Organisms, Chiefly Planktonic. 3 vols. Boston: G. K. Hall, 1974 (LC 74-186491).

______. Oceanographic Index: Regional Cumulation, 1946-1970. 706 p. Boston: G. K. Hall, 1971 (LC 71-166467).

______. Oceanographic Index: Regional Cumulation, 1971-1974: First Supplement. 360 p. Boston: G. K. Hall, 1976 (ISBN 0-8161-0943-5).

______. Oceanographic Index: Subject Cumulation, 1946-1971. 4 vols. Boston: G. K. Hall, 1972 (LC 73-159607).

______. Oceanographic Index: Subject Cumulation 1971-1974; Cumulation 1973-1974--Marine Organisms, Chiefly Planktonic: First Supplement. 2 vols. Boston: G. K. Hall, 1976 (LC 76-357756).

These catalogs are the personal card files of Dr. Mary Sears. They are indexes to journal articles drawn from the nearly 4,000 journals held in the Library of the Marine Biological Laboratory at Woods Hole, Massachusetts, and serve as a cumulated index to the bibliography-abstract section of the journal Deep-Sea Research. They complement the Catalog of the Library of the Marine Biological Laboratory and the Woods Hole Oceanographic Institution (see 400), also published by G. K. Hall, which indexes the library's article reprint collection.

The subject matter of Oceanographic Index is the general field of oceanography, with an emphasis on biological and physical oceanography, and marine chemistry, geology, and meteorology. Excluded from coverage is limnology, terrestrial geology, basic chemistry, fisheries biology, malacology, and algology. The cards are handwritten and occasionally difficult to read. Despite the dates in the titles, coverage originates at the turn of the century, and is international in scope.

The Author Cumulation is a straightforward author index. The Marine Organisms Cumulation indexes articles concerning taxonomic and/or distributional information for genera or species. The first volume has a table of contents giving the volume and page number where entries on different taxonomic groups begin, and also a list of "Organismal Subjects to Genera," which lists the genera in each group of organisms. These serve as a guide to the index.

The Regional Cumulation does not include all of the entries listed in the author cumulation but only those of geographic interest. Geographic subjects are entered alphabetically rather than in a classed arrangement. For example, subdivisions of oceans are entered alphabetically under the name of the subdivision (e.g., Mid-Atlantic Ridge) rather than as a subheading under the name of the ocean. The exceptions are the Arctic and Antarctic regions, which have their subdivisions listed as subheadings.

The Subject Cumulation is arranged alphabetically by author

under subject headings. Some of the subjects are subdivided, but most tend to be quite broad, leading to pages of alphabetically arranged entries about one subject. There is a list of the subject headings used, with see and see-also references, in volume one, but the list is incomplete. Generally the subjects are non-biological, since most articles dealing with specific genera appear in the Marine Organisms Index; however, there are many entries under subjects such as fish, which are then subdivided by scientific and common name. There is also a very long section (over 50 pages) labelled "Translations," which lists articles in Russian with information on where translations may be found.

404. United States. Department of the Interior. Library. Dictionary Catalog of the Department Library. 37 vols. Boston: G. K. Hall, 1967 (LC 73-640211). First Supplement. 4 vols., 1968. Second Supplement. 2 vols., 1971. Third Supplement. 4 vols., 1973. Fourth Supplement. 8 vols., 1975.

The Library of the Department of the Interior was founded in 1949 with the merger of five separate libraries from the following agencies: the Bureau of Biological Survey (established 1885), the Fish and Wildlife Service (1910), the Bureau of Indian Affairs (1824), the Bureau of Mines (1910), and the Office of the Solicitor (1849). This catalog also includes material from the Bureau of Land Management, the National Parks Service, the Bureau of Reclamation, and the Bureau of Outdoor Recreation.

The subjects covered in the library are mines, minerals, petroleum, and coal; fish, fisheries, and wildlife; conservation; land management; land reclamation; public land policy; water; history and development of irrigation in the Western states; energy and power; government relations with Indian tribes; development and maintenance of national parks and monuments; outdoor recreation; and law. The supplements have increased coverage of environmental science topics, especially air and water pollution.

This is a dictionary catalog. Since 1950 the library has used Library of Congress subject headings and forms of entry. There are many cross-references. Included are over 200,000 detailed analytics for numerous journals and reports, mostly printed in the late nineteenth and early twentieth centuries. Also included are books, pamphlets, periodicals, government documents, institutional reports, archival and unpublished material, and doctoral dissertations. The Fourth Supplement includes over 7,000 doctoral dissertations on natural resources and related subjects.

The basic catalog and supplements together contain over one million cards.

405. United States. Geological Survey. Library. Catalog of the United States Geological Survey Library. 25 vols. Boston: G. K. Hall, 1964 (LC 67-987). First Supplement. 11 vols., 1972. Second Supplement. 4 vols., 1975. Third Supplement. 6 vols., 1976.

This is "the largest geological survey library in the world" [Introduction]. It tries for comprehensive coverage of the fields of geology, paleontology, petrology, minerology, ground and surface water, cartography, and mineral resources. Other strengths include mathematics, engineering, certain fields of physics, chemistry, soil science, botany, zoology, oceanography, and natural resources.

This is a dictionary catalog listing bound volumes, pamphlets, some maps, periodicals, and U. S. and foreign government documents. Most of the works are modern, but a few date from the seventeenth and eighteenth centuries. Titles are in English, Russian, and other European languages. Library of Congress subject headings are used with some local adaptations. The library often adds subject headings when it uses Library of Congress printed cards. Cross-references are included.

406. Yale University. School of Forestry. Library. Dictionary Catalogue of the Yale Forestry Library, Henry S. Graves Memorial Library, Yale University. 12 vols. Boston: G. K. Hall, 1962 (LC 72-190317).

The Yale Forestry Library, begun in 1900, is the oldest forestry library in continuous existence in the United States and one of the largest in the world. It holds 90, 000 volumes (in 1962), represented by 250, 000 cards in this catalog. The subject of the collection, of course, is forestry, including forest management, forest protection, wildlife and wilderness areas, the utilization of forest products, plant breeding and botany, agriculture, ecology, and similar subjects.

This is a dictionary catalog. The library uses its own classification system, for which a detailed guide is provided. The subject headings used appear to be modifications of Library of Congress headings. Cross-references are provided.

Included in the catalog are books, periodicals, and analytical entries for periodical articles. There are 38, 000 cards representing periodical articles from the Journal of Forestry and its forerunners during the period 1900-1940, and from all of the leading forestry magazines and lumber journals from 1920 to 1940, when pertinent indexes became available. Books listed in the catalog date from the early eighteenth century to the modern period, and are in English and other Western European languages.

32. BOTANY, AGRICULTURE, AND NUTRITION

Included in this chapter are library collections on plants and plant products. The largest of these collections is that of the United States National Agricultural Library, which has published its catalog in 85 volumes (415). Other catalogs relate more specifically to the science of botany, rather than to agriculture, such as the catalogs of the Royal Botanic Gardens at Kew (410); to specific aspects of botany, e.g., crytogamic botany (408); or to horticulture (411).

Also described here are two catalogs of works on home economics and nutrition: the Catalogs of the Home Economics Library of Ohio State University (413) and the catalogs of the Food and Nutrition Information and Educational Materials Center (417).

407. Barnhart, John Hendley. Biographical Notes upon Botanists. 3 vols. Boston: G. K. Hall, 1965 (LC 78-241179).

This card catalog was maintained at the New York Botanical Garden by John Hendley Barnhart. His purpose in obtaining exact biographical information about botanists and taxonomists was to clarify the botanical nomenclature--since the correct name of a plant is dependent upon when and by whom the name was first published.

The arrangement is by name of the botanist. Each entry gives a birth and a death date (if the botanist was deceased at the time of the entry), and often the place of birth, along with other brief biographical information. There is sometimes a short paragraph clarifying the identity of the individual. Also included are references to journals or biographical reference books where information about that individual may be found. At the beginning of the first volume there is a list of Bibliographical Abbreviations for works that have been consulted often.

There are entries for botanists who were active from the earliest times to the 1940's, and who lived and worked in all parts of the world. Most of the references are to works in German, English, and other European languages.

California. University. Giannini Foundation of Agricultural Economics. Dictionary Catalog of the Giannini Foundation of Agricultural Economics Library. 12 vols. Boston: G. K. Hall, 1971. (see 353)

408. Harvard University. Farlow Library and Herbarium. Catalog of the Farlow Reference Library of Cryptogamic Botany. 6 vols. Boston: G. K. Hall, 1979 (ISBN 0-8161-0279-1).

William Gilson Farlow (1844-1919) was the first Professor of Cryptogamic Botany in the Americas. His library, bequeathed to Harvard College, formed the basis of this collection, which now numbers more than 60,000 items. The subject of the library is cryptogamic botany--the botany of non-flowering plants, or plants that do not produce seeds--especially the Algae, Bryophytes, Fungi, and Lichens. Included are books, monographs, approximately 14,000 periodical titles, pamphlets, and offprints of articles. Works are in Western and Eastern European languages. There is a collection of rare, pre-1850, cryptogamic texts.

The catalog is in two parts. Volumes one to five are an Author/Title Catalog. Most of the cataloging is original, and there are many cross-references to the correct form of name. Biographical material is found after the listing of works by the individual. The library concedes that the Subject Catalog, volumes five and six, is "not consistent or complete." Works are entered under the most specific heading, i.e., the name of the genus or species, rather than under the family. Only pamphlets and offprints are listed in the subject catalog. The classification system used by the library is the Cutter-Sanborn three-figure system.

409. Harvard University. Gray Herbarium. Gray Herbarium Index; Harvard University. 10 vols. Boston: G. K. Hall, 1968 (LC 73-5402). First Supplement. 2 vols., 1978.

This index was begun by Josephine A. Clark in 1894 and has been issued as installments of card sets to subscribers from that time. It is an index of bibliographic references to journals and other sources for newly described or established vascular plants of the Western Hemisphere; e.g., the vascular Cryptogams (Pteridophytes) and the higher plants (Gymnosperms and Angiosperms). All ranks of taxa from genera down are included. Each card contains the scientific name of the plant, an abbreviation of the name of the publishing author, references to the location of the taxon, and a bibliographic reference to the source of the citation. References are highly abbreviated and there is no list of periodicals indexed. There are many cross-references to guide the user from alternate forms of plant names. The original ten volumes contain approximately 265,000 cards; the supplement has a total of 30,000 cards.

Interafrican Committee for Hydraulic Studies. Documentation Center. Catalog du Centre de documentation, Comité interafricain d'études hydrauliques, Ouagadougou, Haute-Volta. 2 vols. Boston: G. K. Hall, 1977. (see 399)

410. Kew, Eng. Royal Botanic Gardens. Library. Author Catalogue of the Royal Botanic Gardens Library, Kew, England. 5 vols. Boston: G. K. Hall, 1974 (LC 74-192649).

________. Classified Catalogue of the Royal Botanic Gardens Library, Kew, England. 4 vols. Boston: G. K. Hall, 1974 (LC 74-192650).

The Royal Botanic Gardens at Kew were begun by Augusta, the Dowager Princess of Wales, in 1759, and acquired by the nation in 1841. The library was started in 1852. Today it holds one of the largest collections of botanical works in the world. Major subject strengths are plant taxonomy and distribution, economic botany, and botanical travel and exploration. The library has significant holdings of early botanical books.

Listed in the catalog are books, pamphlets, and separates (journal reprints), research reports, and scientific publications. There are many analytics for both series and journal articles in both the Author and Classified Catalogues. Works were published in both the nineteenth and twentieth centuries and are in all European languages.

Some of the material appears only in the Author Catalogue, which is generally a main-entry catalog. There are cross-references to the correct form of a name, and from a joint author to a main author.

Most of the Classified Catalogue is arranged by the Dewey Decimal Classification. For systematic works the Bentham and Hooker Botanical Classification is used, and for works about specific flora, the basis is a special geographical schedule used in the Kew Herbarium. There is very little provided in the way of instructions for using the Classified Catalogue and no outline of the classification systems, making the catalog difficult to approach. However, there are indexes. There is a geographic index, which acts as an index to the classification system in the Travel Catalogue and in the Flora Catalogue (both in volume four). There is also a subject index to the main Classified Catalogue. Knowledge of botanical (Latin) plant names is essential in using the index, as there are very few cross-references from common names to Latin names in the index. Included in the Classified Catalogue are major sections on bibliography (volume one, page one) and on biography (volume three, classification number 920), both containing many analytical entries. A few of the items in the Classified Catalogue have been given more than one classification number, but most appear only once in the catalog.

411. Massachusetts Horticultural Society. Library. Dictionary Catalog of the Library of the Massachusetts Horticultural Society. 3 vols. Boston: G. K. Hall, 1963 (LC 75-16209). First Supplement. 441 p., 1972.

The Massachusetts Horticultural Society was founded in Boston in

1829 and the library was started almost immediately. At the time the original catalog was published, the library contained more than 31,000 volumes, "making this the largest and most comprehensive library in its field" [Preface]. Its field is horticulture, especially American horticulture, but coverage is world-wide. The library attempts to obtain every American gardening publication and the best of the foreign publications. It is also strong in pomology (science of fruit growing); herbals and early gardening books; plant monographs, both horticultural and botanical; fine botanical illustrations; home landscaping; and the history of garden design. All phases of gardening are covered: history and collecting expeditions, plant evaluation and selection, basic plant physiology, plant identification, and culture.

This is a dictionary catalog of authors, titles, and subjects. The library has developed its own subject headings, but there are many cross-references for guidance. Included in the catalog are old and rare books, reports of American horticultural societies and special plant societies, government bulletins, records of the American garden club movement, and entries representing 12,600 volumes of serials.

412. New York (City). Botanical Garden. Library. Catalog of the Manuscript and Archival Collections and Index to the Correspondence of John Torrey. Compiled by Sara Lenley, et al. 473 p. Boston: G. K. Hall, 1973 (LC 73-752).

This is a catalog of the manuscripts and letters of important figures associated with the New York Botanical Garden and of other botanical and horticultural figures of the nineteenth and twentieth centuries, including such names as Charles Darwin and John Torrey. Also included are institutional archives of the New York Botanical Garden, containing old maps, architectural drawings, and early photographs of the Garden.

This is a dictionary catalog; most of the entries are for names of individuals. There are many annotations, and many cross-references from variant forms of names. The correspondence of John Torrey is a separate catalog within the volume.

413. Ohio. State University, Columbus. Libraries. Home Economics Library. Catalogs of the Home Economics Library. 3 vols. Boston: G. K. Hall, 1977 (ISBN 0-8161-0054-3).

The School of Home Economics of the Ohio State University was founded in 1896, but a separate library for the school was not established until 1959. By 1977 this library housed 14,000 volumes, including 184 serial titles, theses and dissertations written by students of the school, and 3,500 pamphlets. The latter are not included in the present catalog.

Home economics in the library is defined to include human

development, family relations, human nutrition, food management, home management and housing, textiles and clothing, and home economics education. The library maintains an extensive collection of cookbooks. Material in the library is selected to serve both undergraduates and graduate students.

This is a divided catalog. Volume one is a Subject Catalog, and volumes two and three are an Author-Title Catalog. Library of Congress subject headings and the Library of Congress classification system are used.

414. Torrey Botanical Club. Index to American Botanical Literature, 1886-1966. 4 vols. Boston: G. K. Hall, 1969 (LC 70-5392). First Supplement (1967-1976). 740 p., 1977.

The Torrey Botanical Club, headquartered at the New York Botanical Garden in The Bronx, is believed to be the oldest botanical society in America. Its index has been appearing in the Bulletin of the Torrey Botanical Club since 1886. This publication is a cumulation of the cards from that index. It is an alphabetically arranged author catalog to the botanical literature of the Western Hemisphere, particularly: taxonomy, phylogeny, and floristics of the fungi, bryophytes, pteridophytes, and spermatophytes; the morphology, anatomy, cytology, genetics, physiology, and pathology of these same plant divisions; plant ecology; and general biology including biography and bibliography. Not included are bacteriology, laboratory methods, manufactured products, agriculture, forestry, horticulture, or other fields of applied botany.

The supplement does not include titles in plant physiology and phytopathology.

415. United States. National Agricultural Library. Dictionary Catalog of the National Agricultural Library, 1862-1965. 73 vols. New York: Rowman and Littlefield, 1967-1970 (LC 67-12454).

______. National Agricultural Library Catalog, 1966-1970. 12 vols. New York: Rowman and Littlefield, 1972. Further supplemented by monthly issues, with cumulations.

This library was authorized in 1862 in the same act of Congress that created the Department of Agriculture. By 1965 it had approximately 1,250,000 volumes and had become one of the best agricultural and biological libraries in the world. Subjects covered in depth include general agriculture; agricultural societies; animal science; veterinary medicine; entomology; plant science; agricultural chemistry; agricultural engineering; soils, fertilizers, and soil conservation; forestry; agricultural products; food and nutrition; home economics; rural sociology and rural life; agricultural economics; and statistics. Titles are in many languages with an emphasis on

English and other European languages.

Included in the catalog are monographs, pamphlets, periodicals, theses, and many government publications, particularly those of the Department of Agriculture. There are many analytical entries for monographs in series, but analysis of the contents of journals and of books of botany appears in the library's Plant Science Catalog: Botany Subject Index (see 416).

The library adopted Library of Congress cataloging rules in 1909, but until 1965 it continued to use its own locally devised classification system and its own subject headings in its dictionary catalog. The subject headings often use scientific terms rather than common ones. For science and technology the geographic subdivisions follow the subjects, but for the social sciences subject subdivisions generally follow the geographic name. See and see-also references are included, but tracings have not been reproduced. Volume 73 contains a catalog of translations of articles in the library's collection, arranged alphabetically by author, or by title if there is no author.

The National Agricultural Library closed its catalog in December, 1965. In January, 1966, it adopted Anglo-American cataloging rules and the Library of Congress classification system, and began a new, divided catalog. This new catalog is divided into Names, which includes authors and titles, and Subjects. The library still uses its own subject headings.

Since 1970 the library has been using a computerized system, called CAIN, to produce catalog cards. This system has been available to libraries and individuals for searching online through various bibliographic search services.

The library is located in Beltsville, Maryland.

416. United States. National Agricultural Library. Plant Science Catalog: Botany Subject Index. Compiled by the U.S. Department of Agriculture Library. 15 vols. Boston: G. K. Hall, 1958 (LC 72-288456).

The Plant Science Catalog was begun in 1903 as an index to botanical literature published in books and scientific serials. It was ended in 1952, since the same type of references, but more inclusive in scope, had become available in the United States Department of Agriculture's Bibliography of Agriculture, which had begun publication in 1942.

The subject matter of the catalog is plant science, or botany, including taxonomy, useful and injurious plants, phytogeography, ecology, physiology, anatomy, and plant introduction. Also included are works on voyages and travels, biographies, and textbooks. It does not include plant pathology. Works are in English and in other European languages, and most of the entries are for journal articles.

This is a semi-classed subject catalog. The arrangement is alphabetical by subjects, names of countries, scientific names, and some vernacular names, with appropriate subdivisions. Names of genera are arranged under the name of the family, and species are found under genus. There are cross-references from the name of the genus to the proper family name, and many other see references throughout the catalog. Collective biographies are listed under "Botanists. Biography." There is a table of contents at the beginning of each volume, and the preface in the first volume has a very clear explanation of the arrangement of the catalog.

This catalog is rather dated by now, of course, but it remains useful for historical and taxonomic purposes. A knowledge of Latin names is essential for using it well. The Plant Science Catalog is very similar to the Classified Catalogue of the Royal Botanic Gardens, Kew, England (see 410), and while its monographic entries are not nearly as up-to-date, it provides many more analytical references.

The National Agricultural Library is located in Beltsville, Maryland. Its general dictionary catalog has been published separately (see 415).

417. United States. National Agricultural Library. Food and Nutrition Information and Educational Materials Center. Catalog. 286 p. Beltsville, Md., 1973 (LC 73-602294). Supplement 1. 1974. Supplement 2. 1975. Cumulative Index to the Catalog of the Food and Nutrition Information and Educational Materials Center, 1973-1975. Supplement 3, January-June 1975. Supplement 4, July-December 1975. Supplement 5, January-July 1976. Supplement 6. August, 1977. Supplement 7. 1977.

"The Food and Nutrition Information and Educational Materials Center (FNIC) is designed to disseminate information on school food service training and nutrition education" [Introduction]. Its catalog lists books, journal articles, pamphlets, government documents, reports, proceedings, and media--films, filmstrips, slides, games, charts, audiotapes, and video cassettes--on the subjects of food and nutrition.

The catalog is arranged alphabetically by title under general subject categories. Each entry is annotated. There are subject, personal author, corporate author, and title indexes.

Materials listed in this catalog can be accessed online through interactive bibliographic searching services, since they are listed in the National Agricultural Library's database. However, this catalog and its supplements contain material not to be found in the Dictionary Catalog of the National Agricultural Library or its supplements (see 415).

418. University of the West Indies, St. Augustine, Trinidad. Catalogue of the Imperial College of Tropical Agriculture, University of the West Indies, Trinidad. 8 vols. Boston: G. K. Hall, 1975 (ISBN 0-8161-1190-1).

This collection on tropical agriculture grew from material collected by the Imperial Department of Agriculture in Barbados, which was established by the British government in 1898. In 1922 the department was integrated with the West Indian Agricultural College in Trinidad, which was later renamed the Imperial College of Tropical Agriculture. The Imperial College merged with the University College of the West Indies in 1960, and in 1962 they became the University of the West Indies. The catalog of the library of the Imperial College of Tropical Agriculture was closed in 1961, after the colleges merged; the collection described by the catalog, therefore, covers the period from about 1900 to 1960.

The collection is international in scope, and although English predominates, works in French, Spanish, and Dutch are also included. The emphasis is on tropical agriculture, subtropical agriculture, and related sciences. The catalog lists books, including many early imprints; unpublished reports; scarce West Indiana; lesser-known serial titles from agricultural departments and research institutions all over the world; pamphlets; and government documents of many countries, including the United States. Also listed are a great many entries for journal articles and article reprints, which have been cataloged as fully as monographs.

The cataloging of the library is non-standard, i. e., it does not follow any widely recognized set of cataloging rules. The catalog is divided into six parts: the Author Catalogue is in volumes one to three; the Title Catalogue is in the first part of volume four; the Classified Catalogue is in volumes four to eight; and the Subject Index, Catalogue of Theses and Reports, and Periodicals Catalogue are also in volume eight.

The classification system used in the Classified Catalogue was developed by the library. There is no introduction to it, and no outline of the classification is provided. There is, however, a brief Subject Index to it, consisting primarily of common and scientific names of plants, with some entries for topical or geographic subjects. The index refers the user to the classification number for that subject, but the classification numbers in the Classified Catalogue are not listed on the cards for each item. They appear almost exclusively on guide cards, which are very difficult to locate in the printed catalog. This makes finding a subject in the Classified Catalogue frustrating and time-consuming, but the results, provided one does not want the latest information, can be well worth the effort. Under the names of particular crops, for example, works are organized into particular aspects of the plant, such as pests, storage, weeds, breeding, and fertilizer, and by type of item, such as books, periodicals, papers, and bibliographies.

The Catalogue of Theses and Reports includes student theses from all periods of the college's history, and range from diploma reports and associateship theses of the Imperial College of Tropical Agriculture to masters' and doctoral theses accepted by the University of the West Indies. This is the only catalog that was maintained after 1961, and it includes theses into the late 1960's. The catalog is in two parts: Author and Subject.

The Periodicals Catalogue includes an author and keyword index to the journal Tropical Agriculture, as well as a title list of journals owned by the library, and a short, selected index to articles in journals.

The Title Catalogue is quite short and far from complete.

33. MEDICAL SCIENCES

The most significant of the catalogs on medicine is that of the National Library of Medicine (428), which is limited, however, by the fact that so many different catalogs describe the entire collection. The Author and Subject Catalogs of the New York Academy of Medicine (422) are much easier to use, although the most recent imprints are from no later than 1974.

Hospital and health services administration is the subject of the Catalog of the Library of the American Hospital Association (419), while nursing is the focus of the library maintained by the American Journal of Nursing Company (427).

Dentistry (426) and pharmacy (429) also have their own collections with their own published catalogs. Catalogs of libraries of psychiatry are described in chapter 14, "Psychology."

419. American Hospital Association. Library, Asa S. Bacon Memorial. Catalog of the Library of the American Hospital Association, Chicago, Illinois. 5 vols. Boston: G. K. Hall, 1976 (LC 76-367938).

This library was begun by the American Conference on Hospital Service in 1920 and was taken over by the American Hospital Association in 1929. It is now "considered the most comprehensive single collection of literature on health services administration in the world" [Introduction]. The catalog represents 30,000 volumes on the nonclinical aspects of health care: administration, planning, design, and financing of health care institutions, and the administrative aspects of the medical, paramedical, and prepayment fields. It includes books, some rare books, pamphlets, unpublished reports, government publications, theses, publications of hospitals and nursing homes, and audio cassettes. Of special interest are the collections of American Hospital Association publications, and holdings on voluntary health insurance, especially Blue Cross.

The catalog is a dictionary catalog using subject headings developed by the library's staff. They are the same subject headings used in Hospital Literature Index up to 1978, and are listed in Hospital Literature Subject Headings, published by the American Hospital Association in 1965 and revised in 1977. The catalog includes many see references, and uses Library of Congress classification. Periodicals are listed separately at the end of the catalog, and information on holdings of issues of periodicals is included. There are no analytics; these are provided by Hospital Literature Index, published by the American Hospital Association. Works included are published mainly in this century in English.

420. Francis A. Countway Library of Medicine, Boston. Author-Title Catalog of the Francis A. Countway Library of Medicine for Imprints through 1959. 10 vols. Boston: G. K. Hall, 1973 (ISBN 0-8161-1024-7).

The Francis A. Countway Library of Medicine was established in 1965 and houses the merged collections of the Boston Medical Library and the Harvard Medical Library. This catalog lists imprints from before 1960, and is basically an historical collection. It includes the great medical works of the fifteenth through nineteenth centuries; a great collection of medical Hebraica and Judaica from the sixteenth through the nineteenth centuries; manuscript collections and comprehensive historical collections in obstetrics and gynecology, radiology, surgery, and internal medicine; and works on contemporary medicine, with an emphasis in cardiovascular disease, neoplastic disease, aerospace medicine, and legal medicine. Also included are works on demography and human ecology, modern medical history, and works of biography.

This is a main-entry catalog but it includes entries for works about individuals. The library uses modified Anglo-American cataloging rules and both the National Library of Medicine Classification and the Boston Medical Library Classification. Pamphlets and many rare books are included, and there are analytics for biographical materials and for essays in books. Works are in English and other European languages.

421. London School of Hygiene and Tropical Medicine. Library. Dictionary Catalogue of the London School of Hygiene and Tropical Medicine, University of London. 7 vols. Boston: G. K. Hall, 1965 (LC 74-174278). First Supplement. 441 p., 1971.

Included here are works on preventive medicine of both temperate and tropical climates, public health, and tropical medicine, with a special collection on smallpox. Public health reports, rare books, pamphlets, and maps are all listed in the catalog, as are some reprints of articles in periodicals the library did not regularly subscribe to. Works are mostly in English, French, and other European languages and are from the nineteenth and twentieth centuries.

This is a dictionary catalog. Subject headings, which tend to be quite broad, are subdivided, and the subdivisions are listed at the beginning of the entries for that subject. Bibliographic information tends to be brief--just author, title, and date of publication. There are liberal see and see-also references. The cataloging follows the 1908 Anglo-American Cataloging Code, and the classification system is Barnard's Classification for Medical and

Veterinary Libraries. The Preface mentions that there has never been a cataloging department in the library, and that the catalog has been prepared by library staff in the course of their other duties.

Volume seven is a serials catalog arranged in two sections. The first section lists all periodicals that are regular in publication and contain original or review material. The second section lists administrative reports, calendars, syllabuses, and the like, from corporate bodies.

422. New York Academy of Medicine. Library. Author Catalog of the Library. 43 vols. Boston: G. K. Hall, 1969 (LC 74-171385). First Supplement. 4 vols., 1974.

______. Subject Catalog of the Library. 34 vols. Boston: G. K. Hall, 1969 (LC 74-171312). First Supplement. 4 vols., 1974.

The Library of the New York Academy of Medicine was founded in 1875 and by 1969 had become the second largest medical library in the country, with about 375,000 volumes and 169,000 pamphlets. Government publications and dissertations, particularly foreign dissertations, are also included in the catalog. There are many analytical entries for special journal issues, symposia, parts of series, articles in periodicals and books, and journal reprints cataloged as pamphlets.

The library maintains a divided catalog. The Author Catalog contains main entries, added entries, and cross-references. Modified Anglo-American cataloging rules were adopted in 1967. Certain idiosyncrasies in filing and entry are noted in the Preface. Biographies have been given see references from the name of the biographee to the main entry.

The Subject Catalog uses Medical Subject Headings of the National Library of Medicine (MeSH).

Most of the titles have twentieth-century imprint dates, although some are much earlier. Works are in English, as well as other European languages.

423. New York Academy of Medicine. Library. Catalog of Biographies. 165 p. Boston: G. K. Hall, 1960 (LC 60-50505).

This is the shelflist of the biography section of the Library of the New York Academy of Medicine. The arrangement is alphabetical by name of the subject of the biography. Generally, only monographs are listed. These entries, as well as more recent biographies, are also included in the later Author Catalog of the New York Academy of Medicine, where biographies of an individual can be found via see references from the name of the individual to the author of the biography (see 422).

424. New York Academy of Medicine. Library. Illustration Catalog. Third edition, revised and enlarged. 264 p. Boston: G. K. Hall, 1976 (ISBN 0-8161-0038-1).

The Illustration Catalog was initiated to aid the staff of the Rare Book Department of the New York Academy of Medicine in answering requests for illustrative materials. It is thus historically oriented and would probably be of more use in finding pictures of how seventeenth- and eighteenth-century doctors and laymen viewed the body and medicine than in finding pictures of current medical views of anatomy. Besides anatomy, the catalog lists illustrations of hospitals and other institutions, disease, archaic notions of disease, etc.

This is a subject catalog, with many cross-references, that indexes illustrations in monographs, rare books, and journals. Works date back to the fifteenth century, but twentieth-century materials are also included.

425. New York Academy of Medicine. Library. Portrait Catalog. 5 vols. Boston: G. K. Hall, 1960 (LC 61-587). First Supplement, 1959-1965. 842 p., 1965. Second Supplement, 1965-1971. 593 p., 1971. Third Supplement, 1971-1975. 589 p., 1976.

This catalog contains entries for separate portraits (paintings, woodcuts, engravings, and photographs) of individuals and for portraits appearing in books and journals. The original catalog listed 10,784 separate portraits and 151,792 portraits appearing in books and journals. The First Supplement added 1,073 separate portraits, and 35,976 analytical entries; the Second Supplement 641 separate portraits and 20,000 analytical entries; the Third Supplement 1,658 separates and 21,896 analytical entries.

The arrangement is alphabetical by the name of the individual whose portrait is being described, with cross-references from alternate forms of the name. Symbols indicate if biographical material or an obituary accompanies the picture. The entries often include the year of birth and sometimes the year of death. The portraits are mostly of individuals active in the nineteenth and twentieth centuries, but some of the individuals antedate the Christian era. Coverage is predominantly of American or European individuals and publications.

426. Northwestern University. Dental School. Library. Catalog of the Dental School Library. 8 vols. Boston: G. K. Hall, 1978 (ISBN 0-8161-0239-2).

The Northwestern University Dental School Library was founded in 1896. By the time of publication of its catalog, its holdings totalled 50,946 volumes, including 1,390 rare books, 14,030 pamphlets, 674 current periodical subscriptions, and 2,400 cataloged series. The library has an especially good collection of foreign dental periodicals, complete sets of dental society transactions, and catalogs of almost all of the dental colleges in the United States. It aims to collect comprehensively in the field of dentistry.

This is a dictionary catalog. The library uses its own subject headings and there are many see references. Before 1970 the library used the Black classification system; it now uses the National Library of Medicine classification. Theses are listed under author and subject and under the subject heading "Theses." These include Northwestern Dental School theses plus theses of other schools in the United States and foreign countries. There are separate catalogs for Special Collections and for Periodicals in volume eight. The Periodicals Catalog includes information on which issues the library holds.

427. Sophia F. Palmer Memorial Library. Catalog of the Sophia F. Palmer Memorial Library, American Journal of Nursing Company, New York City. 2 vols. Boston: G. K. Hall, 1973 (LC 74-175946).

This library was established in 1948 by the American Journal of Nursing Company and is still solely supported by that organization. Its subject matter is nursing and related medical topics. Besides books, there are entries here for pamphlets, unpublished reports, and government documents, and some rare books. There are also occasional analytical entries for articles in books. The library has about 10,000 volumes, almost all in English, and bearing mostly twentieth-century imprint dates.

This is a dictionary catalog of authors, titles, and subjects. The subject headings are a combination of the old Bellevue system, headings from the American Journal of Nursing indexes, MeSH headings (Medical Subject Headings from the National Library of Medicine), headings from Education Index for education subjects, and headings from Readers' Guide to Periodical Literature for general subjects. For works cataloged recently, MeSH headings predominate. There are many see and see-also references for assistance, but care must be taken to check all possible subject headings. For example, there are entries under both "Education, Nursing" and "Nursing--Education," but there is a see-also reference only from the latter to the former, not vice-versa. The classification system used was locally developed.

428. United States. National Library of Medicine. Index-Catalogue of the Library of the Surgeon General's Office, United States Army (Army Medical Library). Series 1-5. 61 vols. Washington: Government Printing Office, 1880-1961 (LC 1-2344).

________. Armed Forces Medical Library Catalog: A Cumulative List of Works Represented by Armed Forces Medical Library Cards, 1950-1954. 6 vols. Ann Arbor, Mich.: J. W. Edwards, 1955 (v. 1-3 Authors, v. 4-6 Subjects).

________. National Library of Medicine Catalog: A List of Works Represented by National Library of Medicine Cards, 1955-1959. 6 vols. Washington: Judd and Detweiler, 1960 (Part 1, Authors, v. 1-3; Part 2, Subjects, v. 4-6).

________. National Library of Medicine Catalog: A List of Works Represented by National Library of Medicine Cards, 1960-1965. 6 vols. New York: Rowman and Littlefield, 1966 (v. 1-3, Authors; v. 4-6, Subjects) (LC 51-60145).

________. Current Catalog 1966- . Washington: Government Printing Office. Monthly with quarterly, annual and quinquennial cumulations.

This series of catalogs represents the world's largest medical library, the National Library of Medicine, which is located in Bethesda, Maryland. All items of medical interest are included; the older volumes are perhaps most useful for biographical material. Until the 1950's periodical articles were included in the catalog.

Although the library has always used its own subject headings, they changed radically with the 1960-1965 catalog, when Medical Subject Headings (MeSH) were put into use. These headings are specially devised for the field of medicine and are changed often as new terms and concepts are refined.

The library began using Anglo-American Cataloging Rules in 1966 when it began issuing its Current Catalog, a computer-produced book catalog in three parts: Names, Subjects, and Serials.

Titles with imprint dates of 1965 or later are also included in The National Union Catalog, by main entry (see 13).

429. Wisconsin. University at Madison. F. B. Power Pharmaceutical Library. Catalog of the F. B. Power Pharmaceutical Library. 4 vols. Boston: G. K. Hall, 1976 (ISBN 0-8161-0021-7).

Represented by this catalog is a library of 24,697 volumes of monographs, pamphlets, government documents, journals, microforms, theses, and audio-tutorial sets. There are also several special collections of manufacturers' catalogs, historical college catalogs, and corporation reports.

The subject matter of the library is pharmacy and pharmacology, including pharmacognosy; pharmaceutics; pharmaceutical chemistry and biochemistry; pharmaceutical manufacturing; history of pharmacy; pharmacy jurisprudence; drug literature and evaluation; hospital, retail, and clinical pharmacy; pharmacy and public health; continuing education in pharmacy; social studies of pharmacy; radiopharmaceuticals; pharmacotherapeutics; therapeutics; toxicology; and therapeutic drug evaluations.

This is a divided catalog with separate author-title and subject catalogs. The library uses Library of Congress cataloging rules, classification system, subject headings, and printed cards when available. There are extensive see and see-also references. Included are analytics for monographs in series.

NOTES

1. Charles A. Cutter, "Library Catalogues" in U. S. Bureau of Education, Public Libraries in the United States of America; Their History, Condition and Management, U. S. Dept. of Interior, Bureau of Education Special Report (Washington, D. C.: Government Printing Office, 1876), Part I, p. 549.
2. Charles C. Jewett, On the Construction of Catalogues of Libraries and Their Publication by Means of Separate Stereotyped Titles with Rules and Examples, 2nd ed., Smithsonian Report (Washington, D. C.: Smithsonian Institution, 1853), p. 10.
3. George Thompson, Using Printed Book Catalogs (available from G. K. Hall, Boston, 1979), p. 9. This pamphlet also provides many more examples of the uses of published library catalogs.
4. Eugene P. Sheehy, Guide to Reference Books, 9th ed. (Chicago: American Library Association, 1976), p. 11.
5. For a description of the shelflist conversion project see Richard DeGennaro, "Harvard University's Widener Library Shelflist Conversion and Publication Program," College and Research Libraries 31 (1970):318-331.
6. Sheehy, Guide to Reference Books, p. 12.
7. Nancy Olson, User's Guide to the Library of Congress Shelflist Reference System (Arlington, Va.: United States Historical Documents Institute, 1980), p. v.
8. Lee Ash, compiler, Subject Collections, 5th ed. (New York: Bowker, 1978), p. 412.
9. For a discussion of published library catalogs of interest to anthropologists see Bonnie R. Nelson, "Anthropological Research and Printed Library Catalogs," RQ 19 (1979): 159-170.
10. Colin Steele, Major Libraries of the World: A Selective Guide (New York: Bowker, 1976), p. 268-269.
11. Ash, Subject Collections, p. 47.
12. Ibid., p. 434.
13. Ibid., p. 1105.
14. Ibid., p. 161.
15. Ibid., p. 395.
16. Ibid., p. 419.
17. Ibid., p. 525.
18. Ibid., p. 1026.
19. Sheldon R. Brunswick, review of Catalog of the Arabic Collection, Library Quarterly 41 (1971): 182.
20. Ash, Subject Collections, p. 85.

21. Ibid., p. 87.
22. S. C. Sutton, A Guide to the India Office Library (London: HMSO, 1967), p. 6.
23. Ash, Subject Collections, p. 687.
24. Guy T. Westmoreland, Jr., An Annotated Guide to Basic Reference Books on the Black American Experience (Wilmington, Del.: Scholarly Resources, 1974), p. 4.
25. Ash, Subject Collections, p. 139.
26. Leonard Singer Gold, "Judaica and Hebraica in Book Catalogs," Jewish Book Annual 35 (1977-78): 33-45.
27. Ash, Subject Collections, p. 833.
28. Oswyn Murray, review of The History of Ideas: A Bibliographical Introduction, by Jeremy L. Tobey, The Classical Review n.s., 27 (1977): 293.
29. Donald Goddard Wing, Short-Title Catalogue of Books Printed in England, Scotland, Ireland, Wales, and British America and of English Books Printed in Other Countries, 1641-1700 (New York: printed for the Index Society by the Columbia University Press, 1945-51), 3 vols.
30. Alfred William Pollard and G. R. Redgrave, A Short-Title Catalogue of Books Printed in England, Scotland and Ireland, and of English Books Printed Abroad, 1475-1640 (London: Bibliographical Society, 1926).
31. Etta Arntzen and Robert Rainwater, Guide to the Literature of Art History (Chicago: American Library Association, 1980), p. 13.
32. Ibid.
33. Ash, Subject Collections, p. 989.
34. Steele, Major Libraries of the World, p. 273.
35. Ash, Subject Collections, p. 336.
36. Margaret L. Young and Harold C. Young, Directory of Special Libraries and Information Centers in the United States and Canada, 6th ed. (Detroit: Gale, 1981), p. 1033.
37. Ash, Subject Collections, p. 731.

SUBJECT INDEX

Numbers refer to entry numbers, not page numbers.

INDEX OF LIBRARIES

Included in this index are names of libraries and of other institutions that have produced catalogs, some editors or compilers of catalogs, and titles of catalogs, where the title is distinctive. Numbers refer to entry numbers.